THE ART AND SCIENCE OF
ENTREPRENEURSHIP

THE ART AND SCIENCE OF ENTREPRENEURSHIP

Edited by
DONALD L. SEXTON
RAYMOND W. SMILOR

BALLINGER PUBLISHING COMPANY
Cambridge, Massachusetts
A Subsidiary of Harper & Row, Publishers, Inc.

International Standard Book Number: 0-88730-070-7

Library of Congress Catalog Card Number: 85-22843

Printed in the United States of America

Library of Congress Cataloging in Publication Data

Main entry under title:

The Art and science of entrepreneurship.

  Papers from a conference held in February 1985 sponsored by the RGK Foundation, the IC^2 Institute at the University of Texas at Austin, and the Center for Entrepreneurship at Baylor University.
  Includes index.
  1. New Business enterprises—Congresses.
  2. Entrepreneur—Congresses. I. Sexton, Donald L.
II. Smilor, Raymond W. III. RGK Foundation.
IV. IC^2 Institute. V. Baylor University. Center for Entrepreneurship.

HD62.5.A78 1985   338'.04   85-22843
ISBN 0-88730-070-7

To Carol and Judy
Our entrepreneurial partners in life.

DS and RS

CONTENTS

LIST OF FIGURES

LIST OF TABLES

xiii

PREFACE

Entrepreneurship is one of the great social and economic forces of our time. The surge of interest in entrepreneurial activity reflects a transformation in American society that is characterized by a new wave of business and technological development. If we are truly to grasp the dimensions of this transformation, it is necessary to understand better the dynamics of the entrepreneurial process and to integrate more effectively the theory and practice of entrepreneurship. This was the consensus that emerged from the conference on which this volume is based—State-of-the-Art in Entrepreneurship Research. The conference was sponsored by the RGK Foundation, the IC^2 Institute at the University of Texas at Austin, and the Center for Entrepreneurship at Baylor University, in February 1985.

Entrepreneurship requires the fusion of talent, ideas, capital, and know-how. This fusion process can be risky, uncertain, and sometimes haphazard but is always dynamic. What emerges from the papers in this volume is that an examination of this process shows entrepreneurship to be both an art and a science. Increasing an understanding of the art and science of entreprensurship is the purpose of this book.

Only through communication of research activities can the emerging field of entrepreneurship be broadened to attract new researchers with new ideas, new approaches, and new methodologies that, in turn, can enhance the prospects of success for entrepreneurial ventures. This book, therefore, presents state-of-the-art work in entrepreneurship by leading scholars in an effort to convey what is known about the field, what is not known, and what needs to be done to push the frontiers of research and remain on the cutting edge.

Several conclusions about the current state-of-the-art are readily apparent. First, entrepreneurship is in the early stages of a rapid growth cycle in both industry and academia. How far and how fast the area expands will be a function of our ability to analyze and explain the techniques, interfaces, and causal relationships that exist and are expected to occur.

Second, not all areas have progressed at the same rate. Consequently, while some areas have reached advanced stages, others are still in the exploratory stages.

Third, there is an unfilled obligation to develop convergent theories that provide an overall understanding of the entire entrepreneurial process rather than specific narrow areas and to convey this perspective to a broader audience.

Finally, the study of entrepreneurship has a much more important function than the satisfaction of intellectual curiosity. Basic research must lead to applications in industry and in the public as well as the private sector. State-of-the-art advancements must occur both in academia and in business concurrently for one area to further the body of knowledge in the other. Only in this way can we more effectively link theory with practice and more completely appreciate the art and science of entrepreneurship.

ACKNOWLEDGMENTS

This book is the result of the support, encouragement, and entrepreneurial spirit of many people and organizations.

Dr. George Kozmetsky, director of the IC^2 Institute at the University of Texas at Austin, uniquely combines the finest qualities of the scholar and the practitioner. Without his vision, commitment to research in entrepreneurship, and dedication to linking theory with practice, this book would not have been possible.

Ronya Kozmetsky, president of the RGK Foundation, provided invaluable support for the conference. Her entrepreneurial ability to get things done is surpassed only by her commitment to the educational process.

We wish to thank Linda Teague and Margo Latimer of the IC^2 Institute for their untiring assistance in preparing for the conference. We are particularly grateful to Cynthia Smith of the RGK Foundation, who provided invaluable administrative support.

Elaine Chamberlain of the IC^2 Institute deserves special recognition. She handled conference logistics with élan, solved problems with incredible efficiency, and provided key assistance in helping to compile the manuscript.

We are indebted to the RGK Foundation, the IC^2 Institute, and the Baylor Center for Entrepreneurship. Their ongoing commitment to research and education was the driving force behind the conference and this book.

We want to express our appreciation to Carol Franco, president of Ballinger Publishing Company, for her interest and encouragement, and to David Barber, our editor, for his important help in preparing the manuscript for publication.

We are very grateful to the scholars whose contributions make up this volume.

Finally, each of us wishes to thank his coeditor for making the work on the conference and this book such an enjoyable and productive entrepreneurial adventure.

INTRODUCTION

Kevin Farrell, the Washington Bureau Chief of *Venture Magazine*, in his article in the February 1985 issue titled "There's No Stopping Now," echoed the feelings of many people in the field with his lead statement: "By almost any measure, the 1980's are shaping up as the most entrepreneurial decade in U.S. history." Others quoted in the same article were Donald Burr, CEO of People Express, who said, "We're on the edge of a new golden age that will make previous [entrepreneurial] endeavors look small," and James Botkin, a partner in the Technology and Strategy Group, who declared, "The entrepreneurial explosion will continue through this decade and, quite possibly, to the end of the century. What we are seeing now is really just the beginning."

This volume provides leading edge research in this exciting and growing field of entrepreneurship. Clearly, entrepreneurship has been established as a significant area of inquiry and as an important academic discipline. To address key theoretical and practical issues related to entrepreneurship, this volume is divided into five parts: entrepreneurship characteristics; risk and venture capital financing; high-tech entrepreneurship; growth and entrepreneurship; and research and education.

Part I emphasizes the social as well as the psychological dimensions of entrepreneurship. Howard Aldrich and Catherine Zimmer stress that entrepreneurship is embedded in a social context. Using the population perspective on organizational change, they illustrate the application of network analysis concepts to the study of entrepreneurship. They explore four applications: forces increasing the diversity of networks, increasing reachability through broker roles, the effects of network diversity, and the significance of the resources embedded in entrepreneurial networks.

Robert Brockhaus and Pamela Horwitz examine the psychology of the entrepreneur. They review possible psychological characteristics, assess the effects of demographics (such as age and education), and consider previous business and personal experience. They grapple with various definitions of the term "entrepreneur." They also discuss risk-taking propensity and innovation, need for achievement, locus-of-control beliefs, problem-solving ability and style as well as the interaction of these elements with environmental factors. As an extension of this discussion, Yvonne Gasse suggests a belief-based approach for identifying entrepreneurial potential.

Finally, Robert Hisrich maintains that the risk of failure is perhaps greater for the woman entrepreneur. Not only does she confront all the usual business problems but she also must handle a range of problems associated with being a woman in a traditionally male-dominated arena. Hisrich examines the experiences, problems, and successes of women entrepreneurs. He seeks to provide a framework for understanding this individual who is willing to juggle her life between work and family as well as between work and marriage to create a new venture that will provide independence and satisfaction.

Part II demonstrates the important roles of risk and venture capital financing in supporting entrepreneurial activity. William Wetzel traces the history of risk capital research from its post-World War II infancy to 1984 and concludes with a discussion of aspects of informal risk capital investing that offers opportunities for future research. Albert Bruno provides a structural analysis of the venture capital industry to show similarities and differences to informal risk capital.

David Brophy extends the perspective on venture vapital. The reports on recent developments in the venture capital market reviews selected venture capital research and indicates potentially fruitful areas of research activity. Herbert Kierulff furthers the discussion by commenting on the role that other disciplines may play in extending the frontiers of research on venture capital.

Part III explores the emerging area of high-tech entrepreneurship. Arnold Cooper reviews recent empirical studies to determine factors related to the founding of high-technology firms. He focuses on the characteristics of high-tech entrepreneurs, relationships to incubator organizations, and environmental factors that shape the climate for entrepreneurship. Modesto Maidique studies two related literature streams: new product and new venture success/failure; and research on corporate excellence. He then points to key success factors in the development of high-tech ventures.

Pier Abetti and Robert Stuart review state-of-the-art knowledge on the interrelationships between innovation, technology transfer, and entrepreneurship. They examine two case studies that illustrate the role of the entrepreneur in ensuring effective vertical and horizontal technology transfer with the scientific/technological environment and with the marketplace. In extending the discussion on technology transfer, Donald Myers focuses on the need for a champion of technological innovation and the potential limitations of transferring the role of the champion during the innovation cycle.

Part IV looks at issues associated with corporate entrepreneurship and with maintaining the benefits of entrepreneurial approaches as a company grows larger. Jeffry Timmons emphasizes three driving forces in creating fast-growth, high-potential ventures: the makeup of the founding team; the assessment of the opportunity; and the assembling of the resources necessary for implementation. The challenge is to choose the right mix of these factors depending on circumstances and aspirations.

Ian MacMillan reviews the research literature on corporate venturing. He then focuses on the major strategic and management factors that appear to affect venture success most directly: strategy, structure, planning and control, staffing and reward systems. In response, John Hornaday points to the need for the higher order development of generalizations, theoretical constructs, and "laws" of causal linkages in corporate entrepreneurship ventures.

Part V emphasizes emerging developments in and important needs for research and education in entrepreneurship. Max Wortman develops an interface framework for entrepreneurship and small business and formulates typologies for research in these areas.

Neil Churchill and Virginia Lewis use a four-dimensional classification scheme to examine research in entrepreneurship: research methodology, objective of research, research topic, and the centrality of the study to core problems and issues in entrepreneurship. They find that the research was not closely focused on any small set of topics, that there was a concentration on two methodologies, that both topic and methodology varied considerably depending on whether the study was reported in a journal or a conference proceeding, that the objective of the research was one-third on improving theory and two-thirds on improving practice, and that there was a reasonable degree of centrality present but with room for improvement.

In response, Alan Carsrud, Kenneth Olm, and George Eddy critique the operational definitions for entrepreneurship. They emphasize the need for systematic, empirical research and then suggest a multidimensional model that focuses on the interaction of both micro- and macro-organizational variables that influence entrepreneurial success.

Karl Vesper assesses trends in the number and variety of courses on entrepreneurship, course composition, and class composition. He then reviews extracurricular activities and raises questions that could benefit from more methodological research. In response, Howard Stevenson reports on the recent reemphasis on entrepreneurship at the Harvard Business School. He argues that success will come only if there is balanced progress in four areas: teaching, course development, research, and faculty development.

A number of key general points emerge from these papers. The methodology or means by which hypotheses are proven or disproven, leading to the development of constructs, paradigms, and theories, is an area that requires further development or sophistication as the body of knowledge on entrepreneurship expands. At any point in time in the search for knowledge, the measurement techniques, test instruments, and quantitative methods may range from simple to sophisticated. This occurs because various aspects in the search for knowledge have not progressed at the same rate. Consequently, the need for improved methodological approaches are never completely satisfied. However, this does not mean that researchers should become complacent with current or existing approaches. Rather, they should search for more sophisticated techniques as required by a higher level of research effort.

There is a need for longitudinal studies to provide information that expands the time horizon of the study from a single slice in time to one where the impact of decisions over time can be analyzed. Unfortunately, longitudinal studies require significant periods of time, and in some situations the body of knowledge expands to obviate the needs of the study. Nevertheless, the need for longitudinal studies to evaluate the impact of decisions or changing dimensions over time remains. Specifically, within the area of psychological characteristics, new venture decisions, and the impact of the new ventures on the economic development of an area still represent valid areas in which longitudinal studies are needed to answer ongoing research issues.

Two research issues are of major concern: the development of models that illuminate the interrelationships of the various components of entrepreneurship and the development of a comprehensive theoretical framework. Researchers must now accept as a portion of each research the responsibility to convey the relationship of the particular research to other components and its application to the development of a conceptual framework. These issues are of such importance that they cannot be relegated to one or two persons. What is needed is a cooperative approach with contributions from all serious researchers in the field.

In the area of research on entrepreneurs, we have now conducted a limited number of comparative studies, made inroads into the development and validation of new test instruments, started longitudinal studies, and provided new insights into the relationship between psychological characteristics and sociological factors. Much has been done recently with regard to new venture creation, risk capital, and venture capital. Given the enormous amount of growth in this area and the changing parameter of the field, however, there is need for more work.

In another area—that of the development of a significant data base—efforts are currently underway at Babson College and other organizations to accumulate the data base necessary for large-scale systematic longitudinal studies. Given these data bases, it can be expected that future research efforts will develop well beyond the limited sample sizes of the past.

In the area of venture creation research, a number of basic steps, stages, decision trees, and controversies have emerged. But there has been limited development of a predictive and causal model or set of models that can increase entrepreneurial success when the independent variables are manipulated in appropriate ways.

The interface between small business and entrepreneurship has been an ongoing concern. However, as the distinction between the two areas becomes more clearly defined and as the interface relationships are identified, the relationships between small business, emerging business (entrepreneurship), and large business (corporate entrepreneurship) should provide fertile ground for research efforts.

The importance of entrepreneurship as an academic endeavor has increased substantially in the late five years. The number of new centers and programs under development has resulted in a shortage of senior faculty. Unless more new people can be developed more rapidly, future growth may be stymied. It is necessary, therefore, to assist others through not only a sharing of research but also other aspects that may not be classified as research.

Several specific issues of interest to researchers in the field of entrepreneurship emerge from these papers. With regard to the psychology of the entrepreneur, we are still lacking a generic definition and the development of effective psychological test instruments. There is acceptance of the fact that many entrepreneurs would never initiate their new ventures if their work environments afforded the opportunity for creative expression and innovative activities. The need for longitudinal studies that cover the gamut from aspiring to successful entrepreneurs still exists in order to understand the relationship of psychological traits to both the initiation and growth of the new venture. As suggested by Brockhaus and Horwitz and as supported by Wortman, it might be beneficial to redirect some research efforts in this area towards determining why entrepreneurs succeed or fail, their role in the organization, and their organizational behavior or management style.

The sociological aspects of venture initiation have been studied from both a specific and a broad policy approach. Through the specific studies, a broader conceptual approach can be developed. Aldrich and Zimmer describe the interplay between role models, action groups, and networks that has provided insights into a new research approach in this area.

The woman entrepreneur, an area open for research a few years ago, has now had her role, problems, and motivations more clearly defined in an effort by Hisrich. He provides a framework for understanding this person and for doing additional research.

Wetzel aptly describes the explosion in risk capital: "It is likely that more has been learned about risk capital in the last five years than was discovered in the previous twenty-five years combined." Even with this increased knowledge, informal risk capital has yet to emerge from the exploratory stage. We still do not know what concepts, theories, and hypotheses are relevant. As Wetzel states, "Opportunities to explore the role of individual risk capital investors are virtually without bounds."

The growth of venture capital has paralleled that of informal risk capital. The industry, as Brophy shows, has grown from a fragmented and informal market to one with identifiable components and processes. Venture capital investments have increased by about 155 percent in the last five years. The increased investments have been matched by an increased interest on the part of scholarly researchers. With the development of a comprehensive data base, the opportunity for internally consistent, multifaceted studies of the venture capital process over time are now available. With the data limitations being solved, the area is now ready for the application and adaptation of modern financial economic theories to the venture capital process. This area, like many others, appears to provide ample opportunities for researchers.

Recent research activity in new venture creation has moved beyond steps and stages to the development of models depicting the interrelationships between the founders, the opportunity, and the necessary resources. Further, the research has moved well beyond the creation stage and into the causal relationships associated with growth. This growth factor separates the new venture creation of a small business from the new venture creation of an entrepreneurial or emerging firm. Timmons concludes that "We now see that experience, thought, and action inform each other in the process of venture creation. The process of finding 'the fit' resists simple description, but it is easy to label: it is entrepreneurship."

The broad range of research activities ranging from the small business/entrepreneur interface to the entrepreneur in large corporations has seen considerable activity in the last five years; yet significant effort remains to be done. While the methodological approaches have advanced, we still tend to utilize indiscriminately surveys that do not seem to fit into a logical, coherent framework. The areas of entrepreneurs in government and nonprofit organizations, for the most part, remain virgin territories for research.

Wortman, in his comparative study of research typologies and research studies, notes a number of deficiencies in methodology. He suggests a framework for incorporating the fragmented studies into a theoretical model.

Corporate venture research has made significant strides. Like research in psychological characteristics, however, it is now limited by lack of agreement on fundamental definitions of scope and success.

These problems stand as serious barriers to the advancement of research in this area. A body of knowledge now exists such that, if the definitional problems can be resolved, it is expected that research in the area can move from descriptive material based on case analyses to more rigorous and well-designed studies.

MacMillan suggests the need for research that will explore the causal linkages between critical elements in corporate entrepreneurship, and he presents a model of levels of corporate ventures.

The areas of high-tech entrepreneurship and technology transfer are important areas of serious research. The dynamics of change in these areas is such that research into the impact of change, especially in environmental characteristics and in risk/reward relationships, is clearly needed. Innovation programs and incubator organizations are new to the scene, and our understanding of the role and impact of these structures on entrepreneurship needs to be more fully developed. These are especially important with regard to start-up operations and to their later patterns of performance.

In review of current research in this area, Cooper discusses the distinctive characteristics of high-technology entrepreneurs, their success factors, and their support systems. He also stresses the need for communicating the results of entrepreneurship research to other areas of academia.

Our understanding of the technology transfer process and of the innovation process from which new high-tech ventures are created needs to be expanded. Abetti and Stuart describe different approaches to these processes that have enhanced our understanding of the key factors for success. They provide insights into a growth area comparable to that of risk or venture capital.

Research methodology—our means of proving hypotheses and developing theories—according to Churchill and Lewis is not closely focused on any small set of topics, is not converging equally towards core issues and problems, varies considerably with the topics, and is more oriented toward improving practice than improving theory. At the same time, it does show a reasonable degree of centrality. They provide a convergent model for entrepreneurship research.

With regard to all research, there is a need to show the relationship between the individual research effort and a broader contextual framework. There is also a need to broaden the base in which research efforts are published. Many researchers have expressed concern that research efforts are not being broadly distributed to others outside the entrepreneurship community.

Vesper indicates that entrepreneurship in academia has continued to expand. More schools are adding entrepreneurship courses, and those schools that have had entrepreneurship courses are offering additional courses or developing majors in the area. The requests for information or assistance in establishing new courses or programs seem to be increasing rapidly. While the number of schools with entrepreneurship courses is still relatively small (250), it is clear that entrepreneurship has become established as an area of academic study. As educators as well as researchers, it is important for those doing work in the field to try to measure the results of their efforts in an attempt to improve teaching effectiveness.

Entrepreneurship is a dynamic and creative process that has clearly become an important area of research activity. This book is dedicated to advancing our knowledge of the state-of-the-art in this multidisciplinary field.

I ENTREPRENEURSHIP CHARACTERISTICS

1 ENTREPRENEURSHIP THROUGH SOCIAL NETWORKS

Howard Aldrich
Catherine Zimmer[1]

The formation of new businesses can be conceptualized as a function of opportunity structures and motivated entrepreneurs with access to resources. On the demand side, opportunity structures contain the environmental resources that can be exploited by new businesses as they seek to carve out niches for themselves. On the supply side, motivated entrepreneurs need access to capital and other resources so that they can take advantage of perceived opportunities. A cursory examination of this formulation reveals two essential issues that research on entrepreneurship must address: (1) entrepreneurship is a process and must be viewed in dynamic terms rather than in cross-sectional snapshots; and (2) entrepreneurship requires *linkages or relations* between key components of the process.

Entrepreneurs must establish connections to resources and niches in an opportunity structure, and at some point they must have been affected by relations with socializing agents who motivated them. Stevenson[2] noted that entrepreneurs are driven by opportunity-seeking behavior, not by a simple desire to "invest" resources. By contrast, managers are driven by a concern to invest the resources they manage, treating resources as an end in themselves rather than as a means to an end the way entrepreneurs do. Thus, for entrepreneurs the critical connection is to opportunities, whereas for managers it is to resources.

3

Traditional approaches to research on entrepreneurship neglect the relational nature of the process. Instead, they treat entrepreneurs either as atomized decisionmakers, operating as autonomous entities, or as prisoners of their cultural environment, predisposed to entrepreneurship. The approach we take, by contrast, focuses on entrepreneurship as embedded in a social context, channelled and facilitated or constrained and inhibited by people's positions in social networks. Our critique of traditional approaches and our proposed alternative are based on Mark Granovetter's thoughtful and thorough critique of explanations for "economic action."[3]

TRADITIONAL CONCEPTIONS OF ENTREPRENEURS

Traditional views of entrepreneurship have emphasized psychological and economic models, and a special kind of social-cultural model. In this paper we cannot do full justice to each model and so our objective is to highlight the deficiencies of each in dealing with the embedded nature of social behavior. (The embedded nature of social behavior refers to the way in which action is constrained or facilitated because of its social context.)

Following Granovetter, we have identified two undersocialized approaches to entrepreneurship that treat entrepreneurs as though they were "free agents," operating atomistically in an environment where their cognitions and beliefs drive their behavior.

Personality Theories

Personality-based theories of entrepreneurship posit that people's special personal traits make them prone to behaving and succeeding as entrepreneurs.[4] The list of traits is nearly endless but includes internal locus of control, low aversion to risk taking, aggressiveness, ambition, marginality, and a high need for achievement.

Problems with the Personality Approach

Three problems plague personality-based approaches to explaining entrepreneurship: empirical research does not find strong evidence supporting such approaches, similar approaches in the leadership field have made little progress in finding a generic "leadership" trait, and personality-based models underpredict the true extent of entrepreneurship in the United States.

First, rigorous empirical research has had trouble identifying any traits strongly associated with entrepreneurship, as Brockhaus and Horwitz pointed out at our conference. Most research on entrepreneurs suffers from selection bias—picking successful people and not evaluating their attributes against a comparison group. Research using appropriate comparison groups and other controls has uncovered inconsistent and weak relationships between personality characteristics and entrepreneurial behavior.

Second, a companion tradition in psychology studying leadership has foundered on a similar problem: After three decades of study, using a personality-based approach, investigators still have difficulty identifying leaders outside of the group context in which leadership is displayed. A fair summary would be that no one style of leadership is successful all the time—leadership is very much a contingent phenomenon, with different people exhibiting leadership in different situations.[5]

Third, the personality approach substantially underpredicts the extent of entrepreneurship in the United States as it overstates the extent to which entrepreneurs are different from others. Over their lifetimes, many people attempt, or at least strongly consider, setting up their own business. Hundreds of thousands try every year, and tens of thousands succeed in carrying through by establishing businesses that survive and prosper. All these people cannot be deviant, different, or special, possessing personality traits that the rest of us lack. Considering both the proportion of adults expressing an interest in self-employment and the proportion that actually attempt it, well over half the population must possess "entrepreneurial traits"!

Economic, Rational Actor Theories

Neoclassical economic theories view entrepreneurs as rational, isolated decisionmakers. These models assume that, with clear vision of one's goals and all the required information, a person makes a *decision* to enter self-employment. The motivated person scans the market and chooses the niche that will maximize his or her returns on assets invested in the business. Recent modifications of the neo-classical approach take account of cognitive limits to rationality and information processing, recognizing the level of uncertainty involved in most economic decisions. However, even models of bounded rationality and satisficing behavior retain an emphasis on individual decisionmakers and fail to recognize the embedded nature of economic behavior.

Problems with Economic Approaches

Two problems confront investigators choosing economic, rational actor models of entrepreneurship: Cognitive limits on human behavior are much more stringent than typically recognized, and a strong research tradition in social psychology demonstrates the powerful influence of social factors on cognitions and information processing.

First, empirical research on cognition, perception, and decision-making by social psychologists has found that people do not behave the way atomistic models predict they should. A collection of papers edited by Kahneman, Slovic, and Tversky[6] has brought together a vast body of studies showing that people trying to make decisions have problems with (1) judging the representativeness of the information they receive; (2) making proper causal attributions; (3) limiting themselves only to information easily available, rather than searching for the information necessary to make informed decisions; (4) mistaking covariation for causal connections; (5) being overconfident; and (6) wildly overestimating their ability to make multistage inferences. Treated as isolated individuals, people do not measure up to the standards set by atomistic models.

Second, a person who behaved the way atomistic models describe would be an example of social pathology, not a rational decision-maker, as the person would have to reject all social contact. Ever since the original Sherif[7] autokinetic experiments, social-psychologists have been aware of the effect of social influence on decision-making. Persons do not make decisions in a vacuum but rather consult and are subtly influenced by significant others in their environments: family, friends, co-workers, employers, casual acquaintances, and so on.

American farmers are often cited as a classic example of how decisionmakers behave in a true competitive market, atomized and confined to taking individual actions that are futile in the face of unintended collective outcomes. However, the current predicament of American farmers is *not* because they made decisions as atomized individuals over the past decade but rather because they were influenced by their relations with significant others: bankers and commercial credit lenders, agricultural extension agents, and the farm-oriented business press. Farmers borrowed money to expand when they were advised to do so by persons whom they trusted. Paradoxically, we suspect that those farmers who are best off today are precisely those few who *were* most uninformed and socially isolated over the past decade, thus avoiding the influence of expansionist-oriented influentials!

Deterministic, Oversocialized Models of Entrepreneurship

Some theories posit a "propensity to entrepreneurship" based on national origins, culture, or religion. Certain groups are believed to possess beliefs, values, and traditions that predispose them to succeed in business, regardless of where they find themselves. At one time or another, various groups have been labeled this way, including the Jews, Chinese, Japanese, and Lebanese. Such models are deterministic and oversocialized because they presume the existence of a stereotypical standard that all members of the group display, and presume that behaviors are evoked regardless of the group member's situation.

Problems with the Sociocultural Approach

The major problem with this approach is that the groups alleged to possess a propensity to entrepreneurship display their predisposition only under limited, country-specific and historically specific conditions. Prior to immigration, persons originating from alleged entrepreneurial cultures are mostly indistinguishable from others around them, but in their new surroundings they take on entrepreneurial characteristics. For example, (1) Koreans in their native land versus those migrating to Los Angeles, Atlanta, or Chicago[8] (2) Dominicans in their native land versus those migrating to New York City[9]; and (3) Indians on the Indian subcontinent versus those migrating to England, many of whom come from farming or peasant backgrounds.[10] Research findings strongly suggest that we should attribute the flowering of a group's predisposition to situational, rather than deterministic, conditions.

A strong case is often made for "American exceptionalism," alleging that America is "the land of opportunity" that socializes its citizens into becoming aggressive risk takers. Popular magazines and self-help manuals published today tout the entrepreneurial character of Americans and the rebirth of the entrepreneurial spirit. Were such arguments valid, we would expect the rate of business formation in the United States to be much higher than, say, in Western European nations, and the rate of failure to be lower. In fact, accumulating evidence shows that the rates of business formation and dissolution in Western European nations are much the same as in the United States. Pom Ganguly's research for the British government's Department of Trade and Industry has found that new businesses are being added to the British economy at a rate of about one for every ten existing businesses, and businesses are being dissolved at a rate of about one for every twelve existing businesses.[11] These rates are nearly the same as those found by the U.S. Small Business Administration, using the newly constructed Small Business Data Base.[12] Similar results are emerging for other Western nations.[13] "National character" arguments must give way to models based on an underlying similarity in the economies of all Western advanced industrial societies. Rather than posit overdeterministic models, we should turn our attention to the situational conditions under which entrepreneurs enter business.

THE EMBEDDEDNESS OF ENTREPRENEURIAL BEHAVIOR

As an alternative to under- and oversocialized models of entrepreneurship, we propose a perspective that views entrepreneurship as embedded in networks of continuing social relations. Within complex networks of relationships, entrepreneurship is facilitated or constrained by linkages between aspiring entrepreneurs, resources, and opportunities. We take a population perspective[14] on organizational formation and persistence, recognizing the interaction of chance, necessity, and purpose in all social action.

The Population Perspective

From the population perspective, net additions to populations of businesses reflect the operation of four evolutionary processes: variation, selection, retention, and diffusion, and the struggle for existence.[15]

Any kind of change is a *variation*, and the evolutionary process begins with variations that may be intentional or blind. Some entrepreneurs are driven by a single-mindedness of purpose as they attempt to adapt their plans to environmental exigencies. Other entrepreneurs stumble onto opportunities and resources by chance, perhaps never intending to create a new enterprise until an accidental conjuncture of events presents itself. The process of organizational creation depends only on the occurrence of attempted variations and not on the level of ambitions, foresight, or intelligence people bring to the process. (Of course, whether the attempts succeed is another matter.) The higher the frequency of variations, whatever their sources, the greater the chances of net additions to organizational populations.

Some variations—attempts at forming new enterprises—prove more beneficial than others in acquiring resources in a competitive environment and are thus positively selected. *Selection* criteria are set through the operation of market forces, competitive pressures, the logic of internal organizational structuring, and other forces usually beyond the control of individual entrepreneurs. Organizations founded through maladaptive variations in technology, managerial competence, or other attributes are likely to draw fewer resources from their environments and are therefore more likely to fail. Over time, populations of enterprises are more apt to be characterized by the attributes of surviving organizations than by the attributes of those that failed.

What is preserved through *retention* is the technological and managerial competence that all enterprises in a population use, collectively, to exploit the resources of their environment. The survival of a particular business is not terribly consequential to the survival of the population as a whole, as the total population's survival depends on the total pool of technological and managerial competence. The variations possessed by a particular enterprise contribute to the total pool but do not determine its collective fate.

The competencies of a population are held by the entrepreneurs and their employees. Retained variations are passed on, with more or less variation, from surviving entrepreneurs to those who follow and from old to new employees, some of whom may leave to form their own businesses. Linkages between enterprises facilitate the *diffusion* of beneficial variations, whereas isolated organizations contribute little or nothing to future generations. Not all variations are diffused to new entrepreneurs (because of hostility, pique, mistakes, stupidity, unwillingness to learn, etc.), introducing a large element of uncertainty into the process.

A competitive *struggle over resources and opportunities* occurs, fueling the selection process. Sometimes opportunities are so diverse and resources so abundant that a high proportion of entrepreneurs are successful and the business population grows rapidly. In new industries, first movers have substantial advantages and enjoy rapid growth. As industries evolve, however, or resources become more scarce, shakeouts occur and competition increases the mortality rate, with populations stagnating or declining.

Using evolutionary principles, the population perspective explains how particular forms of organizations come to exist in specific kinds of environments. A specific environment constitutes an opportunity structure containing a resource pool uniquely suited to organizational forms that adapt to it or help shape it. A form well-adapted to a specific environment is probably not the fittest form imaginable and is vulnerable to entrepreneurial successes in founding new organizations with more adapted forms. Nonetheless, it is tolerably fit and probably more fit than previous failed forms.

The population perspective makes minimal assumptions about the cognitive capabilities of humans as information-processors and renders practically irrelevant any speculations about entrepreneurial personalities. People become entrepreneurs through the conjuncture of the four processes outlined above, and entrepreneurship takes on meaning only within the context of these processes. People are intentional or purposeful in their actions, but social conditions are such that we usually cannot attribute organizational formation to any particular, identifiable, intentional act or set of acts.

Environments, as opportunity structures, are diverse, uncertain, and imperfectly perceived, and it is seldom true that a particular individual will both have an accurate view and be aware of it. People are limited by bounded rationality, suffer from limited or biased information and poor communication, and are subject to processes of social influence and reconstructions of reality. Hence, comprehensive explanations of entrepreneurship must include the social context of behavior, especially the social relationships through which people obtain information, resources, and social support.

The Characteristics of Social Networks

The starting point for studying entrepreneurship through social networks is a relation or transaction between two people. Relations may be treated as containing: (1) communication content, or the passing of information from one person to another; (2) exchange content, or the goods and services two persons can exchange; and (3) normative content, or the expectations persons have of one another because of some special characteristic or attribute. The strength of ties depends on the level, frequency, and reciprocity of relationships between persons, and varies from weak to strong. Most research has focused on single content types of relations, and so there is a paucity of information about the effects of types of relations on one another and on the durability of relations composed of different combinations of relations.

Relations between pairs of individuals—entrepreneurs, customers, suppliers, creditors, inventors, and so forth—whatever their content and whatever a person's social role, could be extended and persons included in ways that would expand a unit of analysis indefinitely. A central interest of network theorists, therefore, has been to find ways to set meaningful limits to the scope of a social unit under investigation. The concept of role-set, action-set, and network provide us with some tools for setting such boundaries.

A *role-set* consists of all those persons with whom a focal person has direct relations. Usually the links are single-step ties, but indirect links can be considered by specifying how many steps removed an interacting person can be from the central focal person and still be treated as in the set. We have borrowed the concept of a role-set from Merton, who defined it as "that complement of role relationships which persons have by virtue of occupying a particular social status."[16] Merton gave an example of the status of public school teacher and its role-set, relating the teacher to pupils, colleagues, school principal and superintendent, board of education, and professional organizations of teachers. For entrepreneurs, we could think of partners, suppliers, customers, venture capitalists, bankers, other creditors, distributors, trade associations, and family members.

One of the interesting issues highlighted by the role-set concept concerns conflict produced by divergent expectations from members of an entrepreneur's role-set. Entrepreneurs stand at the center of potentially conflicting demands and expectations from their role-sets, such as between expectations from spouses that some time will be spent at home versus demands from partners that weekends be used to catch up on paperwork. Business survival may depend upon the strategies entrepreneurs adopt to resolve such conflicts.

An *action-set* is a group of people who have formed a temporary alliance for a limited purpose. The concept of action-set has been used by anthropoligists, who have found a specific action or behavior, rather than status, helpful as a frame of reference in studying social change. Rather than the ego-centered analysis of role-set studies, action-set research examines the purposeful behavior of an entire aggregate of persons. Action-sets may have their own internal division of labor, behavioral norms vis-à-vis other persons, or clearly defined principles for the recruitment of new members. An action-set may be centered around the behavior of one individual, as in consortia of high-tech firms led by the enterprise with the most market power, but that is an empirical question.

A *network* is defined as the totality of all persons connected by a certain type of relationship and is constructed by finding the ties between all persons in a population under study, regardless of how it is organized into role-sets and action-sets. Given a bounded system, investigators identify all the links between people within the boundaries. Network analysis assumes that a network constrains or facilitates the action of people and action sets and thus is more than the sum of the individual links that comprise it.

Critical Dimensions of Networks

Before demonstrating the application of network concepts to the explanation of entrepreneurship, let us briefly review three dimensions of networks that are useful in social analysis: density, reachability, and centrality.

The *density* of a network refers to the extensiveness of ties between persons and is measured by comparing the total number of ties present to the potential number that would occur if everyone in the network were connected to everyone else. The simplest measures of density just consider the presence or absence of a tie, but more sophisticated measures take account of the strength of ties.

Reachability refers to the presence of a path between two persons, of whatever distance. Persons can be ranked by how many intermediaries a path travels before one person is indirectly linked with another. An example of the use of indirect ties in connecting distant individuals was provided by Travers and Milgram in their experimental study of communication channels, referred to as the small-world phenomenon.[17] Arbitrarily chosen persons in Nebraska were given letters to send to a target person in Boston, with the stipulation that the letters had to be channeled only through persons known to the senders. Out of 296 starts, 64 letters reached the target person, with the mean number of intermediaries being 5.2. The importance of linking pins was shown in that 48 percent of the completed chains passed through three central individuals before reaching the target.

The *centrality* of a person in a network is determined by two factors: (1) the total distance from a focal person to all other persons, and (2) the total number of other persons a focal person can reach. (For a comprehensive review of the centrality concept, and alternative definitions, see an article by Linton Freeman.[18]) The more persons that can be reached and the shorter the aggregate distance to these persons, the higher the centrality of a focal person. Persons who have extensive ties to different parts of a network can play a key role in entrepreneurial processes. Persons playing central roles may have ties to more than one action-set or other subset of a network, and they can serve three important functions: (1) they serve as communication channels between distant persons; (2) they may provide brokerage services linking third parties to one another by transferring resources; and (3) if they are dominant or high-status individuals, they may serve as role models for others or may use their position to direct the behavior of action-sets or individuals.

NETWORKS AND ENTREPRENEURSHIP

We turn now to four applications of network concepts to the study of entrepreneurship. The first application focuses on the effect of social forces that increase the density of networks, and the second application focuses on the role of "brokers" and other persons or organizations that increase reachability in networks. The third application applies Granovetter's discussion of the importance of linkage diversity to the question of which positions in networks are most likely to produce entrepreneurs.[19] The fourth application focuses on the importance of the social resources embedded in entrepreneurs' networks.

Increasing Density through Raising the Salience of Group Boundaries and Identity

Conditions that raise the salience of group boundaries and identity, leading persons to form new social ties and action-sets, increase the likelihood of entrepreneurial attempts by persons within that group and raise the probability of success. Increasing density can operate at two levels. First, at a local level, increasing density may lead to coalition formation between persons, thus enhancing their collective action capability. Repeated action-set formation, in turn, enhances the institutional infrastructure facilitating entrepreneurship. Second, if density increases not just at a local level but also at the system level—such as for an entire ethnic group or as a result of infrastructural development—then everyone is in a position to collect the combinations of resources necessary for successful ventures. The advantages of local action-sets would thus be eliminated and the entire group would have an advantage over outsiders.

Opportunities are irrelevant unless taken advantage of, and people vary widely in their ability to seize opportunities. Auster and Aldrich, Bonacich, Light, and others have argued that the possibility of exploiting opportunities is linked to a group's internal organizing capacity.[20] Ethnic groups with a high level of self-organization—a densely connected network—provide co-ethnics with a collective capacity for organizing new ventures. Indeed, the most salient feature of early business efforts by immigrant groups is their dependence on an ethnic community for support. Support is provided at two levels: informal support from the friends and relatives of aspiring business owners, and support from the larger network of ethnic institutions, including religious associations, fraternal organizations, and other small businesses. Strong community support, based on ethnic ties, allows small firms some degree of independence from the host community.[21]

Immigration, especially chain migration, may establish densely connected communities of co-ethnics who cooperate when confronted with host hostility.[22] The early opposition towards Japanese immigrants on the west coast of the United States by labor unions, who feared that Asians would replace them at lower wages, obstructed Japanese entry into the mainstream economy. In response, the Japanese pooled their resources and ultimately captured a significant portion of California's agricultural sector until their internment during World War II. The strong ethnic solidarity formed by union and public hostility generated ethnic networks that supported subsequent generations.[23]

Mutual aid, in the form of capital, credit, information, training opportunities, and the regulation of competition, gave Chinese and Japanese immigrants to the United States a strong base on which to develop small business. In contrast, black migrants from the South to Northern cities after World War I and continuing into the 1950s had few collective organizational traditions to follow, except for religion.[24]

Strong ties carry with them a history of past dealings in or out of a business setting that can form a basis for trust. Whereas banks and other formal institutions outside an ethnic group may have little or no objective credit history for an aspiring entrepreneur, within the group strong ties keep alive the memory of past experiences from which to infer trustworthiness, and these relationships may carry strong expectations of trust.[25] Another strength of strong ties is that "strong ties have greater motivation to be of assistance and are typically more easily available."[26]

Mutual benefit associations, cooperative housing and buying arrangements, joint capital raising activities, and other collective actions provide support for potential entrepreneurs. Recent groups in the United States who have followed this model include Cubans in Miami; Dominicans in New York City's garment trade; Koreans in Los Angeles's liquor, wig, and other retail stores; and Indians in California's motel business. Most small firms are capitalized from the owner's savings, but other sources of funds are often sought. The Chinese *hui*, the Japanese *ko* and *tanomoshi*, and the Korean *kye*— rotating credit associations clothed in their respective cultural traditions—have provided simple mechanisms for immigrants to raise business capital.[27] In these cases, social conditions have raised the salience of group boundaries and identity, leading persons to form stronger ties with one another and often to the creation of effective action-sets.

Increasing Reachability and Connectedness Facilitate the Spread of Information and Resources in Networks

Broker roles are central positions in networks, resulting from people's attempts to minimize their transactions costs. Such positions exist because of their function of linking persons having complementary interests, transferring information, and otherwise facilitating the interests of persons not directly connected to one another. Many entrepreneurs enjoy a broker's position, and indeed Schumpeter's classic definition of an entrepreneur as someone who combines old resources in novel ways seems to equate the entrepreneurial with the broker role. However, we are interested in brokers who are not themselves entrepreneurs but who facilitate the actions of entrepreneurs. (Also, we believe many entrepreneurs do not themselves enjoy the advantages of a broker role.) For example, venture capitalists are as important for their broker role as for the funds they provide to struggling entrepreneurs because they bring together technical experts, management consultants, and financial planners to supplement the entrepreneur's limited knowledge and experience.

To illustrate the importance of broker roles, let us consider an example of a population divided into two major types of social roles—such as entrepreneurs and venture capitalists—where some method of interrole communication is desired by persons in each role. Communication is possible if all entrepreneurs are directly linked to all venture capitalists, thus creating a very complex set of relations. The total number of relations established would equal the number of entrepreneurs times the number of venture capitalists, assuming a link is established in each direction. If there were five entrepreneurs and five venture capitalists, the total number of links would be twenty-five.

Each new person added to either side would increase the number of required links linearly (e.g., if another entrepreneur is added, five more links are created). If another person were added to both sides, the number of linkages would increase as the square of the number added (e.g., if one pair is added, the number of ties jumps from twenty-five to thirty-six). In a large population, the maintenance of such a large set of linkages would be extremely costly, especially if the number of entrepreneurs and venture capitalists were increasing rapidly.

The evolutionary model from the population perspective would predict that any innovation or random variation that created a less costly solution to the problem would be quickly selected. Any cost-saving variation would give the entrepreneur using it a relative advantage, and thus a selective survival advantage, over other entrepreneurs in a resource-scarce environment. Similarly, any new organizational form that enabled entrepreneurs and venture capitalists to communicate with one another more quickly would be in a niche with an initially overwhelming advantage, as there would be a strong demand for its services.

If an intermediary or broker organization were created, linking entrepreneurs and venture capitalists—such as venture capital "fairs" or the joint seminars described by David Brophy[28]—the number of connections in the network would be reduced to the number of entrepreneurs plus the number of venture capitalists. That is, five plus five, joined by a central organization, rather than the five times five situation previously. Each person or organization would have one link to the broker, and the process of sorting out the various messages and information channels between them would be internalized by the broker. This is a complex task, but the broker specializes in the role and only a fraction of the ties would have to be active at any one time. Once introduced into a population, we would expect this function to persist, and the concept of the broker should become part of our industrial culture, passed on via imitation and tradition.

Voluntary associations, trade associations, public agencies, and other social units increase the probability of people making connections with one another. Rates of entrepreneurship should be higher in highly organized populations (i.e., populations with a high organizing capacity). The complex pattern of social organization described by Everett Rogers and Judith Larson in their book *Silicon Valley Fever* illustrates the synergistic effects of brokers, central meeting points—such as well-known "watering holes" and restaurants—and family and friendship networks that supported the high start-up rate in the Silicon Valley.[29]

Social networks build slowly, and thus it could be years before an area reaches a density threshold where reachability and hence entrepreneurship is facilitated. Formal studies are lacking, but it is our impression that the time to maturity for the Silicon Valley and the Route 128 complex in Boston was several decades. Accordingly, we expect the Research Triangle of North Carolina to age another decade or so before any significant entrepreneurial activity occurs. At present, the spin-off and new start-up rate appears very low.

The Importance of Diversity in an Entrepreneur's Network: Too Much Solidarity Stifles the Entrepreneurial Soul

Mark Granovetter has developed an argument linking the diversity of ties in which a person is implicated to the scope of opportunities open to that person.[30]

> The argument asserts that our acquaintances ("weak ties") are less likely to be socially involved with one another than are our close friends ("strong ties"). Thus, the set of people made up of any individual and his or her acquaintances will constitute a low-density network (one in which many of the possible relational lines are absent), whereas the set consisting of the same individual and his or her *close* friends will be densely knit (many of the possible lines present).[31]

A potential entrepreneur may have a small group of friends he or she knows well, each of whom knows the others quite well. He or she may also have many casual acquaintances, each of whom also has a circle of close friends. These close friends of his casual acquaintances are unlikely to be known to the potential entrepreneur, and thus his or her only possible ties to them are through the casual acquaintance. The weak tie between the potential entrepreneur and his or her acquaintance is therefore "not merely a trivial acquaintance tie, but rather a crucial bridge between the two densely knit clumps of close friends. . . . It follows that individuals with few weak ties will be deprived of information from distance parts of the social system and will be confined to the provincial news and views of their close friends."[32]

Research in the Boston area by Granovetter has documented that lack of access to the information provided by weak ties puts people at a competitive disadvantage in the labor market, as such people will obtain only redundant information from close acquaintances, who travel in the same circles as the job seeker.[33] People with a more diverse role set, connected to distant others via brokers or other intermediaries, will have access to a wider range of information.

Following the logic of this argument, entrepreneurs are more likely to be found in positions whose centrality is high and which are connected to lots of diverse information sources. Entrepreneurs activate their weak ties for at least two purposes: to gain access to business information and to attract customers. First, information about new business locations, potential markets for goods and services, sources of capital or potential investors, innovations, and standard business practice is likely to be spread widely among individuals. Other things being equal, someone with a small role-set of overlapping ties is at a disadvantage when competing for information with someone who has a large role-set of divergent ties. There is also a disadvantage we might call the "weakness of strong ties," wherein those persons with whom we are tightly linked lead to the introduction of extraneous socio-emotional content into information exchanges, clouding their meaning.

Second, entrepreneurs ask both their strong and weak ties to become customers. Then, in turn, these new customers may tell their strong and weak ties about the new venture. It is the weak ties who can expand the pool of customers; strong ties deliver redundant information.

Perhaps these ideas are a way of rethinking the traditional relation posited between "marginality" and entrepreneurship. Marginality is important but as a characteristic of the social structure, not as a personal characteristic of entrepreneurs. Instead, marginality refers to the weak ties potential entrepreneurs have to diverse information sources and to potential customers, putting them in positions to capitalize on opportunities that remain unknown to the less marginal person.

Nine studies reviewed by Granovetter have tested the strength of the weak ties argument and have provided partial support for it.[34] None of these studies, however, focused on entrepreneurs or on persons classified as self-employed. The theoretical importance of weak ties would be broadened by specific research on how small businesses are founded and how they subsequently fare.

The Importance of Social Resources: It is not just What You Know but Who You Know

Lin and his colleagues have added a component to the strength of ties literature.[35] In his theory of instrumental action, Lin suggested that in a hierarchical social structure, a person in a "position nearer to the top of the structure has greater access to and control of valued resources not only because more valued resources are intrinsically attached to the position, but also because of the position's greater accessibility to positions at other (primarily lower) rankings."[36] He defined social resources as valued resources that are accessible through ties with others. Therefore, all weak ties are not equally useful for acquiring social resources. Weak ties to those contacts with the most social resources—that is, contacts as high in the social hierarchy as possible—will provide the greatest access to social resources. Lin's research on the status attainment of job seekers has weakly confirmed the social resources argument, but his research must be replicated before we can place high confidence in his results.

Extending the argument, successful entrepreneurs will be found in positions with weak ties to people who are in positions to provide timely and accurate information, to people with the resources to act as a customers, and/or to people with resources to invest.

Entrepreneurship is a social role, embedded in a social context. Investigators cannot treat entrepreneurs in isolation as autonomous decisionmakers or lump them together with others with similar social characteristics, without regard to context. It is the effects of social networks in facilitating or inhibiting the activities of potential entrepreneurs.

NOTES TO CHAPTER 1

1. We are deeply indebted to Valerie Haines and Peter Marsden, colleagues at the University of North Carolina, for their comments and suggestions.
2. Howard Stevenson, "A Perspective on Entrepreneurship," Harvard Business School, No. 9-384-131, November 1984.
3. Mark Granovetter, "Economic Action and Social Structure: A Theory of Embeddedness," *American Journal of Sociology* (forthcoming); see also Ronald S. Burt, "Tertius Gaudens, Structurally Autonomous Entrepreneur," Columbia University, 1983. (Unpublished.)
4. See Robert J. Brockhaus and Pamela S. Horwitz, "The Psychology of the Entrepreneur," in this volume.
5. Richard Hall, *Organizations: Structure and Process* (Englewood Cliffs, N.J.: Prentice-Hall, 1982).
6. Daniel Kahneman, Paul Slovic, and Amos Tversky, *Judgment under Uncertainty: Heuristics and Biases* (New York: Cambridge University Press, 1982).
7. M. Sherif, "A Study of Some Social Factors in Perception," *Archives on Psychology* 187 (1935). The autokinetic effect is a visual illusion—a fixed pinpoint of light shown to subjects in a totally darkened room appears to move, smoothly or erratically. Subjects' judgments of the extent to which the light moves are strongly influenced by the reports of others in the room—typically, persons who are confederates of the experimenter.
8. Pyong Gap Min and Charles Jaret, "Korean Immigrants' Success in Small Business: Some Cultural Explanations," Department of Sociology, Georgia State University, August 1984. (Unpublished.)
9. Roger Waldinger, "Immigrant Enterprise and Labor Market Structure," Working paper, Joint Center for Urban Studies, MIT and Harvard University, 1982.
10. Howard Aldrich, John Cater, Trevor Jones, and Dave McEvoy, "From Periphery to Peripheral: The South Asian Petite Bourgeoisie in England," in Ida Harper Simpson and Richard Simpson, eds., *Research in the Sociology of Work*, Vol. 2 (Greenwich, Conn.: JAI Press, 1983), pp. 1-32.
11. Pom Ganguly, "Births and Deaths of Firms in the UK in 1980," *British Business* 29 (January 29-February 5, 1982).
12. U.S. Small Business Administration, *The State of Small Business* (Washington, D.C.: USGPO, 1984).
13. Robert Brockhaus, personal communication,
14. See Howard Aldrich, *Organizations and Environments* (Englewood Cliffs, N.J.: Prentice-Hall, 1979); and Bill McKelvey and Howard Aldrich, "Populations, Natural Selection, and Applied Organizational Science," *Administrative Science Quarterly* 28: 1 (March 1983): 101-28.

15. See McKelvey and Aldrich, "Populations"; and Howard Aldrich, Bill McKelvey, and Dave Ulrich, "Design Strategy from the Population Perspective," *Journal of Management* 10: 1 (Spring 1984): 68–86.

16. Robert Merton, "The Role-Set: Problems in Sociological Theory," *British Journal of Sociology* 8 (1957): 106–20.

17. Jeffrey Travers and Stanley Milgram, "An Experimental Study of the Small World Problem," *Sociometry* 32 (1969): 425–43.

18. Linton C. Freeman, "Centrality in Social Networks: Conceptual Clarification," *Social Networks* 1 (1979): 215–39.

19. Mark Granovetter, "The Strength of Weak Ties," *American Journal of Sociology* 78: 6 (May 1973): 1360–80.

20. See Ellen Auster and Howard Aldrich, "Small Business Vulnerability, Ethnic Enclaves, and Ethnic Enterprise," in Robin Ward and R. Jenkins, eds., *Ethnic Communities in Business: Strategies for Economic Survival* (New York: Cambridge University Press), pp. 39–54; Edna Bonacich, "A Theory of Middleman Minorities," *American Sociological Review* 38 (October 1973): 583–94; and Ivan Light, *Ethnic Enterprise in America: Business and Welfare among Chinese, Japanese, and Blacks* (Berkeley, Calif.: University of California Press, 1972).

21. Kenneth Wilson and Alexandro Portes, "Immigrant Enclaves: An Analysis of the Labor Market Experiences of Cubans in Miami," *American Journal of Sociology* 86: 2 (September 1980): 295–319.

22. Bonacich, "A Theory of Middleman Minorities."

23. Edna Bonacich and John Modell, *The Economic Basis of Ethnic Solidarity* (Berkeley, Calif.: University of California Press, 1980).

24. See E. Franklin Frazier, *Black Bourgeoisie* (New York: The Free Press, 1957), and Nathan Glazer and Daniel Patrick Moynihan, *Beyond the Melting Pot* (Cambridge, Mass.: MIT Press, 1963).

25. Light, *Ethnic Enterprise.*

26. Granovetter, "Economic Action" (forthcoming), p. 14.

27. Mark Granovetter, "The Strength of Weak Ties; A Network Theory Revisited," in Peter V. Marsden and Nan Lin, eds., *Social Structure and Network Analysis* (Beverly Hills, Calif.: Sage, 1982), p. 113.

28. David Brophy, "Venture Capital Research," in this volume.

29. Everett Rogers and Judith Larson, *Silicon Valley Fever* (New York: Basic Books, 1984).

30. See Granovetter, "The Strength of Weak Ties," (1973); Mark Granovetter, *Getting a Job: A Study of Contacts and Careers* (Cambridge, Mass.: Harvard University Press, 1974); Granovetter, "The Strength of Weak Ties," 1982; and Granovetter, "Economic Action" (forthcoming).

31. Granovetter, "The Strength of Weak Ties," 1982, p. 105.

32, Ibid., p. 106.

33. Granovetter, *Getting A Job*. Scott Boorman has suggested that Granovetter's findings may apply only when jobs are scarce. Strong ties may well
be more valuable in other labor market conditions, such as when one needs
to have influence exercised on one's behalf. See Scott A. Boorman, "A
Cominatorial Optimization Model for Transmission of Job Information
through Contact Networks," *The Bell Journal of Economics* 6: 1 (Spring
1975): 216–49.

34. Granovetter, "The Strength of Weak Ties," 1982.

35. See, for example, Nan Lin, W.M. Ensel, and J.C. Vaughn, "Social Resources and Strength of Ties: Structural Factors in Occupational Status
Attainment," *American Sociological Review* 46: 4 (August 1981): 393–
405; and Nan Lin, J.C. Vaughn, and W.M. Ensel, "Social Resources and
Occupational Status Attainment," *Social Forces* 60: 59 (June 1981):
1162–81.

36. Nan Lin, "Social Resources and Instrumental Action," in Marsden and
Lin, *Social Structure and Network Analysis*, p. 131.

2 THE PSYCHOLOGY OF THE ENTREPRENEUR

Robert H. Brockhaus, Sr.
Pamela S. Horwitz

J.S. Mill was the first to utilize the term "entrepreneur" among economists. Mill considers direction, supervision, control, and risk taking to be the functions of the entrepreneur. Mill appears to feel risk bearing is the main distinguishing feature between the manager and the entrepreneur.[1]

Schumpeter, however, stresses the role of innovation as a distinguishing factor for entrepreneurs, since he believes that both managers and entrepreneurs experience risk. He recognizes that the entrepreneurs' challenge is to find and use new ideas. The range of possible alternatives include: (1) developing new products or services, (2) developing new methods of production, (3) identifying new markets, (4) discovering new sources of supply, and (5) developing new forms of organizations.[2] These ideas are supported by Kirzner, who feels that the identification of market opportunities is the fundamental function of the entrepreneur.[3]

Penrose believes that managerial activities should be distinguished from entrepreneurial activities, thus giving birth to the current arguments of how an entrepreneur and manager differ. Penrose states that identifying and exploiting opportunistic ideas for expansion of smaller enterprises is the essential aspect of entrepreneurship.[4] McClelland is less restrictive and believes that an innovative manager who has decisionmaking responsibility is as much an entrepreneur as the owner of business.[5]

Many recent writers are still struggling with the definition of the entrepreneur. Long recognizes three recurring themes emerging from the various definitions—namely, that entrepreneurship involves uncertainty and risk, complementary managerial competence, and creative opportunism.[6] The definitions have changed as business concepts have evolved and ownership forms have changed. It was once felt that one must own a business in order to be considered an entrepreneur. This requirement is no longer believed to be necessary, and in fact many researchers believe it is possible for entrepreneurs to exist as employees of large corporations. Thus the birth of the concept "intrapreneur."

However, there are equally vocal opponents of this concept of entrepreneurship. Indeed, some distinguish between small business owners and entrepreneurs who own businesses. Carland developed the following definitions:

Entrepreneur: An entrepreneur is an individual who establishes and manages a business for the principal purpose of profit and growth. The entrepreneur is characterized principally by innovative behavior and will employ strategic management practices in the business.

Small Business Owner: A small business owner is an individual who establishes and manages a business for the principal purpose of furthering personal goals. The business must be the primary source of income and will consume the majority of one's time and resources. The owner perceives the business as an extension of his or her personality, intricately bound with family needs and desires.[7]

Of course, this viewpoint also is challenged.

A number of other questions about entrepreneurial research exist. There is usually no indication of the type of business the entrepreneur is managing. In addition, some of the research concentrates only on successful entrepreneurs, while other research examines the characteristics of those interested in becoming entrepreneurs with no consideration of their success rate.[8]

It should now be clear that a well-defined entrepreneurial population does not exist and research findings are often difficult to compare. However, despite these difficulties some psychological characteristics are reported in a relatively consistent manner. Three categories of factors that are associated with the decision to become an entrepreneur emerge: psychological influences upon the individual, effects of previous experience, and personal characteristics.

PSYCHOLOGICAL CHARACTERISTICS

Need for Achievement

McClelland's work has been the major contribution to this area of the psychology of the entrepreneur. His research has been based on the need for achievement (nAch). McClelland characterizes individuals with a high nAch as having a strong desire to be successful. He argues that people who are high in nAch possess the following attributes: (1) prefer personal responsibility for decisions, (2) are moderate risk takers as a function of skill, and (3) possess interest in concrete knowledge of the results of decisions (i.e., money as a measure of success). He concludes that a need for achievement drives people to become entrepreneurs.[9]

While the research continues to find that entrepreneurs are high achievers, the same thing has been discovered about successful executives. The most recent research concentrates on the environmental factors that help determine the individual's career path rather than the level of their nAch. The casual link between ownership of a small business and a high need for achievement has not yet been proven. Most small business owners available to be studied were successful, and this success may contribute to their high need for achievement rather than the reverse.

Locus of Control

Closely related to the concept of a high need for achievement is the belief in an internal locus of control. Individuals who cannot believe in the ability to control the environment through their actions would be reluctant to assume the risks that starting a business entail. According to Rotter's locus-of-control theory, an individual perceives the outcome of an event as being either within or beyond his personal control and understanding. Rotter offers a further definition of these two categories of locus of control:

> When a reinforcement is perceived by the subject as following some action of his own but not being entirely contingent upon his action, then in our culture, it is typically perceived as the result of luck, chance, fate, as under the control of others, or as unpredictable because of the great complexity of the

forces surrounding him. When the event is interpreted in this way by an individual, we have labeled this a belief in "external control." If the person perceives that the event is contingent upon his own behavior or his own relatively permanent characteristics, we have termed this a belief in "internal control."

Rotter believed that need for achievement is related to the belief in internal locus of control. He hypothesized that individuals with internal beliefs would more likely strive for achievement than would individuals with external beliefs.[10] More recent studies have supported this hypothesis. Berlew found successful entrepreneurs to desire personal responsibility for their success. Entrepreneurs perform best in situations where they have personal responsibility for results. They tend to be internally rather than externally controlled.[11]

Borland studied locus of control, nAch, and entrepreneurship at the University of Texas with the purpose of discovering what characterized students who intended to become business owners. She found significant differences in internal locus of control between the students who expected to start a company and those who did not. Among those with low nAch, those with higher internal locus of control were found to have a greater expectancy than others of starting a company. The level of internal locus of control made no difference in expectancy of starting a company among those with high nAch. This would seem to indicate that the combination of personality traits might be more crucial than the possession of any single trait. Borland also found that whether or not a student's father has started a company was the most important variable for predicting expectancy of starting a company.[12] This agrees with more recent researchers whose findings supported their belief that the environment had a major impact on the entrepreneurial process.[13]

Brockhaus and Nord compared the locus-of-control beliefs in entrepreneurs and managers. The scores of Rotter's I-E Locus-of-Control scale did not differ significantly between the owners of new businesses and managers. The mean score for both the entrepreneurs and managers were lower than any score reported by Rotter. Both were more internal than the other groups discussed by Rotter. The locus-of-control beliefs did not distinguish entrepreneurs from managers; however, the entrepreneurs did tend to hold more internal locus-of-control beliefs than those reported by Rotter for the general population.[14]

In a later study, Brockhaus compared locus-of-control scores he had collected in 1975 with the success rate of those businesses. The owners of businesses that still existed in 1978 were found to hold more internal locus-of-control beliefs than those whose businesses had ceased to exist. The internal beliefs may have resulted in more active efforts to affect positively the results of the venture rather than attributing less than desirable occurrences to being the result of "luck and beyond the control of the entrepreneur."[15]

When Hull, Bosley, and Udell surveyed over 300 University of Oregon alumni in an attempt to distinguish between the personalities of entrepreneurs and non-entrepreneurs, internal locus of control was the one factor that showed no significant difference.[16] Thus, while an internal locus-of-control belief may be associated with a more active effort to affect the outcome of events, this behavior would seem to hold true for both successful entrepreneurs and successful managers. Therefore, while locus of control fails to distinguish between entrepreneurs and other managers, it could possibly help distinguish successful from unsuccessful entrepreneurs.

Risk-Taking Propensity

McClelland determined that persons with high nAch have moderate risk-taking propensities. As has also been discussed, individuals with high levels of internal locus-of-control beliefs also tend to have high nAch and could thus be classified as moderate risk takers.[17] This concept is of special interest since almost all definitions of entrepreneurs discussed earlier involve risk taking. It is necessary, when considering the idea of risk, to realize there are two parts to the development of the concept: the perceived level of risk in the starting of any venture and the perceived possibility of failure if the venture is unsuccessful. If it is believed that entrepreneurs have a high nAch and a belief in internal locus of control, the apparent contradiction between the definition of entrepreneurs as risk takers and their classification of themselves as moderate risk takers could be resolved. Entrepreneurs have such a high belief in their ability to influence the achievement of business goals that the perceived possibility of failure is relatively low. Thus, the entrepreneur's perceived level of risk is correspondingly lower than that of a non-entrepreneurial personality.

There have been a number of studies supporting the idea that risk bearing is a prime factor in the entrepreneurial character and function.[18] In each of these studies, the establishment of the business was a criteria for being defined as an entrepreneur. Colton and Udell studied the alumni at the University of Oregon. Their results indicated that the personality characteristics most important in identifying entrepreneurial types of individuals are: (1) functional task preference, and (2) personality constructs of creativity, risk, and flexibility. Their results indicate that, with respect to the likelihood of starting a business, the risk scale and creativity scale are much better indicators than nAch and internal locus of control.[19]

Brockhaus cast doubt on the validity of risk-taking propensity as an entrepreneurial characteristic. He found no significant statistical difference in the general risk preference patterns of a group of entrepreneurs and a group of managers.[20] The failure of general risk-taking propensity to distinguish entrepreneurs from managers appears to be a major deviation from the widely held theory that entrepreneurs are the more moderate risk takers. However, the fact that no differences were found does not imply that entrepreneurs are not moderate risk takers. In fact, both entrepreneurs and managers who participated in this study are best described as moderate risk takers because their scores were clustered around the mean score reported by Kogan and Wallach in their original study.[21]

In another study, Sexton and Bowman found that students studying to be entrepreneurs scored higher on the variables of autonomy, change, dominance, endurance, innovation, and self-esteem. They scored lower on level of anxiety, cognitive structure, and performance. Sexton and Bowman found no significant difference in risk-taking propensity of entrepreneur students and those of the general student body.[22] It might be tentatively concluded that general risk-taking propensity is not a determinant in the decision to become an entrepreneur. However, this study does not take into account the perceived probability of failure or a specific business and the perceived consequence of this failure. Students might not be aware of the extensive costs of business failure.

It would appear from the studies performed that risk-taking propensity is not an accurate way of distinguishing entrepreneurs. Their risk-taking propensity varies greatly according to the situation. If business ownership is omitted from the definition of entrepreneur, this would allow the inclusion of corporate entrepreneurs and would reduce risk bearing as a prime factor.

Problem-solving Style and Innovativeness

Hoy and Hellriegel conducted an empirical study of entrepreneurs to assess the model of problem-solving styles suggested by Kilmann and Herden. This model assumes that managers possess relatively permanent cognitive processes by which they perceive data and make judgments. These processes define their problem-solving styles. The study also assumed that the manager's perception of problems and organizational goals is a function of the manager's problem-solving style.[23] Hoy and Hellriegel discovered that the vast majority of the 150 small business managers they studied in Texas were characterized by sensation-thinking problem solving styles.[24] These types of individuals are typified as preferring to deal with "here and now" problems, especially those of a technical or procedural nature.

These small business managers are heavily biased toward identifying their major problems as internal to the organization. Because the firms are small—eight to thirteen employees—the managers may be overwhelmed with the pressure to get the product or service out the door. Their limited resources and concern with day-to-day problems may create tunnel vision. This supports Solomon's findings that entrepreneurs are short-term oriented.[25]

Since entrepreneurs are faced with a number of challenges as they try to implement new ideas and solve the resulting problems, their innovativeness is a major issue. Schumpeter felt that innovation was the central characteristic of entrepreneurial endeavour.[26] Winslow also discussed the idea of innovation and the entrepreneur. He believed that innovation and creativity have occurred under many different business conditions and that innovators seem to believe that puzzles are soluble.[27] In addition, Martin stressed that entrepreneurial creativity is different from literary or artistic creativity in that entrepreneurs do not innovate by creating ideas but by exploring the value of ideas. However, all of these considerations of creativity and innovativeness still do not differentiate the entrepreneur. While the research supports the perception that entrepreneurs are creative, there is nothing in the research that excludes the more traditional business manager from possessing similar creative and innovative ideas.

Values

A consideration of personality characteristics of the entrepreneur must lead to an examination of their value systems. Value orientation might be defined as a generalized and organized conception of nature. This includes an understanding of man's place in the world. More specifically, when discussing entrepreneurs, it refers to the individual's ideas about persons and things.

One of the first major studies of personal values of entrepreneurs was by Hornaday and Aboud.[28] They utilized several objective tests to measure personality characteristics of individuals who had successfully started new businesses. Forty successful entrepreneurs were interviewed and completed the Kuder Occupational Interest Survey (OIS), Gordon's Survey of Interpersonal values, and a questionnaire drawn from Edward's Personal Preference Scale (EPPS). Entrepreneurs scored significantly higher than the general population on the EPPS scale reflecting the need for achievement and on the SIV scale for independence and effectiveness of leadership. They scored lower on the SIV need for support scale. The OIS scales were not significantly different from the general population.

These findings would seem to support the previous discussion of the entrepreneur's high need for achievement and internal locus of control. However, it should be noted that these tests were performed on successful entrepreneurs rather than unsuccessful or prospective entrepreneurs.

Gasse has conducted several studies on the value orientation of the entrepreneur. His studies seem to indicate that the small business owner-manager or entrepreneur has a different function from the large firm manager or executive, and a different set of attitudes and beliefs about the nature of the management process and business in general. On a continuum of business ideology, Gasse identifies two poles: a rational managerial pole and an intuitive entrepreneurial pole. He believes that a rational managerial business ideology tends to be associated with more complex, integrated ways of thinking than an intuitive-entrepreneurial ideology, where simple cognitive structures would be prevalent.[29] This would seem to suggest that certain types of entrepreneurs may be more effective in specific industrial environments.

Using an abridged version of the Dogmatism Scale elaborated by Rokeach, Gasse concluded that the more open-minded the entrepreneur the more he tends to be oriented toward management. Managerial orientation indicates the degree to which an entrepreneur is likely to entertain abstract concepts and to be scientific and rational in his approach to business problems.[30]

There are several studies that support the intuitive, simple structure of the entrepreneurial value system. Solomon found entrepreneurs to be short-term oriented, while Dunkelberg and Cooper characterized entrepreneurs as having orientations toward growth, independence, or craftmanship.[31] Schwer and Yucelt found that the value orientation of the entrepreneur influenced their risk-taking propensity. Risk-taking propensity varied significantly according to respondents' motivation, how they feel about themselves, the probability of improving themselves, and the probability of accomplishing something useful.[32]

These findings seem to support the perception of the entrepreneur as a concrete thinker, who is concerned with the immediate problems and operations of the business. However, as the organization grows, the entrepreneur would have to adjust his interpretation of the world to deal with its increasing complexity.

Overview of Psychological Characteristics

There have been several recent attempts to synopsize those traits that are necessary to become a successful entrepreneur. Welsh and White identify eleven personal characteristics that they consider elements for success in starting a business.[33] They are the need to control and direct, self-confidence, a sense of urgency, good health, comprehensive awareness (maintaining a general overview), realism, superior conceptual ability, allow need for status, an objective approach to interpersonal relations, emotional stability, and an attraction to challenge rather than risk.

When Churchill examined these eleven characteristics of the entrepreneur, he discovered that at least five of the characteristics that make the entrepreneur successful in the beginning stages of the business venture become detrimental when the company achieves success and begins to grow. Self-confidence, a sense of urgency, superior conceptual ability, a low need for status, and an objective approach to interpersonal relations are all important early in the business life but may be detrimental as the business succeeds and grows.[34] All of these factors may make it difficult for the entrepreneur to delegate responsibility and to engage in the internal bargaining that becomes necessary when more individuals join the organization and consensus is necessary.

The research results seem to indicate that there are few psychological characteristics that distinguish the entrepreneur from business managers. This perception is true whether the studies are dealing with the intention to begin an enterprise or with examining those entrepreneurs who have successfully opened their own business. The research studies seldom take into consideration the type of business the entrepreneur is involved in or the measure of the business's success.

EFFECTS OF PREVIOUS EXPERIENCE

Decisions are made not only on the basis of personality but also with consideration of one's past experiences. The decision to become an entrepreneur must be influenced by events that have preceded the decision. There have been several studies that have examined the effect of past experience, especially previous work experience and the existence of role models, on the decision to become an entrepreneur.

Dissatisfaction with Previous Work Experience

Brockhaus studied previous job satisfaction on the part of the entrepreneur. He used the Job Description Index (JDI) developed by Smith, Kendall, and Hulin to measure the employees' satisfaction with the work itself, their perception of supervision, pay, opportunity for promotion, and their attitude toward co-workers.[35] When compared with the normative population used by the developers of the instrument, the entrepreneurs were found to be significantly less satisfied for all subscales except pay. In the case of the pay subscale, the entrepreneurs were significantly more satisfied. Their greatest dissatisfaction appeared to be with the work itself.

Dissatisfaction appears to be the major source of push from one's job. An extreme degree of dissatisfaction with the previous job seems not only to push the entrepreneur from his previous place of employment but also to convince him that no other place of employment may be a satisfactory alternative. If this perception were to be true, the only solution would be to start one's own business.

Weinrauch studied mid-career change and discovered it is becoming more and more prevalent.[36] This trend is expected to grow as more adults reach the ages of thirty-five to fifty, the prime time for mid-career change. It is estimated that one-third of all executives who change careers will end up in a small, one-person business. This movement is also observable in the professionals, government civil service, and military employees who opt for early retirement.

When twenty-one men and women in the Academy of Distinguished Entrepreneurs at Babson College were questioned by Hornaday and Tieken, frustration with current employment was found to be the prime motivator for starting a new business venture.[37]

Prior dissatisfaction may also indirectly contribute to the success of the new venture. Brockhaus compared successful and unsuccessful entrepreneurs and found that the former were more dissatisfied with previous jobs at the time they decided to start their businesses.[38] They may have been even more highly motivated to succeed since the idea of returning to previous careers was so distasteful.

The research concerning previous job dissatisfaction implies several things. First, most entrepreneurs begin by working for someone else and only leave this situation when their needs are not satisfied. It would appear that the employer's lack of understanding of the entrepreneurial personality leads to a work environment full of frustration. This frustration not only deprives the employer of a trained employee but often creates new competition since most entrepreneurs begin businesses in industries with which they are already familiar. It might be beneficial for larger organizations to attempt to provide entrepreneurial personalities with work environments that satisfy their needs for achievement and autonomy.

Role Models

A number of researchers have reported that entrepreneurs have had previous experience in the industry in which they are starting their business. Prior work experience in the particular line of business correlated positively with success.[39] This high correlation between success rate and previous experience should not be surprising since Cooper found over 97 percent of the new high-technology companies studied had at least one founder who had previously worked in the same industry, and approximately 85 percent of the new firms had initial products or services that drew on the founders' previous technical experience.[40] Thus, the large majority of new entrepreneurs, successful or not, have had previous experience in their industry.

Family and friends also seem to serve as role models for aspiring entrepreneurs. Litvak and Maule found successful high-technology entrepreneurs had fathers who were owner/managers.[41] Brockhaus and Nord asked managers and new entrepreneurs if any close relative or friend had owned a business. They found no significant difference between the two groups.[42]

One area where role models appear to be especially important is with women entrepreneurs. Hisrich and Brush surveyed 468 women entrepreneurs and discovered the majority of women state that their fathers were self-employed. Spouses also were predominantly professionals or held technical positions.[43] This provided the women with good role models as well as a supportive, financially sound environment in which to begin a new business venture.

Ronstadt looked at people who considered starting a new venture and decided not to, in an attempt to discover the reason for their negative decision. The individuals who turned away from the entrepreneurial venture were less likely to have parents who were entrepreneurs, had fewer role models among their acquaintances, had poorer education records, and had little experience in the business under consideration.[44]

These findings seem to support the idea that seeing someone else succeed encourages prospective entrepreneurs to take the risk. In summary, the existence of a successful role model encourages entrepreneurial efforts. These models are often present in the work environment and encourage individuals to begin an entrepreneurial venture, especially when the established work environment does not allow the employee room for creativity. In addition, the presence of strong family support is especially important to women and other minority entrepreneurs, who face special problems when trying to begin a new small business. Also, the higher the technological demands of the chosen industry, the more important it is that the entrepreneur has had prior training and has worked with successful technological experts.

PERSONAL CHARACTERISTICS

Several studies have been conducted to try and determine the association, if any, between personal characteristics and the decision to become an entrepreneur. The main areas of consideration are age, education, and residency. A special section will be devoted to the characteristics of women and minorities.

In one of the most thorough studies to date, Petrof collected information from thirty-two participants in the Entrepreneurship Program at Laval University in Quebec, Canada. He conducted a discriminant analysis on twelve variables: age, years of marriage, years in the labor force, number of previous jobs, years of formal education, number of previous attempts to start a business, oldest child in the family, membership in professional and/or trade organizations, profit expectations, outside encouragement, anticipated difficulties, and evaluation of personal shortcomings. The characteristic most frequently associated with the entrepreneurial group was being the oldest child in the family. Holding a large number of previous jobs was associated with the non-entrepreneurial type.[45]

Dunkelberg and Cooper also studied a number of personal characteristics of the entrepreneur. When they surveyed 1,805 small business owners, research findings indicated that substantial differences existed in their background, depending upon how they became owners and their specific industry.[46]

Education

One of the major concerns of those interested in innovation and continued growth of new business is the issue of whether entrepreneurs are born or whether they can be created through training. This makes the education issue an important one. Hornaday and Tieken discovered that many of the successful entrepreneurs felt that, prior to the current generation of young people, special education was less important for entrepreneurs. Now, however, because of the growth of high technology and heavy competition, education was especially important.[47]

Reflecting this concern for education, Vesper expressed the belief that the most likely entrepreneurs to fail would be those with experience but no education. The second most likely entrepreneurs to fail would be those with education but no experience. Conversely, those entrepreneurs who had both experience ane education would be associated with the most profitable business enterprises.[48]

When comparing educational levels of entrepreneurs and managers, Brockhaus and Nord found the level of education to be significantly less for entrepreneurs than for managers.[49] The entrepreneurs averaged 13.57 years of education while the managers averaged 15.74 years. The managers, due to their higher level of education, may have been able to obtain more satisfying jobs. If their jobs proved unacceptable, this level of education allowed them to obtain more desirable employment elsewhere. It should be noted that the education of the entrepreneurs in this study did exceed that of the average person. This finding is consistent with previous research by Howell.[50]

In summary, while experience is perceived as the critical factor in the determination of the business effort's direction, entrepreneurs appear to benefit from both appropriate experience and education.

Women and Minority Entrepreneurs

As more women and minorities have become entrepreneurs, research has been conducted to see how these special groups differ from the white male population that formed the subjects for prior research. During the seventies, blacks were shown to have the lowest participation rates of minority entrepreneurs, while Hispanic and Asian participation rates were showing little increase.[51] In addition, a number of women were beginning entrepreneurial ventures in hopes of overcoming the sex/pay discrimination problem. However, the U.S. Department of Commerce Bureau of the Census report in 1976 indicated that a large gap still existed. There are over 400,000 women-owned businesses, which is approximately 3 percent of all small businesses, yet the female owners' share of total profits was just 0.3 percent.[52] This showed the imbalance between business ownership and monetary receipts of male- and female-owned business ventures.

In addition to profitability, other features of female business owners have been researched in an attempt to discover any distinguishing traits. Schwartz studied twenty female entrepreneurs and found that their major motivations for starting a business were the need to achieve, the desire to be independent, economic necessity, and the need for job satisfaction. These findings seem to correspond with those discovered about the white male population.[53] Also, Sexton and Kent found that female entrepreneurs, just as their male counterparts, differed little in personality characteristics from female managers.[54]

Women entrepreneurs do, however, exhibit some distinctive characteristics. Hisrich and O'Brien found that women entrepreneurs were older and more educated than either the general populace or the male respondents to previous studies. They also had very supportive parents and husbands.[55] This is supported by Smith, McCain, and Warren's research, which profiled women entrepreneurs as having a high educational level.[56]

These findings were further substantiated by two recent studies. Cuba, Decenzo, and Anish collected data from fifty-eight female owners of small businesses.[57] The survey results indicated that successful women owners delegate certain key tasks to employees, are more highly educated, and have more prior work experience than less successful females. Both education and experience were found to be important. In addition, Hisrich and Brush sampled 468 women entrepreneurs in the United States in 1984. The majority were between thirty-five and forty-five, were married and had children, and were the first born in their families. Most had attended college or graduate schools, yet few were trained in technical areas. The majority of women entrepreneurs stated that their fathers were self-employed. Interestingly, but not unexpectedly, 90 percent of the respondents operated service businesses.[58]

A final study to be reviewed is one conducted by DeCarlo and Lyons.[59] Their research explored the characteristics of minority and non-minority female entrepreneurs. The results indicated that the minority females were somewhat older than their non-minority counterparts, and they started their businesses at a later age. A much higher proportion of the minority females reported never having been married. The non-minority females had higher levels of education and higher achievement during their educational experiences. On the personality scale, non-minority females placed a higher value on the scales of achievement, support, recognition, and independence. The minority females placed higher value on conformity and benevolence. Both groups differed significantly from women in the general population on these scales.

These studies seem to indicate that women entrepreneurs have many of the same motivating forces and personality traits of their male counterparts. In both instances, dissatisfaction and the need for achievement were the reasons given for becoming an entrepreneur. There are several characteristics of women entrepreneurs that reflect the difficulties that still exist in terms of discrimination. In order for women to begin and successfully manage their own business, they need more education and stronger support from their families. The lower levels of education of minorities would appear to be reflective of general cultural inequalities.

CHANGING CLASSIFICATIONS OF THE ENTREPRENEUR

The literature is beginning to reflect the belief that a generic definition of the entrepreneur does not exist. Van de Ven warned researchers not to be tempted into the study of traits and personality characteristics. He compared the development of the effort to identify who is going to become an entrepreneur with the historical development of leadership theory.[60]

> Researchers wedded to the conception of entrepreneurship for studying the creation of organizations can learn much from the history of research on leadership. Like the students of entrepreneurship, this research began by investigating the traits and personality characteristics of leaders. However, no empirical evidence was found to support the expectation that there are a finite number of characteristics to traits of leaders and that these traits differentiate successful from unsuccessful leaders. More recently, research into leadership has apparently made some progress by focusing on the behavior of leaders (that is what they do rather than what they are) and by determining what situational factors or conditions moderate the effects of their behavior or performance.

This expresses the current belief of theorists that the appropriate leadership style will change according to the situation. It is possible for almost everyone to be a leader if timing, environment, and situation are right. Similarly, it is possible for almost anyone to be an entrepreneur if the appropriate conditions exist. There is not a single type of entrepreneur, just as there is not a single type of leader.

An example of this new approach to viewing the entrepreneur can be seen in Vesper's work. He has developed an eleven-category range of entrepreneurial styles:[61] (1) solo-self-employed individuals, (2) team builders, (3) independent innovators, (4) pattern multipliers, (5) economy of scale exploiters, (6) capital aggregators, (7) acquirers, (8) buy-sell artists, (9) conglomerators, (10) speculators, (11) apparent value manipulators.

When examining Vesper's classification it is possible to find entrepreneurial types who do not create a new business or even own the business. This continuum recognizes that the environment surrounding the entrepreneurial decision is highly varied. The personality of the individual who could be a successful solo-self-employed business owner would be much different than that of the speculator. While Vesper's approach is only one way to categorize entrepreneurs, such a broad classification system supports the argument that there is no generic entrepreneur. A more meaningful approach might be to attempt to link the background and personality characteristics to the type of entrepreneurial behavior they are likely to exhibit.

Barry offers a different approach to the classification of entrepreneurs.[62] His research suggests that small and medium firms could be classified as either those still controlled by their entrepreneurial founders or those that are traditional family businesses. The entrepreneurial firms reflect the founder's personality, while family businesses are in second, third, or subsequent generations. An expansion of this classification system would be the addition of the category of high-technology entrepreneur. The high-technology entrepreneur was associated initially with the development of a range of high technologies in space and computers. These entrepreneurs tend to be highly educated in the science or technologies and to have studied in business administration and/or have established a team of business associates who have the necessary business skills to launch a high-technology venture.[63]

While high-technology entrepreneurs have more sophisticated educational background, Litvak and Maule reported several characteristics of the high-technology entrepreneur that are similar to those of the traditional small business owner.[64] High-technology entrepreneurs had prior experience in the field and fathers who were either owners or managers and functioned as role models. In addition, their main motivating "push" was from former companies who refused to permit them creative expression.

Many researchers believe that it is possible for entrepreneurs to function successfully within a large corporation. Leibenstein believed that entrepreneurial activity within the organization would be aimed toward the reduction of organizational inefficiency and the reversal of organizational entropy.[65] For large organizations to flourish, entrepreneurial workers must be encouraged rather than restrained. However, most organizations are resistant to change and drive out entrepreneurs. In order for large organizations to keep entrepreneurs, they must provide freedom to make things happen with an environment of few restrictions.[66]

The final approach to identifying entrepreneurs to be discussed is the population ecology school of thought. Freeman and many other population ecologists believe that environmental forces are more important in understanding organizations' creation and survival than are the adaptive actions and attributes of individual entrepreneurs.[67] Several studies support this view. Bruno and Tyzoon discussed environmental studies that have shown that availability of economic resources is conducive to the creation of new ventures.[68] These resources include venture capital, land, real estate, transportation facilities, supporting facilities and a technologically skilled labor force. These studies also revealed factors such as proximity to centers of higher education, entrepreneurial climate, public attitudes, and the quality of living conditions also influence new business development.

In a similar study, when Pennings examined seventy urban areas, the quality of life in terms of economic, education, and health issues was shown to have the most positive impact on the creation of new firms. Contrarily, quality in the political and environmental sector had a negative impact on the creation of new firms.[69] This approach contrasts sharply with the investigations that have dealt with personality characteristics and other psychological attributes as being the determining factors in entrepreneurial decision.

Concluding Comments

The literature appears to support the argument that there is no generic definition of the entrepreneur, or if there is we do not have the psychological instruments to discover it at this time. Most of the attempts to distinguish between entrepreneurs and small business owners or managers have discovered no significant differentiating features.

A few general characteristics of the entrepreneur do emerge, however. The entrepreneur does appear to be achievement oriented and, at least in the early stages of the business venture, have internal locus of control. In general, their values approach has been to concentrate on making short-run decisions and solving immediate problems. This tendency to view the world in concrete, short-run terms could possibly result from the heavy work load assumed by most entrepreneurs. Most entrepreneurs do not usually possess the financial resources or managerial skills to effectively delegate.

From an environmental perspective, most entrepreneurs have a successful role model, either in their family or the work place. However, if the work environment provided more freedom and opportunity for creative expression, most entrepreneurs would probably never open their own businesses.

Entrepreneurs come from both sexes, all races, and a variety of family and educational backgrounds. The female entrepreneur is usually better educated and from a higher social class than her male counterpart. This is probably the result of cultural discrimination rather than a reflection of necessary characteristics of the female entrepreneur.

More and more researchers are recognizing multiple classifications when trying to identify the entrepreneur. Entrepreneurs have been classified by how they have acquired the business ownership: through family inheritance, the purchase of an existing business, or the creation of a new enterprise. They also are frequently grouped by the technological nature of their business.

There have been some serious limitations in most of the research conducted on the psychology of the entrepreneur. The subjects either are aspiring to become entrepreneurs, with no business track record, or are entrepreneurs who have succeeded. One possibility for future research would be a longitudinal study of aspiring entrepreneurs through the creation and managing of their business. This would provide the opportunity to study the traits of both successful and unsuccessful entrepreneurs.

Another limitation of the research is that the types of businesses are seldom identified. The characteristics that lead an entrepreneur to open a service business successfully would be much different from those of a manufacturer. A research possibility might be the comparison of entrepreneurs in several different industries.

It would appear from the research findings that the characteristics of the aspiring or successful entrepreneur vary depending upon the nature and scope of the business venture. Most entrepreneurial ventures result from a "push" from external factors. Either the timing and economic conditions are favorable or the dissatisfaction with other work options so great that starting a business is the best option. It might be beneficial to concentrate research efforts on determining why entrepreneurs succeed or fail. This would allow the development of appropriate training and educational programs and increase the probability of success.

NOTES TO CHAPTER 2

1. J.S. Mill, *Principles of Political Economy with Some Applications to Social Philosophy* (London: John W. Parker, 1848), p. 32.

2. J.A. Schumpeter, *The Theory of Economic Development*, Harvard University Press, Cambridge, Mass, 1934, p. 56.

3. Israel M. Kirzner, "The Theory of Entrepreneurship in Economic Growth," in Calvin A. Kent, Donald L. Sexton, and Karl H. Vesper, eds., *Encyclopedia of Entrepreneurship* (Englewood Cliffs, N.J.: Prentice-Hall, 1982), pp. 272–76.

4. E.T. Penrose, *The Theory of Growth of the Firm* (Oxford: Basil Blackwell, 1968), pp. 46–50.

5. D.C. McClelland, *The Achieving Society* (Princeton, N.J.: D. Van Nostrand, 1961), p. 67.

6. Wayne Long, "The Meaning of Entrepreneurship," *American Journal of Small Business* VIII: 2 (Oct.–Dec., 1983): 47–56.

7. J.W. Carland, F. Hoy, W.R. Boulton and J.C. Carland, "Differentiating Entrepreneurs for Small Business Owners: A Conceptualization," *Academy of Management Review* 9: 2 (1984): 354–59.

8. J.A. Hornaday and J. Aboud, "Characterizations of Successful Entrepreneurs," *Personnel Psychology* 24 (1971): 141–53.

9. D.C. McClelland, *The Achieving Society*, p. 38; D.C. McClelland, "Need Achievement and Entrepreneurship: A Longitudinal Study," *Journal of Personality and Social Psychology* 1 (1965): 389–92; D.C. McClelland and D.G. Winter, *Motivating Economic Achievement* (New York: Free Press, 1969).

10. J.B. Rotter, "Generalized Expectations for Internal Versus External Control of Reinforcement," *Psychological Monographs* 80 (1966): 609.

11. D. Berlew, "The Nature of Entrepreneurs," *Proceedings of Project ISEED* (International Symposium on Entrepreneurship and Enterprise Development). Sponsored by The Ohio Entrepreneurship Office, Columbus, Ohio, 1975, pp. 42–44.

12. C. Borland, "Locus of Control," *Need for Achievement and Entrepreneurship* (Ph.D. dissertation, University of Texas at Austin, 1974), p. 115.

13. John V. Petrof, "Entrepreneurial Profile: A Disciminant Analysis," *Journal of Small Business Management* 19: 4 (October 1981): 13–17.

14. R.H. Brockhaus and W.R. Nord, "An Exploration of Factors Affecting the Entrepreneurial Decision: Personal Characteristics vs. Environmental Conditions," *Proceedings of the National Academy of Management*, 1979.

15. R.H. Brockhaus, "Risk Taking Propensity of Entrepreneurs," *Academy of Management Journal* 23: 3 (1980): 509–20.

16. David Hull, John J. Bosley, and Gerald G. Udell, "Renewing the Hunt for Means of Identifying Potential Entrepreneurs by Personality Characteristics," *Journal of Small Business Management* 20: 2 (March 1982): 11–19.

17. D.C. McClelland, *The Achieving Society.*

18. J.A. Welsh and J.F. White, "Converging on Characteristics of Entrepreneurs," in K.H. Vesper, ed., *Frontiers of Entrepreneurship Research* (Wellesley, Mass.: Babson Center for Entrepreneurial Studies, 1981), pp. 504–15.

19. Robert Colton and Gerald G. Udell, "The National Science Foundation's Innovation Center—An Experiment in Training Potential Entrepreneurs and Innovators," *Journal of Small Business Management* (April 1976): 11–20.

20. R.H. Brockhaus, "Risk Taking Propensity of Entrepreneurs."

21. N. Kogan and M.A. Wallach, *Risk Taking* (New York: Holt, Rinehart and Winston, 1964).

22. Donald Sexton and Nancy B. Bowman, "Comparative Entrepreneurships, Characteristics of Students," in J.A. Hornaday, J. Timmons, and K. Vesper, eds., *Frontiers of Entrepreneurship Research* (Wellesley, Mass.: Babson Center for Entrepreneurial Studies, 1983), pp. 465–78.

23. R.H. Kilmann and R.P. Herden, "Toward a Systemic Methodology for Evaluating the Impact of Interventions on Organizational Effectiveness," *Academy of Management Review* V: 3 (1976): 87–98.

24. Frank Hoy and Don Hellriegel, "The Killmann and Herden Model of Organizational Effectiveness Criteria for Small Business Managers," *Academy of Management Journal* 25: 2 (1982): 308–22.

25. G. Solomon, "Relationship of Selected Characteristics of Small Business Owner-Managers to their Businesses' Probability of Success" (Ph,D. dissertation, The George Washington University, Washington, D.C., 1982).

26. J.A. Schumpeter, *The Theory of Economic Development* (Cambridge, Mass.: Harvard University Press, 1934).

27. Erik K. Winslow, "Product and Innovations: The Human Side," in George Solomon and Bruce Whiting, eds., *Proceedings of Creativity, Innovation and Entrepreneurship Symposium* (Denver, Colo.: Creative Education Foundation Inc., Feb. 1984).

28. J.A. Hornaday and J. Aboud, "Characteristics of Successful Entrepreneurs," *Personnel Psychology* 24 (1971): 141–53.

29. Y. Gasse, *Entrepreneurial Characteristics and Practices: A Study of the Dynamics of Small Business Organizations and Their Effectiveness in Different Environments* (Sherbrooke, Quebec: Rene Prince, 1977).

30. Y. Gasse, "Characteristic Functions and Performance of Small Firm Owner-Managers in Two Industrial Environments" (Ph.D. dissertation, Northwestern University, 1978).

31. W.C. Dunkelberg and A.C. Cooper, "Entrepreneurial Typologies," in K.H. Vesper, ed., *Frontiers of Entrepreneurship Research* (Wellesley, Mass.: Babson Center for Entrepreneurial Studies, 1982), pp. 1–15.

32. Keith R. Schwer and Ugur Yucelt, "A Study of Risk-Taking Propensities among Small Business Entrepreneurs and Managers: An Empirical Evaluation," *American Journal of Small Business* VIII (Jan.-Mar. 1984): 31–37.

33. J.A. Welsh and J.F. White, "Converging on Characteristics of Entrepreneurs."

34. Neil C. Churchill, "Entrepreneurs and Their Enterprises, a Stage Model," in Hornaday, Timmons, and Vesper, eds., *Frontiers of Entrepreneurship Research*, pp. 1–14.

35. R.H. Brockhaus, "The Effect of Job Dissatisfaction on the Decision to Start a Business," *Journal of Small Business Management* 18: 1 (Jan. 1980): 37–43.

36. Donald J. Weinrauch, "The Second Time Around: Entrepreneurship as a Mid Career Alternative," *Journal of Small Business Management* 19: 4 (Oct. 1981): 13–17.

37. John A. Hornaday and Nancy B. Tieken, "Capturing Twenty-One Heffalumps," in Hornaday, Timmons, and Vesper, *Frontiers of Entrepreneurial Research*, pp. 25–29.

38. R.H. Brockhaus, "The Authoritarian Entrepreneur," in Hornaday, Timmons, and Vesper, *Frontiers of Entrepreneurial Research*, pp. 64–67.

39. K.H. Vesper, *New Venture Strategies* (Englewood Cliffs, N.J.: Prentice-Hall, 1980).

40. A.C. Cooper, "Technical Entrepreneurship: What Do We Know?" *Research and Development Management* 3 (Feb. 1973).

41. I.A. Litvak and C.J. Maule, *Canadian Entrepreneurship: A Study of Small Newly Established Firms* (Ottawa: Department of Industry, Trade, and Commerce, 1971).

42. R.H. Brockhaus and W.R. Nord, "An Exploration of Factors Affecting the Entrepreneurial Decision: Personal Characteristics vs. Environmental Conditions," *Proceedings of the National Academy of Management*, 1979.

43. Robert D. Hisrich and Candida Brush, "The Women of Entrepreneur: Management Skills and Business Problems," *Journal of Small Business Management* 22: 1 (Jan. 1984): 31–37.
44. Robert Ronstadt, "The Decision Not to Become an Entrepreneur," in Hornaday, Timmons, and Vesper *Frontiers of Entrepreneurship Research*, pp. 456–62.
45. John V. Petrof, "Entrepreneurial Profile."
46. W.C. Dunkelberg and A.C. Cooper, "Entrepreneurial Typologies," in Vesper, *Frontiers of Entrepreneurship Research* (1982), pp. 1–15.
47. John Hornaday and Nancy B. Tieken, "Capturing Twenty-One Heffalumps," pp. 24–28.
48. K.H. Vesper, "Introduction and Summary of Entrepreneurship Research," in Kent, Sexton, and Vesper, *Encyclopedia of Entrepreneurship*, pp. xxi–xxxviii.
49. R.H. Brockhaus and W.R. Nord, "An Exploration of Factors Affecting the Entrepreneurial Decision.
50. R.P. Howell, "Comparative Profiles: Entrepreneurs Versus the Hired Executive: San Francisco Peninsula Semiconductor Industry," *Technical Entrepreneurship: A Symposium*, Milwaukee: Center for Venture Management, 1972.
51. Bruce Kirchoff, Richard L. Stevens, and Norman I. Hurwitz, "Factors Underlying Increases in Minority Entrepreneurship," in Vesper, *Frontiers of Entrepreneurship Research* (1982), pp. 87–89.
52. U.S. Department of Commerce, Bureau of Census, *Women Owned Business, 1972* (Washington, D.C.: Government Printing Office, 1976).
53. Eleanor B. Schwartz, "Entrepreneurship: A New Female Frontier," *Journal of Contemporary Business* (Winter 1979): 47–76.
54. Donald Sexton and Calvin Kent, "Female Executives Versus Female Entrepreneurs," in Vesper, *Frontiers of Entrepreneurship Research* (1981), pp. 40–45.
55. Robert Hisrich and Marie O'Brien, "The Women Entrepreneur," in Vesper, *Frontiers of Entrepreneurship Research* (1981), pp. 21–29.
56. G. McCain and N. Smith, "A Contemporary Model of Entrepreneurial Style," *Small Business Institute Review* (Summer 1981): 44.
57. Richard Cuba, David DeCenzo, and Andrea Anish, "Management Practices of Successful Female Business Owners," *American Journal of Small Business* VIII: 2 (Oct.–Dec. 1983): 40–46.
58. Robert Hisrich and Candida Brush, "The Women Entrepreneur."
59. James DeCarlo and Raul Lyons, "Comparisons of Selected Personal Characteristics of Minority and Non-Minority Female Entrepreneurs," *Journal of Small Business Management* 19: 3 (June 1981): 23–28.
60. A.H. Van de Ven, "Early Planning, Implementation and Performance of New Organizations," in J.R. Kimberly and R. Miles, eds., *The Organization Life Cycle* (San Francisco: Jossey Bass, 1980), pp. 83–134.

61. K.H. Vesper, *New Venture Strategies.*
62. B. Barry, "Human And Organizational Problems Affecting Growth in the Smaller Enterprise," *Management Review* 5: 4 (Sept. 1980): 14–16.
63. E.B. Roberts, "Business Planning in the Startup of High Technology Enterprise," in Hornaday, Timmons, and Vesper, *Frontiers of Entrepreneurship Research*, pp. 107–17.
64. I.A. Litvak and C.J. Maule, "Some Characteristics of Successful Technical Entrepreneurs in Canada," *IEEE Transactions on Engineering Management*, EM-20: 3 (August 1973): 62–68.
65. Harvey Leibenstein, "Entrepreneurship and Development," *American Economic Review* 58 (May 1968).
66. Richard Molz, "Entrepreneurial Managers in Large Organizations," *Business Horizons* 27: 5 (Sept.–Oct. 1984): 54–58.
67. J. Freeman, "Organizational Life Cycles and Natural Selection Processes," in B.M. Staw and L.L. Cummings, eds., *Research in Organizational Behavior* 4 (Greenwich, Conn.: JAI Press, 1982).
68. A.V. Bruno and T.T. Tyzoon, "The Environment of Entrepreneurship" (Paper for the Conference on Research and Teaching of Entrepreneurship, Baylor University, 1980).
69. J.M. Pennings, "The Urban Quality of Life and Entrepreneurship," *Academy of Management Journal* 25: 1 (1982): 63–79.

THE DEVELOPMENT OF NEW ENTREPRENEURS
A Belief-Based Approach

Yvon Gasse

This paper presents a belief-based approach for dealing with the characteristics of the entrepreneur. Our research results with this approach in the last seven years tend to show that the entrepreneur can be identified and differentiated from the manager and that concrete suggestions can be made for the development of appropriate entrepreneurial styles and behaviors.

COGNITIVE ORIENTATIONS OF ENTREPRENEURS

Although the emphasis on the attributes of the individual entrepreneur does not mean that researchers have ignored the basic requirements for certain skills and a high level of intelligence, it seems, nevertheless, that an important factor may have been neglected. In fact, the actual evaluation of entrepreneurial success, as well as the choice of a particular specialty of managerial activity involves not only deeply rooted personality factors but also situationally as well as culturally defined conditions that may be designated in their most general way as "cognitive orientations" and "values."

An individual who in the general organizational environment of the small business firm might (for personality reasons) become a successful entrepreneur would not do so in a large corporation in which

49

both the cognitive orientations (i.e., the technological and managerial environments) and the values (i.e., professional management as a prestigious role) are different. This consideration is of particular importance if we wish to apply any findings of the relationship between entrepreneurial performance and entrepreneurs' attributes to specific situations.

The cognitive orientations affect not only the actual choice of career (or of types of organization) of a person but also the kinds of emphasis expressed by entrepreneurs on specific functions or activities perceived to be more conducive to managerial as well as organizational performance. Furthermore, there seems to exist a better consensus among authors as to what constitutes cognitive orientations more representative of entrepreneurs as compared to other types of managers. Cognitive orientations make reference to the attitudes, beliefs, and values of the entrepreneur toward various aspects of the business world deemed to be relevant in the dynamic functioning of small business enterprises. With such an approach, the motives of the entrepreneurs will be reflected in their attitudes; these motives for entrepreneurship form a sequence in the attitudes of individual entrepreneurs throughout their business lives.

Consequently, the actual course of action taken by the entrepreneur, in the process of adapting his organization to the environment, depends not only on the requirements of this environment but also (and sometimes mainly) on the beliefs, values, and attitudes of the entrepreneur about certain aspects of his functions, his enterprise, and even the environment. For instance, if the situation in the environment of a small business organization is such that a proper course of action to be taken by the entrepreneur, if he wants his organization to grow, would be to adopt a new product as soon as possible (early imitation), the entrepreneur may choose not to do it because he feels that the risks are too great or that the increase in growth resulting from this strategy would bring additional problems that he is not ready to cope with. Another instance would be the case of a small business organization that has been advised, in order to be more efficient, to adopt some formal techniques and practices of financial as well as manpower control and would not follow this advice because the entrepreneur distrusts these techniques, dislikes to change his habits, and believes that such practices might upset his employees; the entrepreneur may also believe that the best control mechanism for his business is his feeling and intuition. The conse quences for the evolution of the organization of such a conception on the part of the entrepreneur are quite evident; the entrepreneur would not allow his organization to grow beyond a point where he would feel that he could not control directly and personally the operations of his business. Our argument is that the way in which an entrepreneur performs his functions is partly conditioned by the requirements of the environment in which he operates and is partly dependent on the cognitive orientation in terms of attitudes, beliefs, and values of the individual himself. The question is, which attitudes, beliefs, and values are relevant for the entrepreneurial function?

ENTREPRENEUR VERSUS ADMINISTRATOR

The management process in the small business organization will be performed quite differently from the management process in large companies. In fact, the role of entrepreneur is quite different from the role of the professional administrator in large organizations. The term "entrepreneur"—that is, a person in effective control of a business unit—underlines the adaptive nature of managerial processes in the small firm. It has connotations of enterprise, opportunism, individuality, and intuition, in contrast to the connotations of the terms manager and administrator, which are associated with notions of organization, planning, professionalism, rationality, and the predictive management processes. It is our argument that the small business owner–manager or entrepreneur has both a different function from the large firm manager or administrator and a different set of attitudes or beliefs about the nature of the management process and business in general.

The administrator in the large firm is primarily concerned with those activities relevant to predictive management processes—that is, with activities related to prediction and control—whereas the owner-manager of a small business organization needs primarily to perform activities relevant to adaptive management processes, activities that enable him to exploit the advantages of being small. However, the management process as we conceive it is not a dichotomy; it is rather a continuum, and, therefore, incorporates both an administrative element and an entrepreneurial element. The two sets of elements are not mutually exclusive but complementary, both within an organization and, in many cases, within a particular role. It is the emphasis that is necessarily different when considering the demands of large and small firms for these two kinds of management activities, necessarily different because of differences in the environment, in the scale of operations, in the degree of specialization, and in the professionalization of management of the small and the large business organization.

Similarly, just as the entrepreneur would put the emphasis on the entrepreneurial activities of the management process, so too would he hold attitudes related to the entrepreneurial orientation, while the administrator of larger organizations would hold attitudes related to the administrative orientation of the management process.

DOMINANT BELIEFS

Again, the literature on entrepreneurship contains many cases and studies showing that organizational effectiveness is closely related to a particular type of business and managerial orientation. These studies show a high degree of consistency regarding the beliefs claimed to be most appropriate for entrepreneurship. It is not one particular belief that is deemed important but the whole system of beliefs. On the basis of previous studies, the following beliefs were singled out for investigation:

1. *Belief about business firm and businessman.* This deals with the entrepreneur's view of his firm and his role.

2. *Belief about risk taking.* This concerns the extent to which the entrepreneur is willing to take calculated risks.

3. *Belief about wealth and material gain.* An evaluation of the entrepreneur's perception of profits, investment, interests, economic security, and so forth.

4. *Belief about subordinates.* An assessment of the entrepreneur's trust in subordinates.

5. *Belief about business growth.* This taps the entrepreneur's perception of the bounds for the expansion of his firm.

6. *Belief about scientific methods and practices.* This refers to the entrepreneur's attitude toward the methodology developed for the analysis of various problems in the physical and social sciences as well as in the business world.

7. *Belief about competition.* This pertains to the entrepreneur's competitiveness and economic aggressivity.

8. *Belief about uncertainty and change.* An evaluation of the extent to which the entrepreneur is open to change.

9. *Belief about delegation of authority.* An appraisal of the entrepreneur's readiness to delegate authority.

10. *Belief about the control of fate in business.* This concerns the entrepreneur's perception of his influence over his business or the degree to which he relies on chance and external forces.

ENTREPRENEURIAL IDEOLOGY

The attitudes or beliefs just described are somewhat related to one another. They are all about specific aspects of a common phenomenon, the business world; it is quite likely that they form a "cluster." None of these attitudes can be thought of as existing in a complete state of isolation. It is plausible that the degree to which these attitudes form a comprehensive and orderly pattern might be taken as one indication of the degree of unity in the entrepreneur's cognitive orientation. However, only rarely will an entrepreneur or manager exhibit such a high degree of unity of attitudes toward the business world that we would be justified in saying he has a single ideology of business; but it is possible that the effects of attitudinal dissonance upon entrepreneurial behavior would be found to be substantial and pervasive.

Since we assume that these attitudes form a cluster with varying degrees of consonance and interconnectedness, it would be more appropriate, then, to refer to this set of attitudes as a system or, more precisely, as an ideology of business. The business process can be conceptualized as a continuous spectrum of activities ranging from entrepreneurial elements to managerial or administrative elements. Furthermore, each attitude or belief could be represented on a continuum; one section of the continuum would represent the valence of the attitudes deemed to be representative of the entrepreneur, and the other section of the continuum would represent the valence of the attitudes deemed to be representative of the manager in the large firm. For instance, a manager in a large firm would tend to be more favorable with respect to an attitude that stresses the importance of delegation than the entrepreneur in a smaller firm. Therefore, it is possible to conceive of an ideology of business represented on a continuum ranging from entrepreneurial-intuitive at one pole up to managerial-rational at the other end. The advantage of the continuum is that it allows for any intermediate positions between these two extremes.

The concept of ideology or system of attitudes clearly indicates that it is not the effect of one attitude taken in isolation that is important here, but rather the influence of the whole set of attitudes. Rokeach noted that much theory and research are focused on the properties, the determinants, and the measurement of single beliefs or attitudes, rather than on belief systems or attitudes systems.[1] He then argues for a focus on the belief system as a whole, since much of man's behavior can be better understood by relating such behavior to man's belief or attitude systems rather than to the elements of such systems. Then, according to our approach, the way an entrepreneur performs his functions is largely dependent upon his cognitive orientation or, more precisely, his business ideology. Businessmen with an entrepreneurial-intuitive business ideology would tend to view their firm as an extension of the self and the family; they would be conservative risk takers, reluctant to change and suspicious about scientific methods. They would see limits to the size of their firm and take business profits as personal income or gratifications. Paternalism would be the major pattern of superior-subordinates relationships, and they would tend to think that they cannot control much of what happens to their business. Although this description may be conceived of as an ideal type, it does show our argument that this description should be more representative of the views and attitudes of entrepreneurs than of managers in large firms.

Obviously, there are many psychological adjustments to be made by owner-managers of growing organizations. Developing the owner-manager of a small but expanding business from an extrepreneurial orientation toward a managerial one may involve a complete reappraisal of his business ideology during the transitional stages. Not only should we talk about evolution but revolution on the part of the entrepreneur. According to Greiner, in successful transitions the necessary attitude changes on the part of the entrepreneur are made during the crisis stages when the individual is subjected to a multitude of influences and pressures.[2] There is strong evidence that this transition is one of the most difficult problems that entrepreneurs have to face in the course of their business lives. For instance, Greiner suggested that entrepreneurs, realizing that their own managerial styles are no longer appropriate, may even have to take themselves out of leadership positions. He also noted that a management that is aware of the problems ahead could well decide not to grow. It seems that the success of the transition is dependent not only on the rapidity with which it is done but also on some personality characteristics having to do with the structure of the individual's cognitive system, his openness, flexibility, or degree of consonance among his attitudes.

BUSINESS AND MANAGERIAL IDEOLOGY SCALE

A Likert-type scale based upon the beliefs just described was developed. Scores could vary from one pole of a continuum to the other. Again, for the purpose of identification, one pole was categorized as entrepreneurial-intuitive (craftsman type) and the other pole was called managerial-rational (executive type).

This scale has been tested, and the validation procedures have shown metrological qualities equivalent and often superior to similar scales in different areas. The scale has been used in many instances for evaluating the cognitive orientations of entrepreneurs and managers and, in particular, for identifying and helping potential entrepreneurs.[3]

SELECTED RESULTS

In this section, we will present some selected results in using the business and managerial ideology scale and related particularly to the main issues discussed previously. The sample for the main study was composed of fifty-one entrepreneurs of small manufacturing firms in the shoe and plastics industries located in the Province of Quebec, Canada, and employing between 20 and 250 people. The data were collected through semi-constructed interviews conducted by the author and complemented by the business and managerial ideology scale.

Entrepreneurs Compared to Managers

We suggested earlier that one of the main hypotheses underlying the business and managerial ideology scale would be that managers in large corporations would score higher on the scale than owner-managers in small firms. We have been able to test this hypothesis on many occasions. For instance, we have compared the mean scores on this scale between fifty-one entrepreneurs and a group of twenty-six top and middle managers of large corporations (all corporations had more than 2,000 employees). The group of top and middle managers scored, on the average, significantly higher than the entrepreneurs ($t = 3.62$, $p < 0.001$). The same comparisons have been made between 140 high level civil servants, all top administrators in various public departments and agencies of the government of the Province of Quebec. Although the total score is a little lower than that of managers of large corporations, it is still statistically different from the score of entrepreneurs ($t = 2.97$, $p < 0.05$). Finally, the lowest average score we obtained on this scale was from a group of twenty-seven junior managers of small business cooperatives in Africa. These people were enrolled in a special one-year program on cooperative management at the University of Sherbrooke, and they filled out our questionnaire when they were about halfway through their program. Many complex factors may have influenced their answers, but after talking to them, we found that the type and size of their business units were crucial determinants.

Entrepreneurial Beliefs and Management Practices

We had an hypothesis that stated that entrepreneurs with a managerial business ideology would tend to use more organizational techniques and practices than entrepreneurs with an intuitive-entrepreneurial business ideology. The major argument behind this hypothesis was that the managerially oriented businessman would tend to hold favorable attitudes toward formal organizational techniques and practices and would tend to be more rational in his approach to business functions.

Although more research evidence would be necessary to explain the relationships fully, the results tend to show that shoe entrepreneurs are using more organizational techniques and practices mainly because their enterprises are larger and require these techniques and not necessarily because they are more managerially oriented. On the other hand, plastics entrepreneurs make more use of organizational techniques and practices because they are, in general, more managerially oriented. When controlling for size, plastics entrepreneurs tend to be more managerially oriented in their business ideology; furthermore, we observe that when the scores on the business and managerial ideology scale are dichotomized at the mean, at least 50 percent of plastics entrepreneurs as compared to 25 percent of shoe entrepreneurs hold a managerial business ideology.

To summarize, a relationship exists between business ideology and organizational techniques and practices, but the strength of this relationship seems to be conditional either on the size of the firm or on some other relevant structural factors. One of these structural factors that seems very promising for explaining this conditional relationship is the firm's stage of development. Although the aspect of the stage of development of each group of firms was hard to develop, it was already clear that shoe firms and plastics firms were not evolving in general in the same stage of development. Briefly, plastics enterprises as a group could be placed mainly in the stage of dynamic growth on the S-shaped curve while most shoe firms could be spread along the borderlines between dynamic growth and administrative rationalization. The plastics firms were younger, smaller, and had a higher rate of growth than shoe enterprises. Most of the latter did seem to have embarked on the toughest transitional period, a point where the size of the firms already requires a more rational administration from the part of the entrepreneur. More specifically, as to organization practices, stages theory hypothesizes that as firms move along the stages, they move from informal to more formal organization because of accompanying growth.

Entrepreneurial Beliefs and Information

One way of viewing information would be as a particular aspect of formalization. For instance, studies of the stages of growth have found that as firms move along the stages, the information load tends to increase and there is an increasing degree of systematization in the collection of information. Viewed in this perspective, information can be taken as a commodity for which the value and importance vary according to the degree of business sophistication on the part of the entrepreneur's business ideology. For those entrepreneurs with a short-term perspective, day-to-day preoccupations, and a very pragmatic and intuitive problem-solving approach, the search for information would tend to be restricted to few and easily accessible sources. On the other hand, entrepreneurs characterized by a rational-managerial business ideology would tend to value information as an important element in the management of an organization and would tend to increase and diversify their sources of information. Therefore, we hypothesized that the more managerially oriented the entrepreneur, the more sources of information he will use. After controlling for relevant variables, the partial correlation coefficients between business ideology and information for the total sample as well as for both subsamples were all statistically significant.[4]

Entrepreneurial Beliefs and Performance of the Firm

The relationships between the entrepreneurs' cognitive characteristics and the performance of their firms are more problematic because these variables are not operating on the same level of explanation and the length of the linkage between the variables may influence the introduction of various intervening variables. For instance, we found only a slight tendency on the part of managerially oriented shoe entrepreneurs to be more productive than their entrepreneurially oriented counterparts. It is possible here that shoe enterprises are not all evolving in the same stage of development, and this attenuates the relationship. On the other hand, a significant correlation has been observed between the business ideologies of shoe entrepreneurs and the rate of growth of their firms. It seems that shoe owner-managers are influenced by their rate of innovation.[5]

Since most plastics firms in the study seem to be evolving in a stage of dynamic growth, we observed significant relationships between business ideology and productivity and between business ideology and growth, respectively. The stage of dynamic growth calls for an entrepreneurial-intuitive business ideology and a high rate of growth.

Entrepreneurial Beliefs and Education

Two hypotheses were directly related to educational influence. They stated that higher levels of education would orient the entrepreneur's business ideology toward the managerial pole and this influence would be stronger among those having majored in business administration. For the total sample of fifty-one entrepreneurs, these two hypotheses are well supported. We observe a significant correlation of 0.36 between education and business ideology; when entrepreneurs are divided according to their file of study, this correlation increases to 0.59 for those having specialized in business or management as a field of study. This would explain why the correlation between these variables is stronger among shoe entrepreneurs than among plastics entrepreneurs, since 68 percent of the shoe entrepreneurs were educated in commerce and business administration compared to only 27 percent for plastics owner-managers. These findings add to the construct validity of the business and managerial ideology scale.

In fact, these results are not really surprising since the influence of knowledge on the formation and change of attitudes is well known; attitudes are very responsive to knowledge and information. The importance of education for transmitting knowledge and influencing attitudes is well understood when observing the functions of authorities in providing us with ready-made facts and beliefs. It is inevitable that in the complex world in which we live no single individual can hope to ascertain, at first hand, the essential facts about most objects. He must necessarily depend upon what the "experts" tell him. For all individuals, then, facts are frequently mediated by other people as authorities, and the amount of discrepancy between the facts and the individual's beliefs will be dependent upon the validity of the assertions of the authorities and factors that will determine who will and who will not be accepted by the individual as an authority or reliable source of information and knowledge. In the educational system such "authorities" are clearly identified and can largely influence the development of potential entrepreneurs.

To summarize, we feel that the scale on managerial and business ideology meets the minimal requirements of a viable scale. Three major revisions of the scale and its administration to about twenty-five different groups of people all related to management in one way or another (this scale has also been used in France and Belgium) give us some confidence in its usefulness and qualities. It has been largely used for research purposes but also as an instrument for the identification and the development of potential entrepreneurs. The results to date are very encouraging, and we hope to be soon able to use a more simplified instrument in various programs for the development of new entrepreneurs.

NOTES

1. Milton Rokeach, *The Open and Closed Mind* (New York: Basic Books, 1960).
2. L.E. Greiner, "Evolution and Revolution as Organizations Grow," *Harvard Business Review* 50 (July/August 1972): 37–46.
3. Yvon Gasse, "A Comparative Study of the Business and Managerial Orientations of Managers and Entrepreneurs," in John Chamard, ed., *Proceedings of the Second World Congress of the International Council for Small Business*, Halifax, 1983, pp. 72–1 to 72–15.
4. Yvon Gasse, "Information Scanning and Processing in Small Business Firms," *Proceedings of the Administrative Sciences Association of Canada*, May 1980.
5. Yvon Gasse, "Innovation and Management as Strategies for Growth and Productivity in Small and Medium Firms," in Dominique Heau, ed., *Proceedings of the Strategic Management Society*, Paris, 1983, pp. 1–9.

3 THE WOMAN ENTREPRENEUR
Characteristics, Skills, Problems,
and Prescriptions for Success

Robert D. Hisrich

Starting and operating a business entails considerable risk and effort. The risk, both financially and emotionally, can be very high. For the woman entrepreneur, the risk is perhaps even greater as she has the additional problems of being in a male-dominated arena, having few role models, and lacking confidence in her business skills.

In spite of these obstacles an increasing number of women are willing to juggle their lives between work and family, between a career and marriage. Who is this woman entrepreneur? What are her characteristics, skills, and problems? What can be done to make her role as an entrepreneur somewhat less difficult? The answers to these questions will be provided by looking at the role of women in employment; the characteristics of women entrepreneurs; a comparison of male and female entrepreneurs; the problems and prescriptions for success of present and future women entrepreneurs.

ROLE OF WOMEN IN EMPLOYMENT

The role of women in the work place has undergone as dramatic a change in the last thirty years as the view of entrepreneurship over the centuries. Just thirty years ago there were only a small minority of women who owned and operated their own businesses. In fact, in 1940 the entire work force was composed of less than 26 percent

61

Table 3-1. An Historical Perspective.

	25 Years Ago		Today	
	Trend	Impact	Trend	Impact
Education				
	• Women had liberal arts education versus business, engineering or technical	• Women lacked business skills and technical training	• More women studying business, engineering, and science	• More women have training, confidence, and skills to establish their own business
Family				
	• Women were expected to marry and have children	• Women's jobs were part time and secondary to their husband's in importance and wages	• Women's movement	• Women have more supportive husbands
	• Women were caretakers of their family and supporters of their husbands	• Women lived through their spouses' job experiences	• Increased divorce, and single parent families	• Increase in surrogate parenting
			• Postponing of marriage and children	• Increase in women working full-time and having families late
Social				
	• Males were head of the household while women were dependent financially and emotionally	• Women lacked experience in risk taking and negotiating financial matters	• Partnership marriages and family responsibilities	• Self-employment is vehicle for flexible work hours
			• More women are independent and assertive	• Women have more venturesome spirits
	• Activities tended to be sex segregated (clubs and sports)	• Women lacked competitive experience	• Lessening of sex stereotypes	• Women are more confident in male dominated arenas

Occupation

• Occupational stereotypes were common—physician = male; nurse = female; president = male; secretary = female	• Women had limited chances for success in the corporation and in technical fields • Few chances for women to develop management skills necessary in entrepreneurship • Only areas acceptable for women entrepreneurs were retailing, secretarial, child care, or beauty parlors	• Fewer fields are closed to women (legislated changes) • Women have entered medicine, corporate management, and technical fields for careers	• More opportunity for women to gain experience in varied areas; science, medicine, business • Women are more readily accepted in all areas

Economic

• Manufacturing versus service oriented economy—emphasis on producers of goods	• Limited areas where women had experience or training	• More service oriented economy—high technology, communications, and research are popular	• More opportunity for women in areas where specialized labor skills are not required • More flexible jobs and work rules • Opportunities for new businesses in technology and communications to experience high growth

Source: Robert D. Hisrich and Candida Brush, *The Woman Entrepreneur* (Lexington, Mass.: Lexington Books, Inc., 1985).

women in general with most being employed in such occupations as nursing, secretarial work, or teaching. World War II brought many more women into the work force, but such accepted social values as the male being the head of the household and women being dependent by staying home to raise children did not create an environment conducive for women to work unless by necessity. There was even less motivation for women to start their own business. If a woman worked at all, her job was usually secondary to her husband's (or even men in general) and often part-time: of course, lower wages were earned.

These social norms have created occupational stereotypes and of course limited opportunities for women in certain areas such as finance, manufacturing, or research and development. Overall, women were expected to seek employment as nurses, secretaries, or teachers rather than as doctors, engineers, or general managers. Unfortunately, this has not only limited a woman's ability to acquire management experience but has also created obstacles for women business owners trying to establish credibility in atypical areas such as banking, construction, or engineering. In certain fields such as beauty parlors, nursery schools, and some retail stores, women were more accepted as business owners.

Since the turn of the century, women have tried to change some of these accepted social values. For example, Charlotte Perkins Gilman wrote in *Women and Economics* in the 1900s that women's oppression was rooted in their roles as wives and mothers. She indicated that women needed to work to be independent.[1]

In the past twenty-five years, there have been significant social, political, and economic changes that have created opportunities for women as well as given them greater acceptance in the business world. Many things have affected working women: the desire for college students of the sixties and seventies to "find themselves"; the focus on the "me generation"; women's liberation; and legislation prohibiting sex discrimination. Today, most women do not have the social pressure to get married and have children or to stick to a career best suited for child-raising. In fact, over 50 percent of the entire work force today is composed of women, and that figure is growing. More and more women are studying business, law, engineering, and computer science, which means that more women now have the skills and confidence necessary for establishing their own businesses. In addition, demographic trends such as increased divorces, increased single parent families, later marriages, postponement of child-rearing, and partnership marriages have created many changes in business opportunities and acceptance of women in the business world. It is now socially acceptable for women to work and have a family, or to have a career and not be married, or to work in a field dominated by men such as construction, commercial aviation, or medicine. Generally, women have more independence and confidence now than ever before to venture out alone. An overall historical perspective of women twenty-five years ago and today in terms of education, family, social, occupation, and economic perspectives is summarized in Table 3–1.

CHARACTERISTICS OF WOMEN ENTREPRENEURS

In spite of the obstacles and risk, since the 1970s there have been an increasing number of women deciding to start their own businesses. A report of the Bureau of Census using 1972 data indicated that women-owned businesses accounted for only 4.6 percent of all firms in the United States with the receipts from women-owned businesses being only 0.03 percent of all business receipts in the United States. According to a recent Bureau of Labor report female self-employment experienced five times the growth rate of male self-employment between 1972 and 1979. The level of self-employment for females increased from 1,475,000 in 1972 to 2,102,000 in 1979 and 2,334,000 in 1981. More recent statistics put the number of self-employed females at 3,500,000 in 1984. While the percentage of businesses started and operated by women in the United States is small with estimates ranging from 4.6 to 5.7 percent, the absolute number of women-owned enterprises is still large. A report of the Internal Revenue Service indicates that there are 2.8 million female-owned businesses.

Women-owned and -operated businesses vary from state to state. A study by the Small Business Administration found women-owned businesses more prevalent in California, Hawaii, Ohio, Illinois, and states along the east coast. Women-owned firms were least prevalent in Arkansas, South Dakota, Kentucky, and North Dakota. A state-by-state breakdown is indicated in Table 3–2.

Given this greater acceptance of women in the work place and especially as business owners, it is useful to examine the basic characteristics of businesses that women are starting today.

Table 3-2. Percentage of Women-Owned and -Operated Businesses by State.

State	Percentage	State	Percentage
Alabama	20.4%	Montana	25.1%
Alaska	19.6	Nebraska	18.1
Arizona	25.6	Nevada	27.4
Arkansas	15.4	New Hampshire	24.8
California	27.7	New Jersey	22.3
Colorado	24.1	New Mexico	22.2
Connecticut	25.1	New York	23.3
Delaware	23.5	North Carolina	20.4
District of Columbia	32.5	North Dakota	16.8
Florida	24.4	Ohio	23.8
Georgia	20.5	Oklahoma	17.3
Hawaii	32.5	Oregon	20.6
Idaho	17.3	Pennsylvania	20.4
Illinois	25.5	Rhode Island	21.0
Indiana	22.5	South Carolina	25.4
Iowa	18.5	South Dakota	15.5
Kansas	19.9	Tennessee	16.9
Kentucky	16.8	Texas	18.2
Louisiana	17.9	Utah	21.4
Maine	20.7	Vermont	24.6
Maryland	27.4	Virginia	24.9
Massachusetts	22.2	Washington	24.6
Michigan	21.0	West Virginia	25.1
Minnesota	20.7	Wisconsin	20.0
Mississippi	19.2	Wyoming	23.8
Missouri	17.2		

Source: Small Business Administration Study, 1980.

Business Characteristics

Perhaps the most significant characteristic is that the majority of the businesses started by women are young—most being less than five years old. This young age is reflected in the low average gross revenues of the majority of women-owned businesses, less than $500,000 annually, since it is usually two to three years before any business starts turning a profit.

Type of Business

Another characteristic of female-owned businesses is the nature of the business endeavor. Over 90 percent of the businesses begun by women are service related, as opposed to 7 percent in manufacturing and 3 percent in finance. However, more women are starting businesses in high-technology areas such as software production or computer services where high growth opportunities exist. While the type of business venture varies widely, from the very innovative (a private post office) to the male-dominated fields of petroleum products and plumbing, traditionally female areas (such as a travel agency or clothing design) predominate, as is indicated in Table 3–3. The business area most women entrepreneurs are involved in is sales, varying from real estate and insurance to wholesaling and manufacturers' representatives.

The high number of service oriented businesses reflects the educational and occupational background of many women entrepreneurs. Most have a liberal arts college education and a service related occupational experience. This typical background in many cases was a result of the advice of guidance counselors who discouraged women from entering male-dominated fields.

Table 3–3. Nature of Business Venture.

Type of Business	Percentage
Sales	19.7%
Consulting	14.6
Design/Art/Architecture	10.0
Public Relations and Advertising	8.3
Personnel and Business Services	7.7
Computer-Related Business	7.5
Manufacturing	7.0
Secretarial	6.7
Educational Services	6.1
Law/Medical Services	5.4
Distribution and Construction	4.5
Finance	3.0

Source: Robert D. Hisrich and Candida Brush, "The Woman Entrepreneur: Management Skills and Business Problems," *The Journal of Small Business Management* (January 1984): 33.

FEMALE VERSUS MALE ENTREPRENEURS

Even though there has been significant growth in female self-employ-ment, most of what is known about the characteristics of entrepre-neurs, their motivations, backgrounds, families, educational and occupational experiences, and problems is based on studies of male entrepreneurs. This is not surprising since men make up the major-ity of people who have started and own their own businesses. Inter-est in women entrepreneurs is a more recent phenomenon.

Studies of female entrepreneurs have addressed basically the same questions as those of male entrepreneurs. One study of twenty female entrepreneurs found that their major motivations for starting a business were the need to achieve, the desire to be independent, the need for job satisfaction, and economic necessity. These female entrepreneurs tended to have an autocratic style of management while their major problem during start-up was credit discrimination; underestimating operating and marketing costs were subsequent problems.[2]

Another study of 122 black, white, Hispanic, and American Indian women entrepreneurs found that the responses of both minority and non-minority women entrepreneurs differed significantly from those of women in the general population. Differences were also found between minority and non-minority women entrepreneurs, with minority entrepreneurs starting their business at a later age. While non-minority women entrepreneurs scored higher on ratings of need for achievement and independence, minority women entrepreneurs appeared to place a greater value on conformity and benevolence.[3]

Twenty-one women who participated in a study of the demo-graphic characteristics, motivations, and business problems of female entrepreneurs indicated that they had particular problems with col-lateral, obtaining credit, and overcoming society's belief that women are not as serious as men about business.[4]

The characteristics of women entrepreneurs by type of business was the focus of another study. The results indicated that women entrepreneurs have some distinctive characteristics. They were older and more educated than either the general populace or the respon-dents in previous studies and had very supportive parents and hus-bands. Women entrepreneurs in nontraditional business areas (fi-nance, insurance, manufacturing, and construction) also differed from their counterparts in more traditionally female business areas (retail and wholesale trade). The latter group had particular difficulty in gaining access to external financial sources.[5]

A study of twenty female entrepreneurs with one or more years operating a retail or service firm indicated that female entrepreneurs had problems in obtaining funds to start and operate the business, operational problems in the area of record keeping, financial management, and advertising.[6]

Finally, a study reporting the results of a nationwide indepth survey of 468 women entrepreneurs profiled the "typical" women entrepreneur.[7] She is the first-born child of middle-class parents—a self-employed father and a mother who does not work outside the home. After obtaining a liberal arts degree, she marries, has children, and works as a teacher, administrator, or secretary. Her first business venture in a service area begins after she is thirty-five with her biggest problems being in finance, credit, and lack of business training.

As is indicated in this growing body of literature, in some respects women entrepreneurs possess very different motivations, business skill levels, and occupational backgrounds than their male counterparts. Factors in the start-up process of a business for women entrepreneurs are also dissimilar to those of males especially in terms of support systems, sources of funds, and problems. These differences between male and female entrepreneurs are summarized in Table 3–4. For instance, in terms of motivation, men are often motivated by the drive to control their own destiny, to make things happen. This drive often stems from disagreements with their boss or a feeling they can run things better. In contrast, women tend to be motivated by independence and achievement arising from job frustration where they have not been allowed to perform at the level they are capable of.

Departure points and reasons for starting the business are similar for both men and women in that both generally have a strong interest and experience in the area of their venture. However, for men, the transition from a past occupation to the new venture is often facilitated because it is an outgrowth of a present job, sideline, or hobby. Women, on the other hand, often leave an occupation with only a high level of job frustration and enthusiasm for the new venture rather than experience, making the transition more difficult.

Start-up financing is another area where male and female entrepreneurs differ. While males often list investors, bank loans, or personal loans in addition to personal funds as sources of start-up capi-

Table 3-4. An Historical Perspective.

Characteristic	Male Entrepreneurs	Female Entrepreneurs
Motivation	Achievement—strive to make things happen	Achievement—accomplishment of a goal
	Personal independence—self-image as it relates to status through their role in the corporation is unimportant	Independence—to do it alone
	Job satisfaction arising from the desire to be in control	Job satisfaction arising from previous job frustration
Departure Point	Dissatisfaction with present job	Job frustration
	Sideline in college, sideline to present job, or outgrowth of present job	Interest in and recognition of opportunity in the area
	Discharge or layoff	Change in personal circumstances
	Opportunity for acquisition	
Sources of Funds	Personal assets and savings	Personal assets and savings
	Bank financing	Personal loans
	Investors	
	Loans from friends or family	
Occupational Background	Experience in line of work	Experience in area of business
	Recognized specialist or one who has gained a high level of achievement in the field	Middle-management or administrative level experience in the field
	Competent in a variety of business functions	Service related occupational background

Personality Characteristics	Opinionated and persuasive	Flexible and tolerant
	Goal oriented	Goal oriented
	Innovative and idealistic	Creative and realistic
	High level of self confidence	Medium level of self confidence
	Enthusiastic and energetic	Enthusiastic and energetic
	Must be own boss	Ability to deal with the social and economic environment
Background	Age when starting venture 25–35	Age when starting venture 35–45
	Father was self-employed	Father was self-employed
	College educated—degree in business or technical area (usually engineering)	College educated—degree in liberal arts
	Firstborn child	Firstborn child
Support Groups	Friends; professional acquaintances (lawyers, accountants)	Close friends
	Business associates	Spouse
	Spouse	Family
		Women's professional groups
		Trade associations
Type of Business Started	Manufacturing or construction	Service Related—educational services, consulting, or public relations
	Average net income—$7,100/year	Average net income—$2,200/year

tal, women in nearly all cases have relied solely on personal assets or savings.

Occupationally, there are also differences between men and women entrepreneurs. Although both groups have experience in the field of their ventures, men usually have more competence in many business skills. In addition, the nature of the experience of men entrepreneurs is often in manufacturing, finance, or technical areas. In contrast, most women entrepreneurs' administrative experience is limited to the middle management level in more service related areas such as education or retail sales.

In terms of personality, there are strong similarities between male and female entrepreneurs. Both tend to be energetic, goal oriented, and independent. However, men are often more confident and less flexible and tolerant than women, which can result in different management styles. A study of seventy-six female entrepreneurs in the San Francisco area indicated that female entrepreneurs were different in behavior and attitudes from male entrepreneurs and tended to be more opportunistic—more adaptable in their entrepreneurial style.[8]

The backgrounds of male and female entrepreneurs tend to be similar except that most women are a little older when they embark on their first significant venture (35–45 versus 25–35) and their educational backgrounds are different (more liberal arts versus business and engineering).

Support groups also provide a point of contrast between the two. Men usually list outside advisors (lawyers, accountants) as most important supporters with the spouse being second. Women list their spouses first, close friends second, and business associates third. Moreover, women usually rely heavily on a variety of sources for support and information such as trade associations and women's groups while men are not as likely to seek as many outside supporters.

In general, most businesses started by men and women entrepreneurs differ in terms of the nature of the venture. Women are more likely to start a business in a service related area—public relations, sales, or educational services—whereas men are more likely to enter manufacturing, construction, or high-tech fields. The result is often lower earnings for women-owned businesses.

PROBLEMS OF WOMEN ENTREPRENEURS

All entrepreneurs have problems with their businesses either during start-up or current operations, or both. Obtaining credit, weak collateral position, and problems in financial planning tend to be the most pressing problems faced by women entrepreneurs (see Table 3-5). While financing is a problem for every entrepreneur, for women entrepreneurs the problem is often more acute for two reasons.

First, women often lack a financial track record in business, which results in difficulties in dealing with lending institutions. When considering a request for funds, most commercial lending institutions or venture capital firms are primarily interested in a track record, management experience, the market, and the proprietary nature of the product of service. For a woman entrepreneur who lacks experience in executive management, has had limited financial responsibilities, and proposes a non-proprietary product, the issue of a track record is even more important to a potential financier. As a result, women must often either have their husbands cosign a note, seek a co-owner, or use personal assets or savings. While it is important for lending institutions to understand the nature of women entrepreneurs, it is equally important for the woman entrepreneur to know how to approach a lending situation.

Table 3-5. Major Problems in Start-up and Current Operations.

Start-up Problems		Current Operations Problems	
Lack of business training	20%	Lack of experience in financial planning	18%
Obtaining lines of credit	28		
Lack of experience in financial planning	20	Demands of company affecting personal relations	15
Weak collateral position	21	Weak collateral position	13
Lack of guidance and counseling	21	Obtaining lines of credit	11
		Lack of business training	11

Source: Adapted from Robert D. Hisrich and Candida Brush, "The Woman Entrepreneur: Management Skills and Business Problems," *Journal of Small Business Management* (January 1984): 36.

A second reason that women entrepreneurs often encounter difficulties in the area of finance is their lack of skills and experience in financial planning, accounting, marketing, and operations. Experience in dealing with money, negotiating, and performing financial responsibilities, and having expectations to be the boss inspires confidence in these areas. Most women entrepreneurs have not had the exposure or opportunity to develop confidence in business management and negotiating financial matters. Most women entrepreneurs lack experience in finance, considering it their weakest business skill. This lack of experience and confidence in negotiating financial matters in effect increases the risk in the eyes of the lender.

A final area that women entrepreneurs often mention as a business problem is the lack of respect for business women. Although this is not as big a problem as lack of financial capabilities, some women entrepreneurs have felt this particularly in the start-up phase of their business. This issue is somewhat more prevalent in fields where women business owners are fewer in number, such as construction, manufacturing, or finance.

PRESCRIPTIONS FOR SUCCESS

There are several key factors that contribute to success for women entrepreneurs. These include establishing a track record, continuing education, previous experience, the ability to set priorities in personal responsibilities, development of a support system, and determination.

Track Record—Experience in Dealing with Money

First, a track record needs to be established. Aspiring women entrepreneurs should study the lending pattern of banks and select one for a short-term loan even if a loan is not needed. Although more women have credit ratings than previously, a good credit rating needs to be established. By applying for and paying off a personal or business loan on time, a woman entrepreneur will not only establish or strengthen a track record but will acquire needed experience and develop confidence in dealing with financial institutions.

What are some other ways to establish a track record? Women entrepreneurs have offered several suggestions. One way is for the potential entrepreneur to manage the family finances. By setting up a family budget based on projected income and expenses and accounting for any variances between the projected and actual, basic experience in planning and budgeting is obtained. Another is to do the family taxes or, whenever possible, obtain experience bookkeeping in a volunteer organization or trade association.

Continuing Education and Hiring Experts

Women entrepreneurs, lacking educational experience or business skills, should compensate by hiring experts or by taking advantage of seminars and minicourses that are application oriented and taught by someone who has owned a business. These seminars will provide the needed guidance and familiarity with financial, legal, marketing and planning matters.

The overall assessment of business skills by women entrepreneurs indicate strengths in dealing with people, product innovation, and idea generation; average skills in marketing and business operations; and weaknesses in finance (see Table 3-6). This self-appraisal may be skewed particularly in the areas of marketing and business operations since many women entrepreneurs surveyed were just starting their businesses and were not yet confident of their business management skills. This low assessment of skills in finance, marketing, organizing, and planning may mean further barriers to the future growth of the business.

Women entrepreneurs need to make an honest self-appraisal of their strengths and weaknesses and then overcome any deficiencies by seeking further education. Many women entrepreneurs have strengths in important management skills such as dealing with people, product innovation and idea generation. These strengths are an important factor in the way they run their businesses. Women may also tend to be more tolerant and understanding of human relations and willing to work things out as well.

While in high school and college, women aspiring to be entrepreneurs should be encouraged to study engineering, science, technical, or business related subjects in addition to liberal arts. The educational system as well as the environment should provide encouragement for women to concentrate in science, engineering, or computer technology equally with English, nursing, or education.

Table 3-6. Women Entrepreneurs' Self-Appraisal of Their Management Skills.

Management Skill	Poor	Fair	Good	Very Good	Excellent	No Opinion
Finance—securing capital forecasting, budgeting	15%	32%	27%	15%	6%	4%
Dealing with People—management development, and training	2	10	28	33	27	—
Marketing/Sales—marketing research, promotion, selling	6	20	20	33	22	—
Idea Generation/Product Innovation	3	10	26	27	33	1
Business Operations—Inventory, production, day to day operations	3	18	32	30	17	—
Organizing and Planning—business strategy, organizational structure, policies	4	15	29	29	23	—

Source: Adapted from Robert D. Hisrich and Candida Brush, "The Woman Entrepreneur: Management Skills and Business Problems," *Journal of Small Business Management* (January 1984): 36.

Besides education, another tactic for overcoming deficiencies is to hire experts. Many women entrepreneurs have done so, not being threatened by the prospect of relying on an outsider to provide knowledge and skills.

Occupational Experience

Aspiring women entrepreneurs should try to obtain occupational experience in middle management or technical areas. Experience in managing helps develop confidence in decisionmaking while providing exposure to planning, marketing, and financial matters.

Organization and Prioritization in Personal Responsibilities

When a family is present, the entrepreneur should assess her family situation before launching a new venture. Organizational skills must be strong to manage both family and business in even the best of circumstances. These skills are needed at an almost impossible level when family problems occur. Women entrepreneurs with families should not be afraid to prioritize both household and business responsibilities and delegate readily when necessary.

Organizational skills and priority setting are important attributes that allow women entrepreneurs to balance their dual role in the home and business. While the role conflict of work versus motherhood is difficult for any working woman, for the woman entrepreneur the problem and anxiety are compounded because, as a business owner, she is responsible for the profit and loss of the venture. Since this takes a much greater commitment than the 9 to 5 workday, the ability to manage one's time and to adapt become even more essential for success.

Support System and Mentor

A strong moral support system of family and friends, clients, and business associates should be established by every woman entrepreneur. A cheering squad is important in successfully establishing and operating a new venture. Women entrepreneurs can benefit from contacts with role models or mentors and should seek out experts or entrepreneurs in other fields as well as their own. For women entrepreneurs there may be fewer role models given the smaller number of women business owners, and working through or establishing an "old girl network" may be advantageous. Successful women entrepreneurs should remember the importance of being a mentor or role model for someone else.

Women entrepreneurs generally have, in addition to supportive husbands, strong support from friends or business associates and women's professional groups. Many have mentors to guide and assist them as well.

Some women entrepreneurs felt that their support systems were the key to their success. Mentors frequently provide women entrepreneurs knowledge and guidance in areas where they lacked confidence or were deficient, such as in law, finance, or organizational planning. Mentors were also able to lend credibility to the venture often by being on the board of directors of the woman entrepreneur's company.

Determination and Professionalism

Entrepreneurs, no matter what their gender, need to be determined to work for the success of their endeavor and be professional in their approach. These attributes are especially important for women entrepreneurs because determination will help them succeed in establishing their business and professionalism will contribute to their being taken seriously.

For the women entrepreneurs who have succeeded in establishing their own businesses, motivation was a factor in their level of determination. The major motivations of a woman entrepreneur are more independence, achievement, job frustration, and job satisfaction than money and power. This job frustration, desire for independence, and self-fulfillment provide a strong resolve to succeed and an openness to continue education or seek expert assistance when needed.

For a woman to be taken seriously in her business, gain respect, and establish business contacts, especially in male-dominated fields, it is important for her to be professional. A professional atitude is important in handling all the activities of the business.

In general, women entrepreneurs have a conservative risk-taking posture in terms of product or service idea. The result is that the businesses started by the women entrepreneurs will not likely grow to a significant size. The exceptions are individuals who either took substantially greater risks or entered a field atypical of the majority of women entrepreneurs.

Even though the majority of the businesses started by women are young and small in terms of gross revenues and number of employees, the question arises, is size a sign of success? In fact, the realism and caution exhibited by the women business owners in undertaking initial risk and in business expansion may actually insure the success of the endeavor over time. Their reasons for starting their own business are rooted in their knowledge of the area and job frustration. In fact, for many, the end is not profit but self-fulfillment. This is not to say that women entrepreneurs are not concerned with the bottom line; they just seem to be more concerned with quality than quantity. This is certainly a good objective since once a quality product or service is developed there is usually opportunity for expansion.

THE FUTURE

The future for women entrepreneurs appears very bright. Over the past twenty-five years there has been significant growth in women-owned businesses as well as more opportunities in many fields. Today women entrepreneurs are more confident, better skilled, and willing to take more risks than ever before. However, there may be still some time before a woman entrepreneur has complete acceptance in all fields and industries. The roles of business, society, and education will play an important role in the future of women entrepreneurs.

The growth of women-owned businesses has been increasing at a substantial rate. From 1979 to 1981, the average growth of women-owned businesses per year was less than 5 percent; from 1981 to 1984 this rate approached 17 percent per year. If the 17 percent growth rate continues for the next six years, by 1990 the estimated number of women-owned businesses will grow from 3,500,000 to about 9,000,000. From a business perspective, this will have significant impact as women entrepreneurs will no longer be a minority in absolute numbers. They will comprise much greater than the present 5.6 percent of all businesses in the United States. Financial institutions, the government, and industry will be more familiar with and accepting of female-owned businesses as women entrepreneurs will no longer be uncommon.

Second, since many women-owned businesses are less than five years old, there will be significant growth and expansion in the future. This increase in size will further aid in establishing the presence of the woman entrepreneur in the business community. This maturing and growth will, of course, mean new problems such as expansion, harvesting products, meeting intense competition, declining markets, rising wages, and business reorganization.

Cultural norms and activities assigning women the responsibility for home and family are in the process of undergoing change. Even though most men are more accepting of family partnerships, role reversals and shared household duties, the sex and role stereotypes still remain. As more women become economically and emotionally independent through careers or self-employment over the next decade, negative attitudes about women entrepreneurs and their dual roles should be less closely held. The women entrepreneurs of the sixties, seventies, and eighties have laid the groundwork for more social acceptance of occupational choices. Hopefully by 1990, the pressure for women entrepreneurs to "do it all" will be less, and adjustments for family responsibilities and household duties will be routine rather than the exception.

Perhaps even more important in the future of women entrepreneurs is the role of education. While the majority of previous research studies have not focused on women entrepreneurs, there is a major effort underway to learn more about their distinct characteristics and problems. Recent hearings before the United States Senate Sub-Committee on Small Business have amplified the need for more data on women-owned businesses. It is expected that as the number of women entrepreneurs increase and the established businesses continue to grow, the body of literature on women entrepreneurs will have a corresponding increase.

Women entrepreneurs who have successfully established a business can contribute greatly to the educational process by participating in high school or college classes as guest speakers, by hiring women students, or by being a mentor or role model for a potential woman entrepreneur. This type of support is invaluable and can create motivation and inspiration for a future woman entrepreneur.

In all, the future for women entrepreneurs is bright. Still, of course, the real concern for a woman is whether or not to become an entrepreneur in the first place.

NOTES TO CHAPTER 3

1. Sookie Stambler, *Women's Liberation—Blueprint for the Future* (Ace Books, 1970), p. 267.
2. Eleanor B. Schwartz, "Entrepreneurship: A New Female Frontier," *Journal of Contemporary Business* (Winter 1979): 47–76.
3. James DeCarlo and Paul R. Lyons, "A Comparison of Selected Personal Characteristics of Minority and Non-Minority Female Entrepreneurs," *Journal of Small Business Management* (December 1979): 22–29.
4. Robert D. Hisrich and Marie O'Brien, "The Woman Entrepreneur from a Business and Sociological Perspective," in K.H. Vesper, ed., *Frontiers of Entrepreneurship Research* (Wellesley, Mass.: Babson Center for Entrepreneurial Studies, 1981), pp. 21–39.
5. Robert D. Hisrich and Marie O'Brien, "The Woman Entrepreneur as a Reflection of the Type of Business," in K.H. Vesper, ed., *Frontiers of Entrepreneurship Research* (Wellesley, Mass.: Babson Center for Entrepreneurial Studies, 1982), pp. 54–67.
6. Eric T. Pellegrino and Barry L. Reece, "Perceived Formative and Operational Problems Encountered by Female Entrepreneurs in Retail and Service Firms," *Journal of Small Business Management* (April 1982): 15–24.
7. Robert D. Hisrich and Candida Brush, "The Woman Entrepreneur: Management Skills and Business Problems," *Journal of Small Business Management* (January 1984): 30–37.
8. Norman R. Smith, Gary McCain, and Audrey Warren, "Women Entrepreneurs Really Are Different: A Comparison of Constructed Ideal Types of Male and Female Entrepreneurs," in K.H. Vesper, ed., *Frontiers of Entrepreneurship Research* (Wellesley, Mass.: Babson Center for Entrepreneurial Studies, 1982), pp. 68–82.

RISK AND VENTURE CAPITAL FINANCING

4 INFORMAL RISK CAPITAL
Knowns and Unknowns

William E. Wetzel, Jr.

The overwhelming majority of risk capital research has been devoted to studies of the institutional risk capital markets, despite the fact that investigators typically acknowledge that informal risk capital may well represent an even larger pool of funds for entrepreneurs.

The paper opens with a section titled "Playing With Numbers." It is a flight of fancy designed to locate the outer limits of the invisible informal risk capital market and to contrast those limits with the scale of the institutional risk capital market. In a sense, the discussion puts some boundaries on our ignorance. The numbers are crude. They are intended to provide a sense of perspective and to whet the appetites of investigators interested in risk capital research.

The second section traces the record of informal risk capital research. Research completed is summarized. Research completed from 1980 to 1984 is discussed in more detail and studies known to be currently in process are cited. The paper concludes with a brief discussion of research opportunities in the informal risk capital markets.

In the research summaries that follow an attempt has been made to highlight key characteristics of informal risk capital and to contrast these emerging characteristics with the characteristics of institutional venture capital. Clearly, the research summaries have been filtered through the eyes of the author in terms of the selection of conclusions and inferences upon which to comment. The potential for bias, however inadvertent, is acknowledged.

85

Informal risk capital research is linked by a number of more or less common objectives, or lines of inquiry. These commonalities include the following questions:

- What is the scale of informal risk capital investing—both in numbers of investors and dollars invested?

- What are the communications channels that link entrepreneurs with informal investors and informal investors with each other?

- Are there regional differences in the absolute and/or effective availability of informal risk capital?

- What are the characteristics of the screening and evaluation models employed by informal investors? How diverse are informal investor decision models? Do they differ from the models employed by professional venture capitalists?

- Does informal risk capital complement or compete with institutional venture capital? Are there circumstances under which it is more appropriate for an entrepreneur to seek funds from an angel than from a professional venture capital firm?

- Is informal risk capital more or less expensive than professional venture capital?

- Are there subsets of informal investors that tend to behave differently (e.g., active vs. passive investors, more affluent investors vs. less affluent investors, self-made investors vs. those with inherited wealth)?

- Are informal investors motivated exclusively by monetary rewards or do they sometimes seek nonfinancial returns? What are these nonfinancial considerations and how powerful are they?

PLAYING WITH NUMBERS

The mental exercises that follow are seldom found in papers presented at "respectable" academic conferences. If the state of informal risk capital research were further advanced the exercises would not be needed here. However, the hunt for angels and gnomes, like the hunt for the source of dynamic entrepreneurial performance, still has much in common with the hunt for the Heffalump.

The Heffalump is a rather large and very important animal. He has been hunted by many individuals using various ingenious trapping devices, but no one so far has succeeded in capturing him. All who claim to have caught sight of him report that he is enormous, but they disagree on his particularities. Not having explored his habitat with sufficient care, some hunters have used as bait their own favorite dishes and have then tried to persuade people that what they caught was a Heffalump. However, very few are convinced, and the search goes on.[1]

The following quasi-facts and machinations are designed to put some boundaries on the extent of our ignorance. The quasi-facts precede the pure fancies:

1. The number of corporations in the United States exceeds two million. Of the total corporate population only one in one hundred (20,000) is publicly traded, only one in two hundred (10,000) is large enough to be required to report regularly to the SEC, and only one in four hundred (5,000) is listed on an organized stock exchange. In other words, 99 percent of U.S. corporations are privately held. The number of firms entering the public equity market annually is approximately 500 (over the last fifteen years the number of initial public offerings has ranged from less than fifty to over one thousand). In 1983 public underwritings of companies with a net worth of $5 million or less totalled $3.7 billion for 477 firms, an average of about $7 million each. In view of infant mortality rates, it is not unreasonable to assume that well under 1 percent of corporate start-ups will both survive and ultimately develop a public market for their shares.

2. The number of firms financed by the institutional venture capital community is under one thousand per year and less than half are start-ups. The rate of institutional venture capital investing is currently about $2.5 billion per year, an average of about $2 million per transaction. The prospect of a public offering or merger with a larger firm within five to ten years is a necessary condition to attracting institutional venture capital.

3. The number of business start-ups exceeds 500,000 per year. If 95 percent of these start-ups are too small to require outside equity financing, there are still 25,000 start-ups that need outside equity capital and apparently succeed in raising it. To carry this flight of fancy one step further, if these start-ups raise an average of $200,000 apiece, the aggregate equity funding for these ventures totals $5 billion annually.

Question: If institutional venture capitalists finance less than one thousand start-ups annually, where do the other 24,000 (or whatever figure you prefer) find their equity capital? The answer: from informal investors. The figures suggest that informal investors finance as many as twenty times the number of firms financed by institutional venture capitalists and that the aggregate amount they invest is perhaps twice as big.

Similar conclusions can be reached by playing with the numbers of potential investors:

1. The Forbes Four Hundred Richest People in America[2] represent a combined net worth of $125 billion, an average of $315 million each. Forty percent (159) of the Four Hundred were described by Forbes as "self-made." The combined net worth of the richest self-made people is about $50 billion. If 10 percent of their net worth is available for venture-type investing, the pool of funds available from these one hundred fifty-nine individuals alone is $5 billion. In addition to their role as potential angels, the very wealthy are also significant investors in professional venture capital firms. Individuals and families provided 21 percent of the $3.4 billion committed to independent private venture capital funds in 1983.[3]

2. There are over 500,000 individuals in the United States with a net worth in excess of $1 million. If 40 percent of these potential angels ("accredited investors" by one of the SEC's new Regulation D criteria) are also self-made and presumably interested in backing entrepreneurs, the effective angel pool numbers about 200,000. If half of these angels invest in any given year and ante up $50,000 apiece, that puts the total number of active angels at 100,000 annually and the amount invested at $5 billion. If the typical deal involves four angels co-venturing, then the number of ventures financed is on the order of 25,000, each receiving an average of $200,000. Note that these numbers were conveniently rigged to conform with the earlier estimates of the number of ventures financed by informal investors.

The extent of our ignorance is measured by the fact that we know next to nothing about the ventures, the investors, or the processes involved in the funding of approximately 25,000 firms and approximately $5 billion of informal risk capital investing per year.

CHRONOLOGY OF INFORMAL RISK CAPITAL RESEARCH

The trail of research related directly or peripherally to the informal risk capital markets began, as can best be determined, about twenty-five years ago with the Federal Reserve studies that preceded passage of the Small Business Investment Act of 1958, the act that created the Small Business Investment Company (SBIC) program. A study by Albert Rubinstein was part of the Federal Reserve research.[4] The record of research since 1958 is chronicled below. Apologies are extended to any investigators whose work has been overlooked. Additions to the list of informal risk capital research are welcomed.

Pre-1980

1964—Gordon Baty.[5] Baty examined the initial financing of new, research-based organizations in New England. Baty reported that the work of Rubinstein, the Federal Reserve System, and others revealed that the individual private investor is indisputably the most important source of initial equity for the small firm. Baty concluded that private individual investors are not only more likely to supply initial risk funds than venture capital organizations but are likely to supply them on rather more liberal terms. Baty found that initial investors in new, research-based enterprises were predominantly affluent individuals. Baty speculated that those who inherited wealth tended to be less venturesome than those who were self-made. He further speculated that those who were self-made identified themselves with the industry in which they made their wealth, while those who inherited wealth tended to be members of the financial community. Baty also noted the subjective nature of the individual investor's decision process and the apparent influence of non-economic variables.

1972—Cary Hoffman.[6] Hoffman's Ph.D. dissertation at the University of Texas is required reading for anyone interested in the informal risk capital markets. Hoffman reviewed the existing literature and then explored the process by which individual investors identify, evaluate, and structure their investments in new, small companies. Data were collected from thirty-nine individual investors in two

Texas cities, Waco and Austin. He also examined the relative significance of venture investors in the economic growth of the two Texas communities. Hoffman's study reached a number of provocative conclusions. Among them were:

1. Investment decisions appeared to be determined most frequently on the basis of investor-centered factors, such as personal preference, previous investment experience, personal biases, tax position, and so forth.

2. Venture capital intermediaries were found to play a critical catalytic role in the venture capital investment process, particularly since few individual investors actively sought out new, small companies in which to invest.

3. Differences in the venture capital investment process between more developed and less developed areas are likely to relate more to the investment practices and dynamics of the local venture capital networks than to the absolute availability of venture capital, the number of venture capitalists, the opportunities to invest, or the absolute propensity to invest.

4. The data suggested substantial variations in investor decision models. Often the same company would be considered favorably by one investor and unfavorably by another—even among investors who were business or investment associates.

5. Friends and business associates referred more new and small companies to the investors than any other source.

6. Relatively few capital seekers were cognizant of venture capitalists as a group or of the identity of specific ones in their city.

1974—David Brophy.[7] Brophy studied the financial support for new, technology-based firms that were incorporated and operating from 1965 to 1970. Brophy's data shed light on the significance of individual investors and revealed regional disparities in the availability of financing for new, small technology-based firms. In a sample of Boston-area firms, private individuals (excluding founders, friends, and relatives) provided 14 percent of total financing. SBICs and private venture capital firms provided 15 percent. The figures for a sample of Ann Arbor/Detroit firms were 16 percent from individuals and 2 percent from venture capitalists. Bropny also noted the loosely joined networks linking sources of capital.

1974—Bean, Schiffel, and Mogee.[8] These authors examined existing evidence and found little support for assertions that technological innovation by new/small firms is impeded by an inadequate supply of capital. However, they noted that the majority of venture capital firms do not fund start-up ventures. For purposes of this chronology, one of their assertions is worth noting:

> The issue of little knowledge of the venture capital/new technological enterprise is multi-faceted. Entrepreneurs and potential entrepreneurs seem to need better information on financial sources while capital suppliers seem to need better information on new venture/technological investment opportunities.

1976—Charles River Associates.[9] As part of a study of capital market imperfections, Charles River Associates (CRA) examined the composition of external funds received by small, technology-based firms prior to making initial public offerings. The study revealed that between 1970 and 1974 "unaffiliated individuals" accounted for 15 percent of external funds while "venture capitalists" accounted for 12 percent. When the data were classified by stage (age of venture), unaffiliated individuals provided 17 percent of external capital during the start-up year, while venture capitalists provided 11 percent. CRA explicitly excluded from their study of capital market imperfections "individuals who act informally as providers of venture funds." Yet CRA commented that ". . . they may represent the largest source of venture capital in the country."

While the CRA study found "no evidence of substantial market imperfections that restrict the flow of funds to small, technology-based firms," it also raised the following question: "It is not clear whether the existing system for generating and disseminating information about investment opportunities is efficient." In other words, it is not clear whether it could be improved in a cost-effective manner.

CRA also pointed out that the absence of market imperfections does not necessarily imply that the flow of funds to new, technology-based firms is in some sense ideal in view of the external benefits generated by entrepreneurial ventures: "To the extent that investments in small, technology-based firms produce external economies, too few resources will be allocated to all phases of investing in them, including generating information about investment opportunities."

The existence of substantial external economies (social rates of return in excess of private rates of return) associated with technological entrepreneurship has been confirmed by Edwin Mansfield. In a sample of seventeen industrial innovations Mansfield estimated the median private rate of return at 25 percent and the median social rate of return at 56 percent.[10]

1980–1984

1981 – Semour and Wetzel.[11] Seymour and Wetzel collected data from 133 individual investors in New England. Their research focused on the role of informal investors as a source of funds for three types of investment situations: financing for technology-based inventors, start-up and early stage financing for emerging firms, and equity financing for small, established firms growing faster than retained earnings can support.

The three areas addressed represent investment situations that seldom attract financing from institutional venture capital sources. Their sample of angels reported risk capital investments totaling over $16 million in 320 ventures between 1976 and 1980, an average of one deal every two years for each investor. The average size of their investments was approximately $50,000, while the median size was about $20,000. Thirty-six percent of their investments involved less than $10,000, while 24 percent involved over $50,000. In 60 percent of their investments these investors participated with other investors in larger transactions. Participation with other investors permits venture financing that approaches the $500,000 interest threshhold of institutional venture investors. Additional conclusions of interest include:

1. Forty percent of past financings were start-ups, and 80 percent involved ventures less than five years old. Sixty-three percent of their investments were in companies that had not achieved break-even operations (another definition of start-up). With respect to future investments, 78 percent reported a strong interest in start-up and early stage financing for emerging firms. One third of the sample expressed a strong interest in prestart-up financing for technology-based inventors. The principal investment criterion cited by investors interested in inventors was that the technology be in a field that they understood and could evaluate for themselves.

2. The angels in Seymour and Wetzel's study were a well-educated group and experienced in the management of start-up situations. Ninety-five percent held four-year college degrees and 51 percent had graduate degrees. Of the graduate degrees, 44 percent were in a technical field and 35 percent in business or economics (generally an MBA). Seventy-five percent had been involved in the start-up of a new venture. Eighty-four percent reported that they expect to play an active role with the ventures they finance—typically an informal consulting role or service on a working board of directors.

3. The tendency of informal investors to maintain close working contact with ventures they finance is reflected in the geographic distribution of their portfolios. Three-quarters of the firms financed by these investors were within 300 miles of the investor (roughly one day's drive), and 58 percent were within fifty miles. The tendency of informal investors to invest close to home may also reflect the absence of systematic channels of communication between investors and entrepreneurs. The likelihood of an investment opportunity coming to an individual investor's attention increases, probably exponentially, the shorter the distance between the two parties.

4. While the interests of the investors in the Seymour and Wetzel sample covered the entire spectrum of business and industry categories, there was a clear preference for manufacturing enterprises in general and for high-technology manufacturing in particular. Sixty-four percent expressed a strong interest in high-technology manufacturing, 33 percent in industrial product manufacturing, and 30 percent in service firms. Only 5 percent expressed a strong interest in wholesale trade, 3 percent in retail trade, and 1 percent in transportation firms.

5. Risk capital is "patient money." The patience level of informal investors was tested in terms of expected holding periods. The median expected holding period was five to seven years. However, 24 percent either considered the holding period unimportant or expected to hold their risk capital investments longer than ten years, a patience level well in excess of the exit expectations of institutional venture capitalists. Forty-seven percent of the investors reported that provisions for liquidating their investment were "definitely" or "generally" included in their initial investment agreement.

6. The typical angel seriously considers and rejects two or three investment opportunities each year. The most common reasons cited for rejection were lack of confidence in management; unsatisfactory

risk/reward ratios; absence of a well-defined business plan; the investor's unfamiliarity with products; processes, or markets; or the venture was a business that investor "did not want to be in."

7. Investors perceive significant differences between the risks associated with investing in early stage situations and those associated with later stage financing. Median expectations of losses exceeding 50 percent of their investment were anticipated for investments in seven out of ten inventors, six out of ten start-ups, five out of ten firms under one year old, four out of ten firms under five years old, and two out of ten established firms. Reward expectations for successful investments reflected the perceived risk of losses. With respect to successful investments, investors anticipated median five-year capital gains of ten times for inventors and start-ups, six times for firms under one year old, five times for firms under five years old, and three times for established firms. Median minimum portfolio expectations were a consistent 20 percent per year for all types of portfolios (inventors, start-ups, etc.) except for portfolios of established firms where the median expectation was 15 percent per year. While risk capital is clearly expensive, and deserves to be, the reward expectations of informal investors seem low when compared to the range of expectations usually attributed to professional venture capital firms. The relatively low cost of informal risk capital may be due in part to the non-financial rewards that often motivate individual investors.

8. As distinguished from professional venture capitalists, informal investors often look for nonfinancial returns from their risk capital portfolios. These nonfinancial returns fall into several categories; some of them reflect a sense of social responsibility of many informal investors and some seem to reflect forms of "psychic income" (or so-called "hot buttons") that motivate individuals. The list of nonfinancial considerations includes creating jobs in areas of high unemployment, ventures developing socially useful technology (e.g., medical or energy-saving technology), ventures contributing to urban revitalization, ventures created by female or minority entrepreneurs, and the personal satisfaction derived from assisting entrepreneurs build successful ventures. A significant fraction of the sampled investors reported that they would accept a lower return (or undertake a higher risk) in situations providing some form of nonfinancial reward. Forty-five percent of the sample consider "assisting entrepreneurs" a form of nonfinancial reward. Between 35 and 40 percent reported that they would accept lower returns when their investment

helped create employment in their communities or contributed to the development of socially useful technology. Median rate of return reductions of 20 percent were associated with investments that create employment and that assist minority entrepreneurs.

9. Informal investors in the Seymour and Wetzel study typically learn of investment opportunities through a network of friends and business associates. Fifty-two percent cited "business associates" as a frequent source, 50 percent cited "friends," and 41 percent cited "active personal search." The next most common source, "investment bankers," was cited as a frequent source by 15 percent of the investors. All other sources, including business brokers, commercial bankers, attorneys, and accountants were insignificant. Since individual investors tend to be found in clusters, these data may underestimate the significance of professional intermediaries in the referral process. While most investors learn of investment opportunities from friends and business associates, the opportunity may often be introduced to one member of the cluster by a banker, broker, attorney or accountant.

10. Investors totally dissatisfied with existing channels of communication between entrepreneurs and individual investors outnumbered "definitely satisfied" investors by over four to one. Fifty-eight percent expressed a strong interest and 38 percent a moderate interest in an experimental referral service that would direct investment opportunities to their attention. See the discussion of Venture Capital Network, Inc. below.

1983—Shapero.[12] Albert Shapero examined the initial financing of new ventures in two mid-western cities. Shapero collected data from thirty-three private individuals who made investments in start-ups or very young companies. His methodology paralleled Hoffman's study, as did his conclusions. Several of Shapero's conclusions and inferences are of particular interest.

1. Individuals most likely to invest in new ventures appear to be those who have "made it themselves"—first generation money.

2. In both cities (Columbus, Ohio, and Louisville, Kentucky) the great majority of respondents would not invest alone but would try to interest others in investing with them.

3. An important difference between communities with regard to propensity to invest is the existence or nonexistence of venture investment networks among potential investors. Shapero defines a ven-

ture investment network as a group of two or more venture investors who share investment information with each other and who often invest together. According to Shapero, any examination of the nation's apparent "hot spots" of investment in particular kinds of new ventures such as Boston and the San Francisco areas reveal several informal networks of venture investors in each. Rubinstein, in his 1958 research, pointed out that private investors are far more dependent on their informal networks than are the large venture capital institutions:

> The fraternity of individual backers of small businesses appear to be rather close knit at least on a local level. A good deal of information is passed about by word of mouth. If one investor who enjoys considerable prestige among his associates believes a situation to be promising and recommends it to others, his friends may participate merely on the basis of his recommendations. . . . [13]

The significance of a respected lead investor in attracting the participation of other individual investors was evident in a recent case study of the Taplin & Montle Development Fund, an informal association of individual investors in the Boston area.[14]

The importance of informal venture investment networks was also cited by the Panel on Venture Capital of the U.S. Department of Commerce Technical Advisory Board. The panel reported that they:

> . . . became increasingly aware of an informal network of people, institutions and relationships that are significant in the process of financing new enterprises. . . . it is apparent that the network does not operate with the same degree of effectiveness in every geographic region of the country.[15]

4. The decision to consider an investment is highly related to personal knowledge of the business field or the entrepreneur or a high regard for the third party who brings the investment opportunity to the investor for review. What may appear as idiosyncratic decisions on the part of investors are, in reality, an expression of a rational assessment of the value of information and the importance of personal interest in the investment situation.

1983—Obermayer.[16] Judith Obermayer collected data from 101 small, high-technology companies to test the sufficiency of capital resources available to meet current and anticipated capital needs.

Obermayer concluded that there is " . . . a clear gap in the capital available for the very early stages of corporate development before there are significant sales." The gap Obermayer documented was for very early stage financing in amounts ranging from $50,000 to $200,000. She cited private investors as the only source likely to provide small amounts of seed capital. Twelve of her sample of 101 firms had raised funds from private investors. Obermayer recommended tax incentives to attract capital away from tax sheltered oil and gas and real estate investments and better mechanisms for connecting investors and investment opportunities.

1983 — Schell. [17]   Douglas Schell studied entrepreneurial development in the area surrounding the Research Triangle Park in North Carolina. He found that the rate of formation of technology-based ventures lagged the rates of new enterprise development in other areas of the United States. He concluded that the lower rate of new enterprise formation was due in part to " . . . the absence of a critical mass of local venture capital, both formal and informal." Another study, cited by Schell, reported that there is an informal investor market in North Carolina sufficient to finance about 235 ventures a year. The same study also concluded that the potential of the informal investor market is about as large as past institutional venture capital activities in the state. [18]

Schell reported that informal venture capitalists in North Carolina tend to look outside the state for investment opportunities. He cited the need for studies to determine if lack of opportunities is a major reason or whether there is an insufficient flow of information between entrepreneurs and investors. North Carolina informal investor research has indicated that the strength of information networks in the state is based on extended family relationships that use middlemen to buffer entrepreneur/inventors from wealthy investors. The middlemen are not usually part of the group of wealthy individuals. According to Schell, the linkages between these individuals appear to be more pervasive than those in New England.

1983 — Krasner and Tymes. [19]   O. J. Krasner and Elna Tymes replicated the Seymour and Wetzel study in the San Francisco Bay area. Data were collected from forty-one investors, thirty of whom were private individuals and eleven were professional venture capitalists. Krasner and Tymes' results were consistent with the basic findings of the Seymour and Wetzel study of New England investors. A few differences and similarities are worth noting.

1. The California investors typically share their investments with other individuals. Seventy-eight percent preferred to participate with other individual investors. Only 6 percent preferred to be the sole investor.

2. Seventy-eight percent of the California investors maintained an active working relationship with ventures they financed. However, they appeared to be willing to invest further from home than the New England investors.

3. The sample of investors differed significantly from New England investors in their risk/reward expectations, possibly a reflection of the "Silicon Valley" phenomenon. The California investors perceived significantly less risk in all types of risk capital portfolios, from inventors through established firms. For example, they anticipated losses exceeding 50 percent of their investment in only five out of ten inventors (versus seven out of ten in New England), and three out of ten start-ups (versus six out of ten in New England). California investors also anticipate significantly higher rewards—80 percent to 100 percent per year from successful inventors and start-ups (versus 50 percent per year in New England). Overall portfolio expectations were also higher—50 percent per annum from inventor and start-up portfolios compared to 20 percent in New England.

4. Many individual investors in California also look for nonfinancial returns from their investments. For example, between 40 and 45 percent would accept a lower return or undertake a higher risk when their participation contributed to the development of new technology or aided an entrepreneur in building a successful venture.

5. Investors relied upon the same informal network of friends and business associates for most of their investment opportunities. Compared to New England investors, the California investors were more dependent upon business associates than upon friends.

6. Another striking contrast between the New England and California investors appeared in their satisfaction with the informal network as a source of investment opportunities. Compared to 28 percent in New England, 61 percent of the California investors were either definitely satisfied or basically but not totally satisfied with the effectiveness of existing channels of communication between entrenreneurs and investors.

1984—Wilson.[20] Wilson collected data from eighty-three New Hampshire firms, a 75 percent response rate from a sample of 110 independent companies with at least fifty employees and growing at rates in excess of 15 percent per year. The study was designed to assess the equity and long-term debt needs of growth companies and to determine the relative availability of expansion capital in the state. Sixty percent of the respondents reported that problems raising expansion capital had not been an obstacle to growth. However, Wilson's analysis of the 40 percent reporting problems raising capital suggested that the equity and long-term debt needs of small, rapidly expanding companies were not being met. Capital problems appeared to be particularly acute for companies with under one hundred employees, less than $5 million in annual sales, and growing at rates in excess of 30 percent per year. These small, high-growth firms reported that the lack of adequate financing was curtailing growth and creating cash flow problems due to forced reliance on short-term debt. These findings are consistent with data contained in research by Tyebjee and Bruno.[21] In looking at "the effect of capitalization on performance" (the cause and effect relationship probably operates in the opposite direction), Tybjee and Bruno related several measurable financial characteristics (liquidity, leverage, and productivity) to growth. Using current ratios, quick ratios, working capital turnover, debt to equity ratios, sales per employee, and sales per customer, Tyebjee and Bruno found that high growth is associated with lower liquidity, higher leverage, and higher productivity.

Wilson's data suggest that professional venture capital firms and private investors serve distinct categories of growth firms. Individuals tend to be active in companies with less than one hundred employees, less than $5 million in sales, and with employment growth rates in excess of 40 percent. Professional venture capitalists were more active in companies with over one hundred employees, over $5 million in sales, and growing at less than 40 percent per year. Twenty-eight firms, 39 percent of the sample, felt that more efficient access to individual equity investors would have contributed to company growth.

1984—Securities & Exchange Commission.[22] Regulation D under the Securities Act of 1933 became effective 15 April 1982. Regulation D was developed by the SEC in accordance with the provisions of the Small Business Investment Incentive Act of 1980. Regulation D exempts certain private and limited offerings from the registration requirements of the 1933 Act and replaces the SEC's Rules 240, 242, and 146. The SEC examined the characteristics of the issuers and offerings using the Regulation D exemption during the first year it was in effect. The study sheds some light on the scale of limited offerings. Note that the provisions of Regulation D do not apply to intrastate financings that are exempt from registration under Rule 147.

Issuers claiming an exemption under Regulation D in its first year offered an estimated $15.5 billion of securities in over 7,200 filings. Partnerships accounted for 55 percent of the value ($8.6 billion) and 66 percent of the number of Regulation D offerings. Corporations accounted for 43 percent of the value ($6.7 billion) and 32 percent of the offerings (2,304).

Corporations claimed more Rule 504 exemptions (limited offerings under $500,000) while partnerships claimed the majority of Rule 505 (limited offerings under $5 million), Rule 506 (private placements), and multiple exemptions. Under Rule 504, 1,103 corporations raised $220 million, an average of $200,000 and a median of $150,000. The typical corporate issuer tended to be small, with five or fewer employees (60.7%) and an operating history of two years or less (68.8%). The typical corporate issuer had less than 10 stockholders (64.3%), revenues and assets of $500 thousand or less (75.5% and 71.3% respectively), and stockholders equity of $50,000 or less (87.9%). Seventy-seven percent were not operating at a profit.

1984—Tyebjee and Bruno.[23] The Tyebjee and Bruno research is actually five separate studies, each dealing with a different aspect of the financing of new, technology-based ventures. While their research deals primarily with professional venture capital, it deserves citation in this paper for several reasons. First, the research contains some incidental data on the role of private individuals in the financing of new, technology-based ventures. Second, the research is one of the most comprehensive studies of venture capital to be completed in recent years and provides solid background reading for anyone interested in venture investing, whether by individuals or professionals. Third, a useful model of venture capital investment activity was developed. The model is in the form of a sequential process involving five steps: deal origination, screening, evaluation, structuring the deal, and post-investment activities.

Of particular interest is the modelling of the venture capitalist's evaluation process. Their evaluation model employs twenty-three criteria grouped by factor analysis into five areas of interest: market attractiveness, product differentiation, managerial capabilities, resistance to environmental threats, and cashout potential. In a sample of ninety deals evaluated by forty-one venture capitalists, the model predicted 68 percent of the deals that were rejected and 95 percent of the deals that were accepted. The evaluation model provides significant new insights to the venture capital decisionmaking process. Both the model of venture capital investment activity and, in particular, the evaluation model provide an analytical framework that should be useful when applied to the activity and investment decisions of individual investors. Differences and similarities between the two markets are more susceptible to comparative analysis thanks to Tyebjee and Bruno.

In their survey of start-up ventures, Tyebjee and Bruno found that venture capital is more expensive than other outside investments. When the outside equity was largely (80%–100%) from venture capital firms the average equity given up was 58 percent, whereas if the same percentage of outside equity capital was derived from non-venture sources the average equity relinquished was 36 percent. They caution that the interpretation of this result needs to be tempered by the fact that venture capital typically invests funds of an order of magnitude larger than other types of outside investors.

They also found that the average new investment per investor in first round financing was $559 thousand for venture capitalists and $73 thousand from private individuals. Roughly similar differences were found in second and third round financings.

Research in Process

Aram—Aram Research Associates.[24] John Aram, Aram Research Associates, is attempting to replicate the Seymour and Wetzel study in an area encompassing the eastern Great Lakes region: essentially southeast Michigan, eastern Indiana, all of Ohio, western Pennsylvania, and upstate New York. SBA contract specifications require close compatibility with the Gaston research described below. Therefore, Aram will attempt to reach individual investors through the firms they have financed. His sample of firms will be drawn from the SBA's Small Business Data Base. Aram will also use the same survey instrument employed by Gaston but with the addition of questions dealing with investor interest in an investment opportunity referral service. Aram's research is awaiting OMB approval of the survey instrument. Final research results are expected to be available by early fall 1985.

Gaston—Applied Economics Group, Inc.[25] Gaston is using the same survey instrument employed in the Seymour and Wetzel study. Gaston's research differs primarily in the methodology employed to identify individual investors. Using the SBA's Small Business Data Base, Gaston has drawn a sample of 100,000 firms, stratified by size from the one from Pennsylvania through the southeast and west to New Mexico. The sample firms will be asked to identify individual investors from whom Gaston will then collect data. Based upon the results of test mailings, Gaston projects an ultimate investor sample of three thousand to five thousand individuals. Gaston anticipates that his research will be completed by early summer 1985.

MacMillan and Kobernick—New York University.[26] MacMillan and Kobernick are in the design stage of an exploratory study of the informal venture capital market—"individuals who risk their personal funds to support embryonic ventures with seed capital." The researchers are attempting to identify segments of this network of investors so that they can later study the way that this market works. The objective of the study is a better understanding of the factors that drive investment decisions in this important and little known market.

Neiswander—Case Western Reserve University.[27] Neiswander is engaged in several projects involving informal investors, including plans for a seed capital conference bringing together individual investors and entrepreneurs at the research, start-up, or early post-start-up stage.

Neiswander began an informal investor research project in December 1984. A brief questionnaire was developed to collect data from individual investors in the Cleveland area. It is particularly interesting to note that an initial group of six individual investors was able to provide referrals to 113 additional investors. Most of the six provided introductions to three or four individuals, but one investor provided thirty-nine referrals and another provided twenty-five. The questionnaire deals with investor interests, capabilities, and attitudes toward an investment opportunity referral service in the Ohio area.

Wetzel—Venture Capital Network, Inc.[28] Venture Capital Network, Inc. (VCN) is a private sector experiment in mobilizing informal risk capital for entrepreneurs in the six-state New England region. VCN solicits and profiles opportunities for risk capital investment in new or emerging ventures, identifies active informal investors and profiles their distinguishing investment objectives, and provides a timely, objective, and confidential referral system serving both entrepreneurs and investors. VCN is designed to minimize the cost of an entrepreneur's search for informal risk capital and to provide informal investors with a convenient system for examining investment opportunities that meet their preliminary screening criteria, without disclosing the identities of either party until an introduction is requested by an investor. VCN assumes no fiduciary, advisory, or evaluative function in providing its services.

VCN will test the hypothesis that the existing system for generating and disseminating information about risk capital investment opportunities can be improved in a cost-effective manner. With the assistance of financial intermediaries and using computerized data base management technology, VCN expects to become self-sufficient within two years, supported entirely by user fees.

By minimizing the cost of information, VCN hopes to have a significant impact upon the effective availability of informal risk capital in New England. Entrepreneurs will be able to locate the most appropriate sources of funds and investors will be able to locate the most attractive investment opportunities. VCN should also overcome some of the "discouragement effect" of market imperfections.

Analogous to the discouragement effect in labor markets that lowers the official number of job seekers, there is undoubtedly a similar discouragement effect operating among unsuccessful seekers of venter capital, would-be seekers of venture capital, and would-be entrepreneurs.[29]

For entrepreneurs prematurely abandoning the search for funds, the effective cost of risk capital is infinite, and society bears the cost of lost opportunities to establish new ventures or expand old ones. By offering a systemmatic approach to fund raising, VCN expects to overcome some of the social costs associated with the discouragement effect.

Since the inception of operations in May 1984, VCN has enrolled approximately one hundred individual investors and serviced approximately fifty entrepreneurs. VCN maintains an investor's profile or an entrepreneur's investment opportunity in an active data base for a twelve-month period. Through November 1984, over twelve hundred Stage I matches, over two hundred Stage II matches, and over fifty introductions of investors to entrepreneurs had been concluded. A Stage I match is computer generated and results in a blind copy of an entrepreneur's registration form being forwarded to an investor. A Stage II match occurs when an investor requests a copy (blind) of a two-page executive summary of the entrepreneur's business plan, submitted to VCN with the entrepreneur's registration. An introduction occurs after Stage II when requested by an investor. Any sales or purchases of investment interests resulting from a VCN introduction are on a negotiated basis between the entrepreneur and the investor(s) without any participation by or remuneration of VCN.

VCN does not make any independent investigation to verify the factual information submitted by entrepreneurs or investors and makes no representations or warranties regarding the accuracy or completeness of the information provided by entrepreneurs or investors. VCN does not solicit any character or credit references from entrepreneurs or prospective investors and does not evaluate or endorse the merits of any investment opportunities presented through its services. Since VCN does not become involved in investment negotiations, it has no systemmatic method for tracking the outcome of introductions.

INFORMAL RISK CAPITAL RESEARCH:
ISSUES AND IDEAS

Probably more has been learned about informal risk capital since 1980 than was discovered during the previous twenty-five years combined. But that statement is neither as powerful nor as comforting as it sounds. While we may have developed an increased appreciation for the significance of informal risk capital in the financial life-cycle of entrepreneurial ventures, we still know very little about informal investors themselves, the decision models they employ, or the information networks that link them.

Informal risk capital research has yet to emerge from the exploratory stage—the discovery of what concepts, theories, and hypotheses are relevant. Some notable progress has been made toward the formation of testable hypotheses. Tyebjee and Bruno's investment decision model is one example of an hypothesis that can be tested with informal investors. Venture Capital Network, Inc. is an example of an hypothesis currently undergoing field tests. Despite this movement toward traditional research methodology, it seems reasonable to conclude that the "state of the art" in informal risk capital research is still exploratory in nature. A citation from Hoffman's 1972 dissertation is as appropriate now as it was then.

> . . . in the enterprise of exploration we keep our theory fluid. It can be changed to fit the discovered facts and we can change the categories of facts we are interested in as relationships become clearer to us. The result of exploratory research is a network of meaning, however incomplete and tenuously supported, constructed after the fact to fit the observed events. It should lead to a more elaborate theory, to more precisely defined, hypotheses.[30]

A review of the record of informal risk capital research suggests the following issues that deserve further exploration and analysis:

- What is the scale of informal risk capital investing—both in numbers of investors and in dollars invested?

- What are the personal characteristics of informal investors? Are there subsets of informal investors that can be distinguished by their investment behavior—for example, active versus passive investors, very wealthy versus less wealthy investors, self-made investors versus investors with otherwise acquired wealth?

- Can the decision processes of informal investors be modelled? If so, how do these models differ from the decision models of professional venture capitalists?

- What are the characteristics of the information networks that link informal investors? Are there geographic differences in the nature or effectiveness of these networks?

- Is informal risk capital more or less expensive than professional venture capital? To what extent are informal investors motivated by nonfinancial as well as financial rewards?

- Do clusters of informal investors tend to be characterized by the presence of one or more lead investors who influence the propensity to invest of other investors?

- To what extent do informal investors and professional venture capitalists compete with or complement one another? Are there types of entrepreneurial ventures or stages in the life cycle of entrepreneurial ventures that tend to fit the investment objectives of one class of investor better than another?

- To what extent do financial intermediaries influence the effective availability of informal risk capital in a community?

- What are the most effective methods for locating informal investors and/or entrepreneurs looking for risk capital?

It seems to be generally agreed that the United States is experiencing the greatest explosion of entrepreneurship in its history. Risk capital is a critical factor in the entrepreneurial process and individual investors are a major but largely invisible segment of the risk capital markets. Opportunities to explore the role of individual risk capital investors and thereby contribute to the vitality of an entrepreneurial economy are virtually without bounds.

NOTES TO CHAPTER 4

1. Peter Kilby, ed., *Entrepreneurship and Economic Development* (New York: The Free Press, 1971).

2. "The Four Hundred Richest People in America," *The Forbes Four Hundred*, 1 October 1984.

3. *Venture Capital Journal* (January 1984).

4. Albert H. Rubenstein, *Problems of Financing and Managing New Research-Based Enterprises in New England*, Federal Reserve Bank of Boston, Boston, Mass., 1958.

5. Gordon B. Baty, *The Initial Financing of the New Research-Based Enterprise in New England*, Federal Reserve Bank of Boston, Boston, Mass., 1964.

6. Cary A. Hoffman, "The Venture Capital Investment Process: A Particular Aspect of Regional Economic Development" (Ph.D. dissertation, the University of Texas at Austin, 1972).

7. David T. Brophy, "Venture Capital Research," in C. A. Kent, D. L. Sexton, and K. H. Vesper, eds., *Encyclopedia of Entrepreneurship* (Englewood Cliffs, N. J.: Prentice-Hall, 1982).

8. A. S. Bean, D. Schiffel, and M. E. Mogee, "The Venture Capital Market and Technological Innovation," *Research Policy* 4 (1975).

9. Charles River Associates Inc., *An Analysis of Capital Market Imperfections*, prepared for the Experimental Technology Incentives Program, National Bureau of Standards, Washington, D.C., 1976.

10. Edwin Manfield, "Entrepreneurship and the Management of Innovation," in J. Bachman, ed., *Entrepreneurship and the Outlook for America* (New York: The Free Press, 1983).

11. C. R. Seymour and W. E. Wetzel, *Informal Risk Capital in New England*, University of New Hampshire, Durham, N.H., 1981. See also W. E. Wetzel, "Angels and Informal Risk Capital," *Sloan Management Review* (Summer 1983).

12. Albert Shapero, *The Role of the Financial Institutions of a Community in the Formation, Effectiveness and Expansion of Innovating Companies*, Shapero-Huffman Associates, Columbus, Ohio, 1983.

13. Rubenstein, *Problems of Financing.*

14. W. E. Wetzel, "Taplin & Montle Development Fund: A Case Study in Finance," in J. Hornaday, J. Timmons, and K. Vesper, eds., *Frontiers of Entrepreneurship Research* (Wellesley, Mass.: Babson College, 1983).

15. U.S. Department of Commerce, *Financing New Technological Enterprise*, Report of the Panel on Venture Capital to the Commerce Technical Advisory Board, Washington, D.C., 1970.

16. Judith H. Overmayer, *The Capital Crunch: Small High-Technology Companies and National Objectives During a Period of Severe Debt and Equity Shortages*, Research & Planning, Inc., Cambridge, Mass., 1983.

17. Douglas W. Schell, "The Development of the Venture Capital Industry in North Carolina: A New Approach," in J. Hornaday, F. Tarpley, J. Timmons, and K. Vesper, eds., *Frontiers of Entrepreneurship Research* (Wellesley, Mass.: 1984).

18. John S. Hekman and Mike E. Miles, *North Carolina Study of Venture Capital Markets* (Chapel Hill, N.C.: University of North Carolina, 1982).

19. O. J. Krasner and Elna R. Tymes, "Informal Risk Capital in California," in J. Hornaday, J. Timmons, and K. Vesper, eds., *Frontiers of Entrepreneurship Research* (Wellesley, Mass.: Babson College, 1983).

20. Ian G. Wilson, *Financing Growth Companies in New Hampshire*, Department of Resources and Economic Development, State of New Hampshire, Concord, N.H., 1984.

21. Albert V. Bruno and Tyzoon T. Tyebjee, *Venture Capital Allocation Decisions and Their Performance* (Santa Clara, Calif.: University of Santa Clara, 1984).

22. *An Analysis of Regulation D*, Directorate of Economic and Policy Analysis, U.S. Securities and Exchange Commission, Washington, D.C., 1984.

23. Bruno and Tyebjee, *Venture Capital Allocation Decisions.*

24. John Aram, Aram Research Associates, Cleveland, Ohio.

25. Robert J. Gaston, Applied Economics Group, Inc., Knoxville, Tenn.

26. J. M. Kobernick and Ian C. MacMillan, New York University, New York, N.Y.

27. Kirk Neiswander, Case Western Reserve University, Cleveland, Ohio.

28. William E. Wetzel, University of New Hampshire, Durham, N.H.

29. Myles G. Boylan, "What We Know and Don't Know About Venture Capital" (Paper for the American Economic Association Annual Meeting, December 1981).

30. B. G. Glaser and A. L. Strauss, *The Discovery of Grounded Theory: Strategies for Qualitative Research* (Chicago, Ill.: Aldine Publishing Co., 1967).

A STRUCTURAL ANALYSIS OF THE VENTURE CAPITAL INDUSTRY

Albert V. Bruno

The existing literature on venture capital falls into two categories. The first is the deal flow and management process in venture capital firms including sources of deals, workflow, deal selection, and rejection. This area has been the focus of a number of studies. These studies have relied upon mail questionnaires and personal interviews to develop descriptive statistics characterizing the search, screening, and evaluation process in the venture capitalist's involvement in venture management.

The second area is concerned with whether the venture capital market is efficient, and particularly if there are any barriers to the flow of venture capital to innovative ventures. Recently, as venture capital research has sought to move beyond the exploratory stage, authors have begun to formulate conceptual models and postulate hypotheses regarding the complex phenomena of venturing. The discussion that follows seeks to contribute to the understanding of the venture capital industry by analyzing its structural characteristics. The similarities and dissimilarities between informal risk capital investors and institutional venture capital investors are examined in this context.

The structural analysis of the venture capital industry follows the format espoused by Michael Porter.[1] This approach examines the structural features of industries that influence the potential profitability and ongoing success of entities competing in the industry.

Porter argues that the success of these entities is determined by the intensity of rivalry within the industry, the intensity of rivalry with substitutable products produced by closely related industries, the relative bargaining power of suppliers and customers, and ease of entry.

SUPPLIERS

Money is the "raw material" for the venture capital industry. Capital is available from many sources, but pension funds, corporations, insurance companies, endowments and foundations represent 63.6 percent of the 1983 capital committed to independent private venture groups.[2] This trend toward an institutionalization of the industry shows a progressive reinforcement of the suppliers' power because:

1. The money invested in the venture capital industry by institutions is a very small fraction of their total assets whereas it is more than half of the funds raised by the venture capital industry. Pension funds alone invested $2 billion in venture capital firms between 1978 and 1983. That is only two-tenths of one percent of their total assets, estimated to total $920 billion at 31 December 1983.[3]

2. There is a credible threat of forward integration. Some pension funds, for example, have already turned to direct venturing. Internally managed pension funds and large corporations may prefer to have direct venture capital exposure because of closer contact with new technologies, opportunity for later public investment in a new industry discovered through venturing, and possible future acquisitions of the new ventures.

3. The institutional investors to some extent are also suppliers of the substitutes, the different types of financing alternatives that are available. Selected venture groups exercise considerable power. For example, according to the *Venture Capital Journal* very experienced venture capital firms (with some partners having over ten years experience) received 66 percent of pension funds commitments in 1983, whereas inexperienced firms (no previous venturing) attracted only 1 percent.[4] In a sense, then, the suppliers are imposing barriers to entry.

Among the other suppliers of funds, in recent years foreign investors played an increasingly important role, committing $531 million in 1983, compared with $188 million in 1982.[5] There is also a trend among foreigners toward direct investing because it provides access to technology and markets, whereas investing in blind pools simply provides better returns than that provided from investments in their own countries.

The magnitude of the role of individuals and families, the informal risk capital as described by Wetzel, who were the initiators of the venture capital industry as we know it, is unclear.[6] On the one hand, this source seems to pale in comparison to the huge amount of institutional money that was poured into the industry in recent years and by the large capital expenditures that new high technologies require for a start-up. On the other hand, as Wetzel suggests the magnitude of these funds from informal sources, could conceivably have substantially more impact than previously thought.

A major source of power for all the capital suppliers, is the capability to switch to other forms of investments whenever the reward/risk ratio for the venture capital industry is perceived to be marginal.

BARRIERS TO ENTRY

Entering the venture capital industry is challenging. Availability of funds is not the only barrier; experienced management and deal sourcing can be critical barriers. Moreover, fund raising has not become significantly easier as tax law and regulation changes have made sources of capital more available. The selectivity and the nature of the institutional investors have enhanced the role of the larger, more experienced firms rather than new entrants. According to industry publications, "the competition for capital is fiercer than ever."[7] There is confusion in the market because of concerns for less successful venture investment cycles and because of the number of groups asking for funds.[8]

Because of these difficulties, new entrants are obliged to develop a clear entry strategy in order to succeed. These strategies exploit the competitive advantage of the entrant: If it is a spin-off group of a large venture capital firm, it will offer experienced management. If it is a corporation or a bank, it will have relatively easy access to funds. If the venture capital entity is neither of the above, it will look for a niche—a specialized investment area in order to generate a good deal flow.

In the venture capital industry, there are very few economies of scale; to maintain the "quality" of the investment, the ratio between the number of deals and the number of senior managers must be held relatively constant.[9]

It is possible to define product differentiation for the industry. In fact, the venture capitalist's assistance can be thought of as value added. It is highly sought by some entrepreneurs. The quality of expertise available differentiates the participants in the industry. Moreover, the trend to niche entry strategies has brought specialization that will create barriers in the future. Examples of differentiations are internationalization, specialization (franchising, R&D, merchandising), industry focus, a geographic orientation, and financing stage specialization.[10]

With regard to exit barriers, there is not a "technical" obstacle: Dissolving funds is primarily a liquidation problem. At least, three funds (for example, Cal Fed Venture Corporation) had been dissolved by the first half of 1984.[11]

BUYERS

Entrepreneurs seeking capital have power within the industry only if their venture ideas are truly outstanding or "if too much money is chasing too few deals." The latter situation, although relatively rare, occurred during the boom venture capital availability period that just ended. According to H. E. Bigler of Bigler Investment Company, even during the recent boom period only the less experienced venture capital firms found themselves chasing inappropriate investment opportunities.[12]

Since 86 percent of the total venture capital disbursements in 1983 was invested in high-technology related products, the whole spectrum of new or expanding businesses searching financing is impacted by choice of industry considerations.[13] On the other hand, being undercapitalized is normal for fledgling entrepreneurial ventures. Usually they seek venture capital when it is impossible to obtain debt or to launch a public offering. Even though many entrepreneurs look for the advice and the technical expertise of the venture capital firm, some of them resent the loss of operating control and the high dilution of equity when venture capital funds are committed to their company.

The question of bargaining power is an interesting one. For example, seed capitalists (who finance at the idea or concept stage) tend to ask for less equity so that sufficient equity remains to provide incentive for the entrepreneurs. Sometimes the technology dictates easier terms for the entrepreneurs. For example, with the continued evolution and specialization of the semiconductor industry, some firms, such as Cypress Semiconductor Corporation of San Jose, California, are heavily courted by venture capital investors.[14]

SUBSTITUTES

Currently, there seems to be little serious pressure from substitute financing. However, there are signs that this may be changing. A recent article in *Inc.* magazine reports numerous examples of entrepreneurs who looked for different routes to finance their ventures than venture capital.[15] For instance, Ashton Tate, the software company launched in 1980, did not accept venture capital funds that were offered to it but rather "secured a $6 million line of credit from Bankers Trust." Even if it is not possible to speak of "denied venture capitalists" as it was done for denied entrepreneurs, there is enough evidence that the institutional involvement in the industry has also distorted the relationship with entrepreneurs.[16] Perhaps the informal risk capital as described by Wetzel will become more organized and represent a significant form of substitute in this industry.[17] An example of the possibilities is the Venture Capital Network Incorporated, the University of New Hampshire private sector experiment in mobilizing informal risk capital for entrepreneurs in the six-state New England region.

INTERNAL RIVALRY

In addition to the continuing fund-raising challenges mentioned earlier, there is also pressure to analyze new proposals promptly and efficiently in order to invest the capital that is available. It is useful to consider the basis of internal competition at two levels: at the macro level, where the motivations and the strategies depend on the organizational structure of the venture capital entity, and at the micro level, where market position and competitive strategies give some industry participants a significant competitive advantage.

VENTURE CAPITAL ORGANIZATIONS AND COMPETITION

The industry segments that play the most important role in the competitive environment are:

1. Private independent firms ($8.5 billion of controlled capital in 1983.)
2. Small business investment companies (SBICs) ($890 million of private capital, $826 million from SBA)
3. Public firms (or BDC, business development companies, $500 million)
4. Corporate subsidiaries ($2.4 billion)
5. Informal risk capital ($5.0 billion) as speculated by Wetzel. Other sources, such as R&D partnerships, state sponsored venture capital funds, specialty funds, and foreign direct investments can be considered minor participants at the time of this writing.

Private venture capital partnerships are the organizations most likely to succeed in the industry structure. The significant competitive advantage enjoyed by these partnerships is the consequence of the involvement of experienced, well-connected full-time senior management. These general partners are highly remunerated for their management skills; they typically receive up to 2.5 percent of committed capital as annual fees plus 20 percent of the net long-term capital gains. Ordinary income (dividend or interest) is used to cover expenses, whereas the taxation is on the individual partners, whose liability is limited to their interest in the partnership. The high incentives, the concentration of responsibility, and the consequent operational efficiency result in the competitive advantage of this organizational form.

SBICs were created by an Act of Congress in 1958 to stimulate small business development. They receive initial capitalization from private sources, which enables them to obtain funds from the federal government or through government guaranteed loans. As an incentive, investors in SBICs have selected tax advantages (for example, they can treat gains on sales of SBICs stock as long-term capital gains). However, some regulations reduce their room to maneuveur compared with the rest of the industry. For instance, investment is permitted only in businesses with a net worth of less than $6 million.

The recent increasing availability of venture funds was beneficial also to the SBICs, even if not to the same degree as the rest of the industry. The competitive advantage of SBIC leverage is offset not only by the restrictive regulations but also by the SBICs complete dependence upon legislation. Their attractiveness is only in the benefits given by legislation, whereas a leverage shortfall can force them to reduce their activity drastically.[18] The secondary role of SBICs is emphasized by the fact that large venture capital firms, such as TA Associates, use them primarily for investments that can be highly leveraged in lower risk situations.

P. R. Liles, in his analysis of the experience of American Research and Development Corporation (ARD) and Boston Capital Corporation, concludes that the substantial period of illiquidity imposed makes the venture capital form of investment generally inappropriate for the investing public.[19] The concept of a public venture capital concern is a contradiction in terms for many observers, even after Congress created the BDCs in 1980. This type of publicly held company, unlike mutual funds, is permitted to compensate managers according to performance, and, under current law, distributions are considered non-taxable returns on capital.[20]

The net asset value (the difference between assets at market value and liabilities, divided by shares outstanding) heavily influences the price of the stock. If a BDC is selling at a discount, an equity offering is not a viable option and borrowing money is the only solution. This drives the management philosophy and strategy toward a diversified portfolio and conservative choices. Moreover, the books of the BDCs are difficult to read for the shareholders. Investments in private companies are carried at values determined by the board. Equity is raised through off-balance sheet methods to avoid dilution of stockholders' equity. These considerations are probably among the reasons why Heizer Corporation and Naragansett Capital Corporation, the two largest companies of the BDC segment, left the battlefield (the first one liquidated, the second one was offered a buy-out) a few years after the new status was approved.[21]

Corporate venture subsidiaries have a "philosophy" problem when compared with private partnerships. The motivation behind the corporate venture activity is often the "window on technology" or a means to sustain growth. The corporate venture capitalist may also be instructed to invest only in technologies related to the parent corporation, offsetting the parent's competitive advantages, such as technological and marketing synergies with lack of investment diversification.

Investment banking firms, which usually trade in more established securities, occasionally (and more often) form investor syndicates for venture proposals. Their strategy is often biased by the tendency to overfinance young companies in order to keep them as future clients.

In this context, the research and development (R&D) limited partnership seems to have a future in the venture capital industry. Investors in these partnerships receive the right to tax deductions for R&D expenses, and for licensing fees or capital gain for any developed technology, whereas the sponsoring companies can pursue research and development without sacrificing equity or debt. The structure given to these firms fulfills many needs of emerging companies and provides tax-sheltered investment opportunities.[22] All of this, of course, is subject to continued favorable treatment from the Internal Revenue Service, which is in question. The informal risk capital phenomena described by Wetzel will not be discussed again here. Suffice to say that the impact of this form of risk capital could be substantially understated in published data on venture capital formation.

A final consideration should be given to the leveraged buy-out (LBO) oriented venture capital firms. In fact, if there is no link between the strategy and the structure, as in the other cases, some firms specialize and find their competitive role in private purchases of a going concern by heavily borrowing funds. When all goes well, the acquired assets generate sufficient earnings to pay off the debt and to enrich the investors through the public sale of shares in the company they have bought out.

Professor Wetzel's chapter provides a significant beginning to understanding one aspect of the industry, the informal risk capital community. It is possible to speculate, as Wetzel has, on important pieces of knowledge that would contribute to a higher level of understanding of the industry. This speculation could be made in the context of what are or will be the critical factors for success in the industry. These include: *deal sourcing*, the access to viable deals; *deal evaluation and selection*; *significant management advice* to entrepreneurial ventures subsequent to investment; *deal structuring and portfolio management*; and *access to funds*.

NOTES

1. M. E. Porter, "Note on the Structural Analysis of Industries," Harvard Business School, Intercollegiate Case Clearing House, 1975.
2. *Venture Capital Journal*, Special Report (July 1984): 10.
3. "Capital Transfusions 1983," *Venture Capital Journal* (January 1984): 10.
4. *Venture Capital Journal*, Special Report.
5. *Venture Capital Journal*, Special Report.
6. William E. Wetzel, Jr., "Informal Risk Capital—Knowns and Unknowns, "Proceedings, *State of the Art in Entrepreneurial Research*, Austin, Texas, 21–22 February 1985.
7. L. Kravitz, "Venture Funds Stop To Catch Their Breath," *Venture* (June 1984).
8. *Venture Capital Journal*, Special Report: 7.
9. J. Thackray, "The Institutionalization of Venture Capital," *Institutional Investor* XVII: 8 (August 1983).
10. S. Davidson and M. Tercek, "Venture Capital Industry Survey," (Unpublished.)
11. J. Kotkin, Venture Capital, Inc., August 1984.
12. Bigler Investment Management Company, Inc., "Venture Capital, A Perspective," 1983.
13. *Venture Capital Journal*, Special Report (May 1984): 8.
14. "Start Up Semiconductor Firms Find Funds," *The Wall Street Journal*, 21 September 1984.
15. Kravitz, "Venture Funds."
16. A. V. Bruno and T. T. Tyebjee, "The One That Got Away: A Study of Ventures Rejected by Venture Capitalists." (In process.)
17. Wetzel, "Informal Risk Capital."
18. *Venture Capital Journal*, Special Report (October 1983): 6.
19. P. R. Liles, "Sustaining Venture Capital Firms," Management Analysis Center, 1977.
20. G. Kozmetsky, M. D. Gill, and R. W. Smilor, *Financing and Managing Fast Growth Companies: The Venture Capital Process* (Lexington, Mass.: Lexington Publications, forthcoming).
21. "Now Anyone Can Be a Venture Capitalist," *Business Week*, 26 March 1984.
22. Bigler Investment Management Company, Inc., "Venture Capital."

5 VENTURE CAPITAL RESEARCH

David J. Brophy

INTRODUCTION

Venture capital may be defined as financing extended to an emerging growth company, in the form of equity or long-term subordinated convertible debt, at a stage in the firm's life when access to funding from banks, other financial institutions, and the public equity and debt markets is either not yet available or still relatively expensive. Such capital is provided by its ultimate investors through private placement and management by venture capital investment specialists to companies expected to grow rapidly and to generate unusually high returns. The market for venture capital finance and investment has expanded and deepened since 1950, developing from a fragmented and informal market to one with identifiable components and processes. The market, which has been highly concentrated with respect to geography, sources of funds, and distribution of funds is in a continuous process of deconcentration, expanding regionally and internationally, employing funds from a widening array of sources, and servicing investment demand in an ever-increasing variety of outlets, all innovative and entrepreneurially driven, and mostly technology based.

To put the role of venture capital in context, it is useful to think of it as a key part of the economic growth process now facing much of the United States and other countries as well. The venture capital

119

process is important in marshalling resources for the attainment of benefits for government, business, and the public at large. This representation should not be interpreted as suggesting that venture capital finance is of greater importance than other elements. It should be thought of as "necessary but not sufficient" for generating these benefits. It is more to the point to think of the financier as the overseer of the market exchange system, in a sense deciding through financing decisions, on behalf of society at large, what new projects should go forward and which should not. This is an important function in the economic transition now facing many economies. It is unlikely that a country or area can be competitive in commercial exploitation of innovative processes, products, and service without a strong local venture capital community. While venture capital does flow geographically, investments tend to be made close to the home base of the venture capital investment firm. Aside from occasional investments, funds flow systematically through co-investment among professional venture capitalists. Funds flow more easily, in greater volume, at more favorable terms to those areas in which local professional venture capital firms exist and are active market participants.

SOURCES AND DISTRIBUTION OF VENTURE CAPITAL INVESTMENT FUNDS

The visible supply of funds committed explicitly to venture capital investment at any moment is reflected in the "funds under management" by venture capital investment firms. These firms are generally established as limited partnerships, small business investment companies (SBIC), or business development corporations (BDC). The amount outstanding at year end and the annual change for the period 1969–83 is presented in Table 5–1. Several points are worthy of note. First, the absolute amount of funds under management is very small in relation to other macroeconomic statistics. Second, the rapid expansion of total capital in the 1978–84 period followed a period of decline and recovery from 1969 through 1977. Third, the net cash flow (capital pool plus additions minus distributions to investee firms) has been negative in each year except 1978 and 1983, suggesting a steady pressure on the liquid resources of the venture capital industry. This negative net cash flow has led to the continuous de-

Table 5-1. Flow of Investment Funds in the U.S. Venture Capital Industry.

Year	Capital Pool, Start of Year	Invested In V.C. Funds	Disbursed to Investees	Net Cash Flow
1969	3,000	171	450	−279
1970	2,900	97	350	−253
1971	2,800	95	410	−315
1972	2,800	62	425	−363
1973	2,700	56	450	−394
1974	2,700	57	350	−293
1975	2,800	10	250	−240
1976	2,900	50	300	−250
1977	3,000	39	400	−361
1978	3,500	570	550	20
1979	3,800	319	1,000	−681
1980	4,500	900	1,100	−200
1981	5,800	1,300	1,400	−100
1982	7,600	1,700	1,800	−100
1983	11,500	4,100	2,800	1,300
Totals:		9,526	12,035	−2,509

Source: David Arscott, Partner, Arscott and Norton, San Francisco, Calif.: 7 June 1984.

mand for more funds to be committed to satisfying the needs of investee firms.

The time pattern reflected in Table 5-1 may be explained in terms of investment opportunities and tax-related incentives. Following a strong market demand for equities of emerging technology-based firms in the late 1960s, investors lost interest in this type of investment in the early 1970s. This was due in large measure to the reduction in federal government funding support for technological research and development and the cutback in the space and military spending programs, both major sources of product demand from technology-based firms. To these problems were added the debilitating effects of the generally poor economic conditions of the early to mid-1970s, during which time young innovative firms were especially hard hit by rising rates of inflation, recession, and cost of funds.

With respect to technology, a major contribution of this early 1970s period was the application of the semiconductor to consumer and industrial applications (e.g., hand-held calculators, early microcomputers). This dramatically influenced the orientation of emerging technologically innovative firms away from full dependency on government funding and purchasing policy to a market base increasingly extended to include heavy private sector consumer and industrial demand. This development positioned such firms to move ahead rapidly across a broad front characterized by a strong trend to technological innovation.

In 1978, the capital gains tax differential—removed by the Tax Reform Act of 1969—was restored, with capital gains tax reduced to 28 percent. This was subsequently lowered for individuals to 20 percent in 1980. At this same time, the Employee Retirement Investment Security Act (ERISA) was clarified to the satisfaction of pension fund investment managers interested in venture capital investments. These changes provided incentives for, on the one hand, tax-paying investors (financial and nonfinancial corporations) and, on the other hand, the nation's major tax-exempt investment pool to seek opportunities for investment with capital appreciation potential.

The results of these developments are reflected both in the aggregate volume of funds invested over time (Table 5-1) and in the distribution of funds by investor source. The sources of funds for venture capital firms are shown in Table 5-2, which reflects the growing importance of pension funds as ultimate investors. The growth of these firms, in dollar volume and in professional human resources, is reflected in Table 5-3. These data show that the change in capital per firm over the 1977-83 period has been greater than has the increase in capital per professional, indicating that investment firms are staying ahead of their capital growth in the addition of professional personnel. What is not shown in this table is the fact that the average tenure in venture capital of the professional base is now between three and four years, with a bimodal distribution between veterans (fifteen to twenty years) and newcomers to this relatively young industry. The geographic distribution of venture capital investment resources has become proportionally more concentrated in the 1977-83 period, as shown in Table 5-4. While California clearly dominated this pattern, it is important to note that venture capital resources have appeared for the first time in some states and have increased in absolute and proportional importance in an increasing number of states over time.

It is also important to understand the investment pattern of professional venture capital managers with respect to stage of life-cycle

Table 5-2. Venture Capital Commitments, 1982-84 (Independent Private Firms Only).

	Total Capital Committed (millions)			Percent of Total Capital Committed		
	1982	1983	1984 (6 Mos.)	1982	1983	1984 (6 Mos.)
Pension Funds	$ 474	$1,070	$ 653	33%	31%	36%
Foreign	188	531	349	13	16	20
Individuals and Families	290	707	274	21	21	15
Corporations	175	415	239	12	12	13
Insurance Companies	200	410	194	14	12	11
Endowments and Foundations	96	267	95	7	8	5
Total	$1,423	$3,400	$1,804	100%	100%	100%

Source: *Venture Capital Journal* (July 1984).

Table 5-3. Growth of Capital and Professional Resources of Venture Capital Firms, 1977–83.

| | Average Capital/Firm ($ millions) | | | Median Size ($ millions) | Average Capital/Professional ($ millions) | | |
	1977	1983	Percent Increase	1983	1977	1983	Percent Increase
Independent–private	$ 9.0	$36.4	304%	$18.0	$3.8	$ 9.5	150%
Corporate–financial	25.4	35.9	41	14.5	7.7	8.5	10
Corporate–industrial	8.9	37.9	326	10.0	4.0	12.9	223
Other V.C. SBICs	5.9	5.3	(10)	2.0	2.4	2.3	(4)
Total Industry	$10.6	$27.0	155%	$10.0	$4.2	$ 8.1	93%

Source: *Venture Capital Journal* (July 1984).

Table 5-4. Geographic Distribution of Venture Capital Resources by Leading States.

	Capital ($ millions)				Firms			
	1977	Percent of Total	1983	Percent of Total	1977	Percent of Total	1983	Percent of Total
California	$524	21%	$3,656	30%	44	19%	142	26%
New York	718	28	2,559	21	56	24	89	17
Massachusetts	334	13	1,549	13	28	12	45	8
Illinois	255	10	715	6	14	6	18	3
Connecticut	89	4	683	6	10	4	17	3
Texas	83	3	473	4	14	6	45	8

Source: *Venture Capital Journal* (July 1984).

Table 5-5. Venture Capital Disbursements by Financing Stage.

	Percent of Number of Financings*		Percent of Dollar Amount Invested		Average Size Financing (000)	
	1983	1982	1982	1982	1983	1982
Seed 1	6%	5%	3%	2%	$1,300	$ 800
Startup	16	20	11	17	2,000	1,600
Other Early Stage	21	18	19	17	2,700	1,800
Total Early Stage	43%	43%	33%	36%	$2,300	$1,600
Second Stage	29%	24%	35%	30%	$3,850	$2,400
Later Stage	19	21	20	22	3,200	2,000
Total Expansion	48%	45%	55%	52%	$3,650	$2,200
LBO/Acquisition	6%	5%	9%	8%	$4,850	$2,800
Other	3	7	3	4	3,000	1,050
Total Other	9%	12%	12%	12%	$4,250	$1,800
Total	100%	100%	100%	100%		

*Percentage of number of financing rounds rather than number of companies because a company may receive different stages of financing in the same year.

Source: *Venture Capital Journal* (July 1984).

of investee firms and to see how it has changed over time. Data on venture capital disbursements are presented in Table 5-5. In the 1960s, venture capital investment stressed new business formation rather than ongoing development of firms. During the mid-1970s, expansion financing dominated and start-up financing declined to less than 10 percent of total activity. While the initial investment focus after the increase in available funds in 1978 was toward expansion financing, a strong shift toward start-up financing has appeared since 1980. This reflects both the increased number of entrepreneurs attracted to the idea of starting a new business and competition among venture capitalists to capture the emerging "hot" companies at an early stage when the prospective returns are highest.

As professional venture capital managers seek exceptional rates of return for their investors, they exhibit a preferred habitat for their investments which has changed only slightly in recent years. This preference is reflected by the concentration of disbursements to

Table 5-6. Geographic Distribution of Venture Capital Disbursements, 1982–83.

	Percent of Number of Companies Financed		Percent of Dollar Amount Invested	
	1983	1982	1983	1982
California	38%	37%	47%	45%
Massachusetts	14	14	11	13
Texas	7	8	5	8
New York	6	7	6	8
Four State Total	65%	66%	69%	74%
Northeast (CT, DE, ME, MA, NH, NJ, NY, RI, PA, VT)	28%	28%	24%	26%
Southeast (AL, DC, FL, GA, MD, MS, NC, SC, TN, VA, WV)	8	7	7	5
Midwest/Plains (IL, IN, IA, KS, KY, MI, MN, MO, NE, ND, OH, SD, WI)	11	9	7	8
Southwest/Rockies (AZ, AR, CO, ID, LA, MT, NV, NM, OK, TX, UT, WY)	12	15	10	13
West Coast (CA, OR, WA)	41	41	5	48
Total	100%	100%	100%	100%

Source: *Venture Capital Journal* (July 1984).

entrepreneurial firms by geography, industry, and stage of life of the investee, and its consistency over time. The geographic concentration of venture capital disbursements is shown in Table 5-6. It is evident that the northeast and west coast regions have been the primary recipients of venture capital disbursements. The fact that these are also the regions to which the largest volume of commitments of capital to venture capital funds have flowed indicates that both investment managers and investee firms tend to cluster in the same location and that, on balance, venture capital funds tend to be invested close to home. A review of the distribution of investment by industry sharpens the focus of this geographic pattern. As shown in Table 5-7, the bulk of venture capital investment is directed toward tech-

Table 5-7. Venture Capital Disbursements by Industry Category.

	Percent of Number of Companies Financed		Percent of Dollar Amount Invested	
	1983	1982	1983	1982
Computer Hardware and Systems	28%	29%	39%	37%
Software and Services	12	8	7	6
Telephone and Data Communications	9	7	11	7
Other Electronics	10	11	10	13
Total Electronics Related	59%	55%	67%	63%
Medical/Health Care Related	11%	8%	9%	7%
Commercial Communications	3	3	2	3
Genetic Engineering	3	3	3	3
Energy Related	3	6	3	6
Industrial Automation	3	5	2	3
Industrial Products and Machinery	3	5	2	4
Consumer Related	7	6	7	5
Other Products and Services	8	9	5	6
Total	100%	100%	100%	100%

Source: *Venture Capital Journal* (July 1984).

nology-based industry such as telecommunications, electronics, computers, and biomedical firms. These are industries in which explosive growth has been obtained over the past twenty years. Even the casual observer is aware of the concentrations of technology-based industry in California and Massachusetts. It should come as no surprise to find venture capital activity concentrated in those areas in which technology-based firms are clustered.

THE ROLE OF THE PUBLIC EQUITY MARKET

Going public—the sale through a registered offering of equity securities to the public at large—is an attractive exit route or source of investment liquidity for the entrepreneur, the venture capitalist, and the ultimate investor. Demand for such shares in the initial public offering (IPO) market has been related procyclically to broad stock market indices, with periodic "hot market" or "speculative bubble" characteristics. For most of its history the IPO market, and its over-the-counter (OTC) after-market, have been highly unstable. They have been considered unreliable both by fund-raising companies and by investors. For much of the 1978–83 period, however, the IPO market experienced a steadily increased volume of new issues. The demand for these shares, though variable, rose as well on average, lifting secondary market (OTC) prices to attractive premia over broad market indices.

The relationship between the IPO market and its secondary OTC market performance, on the one hand, and the venture capital market, on the other, has at least two important dimensions. The existence of a strong and reasonably stable investment demand (largely from institutional investors) for IPO shares encourages earlier stage venture capital investment by promising an early opportunity to realize capital gains on the IPO issue and subsequent public sales of stockholdings. Also, the IPO market provides a vehicle for "price discovery" by those negotiating venture capital financings. In more than a few cases, qualifying young companies chose to go public instead of raising funds through the private venture capital route.

In the last part of 1983 and through 1984 the IPO market imposed a much finer "filter" on prospective issues, thus lowering the quantity of issues and the price paid on average for these shares and raising the quality of issues sold. This is reflected in Table 5–8. De-

Table 5–8. Initial Public Offerings for 1983, 1984.

	Number	Index of Offerings for 1984 Dollars Underwritten (millions)	Number	Index of Offerings for 1983 Dollars Underwritten (millions)
January	43	$ 353.21	19	$ 163.38
February	24	146.57	26	345.06
March	27	141.19	42	431.71
April	19	88.63	29	267.73
May	23	134.72	42	348.79
June	16	96.36	68	931.90
July	20	109.55	75	771.94
August	22	187.57	64	678.51
Total	194	$1,257.80	365	$3,939.02

Source: *Venture Capital Journal* (October 1984).

spite this cooling off, the IPO market has not disappeared as it has in years past. Thus, it still provides a net positive incentive for venture capital investors interested in "cashing out" after reasonably short (three to five year) holding periods.

THE OUTLOOK FOR THE VENTURE CAPITAL MARKET

Despite the euphoric excitement surrounding the "discovery of high tech" by most of the investment world since 1978, the venture capital industry has made substantial net gains since that time. Perhaps most important is the movement—not yet complete—toward a degree of structure, professionalism, and sense of mission in the venture capital industry significantly greater than that of the informal, fragmented, ad hoc business of the fifties, sixties, and early seventies. Venture capital firms are staffed by people better equipped to build businesses—people with strong backgrounds in technology, operations, and marketing. This is a marked change from the historical model, which featured partners trained principally in financial analysis and the law. The increased supply of investment funds is now emanating from investors who are much more sophisticated about technological assessment and market analysis than were their predecessors. The result is that the large volume of finance available to venture capital funds is coming from a better informed clientele who demand superior results in an increasingly competitive market environment.

The application of technology to economically important problems has developed at an impressive rate. Much of the technology being applied today is based on "old" science, and the competition driven by the ability to form and fund new, technology-based firms is accelerating technology transfer through this vehicle. It appears unwise, therefore, to adopt the view that there is "too much money and too few deals" except in the most parochial and limited sense.

For these and other reasons it is highly likely that 1985 will see a level of new venture capital funding of $2.5 to $3.5 billion, mostly in the form of extensions of existing funds. Disbursements will likely be higher than in recent years, partly due to a more selective IPO market posture. The venture capital investment process will become more fully accepted by a broader range of financial institutions, and the range and volume of private placement capital and services available to emerging growth companies will continue to increase. This will push the economy in the direction in which it began to move ten years ago—from the stable, large-firm model of industrial activity to the innovative, entrepreneurial risk-taking, inherently unstable smaller firm model, which will increasingly influence the U.S. economy in the years ahead. The provision of venture capital to form and fund such firms is critically important to this type of industrial development.

REVIEW OF VENTURE CAPITAL RESEARCH

The previous sections of this paper have been devoted to showing how the venture capital market has developed over its modern (i.e., post-1960) history. As this development has progressed, generating widespread interest in the processes involved, an impressive volume of investigative research on venture capital has appeared.

The 1960s

Very little scholarly research on venture capital was generated in the 1950s,[1] In the 1960s, a considerable amount of work was produced on the role of finance in the development of the entrepreneurially driven emerging growth company—in particular, the technology-based "spin-off" firm. This interest came principally from researchers in the field of general management who, through work on entrepreneurship, became aware of the importance of the problem of providing external funds for these highly risky young firms. The most notable examples of this work are Cooper, Shapero, and Roberts.[2] These management scholars, recognizing the special role being played by finance in the entrepreneurial process, stimulated the production of a series of theses, dissertations, and articles focused upon the financing of emerging growth companies. Among the most significant of these are Baty, Briskman, Rogers, Aguren, Hall, and Shapero, et al.[3] In many respects these studies were by necessity descriptive and confined to limited samples. An important characteristic of these research pieces is their scope: A review of the work shows that most of the questions being addressed in these early papers are still being addressed today, and, indeed, a great similarity in methodology between the two time periods is evident. Without a comprehensive information base scholars spent most of their resources and effort gathering data suitable for analysis. While some researchers proceeded with the "pick and shovel" work needed to raise and maintain data bases suitable for longitudinal study [see, for example, Cooper and Bruno[4]], most proved to be "one shot" authors who did not develop a sustained body of work in this field. A discouraging result of this pattern was the absence of any unified, consistent set of information on which significant research continuity could be built.

The 1970s

In the 1970s important pieces of scholarly research appeared that expanded the knowledge of the underlying processes involved in venture capital and provided a link between venture capital and the emerging modern theory of finance. For example, Donahue developed a generalized risk model (employing Monte Carlo simulation) and applied it to the analysis of large corporate ventures, thus illustrating how formal risk analysis techniques might supplement intuition in evaluation of venture opportunities.[5] Throughout the balance of the 1970s a series of scholarly investigations of the venture capital investment decision process appeared. The first of these, by Wells, was based upon a study of seven venture capital firms.[6] This work provided insight on the management of the venture capital funds and on the processes and procedures involved in finding, selecting, monitoring, and exiting venture capital investments.

Hoban took a slightly different approach and studied the characteristics of fifty investee firms from four different venture capital funds.[7] This study provided insights concerning the investment performance of the fifty firms and of the funds that had invested in them. An interesting conclusion was that the market for venture capital finance appeared to be efficient with respect to observed risk-return relationships.

The question of market efficiency was directly addressed by Poindexter, who applied the capital asset pricing model (CAPM) in a comparison between the public equity markets and a set of venture capital investments.[8] While the study produced unacceptable results in its attempt to modify CAPM to fit the venture capital market, it concluded—on the basis of "intuitive" evidence—that the market is efficient.

Research up to this point had brought recognition to the relationship between the venture capitalist and entrepreneur. To this body of descriptive information and intuitive conclusions, Ian Cooper added a new high level of insight and analytical rigor.[9] This study provided the first attempt to model the venture capitalist-entrepreneur interaction across time and is a valuable piece of foundation research for those interested in the dynamics of the processes involved.

At the same time, a study by Dorsey focused upon characteristics of venture capital funds and especially on those characteristics that effect successes.[10] This study is important because it provides information on certain parameters of venture capital funds that gives insight concerning their operations. A later study by Meade presents a model of the venture capital fund's portfolio management problem.[11] This study is an important extension of the work of Cooper and, to a lesser extent, of Dorsey. The main point is the concentration of attention on the dynamic programming aspects of venture capital fund management in a portfolio sense across time.

As a useful addition to the work of Poindexter and of Hoban, Howat studied 397 investments in small businesses by six small business investment companies.[12] This study concluded that the small business investment companies were not compensated sufficiently (via realized returns) for the risk present in the investments studied. These results are provocative in light of previous conclusions of market efficiency in the studies by Poindexter and by Hoban.

The issue of market efficiency was also addressed through the 1970s in terms of the allocative efficiency of the venture capital market, given the observed concentration of venture capital firms and of their preferred type of investee firm. Brophy and Welch, in a 1973 study, compared the financing experiences of matched sets of new, technology-based firms located in Boston and Ann Arbor, finding that the Boston firms (located in the midst of a cluster of venture capital firms) received more funds at an earlier stage of life and at lower cost than did the matched set of Ann Arbor firms (located in Michigan, which at the time had only one venture capital firm).[13] The Charles River Association study for the National Bureau of Standards concluded that no geographic barriers to the free flow of venture capital exist and that the market is geographically efficient.[14]

Brophy demonstrated that significant differences in net "balance of venture capital flows" existed among the major regions of the United States, with many regions that claimed to need venture capital for economic development actually being net exporters of venture capital to other regions.[15] Brophy demonstrated the linkage between finance, entrepreneurship, and economic development, an approach that has been productively continued and extended by Wetzel.[16] These studies are useful complements to dissertations by both Hoffman and Benoit.[17]

The 1980s

There is evidence that the interest of scholarly investigators in venture capital research has increased in the 1980s and that the prospects for improved empirical and theoretical research are very good. While this is due in part to the growing awareness of the venture capital market, it may also be traced to researchers' interest in speculative markets, especially ones in which price discovery is such a problem and the need for complex securities and contracts is so high. In short, venture capital research offers an attractive avenue through which to test emerging theory in finance. It may also be the case that the venture capital market offers the same opportunities to scholars interested in technology assessment, organizational theory, marketing, the law, and other fields.

In a 1981 study, Pence investigated the factors involved in the venture capital investment decision process,[18] Thirty-five venture capital firms provided information concerning three hypothetical venture investment opportunities. This study gives some insight concerning the "portfolio fit" characteristic and the evaluation of risk and return on specific investments. From a methodological aspect the study is important inasmuch as it involves principals of venture capital firms with whom interviews were conducted and with whom hypothetical case study research instruments were used.

In 1981, a study by Brophy of seventy-six venture capital firms provided detailed information on the portfolio characteristics and investment intentions of the firms studied.[19] This type of research has been extended by Bygrave, Timmons, and Fast utilizing the first comprehensive data base—owned by Venture Economics, Inc.—suitable for venture capital research.[20] This research, and the information set upon which it is based, promises to provide the opportunity for internally consistent, multifaceted studies of the venture capital process over time. It is, therefore, one of the most encouraging developments to occur in venture capital research to date. Independent of the Bygrave, Timmons, and Fast research, important progress in the empirical analysis of the venture capital investment process has been made by Bruno and Tyebjee.[21] Their efforts have produced a unique set of survey information that has yielded rich insight on the factors and considerations involved in the venture capital investment process. Still a different type of empirical study is that of Martin and Petty, who analyzed the investment performance of selected publicly traded venture capital investment companies.[22] While results of that study were not entirely conclusive, the paper introduced and proved useful some new approaches to empirical research on venture capital.

Progress continues in the development of analytical models and in the linking of venture capital investment with modern financial theory. A 1982 paper by Brophy, Amonson, and Bontrager provides a model for pricing and structuring venture capital investments.[23] Probably most significant in this analytical approach is a study by Chen that provides a theoretical model of the relative positions, roles, and functions of investor, venture capitalist, and entrepreneur.[24] This study independently supports further work by Tyebjee and Bruno conerning the linkage between venture capitalist and entrepreneur.[25] Chen's study is also important because, like Cooper's, it represents application of state-of-the-art finance theory to the unique conditions found in the venture capital market. Its value is enhanced by the likelihood that it will attract other financial economists to the venture capital field as a test ground for emerging theoretical work. In this sense it extends an important review of the applicability of modern finance to the small firm by McConnell and Pettit.[26]

DIRECTIONS FOR FUTURE RESEARCH

The venture capital market and the processes central to it are becoming part of the economic fabric of this country and, to an increasing extent, of other countries as well. The development of this field has been broad and it has moved ratchet-like to a permanently higher level of significance in our economic system and in our research interests.

The Need for Case Studies and Comprehensive Information

Research on venture capital has been hampered by a lack of comprehensive and consistent information. Since the investee firms and venture capital investment funds involved are not publicly held, no trading price-volume information or annual reports to investors are generally available.

The best sources of published information potentially available to scholars are Venture Economics, Inc., Wellesley, Mass. (publisher of *Venture Capital Journal*) and Howard Publications, Inc., Philadelphia, Penna. (publisher of *Going Public—The IPO Recorder and Private Placements*). Both are relatively expensive and neither provide information in machine-readable form; however, their main advantages are their superiority to the "pick and shovel" data gathered by individual investigators mentioned earlier.

Along with using information from such secondary sources, researchers should be encouraged and supported financially in performing case study analyses on investors, venture capital firms, and emerging growth companies. This type of study is demanding, expensive, and difficult to build into a publishable work product unless combined with complementary pieces of work. Nonetheless, if we wish to understand the processes of financing and building successful young companies we must assemble a set of clinical case observations that may be studied, compared, and differentiated on a continuous longitudinal and cross-sectional basis. It is especially important that these case studies embrace as many of the players (investor, venture capitalist, entrepreneur) as possible and record for analysis the viewpoint and position taken by each over time. We have evidence from the research cited above that survey and interview techniques are feasible and productive in this field of research. In particular, we have reason to be confident of the willingness of the players to contribute the time and (within limits) the information needed for such case work.

The Need to Apply and Adapt Modern Financial Economics Theory to the Venture Capital Process

Research on venture capital and the emerging growth company have fallen short of comprehensive understanding of the processes involved. In part this is due to the data limitations mentioned above. It is also due to the fact that researchers have been slow to employ, test, and modify modern financial economics theory in our research.

In the study of venture capital finance and investment, several areas of finance theory provide attractive research opportunities. Certainly modern portfolio theory should be applied to the venture capital activities of large investors in analyzing the issues involved in selecting among and appraising the performance of competing venture capital funds with differing investment philosophies. At the level of the investee firm, the applicability of the theory of capital budgeting—currently dominated by the capital asset pricing model—provides a potentially useful theoretical framework for research. The dynamic programming aspects of this process offer a particularly promising approach to understanding the sequencing of investments in the emerging growth company. Along these same lines, financial economists have long professed that, in theory, the valuation of investment projects and securities is best done in a state-contingent framework. From a practical viewpoint this approach has been slow to gain acceptance because of difficulties in conceptualization and implementation by practitioners. Venture capital professionals and entrepreneurs deal intuitively with a state-contingent framework in their deliberations on business plans and negotiations on pricing of capital. Application of this approach in trying to understand venture capital processes could yield results useful to financial economics in general as well as to the interaction of finance and entrepreneurship.

With respect to capital structure, financial economists have spent time and effort trying to determine whether or not an optimal capital structure may be attained by a firm and, if so, how it is done and why it is optimal. In this continuing debate a noncontroversial argument is that the market is the final judge, with that judgment expressed in prices paid for the firm's equity and debt. In the emerging growth company the same issues exist but there is no avenue (i.e., no public market) for open-market judgment to be observed. Researchers have begun to study the use of complex securities and monitoring systems as devices to achieve the equivalent of the "discipline of the marketplace" in situations where agency risk exists and in which no trading in the firm's securities occur. The venture capital market provides an attractive arena in which to conduct this type of research.

These several suggestions are not exhaustive or limiting but are intended to suggest that opportunities exist to use theoretical frameworks in financial economics, and probably other fields as well, to extend and deepen our understanding of the venture capital process.

Research Questions of Current Interest

Presuming that researchers are able and willing to develop data and employ modern theory, what venture capital research questions present themselves? Fortunately there is no shortage and the topics suggested here should be considered representative and not comprehensive.

Investor-related Questions. The period 1977–84 saw a strong surge of funding enter the venture capital business. No analysis of performance results of this investment and no evaluation of the benefits (financial and nonfinancial) accruing to the investors have been conducted. This is an important area of research inasmuch as the flow of such funding is of critical significance to the continued existence of the ability to finance emerging growth companies. There is the opportunity for effective work on the portfolio management impacts of venture capital investment, the setting of consistent objectives for the interested institutional investor, and the evaluation of performance against those objectives. Fairly direct studies of investment strategies (e.g., specialty funds, diversified funds, or investment in a "fund of funds") are both feasible and valuable. Such work is also of great interest to practitioners—that is, to institutional investors and the venture capital intermediaries who manage their venture-dedicated funds. The regulatory and tax policy issues implicit here make such research of interest to government agencies as well. It is particularly important, for example, to address the role of tax incentives in the flow of venture capital so that we fully understand their importance and are able to intelligently address questions of their continuance.

Intermediary-related Questions. The average capital per firm and per professional employee have both increased since 1977. Despite this change in size and evidence that the operation of a venture capital fund is becoming increasingly complex, little systematic study of managing the venture capital fund has been done. This area is rich in research questions given the problems of agency, conflict of interest and objectives, and investment monitoring that abound. Several specific topics of potential interest are:

- How does management differ in the salary-plus-bonus reward system fund compared to the carried interest type fund?
- How are the core processes (deal origination, valuation, structuring and monitoring) carried out across venture capital funds?
- How is strategic planning done in the venture capital firm?
- How does the venture capital intermediary interact with the ultimate investors, venture capital syndicate members, and portfolio companies?

Investee-related Questions. Perhaps the richest trove of research questions is to be found on the level of the investee firm. We still understand little about entrepreneurship and of the processes that produce "winners." Continued "clinical" research is needed if we are to learn more about this fundamentally important economic force. From the perspective of the venture capital process a variety of research issues present themselves. Some of them are addressed below:

1. Compensation of the entrepreneurial team is an issue that begs for study. Complex equity participation arrangements and covenants are the general rule, with confusion and a lack of trust often resulting from the lack of clarity present. Quite often, instead of a bonding agent to pull "the team" together to drive the venture, the initial structuring is adversarial at its core and may be so disruptive as to spoil the venture. Analyses of alternate structures and identification of simplified and clear approaches represents a good and useful research objective.

2. Technology assessment at the earliest stage in a venture is a currently important issue. Evidence should be collected concerning methods used and the relative success of various approaches. This is of growing importance since alternate approaches to technological

innovation abound and the capital costs required for development are increasing.

3. Valuation of the economic opportunity presented. Research is needed on the valuation process, to determine how decisions are now made, and whether they represent "fair" value equivalent to what would be achieved in an "efficient" market.

4. Ongoing financial management issues in the emerging growth company setting provide good research opportunities because of the size and scale factor differences (versus large, stable firms) and the inherent risk differences involved. A basic research question might address the issues of managing a venture capital financed emerging growth company as opposed to managing a small business in which such constraints may not exist.

5. "Cashing out" issues involve an especially important set of research questions. They revolve around the preparations, benefits, and costs of going public or disposing of the firm through sale to a larger company. Related to these specific issues is the question of managing and financing across the full range of the growth cycle and the skills and input factors required to keep the investee company on track.

These suggested research areas represent only an indication of the directions which research efforts might profitably take in the years ahead. Perhaps the most heartening characteristics of this whole field of research is the fact that these and other questions are of growing importance to providers of the information and financial support necessary for publishable research to be carried out. It is likely that research effort, once drawn into this field, will discover and generate a wide and complex array of topics, the limits of which cannot be estimated here.

CONCLUSIONS AND RECOMMENDATIONS

The venture capital business has grown and acquired the characteristics of an industry. Its visibility and importance as an economic force focuses increased attention on the processes involved. Both macro- and microeconomic implications are present for the private sector and important policy issues exist for public sector agencies involved with economic development and national revenue.

Basic research questions have, in the main, been addressed repeatedly over the past twenty years. The lack of comprehensive, definitive answers reflects difficulty in attaining information and, to a lesser extent, a failure to approach these questions in a theory-based analytical fashion as opposed to a descriptive manner of study. Evidence presented argues that the potential clearly exists for higher level studies of venture capital.

As a more sophisticated, generalized, and useful approach is taken to venture capital research, the rate of scholarly publication in this field will grow. As the volume and quality of publications increases, it will provide a base on which educational programs may be built. In this way, an understanding of the fundamental issues involved in venture capital may be transmitted to entrepreneurs, public policy agencies, venture capital intermediaries and their ultimate investors.

NOTES TO CHAPTER 5

1. H.Y. Hussayni, "Corporate Profits and Venture Capital in the Postwar Period," (Ph.D. dissertation, University of Michigan, 1959).

2. Arnold C. Cooper, *The Founding of Technology-Based Firms* (Milwaukee: The Center for Venture Management, 1971); A. Shapero, et al., *The Structure and Dynamics of the Defense R&D Industry: The Los Angeles and Boston Complexes* (Menlo Park, Calif.: Stanford Research Institute, 1965); E.B. Roberts, "Entrepreneurship and Technology," in W.H. Gruber and D.G. Marquis, eds., *Factors in the Transfer of Technology* (Cambridge, Mass.: MIT Press, 1969), pp. 219–37.

3. Gordon B. Baty, "Financing the New Research Based Enterprise in New England" (M.S. thesis, Massachusetts Institute of Technology, 1963); Eugene F. Briskman, "Venture Capital: The Decision to Finance Technically-Based Enterprises" (M.S. thesis, Massachusetts Institute of Technology, 1966; Claude E. Rogers, "The Availability of Venture Capital for New Technically-Based Enterprises" (M.S. thesis, Massachusetts Institute of Technology, 1966); Wayne F. Aguren, "Large Nonfinancial Corporations as Venture Capital Sources" (M.S. thesis, Massachusetts Institute of Technology, 1965); David R. Hall, "A Study of the Capital-Seeking Process of the Technical Entrepreneur" (M.S. thesis, Massachusetts Institute of Technology, 1967); A. Shapero, K.P. Draheim, C. Hoffman, and R.P. Howell, *The Role of the Financial Community in the Formation, Growth and Effectiveness of Technical Companies* (Austin, Texas: Multi-Disciplinary Research, Inc., 1969).

4. Albert V. Bruno and Arnold C. Cooper, "Patterns of Development and Acquisitions for Silicon Valley Startups," *Technovation* (Amsterdam: Elsevier Scientific Publishing Company, 1982), pp. 275-90.

5. Thomas W. Donahue, "An Application of a Generalized Risk Model to the Analysis of Major Capital Ventures" (Ph.D. dissertation, University of Southern California, 1972).

6. William A Wells, "Venture Capital Decision-Making" (Ph.D. dissertation, Carnegie-Mellon University, 1974).

7. James P. Hoban, "Characteristics of Venture Capital Investments" (Ph.D. dissertation, University of Utah, 1976).

8. John B. Poindexter, "The Efficiency of Financial Markets: The Venture Capital Case" (Ph.D. dissertation, New York University, 1976).

9. Ian A. Cooper, "A Model of Venture Capital Investment" (Ph.D. dissertation, University of North Carolina, 1977).

10. Terry K. Dorsey, "The Measurement and Assessment of Capital Requirements, Investment Liquidity, and Risk for the Management of Venture Capital Funds" (Ph.D. dissertation, University of Texas at Austin, 1977).

11. J. Meade, "Risk Analysis in the Venture Capital Portfolio," *Operational Research* (London: June 1974): 110-20.

12. John D. Howat, "An Analysis of the Investments of Small Business Investment Companies" (Ph.D. dissertation, University of Illinois, 1978).

13. David J. Brophy and William W. Welch, "The Financing of New, Technology-Based Firms," The University of Michigan, Occasional Paper, 1973.

14. Charles River Associates, "An Analysis of Venture Capital Market Imperfections," NTIS Report PB-254996, National Bureau of Standards, Washington, D.C., 1976.

15. David J. Brophy, "Cost and Availability of Venture Capital," White House Conference on Small Business, 1980.

16. David J. Brophy, *Finance, Entrepreneurship and Economic Development* (Ann Arbor: The University of Michigan, Institute of Science and Technology, 1974); William E. Wetzel, "Venture Capital Network, Inc.: An Experiment in Capital Formation," in J.A. Hornaday, F. Tarpley, J.A. Timmons and K. Vesper, eds., *Frontiers in Entrepreneurship Research* (Wellesley, Mass.: Babson Center for Entrepreneurial Studies, 1984), pp. 335-57.

17. Cary A. Hoffman, "The Venture Capital Investment Process: A Particular Aspect of Regional Economic Development" (Ph.D. dissertation, The University of Texas at Austin, 1972); Jean-Louis Benoit, "Venture Capital Investment Behavior: The Risk-Capital Investor in New Company Formation and Expansion in France" (Ph.D. dissertation, The University of Texas at Austin, 1975).

18. Christine C. Pence, "The Making of an Investment Decision: The Venture Capitalist's Case" (Ph.D. dissertation, University of California, Irvine, 1981).

19. David J. Brophy, "Flow of Venture Capital, 1977–1980," in K.H. Vesper, ed., *Frontiers in Entrepreneurship Research.* Wellesley, Mass.: Babson Center for Entrepreneurial Studies, 1981).

20. W.D. Bygrave, J.A. Timmons, and N.D. Fast, "Seed and Startup Venture Capital Investing in Technological Companies," in J.A. Hornaday, F. Tarpley, J.A. Timmons, and K. Vesper, eds., *Frontiers in Entrepreneurship Research.* Wellesley, Mass.: Babson Center for Entrepreneurial Studies, 1984), pp. 1–17.

21. Tyzoon T. Tyebjee and Albert V. Bruno, "A Model of Venture Capitalist Investment Activity," *Management Science* 30: 9 (September 1984): 1051–66.

22. John D. Martin and William Petty, "An Analysis of the Performance of Publicly Traded Venture Capital Companies," *Journal of Financial and Quantitative Analysis* 18: 3 (September 1983): 410–21.

23. David J. Brophy, Edward Amonson, and Philip Bontrager, "Structuring and Pricing of Venture Capital Investments," in J. Hornaday, J. Timmons, and Karl Vesper, eds., *Frontiers in Entrepreneurship Research*.

24. Yuk-Shee Chen, "On the Positive Role of Financial Intermediation in Allocation of Venture Capital in a Market With Imperfect Information," *Journal of Finance* XXXVIII: 5 (December 1983): 1543–68.

25. Tyzoon T. Tyebjee and Albert V. Bruno, "Venture Capital: Investor and Investee Perspectives," *Technovation* 1: 3 (June 1984): 185–208.

26. John J. McConnell and R. Richardson Pettit, "Application of the Modern Theory of Finance to Small Business Firms."

Discussant

ADDITIONAL DIRECTIONS FOR RESEARCH IN VENTURE CAPITAL

Herbert Kierulff

Professor Brophy has provided us with a fine overview of the emerging venture capital industry from the late 1960s to the present. To the tabular data, important historical information and interpretation has been added that is helpful in understanding the monumental changes that have occurred in just a decade and a half. Brophy has also noted the impact of changes in the initial public offering (IPO) market on investment decisionmaking in the industry.

Brophy's Directions for Future Research Section contains a wealth of good ideas that should keep researchers productively engaged for some time. The clinical approach of case studies provides insights to the researcher that simply cannot be duplicated by a mail or telephone questionnaire or statistical manipulation of quantitative data.

The purpose of this paper is to provide additional research topics that are of interest to these in clinical work and to expand upon the author's comment that " . . . venture capital research offers an attractive avenue through which to test emerging theory in finance. It may also be the case that the venture capital market offers the same opportunities to scholars interested in technology assessment, organizational theory, marketing, the law, and other fields." This is a very insightful comment, worthy of further discussion.

In the 1970s, it was common to see lists of characteristics of the entrepreneur—those personality traits that were important to success as an entrepreneur. It was believed that if these traits could somehow be defined, a venture capitalist would have an easier time picking winners. These lists have lost some of their charm as we realized that many different kinds of people can and have launched new ventures.

Yet the issue of leadership, elusive as it is, has lost none of its importance. Management still remains as a key to successful venturing. Given its importance to the field, perhaps we should continue our questioning but place more emphasis on the venture team. Specifically, we need to know more about the interpersonal dynamics of these teams.

Clearly, members are chosen to fill a functional role—marketing, engineering, production, finance—and they must have certain backgrounds of experience and education that qualify them. At the same time, the team must function well as a team under continued stress.

How does the venture capitalist assure himself that a team will operate smoothly? And what are his roles in the interpersonal dynamics of a functioning venture team? Professor Brophy mentioned compensation of the team as one factor that may spoil a venture. How does the venture capitalist deal with this potentially explosive issue?

The second area has to do with ethics and social responsibility. As the venture capital industry matures and becomes even more visible, the subjects of ethical and socially responsible behavior will come up more frequently. Only a few years ago, the venture capitalist enjoyed a knight-in-shining-armor image. Steve Brandt in his 1982 book, *Entrepreneuring*, wrote: "Venture capitalists are suddenly national heros as young microcomputer and biomed companies go public and make capital gains respectable, even patriotic, again."[1]

Two short years later, *Inc.* magazine's cover carried the title "Why Smart Companies Are Saying NO to VENTURE CAPITAL."[2] Inside, various horror stories related the difficulties fledgling entrepreneurs were having obtaining and getting along with their financial partners. Subsequent letters to the editor supported the article and added more stories.

What constitutes ethical and unethical behavior in the industry? How is unethical behavior policed? How does/can the industry maintain an image of responsibility to the public good? These and related questions could make for interesting research.

At the same time, we should ask how venture capitalists view and deal with ethics as it relates to the firms they finance. To what extent, for example, is the venture capitalist the one who sets the ethical tone in an entrepreneurial venture? And how does ethics influence the investment decision?

As Professor Brophy points out, the bulk of professionally managed venture capital funds flow to only a relatively few industries and only in a few areas of the country. Furthermore, other studies and interviews indicate that the industry tends to prefer investing at the later stages of the innovation/business development process rather than at the start-up or pre-start-up phases where the risks are higher.[3]

How, then, is early stage innovation in non-choice industries and locations to be financed? Given that it is in the national interest to develop and maintain an economy with a broad technological base, who should do it? And how should it be done? The obvious answer, of course, is the private corporation funding internal research and development or licensing it from inventors, and then bringing it to market. Another approach may involve the participation of the federal government. The Japanese, for example, have a massive network of programs and institutions to assist inventors, and these are administered and financed cooperatively by the private and public sectors.

In the United States there is at least one program—the Energy Related Inventions Program—that provides seed capital to investors and entrepreneurs with promising energy technology. The program, jointly administered by the National Bureau of Standards and the Department of Energy, is relatively new, but it has funded about 200 small proprietorships and corporations.

In any case, the roles and responsibilities of the private and public sectors in financing the commercialization of technology are not clear. Significant work can be done in this area.

A fourth research area covers those intervention decisions when the venture encounters serious problems and becomes a turnaround situation. Many decisions need to be made, not the least of which is to recognize the situation as a turnaround requiring a complex of actions designed to resolve the issue favorably. Timing is critical since the earlier the decision is made, the greater is the likelihood of a successful intervention.

However, a number of factors must be dealt with at that point. Perhaps the most difficult is convincing the entrepreneur that there is a problem. At the same time, other interested parties (including other participating venture capitalists) must be consulted. Research into how this process works and how the turnaround proceeds can yield useful information. Of particular interest are the decisions to invest further in the face of negative cash flows and the problem of what to do with management. Often a venture in trouble will appear to be a black hole pulling in money that then seems to disappear. And yet there is always hope to the hopeful. When does one cut the cord?

This author is in agreement with Brophy that the venture capital field does offer "an attractive avenue through which to test emerging theory" in a number of disciplines. The field of entrepreneurship in general and venture capital in particular presents extreme or border-line conditions for the testing of business theory. The firms involved are small to the point of being miniscule. The risk is high, as is the potential reward. Growth from a small base like that presented by a start-up can be astronomical in percentage terms. Reorganization is sometimes the only constant the entrepreneur and venture capitalist can count on for the first few years.

A theory in any of the functional business disciplines—finance, accounting, marketing, management, business economics—is comprehensive only to the extent that it can explain and predict behavior in extreme cases. Thus, if a theory does not work well in the entrepreneurial arena, it is most important to find out why. If the theory will not explain and predict well in our field, it may not do so elsewhere, and this may lead researchers to examine its application more carefully. If the theory begins to collapse, researchers are then encouraged to develop new approaches to replace it.

On the other hand, one can appreciate the frustration that the researcher must feel when he attempts to apply, say, the capital asset pricing model (CAPM) to new venture investments. CAPM was developed by researchers investigating returns on publicly traded companies and begins with an efficient market in equilibrium and an historical trail of price and dividend information for the assets under study. Similar frustrations will accompany him should he attempt to apply the relative newcomer to the block—the arbitrage pricing theory—to venture investments because it, too, relies upon past pricing data and an efficient market. As Brophy states, "Valuation is difficult because it lacks an objective base."

Nevertheless, if useful work does come out of this effort, it may be applied elsewhere with benefit. For example, the manager in a large corporation making a decision to launch a new product, enter a new market, or undertake certain research and development work faces the need to establish appropriate discount rates for these decisions. And he is in a position similar to that of a venture capitalist.

In sum, Professor Brophy has provided a number of insights into the development of the venture capital industry and the nature of the research efforts to date. Brophy has also given the challenge of major research yet to do and the important suggestion that work done in the functional fields of business and economics should be tested against the realities of the venture capital market.

NOTES

1. Steven Brandt, *Entrepreneuring* (New York: New American Library, 1982), p. ix.
2. Joel Kotkin, "Why Smart Companies Are Saying NO to VENTURE CAPITAL," *Inc.* (August 1984): 65–75.
3. Marcia Rorke, Herbert Kierulff, and Arthur Ramseur, "Roles and Responsibilities of the Private Sector in Applied Research and Development," Division of Policy Research and Analysis, National Science Foundation, March 1984.

HIGH-TECH ENTREPRENEURSHIP

6 ENTREPRENEURSHIP AND HIGH TECHNOLOGY

Arnold C. Cooper

INTRODUCTION

At a time when entrepreneurship has attracted the support of government, the attention of the media, and even respectability within academia, particular attention has been focused upon new, high-technology firms. There are several reasons for this:

1. High-technology firms offer possibilities for great growth. Actual growth may vary widely, but the possibilities are illustrated by Apple Computer, which achieved sales of $1.5 billion in nine years, and Compaq Computer, which grew to $325 million in three years. The job creation inherent in such growth clearly attracts those concerned with regional economic development. The potential financial returns make such firms of particular interest to the financial community. (One study estimated that 60 to 70 percent of investments by the leading venture capital firms were in technology-based firms.)[1]

2. From the standpoint of regional economic development, these firms seem highly desirable. They often produce little noise or pollution, and they employ highly paid engineers and technical managers. Each successful new firm creates a corporate headquarters, with professional employees with a commitment to the community.

3. Small high-technology firms appear to account for a disproportionately high share of major technological innovations. (At least eight studies, covering a variety of industries and periods, indicate that small firms play an unusually important role in innovation.)[2] In addition, small companies seem to bring new products to market more quickly and to be more efficient in product development.[3,4]

4. For potential entrepreneurs, the relatively high success rate of new, high-technology firms can offer particularly attractive risk/return relationships.[5] Furthermore, these firms offer alternative career prospects for those managers and engineers who function most effectively in the less structured environment of a small firm.

5. They add to the vitality and flexibility of our economy, serving as new sources of competition and challenging established firms. In developing industries, in which it is by no means clear which technical or strategic approaches will dominate, they constitute hundreds of independent centers of innovation, each testing particular product configurations and strategies.

Some of the major issues of our time relate to job creation, international competitiveness, the fostering of innovation, and the replacement of "sunset industries." New high-technology firms, with their special characteristics, are a unique resource for dealing with these problems.

High-Technology Firms

High-technology firms might be defined in different ways, but presumably they are characterized by substantial emphasis upon research and development, the employment of people with technical training, and participation in industries with high rates of technical change. Based upon such reasoning, some researchers have focused upon firms within particular SIC groups, involving such products as electronic components, computers, and pharmaceuticals.

However, even within the same industry, there may be wide differences in the extent to which firms place emphasis upon new technology. Some companies may be technological leaders, emphasizing research and development as a competitive weapon and competing in rapidly-changing segments of their industries. Other firms, even within the same broad industry, may be doing relatively routine manufacturing and utilizing technology that is widely available and relatively unchanging. To complicate the definitional problem more fully, it can be observed that some firms in "low-technology" industries follow strategies that emphasize the development of new technology.

However, in reviewing prior literature, we must recognize that previous studies appear to use a variety of definitions. Sometimes samples are not clearly described or appear to include a wider set of firms, only some of which are high-technology companies. Recognizing that the boundaries of the studies reported here are somewhat fuzzy, our primary focus will be upon firms founded by technically trained people, competing through emphasis on technological innovation, and participating in industries characterized by technological change.

Relevant Literature

In studying the founding of high-technology firms, much of the literature on entrepreneurship appears to be broadly applicable. Problems associated with team formation, working with professional advisors, or raising venture capital may arise in almost any entrepreneurial setting. Many of the characteristics of entrepreneurs probably do not vary much according to the nature of the firm founded.

The literature on high-technology entrepreneurship might be considered according to the following typology: (1) discursive writings—based upon wisdom, observation, and general experience, usually prescriptive in character; (2) case studies—based upon intensive study of selected cases; data can be from secondary sources or field studies; (3) field surveys—data gathered from many respondents through survey techniques; and (4) field research—includes comparative case studies, longitudinal studies, field experiments.[6]

There are a substantial number of discursive writings giving guidance to prospective technical entrepreneurs. These writings include checklists, discussions of typical problems, and advice on how to raise capital, investigate markets, and so forth.[7] The wisdom may be sound but is normally not presented in a way which enables the reader to consider the evidence on which the conclusions are reached.

There are also a large number of case studies on high-technology entrepreneurship, including some cases written for classroom use and a very large number of magazine articles about new high-technology firms. There are also many books and articles on the history of invention and on the histories of some of the major high-technology firms. Many of these case studies are fascinating and are rich sources of information about the entrepreneurial process. However, for purposes of answering research questions, most might be viewed as raw data, requiring further systematic study in order to draw generalizations that might be broadly applicable.

There are a substantial number of field surveys, many focusing upon technical entrepreneurs in a particular geographical area. Most are cross-sectional studies, examining particular aspects of a number of founders or new firms at a particular time.

Although less extensive than the field survey literature, there is a growing body of field research. Included are some longitudinal studies and some reports on the results of field experiments, most notably the results of programs intended to stimulate and support entrepreneurship.

INFLUENCES ON ENTREPRENEURSHIP

The decision to found a new firm seems to be influenced by three broad factors.[8] They are: (1) the entrepreneur, including the many aspects of his or her background affecting perceptions, skills and knowledge; and motivations; (2) the organization for which the entrepreneur had previously been working, whose characteristics influence the location and the nature of new firms, as well as the likelihood of spin-offs; and (3) various environmental factors external to the individual and the previous organization, making the climate more or less favorable to the starting of a new firm.

The Entrepreneur

In reviewing the literature since 1980, it is clear that the characteristics of the entrepreneur have received the most attention.

Family backgrounds were examined in five different studies conducted in Pittsburgh,[9] Sweden,[10] Canada (2 studies),[11] and Massachusetts.[12] Founders were found to be from families in which parents owned a business in 41 percent of the cases in Pittsburgh, 45 percent in Sweden, 50 percent in Canada, 20 percent in Canada, and

33 percent in Massachusetts. These percentages, although much higher than for the population as a whole, appear somewhat lower than found in some earlier studies of nontechnical entrepreneurs. Previous studies of nontechnical founders in the United States disclosed that 50 to 58 percent had family backgrounds of business ownership.[13] At any rate, it appears that both technical and nontechnical entrepreneurs are influenced by growing up in families in which there are role-models of entrepreneurship, as well as the learning experience of being around a family business.

In four different studies, technical entrepreneurs were found to have substantial formal education. They were discovered to have graduate degrees in 35 percent of the start-ups in Pittsburgh, 50 percent in Canada, 55 percent in Massachusetts, and 75 percent in Sweden. Interestingly, one Swedish study found no distinguishable difference between the academic grades of company founders and other students.[14] These educational levels are, of course, much higher than for the population and are not surprising for firms dependent upon the development of new technology. Previous studies of nontechnical entrepreneurs have found widely differing patterns, with one recent study discovering 36 percent with college degrees and 60 percent with education beyond high school.[15]

Most technical entrepreneurs started their firms when they were in their thirties. The average age in seven studies ranged from thirty-four to forty-two with a median of thirty-seven. This does not seem to vary much from previous studies of nontechnical founders and suggests that, for many, there is probably a window of opportunity when they have some financial resources, relevant experience, and a track record of success but have not yet reached a point when they are reluctant to risk what they have.[16]

At the time of founding, most seem to have had some experience across different companies but not to have been "job-hoppers." Mean or median number of prior jobs was 2.7 in Pittsburgh, 3 in Sweden, 4 in Canada, and, as found by Bruno and Tyebjee,[17] 5 in Silicon Valley. One of the most surprising findings was the extent to which these founders had previously owned or started a company. Prior business ownership was found in 67 percent of the cases in Pittsburgh, 45 percent in Sweden, and 32 percent in Massachusetts. These percentages are higher than in many previous studies of both technical and nontechnical entrepreneurs. One earlier study of thirty technical founders involved 27 percent who had previously owned a business, and a study of 1,805 nontechnical business owners found 11 percent.[18] This may mean that, within a region, one of the best predictors of future entrepreneurial activity is the presence of experienced technical entrepreneurs.

As in previous studies, many of these founders started with one or more partners. In ten studies, the median percentage of founders with partners was about 70 percent. This is somewhat higher than found in earlier research involving technical entrepreneurs, in which about 60 percent had partners.[19] Nontechnical entrepreneurs seem to be much less likely to have partners. Since both prior entrepreneurial experience and the presence of teams are thought to increase the chances of success, it is interesting that high and increasing percentages of high-technology start-ups seem to involve this combination.

There have been a few studies looking at the psychological make-up of these founders. Two investigations, in Pittsburgh and Canada, found desire for independence and self-achievement to be major motivating factors.[20] Interestingly, and consistent with one prior study of nontechnical founders, the entrepreneurs in one Canadian study did not perceive the act of starting a company to be highly risky.[21] After founding, those with motives involving self-achievement, avoiding risk, seeking feedback, personal innovation, and a positive orientation to the future were more likely to have faster growing firms.[22]

These, then, are characteristics of technical entrepreneurs who have been studied. However, we should remember that these founders were successful, in the sense that they got companies started and those companies survived long enough to be included in these samples. It may be that founders who never got beyond the part-time stage or who did not succeed in raising capital or becoming visible have somewhat different profiles.

Previous Organization of the Entrepreneur

The organization where the entrepreneur was located before leaving to start a business, which might be termed an incubator, appears to influence the entrepreneurial process in several ways. Technical entrepreneurs often seem to start businesses closely related to what they did before. In seven studies, the percentage whose firms had products closely related to their prior organizations (or which transferred substantial technology from them) ranged from 62 to 93 percent, with a median of 73 percent. Because of different definitions of relatedness, it is difficult to compare findings. However, it does appear that nontechnical firms are somewhat less likely to show this relationship, with two earlier studies showing this connection in 50 percent to 55 percent of the cases.[23] Clearly, high-technology firms are dependent upon current knowledge of technical and market opportunities, and this knowledge is most likely to be acquired in a corporation or university already active in a given technology. Thus, high-technology entrepreneurship and the nature of firms started in a given region may be particularly dependent upon the character of organizations already there.

Entrepreneurs may be motivated to start their firms, in part, because of negative "pushes" within their incubator organizations. Although there has not been much recent examination of the influence of the incubator on entrepreneurial motivations, two recent studies have considered this. One found that 15 percent of the founders in Pittsburgh were fired or laid off, and 56 percent reported being frustrated in their previous jobs.[24] A Swedish study reported that many founders said that a problem in their last employment was one factor in deciding to start out. One earlier study by this author of technical entrepreneurs, based upon personal interviews, found that 83 percent appeared to be strongly influenced by pushes in their prior positions. By contrast, one large study of nontechnical entrepreneurs, based upon questionnaire data, found only 22 percent so influenced.[25] Whether technical entrepreneurs are more often motivated by negative pushes or whether the differences primarily reflect contrasting research methodology is an open question.

The incubators for technical entrepreneurs often seem to be smaller organizations. Four studies have examined this. In Sweden, 83 percent were from organizations with less than 500 employees; in Silicon Valley, 77 percent were from organizations with less than 1,000 employees; and in Philadelphia, Freedman found only 7 percent were from "large" corporations.[26] However, a Canadian study discovered 64 percent from government or from firms with more than $10 million in annual sales. This is consistent with Cooper's earlier study of high-technology entrepreneurship finding spin-off rates from firms with less than 500 employees to be ten times as high as for larger firms. One large study of nontechnical firms found 63 percent from businesses with less than 100 employees and 13 percent not previously in the work force or from nonprofit organizations.[27] It does appear that, for both technical and nontechnical entrepreneurs, smaller organizations often make good incubators.

Incubator organizations also influence the location of new firms. One recent study found 85 percent of the new firms in the same general location as their incubator organizations.[28] A Philadelphia-based study found most of the new firms started by founders who already lived there; however, it also reported that some entrepreneurs not included in the study had apparently moved away in search of capital. Earlier examinations of technical founders indicated very high tendencies to stay in the same location when starting, usually 90 percent or more. One large study of nontechnical founders found a surprisingly high 25 percent who moved when starting.[29] Nevertheless, it is clear that regional entrepreneurship draws upon the people already living in an area, although technical entrepreneurs may be somewhat less likely to move than their nontechnical counterparts.

Recent research seems consistent with earlier studies in suggesting that incubator organizations do influence entrepreneurship and that the effects may be somewhat stronger for high-technology firms.

Environmental Influences

A number of environmental factors help to shape the climate, making it more or less favorable for entrepreneurship. One important determinant is the availability of capital, including attitudes of bankers and investors. In reviewing the literature since 1980, it is clear that this has been a fruitful area of research, with a substantial number of these studies centering upon the financing of high-technology ventures.

The studies considered here, none of which focus solely on financing, indicate the importance of personal savings as a source of capital. In the four studies that examined financing by source, the percentage reliance on personal savings ranged from 47 to 73 percent. Interestingly, professional venture capital sources did not play a very important role in start-up financing, even for these high-technology firms. Other important aspects of financing, including the availability of seed capital, attitudes of lenders, and the processes by which founders and investors get together, probably vary over time and from region to region. The upshot is that, despite the importance of personal savings as a financing source, some periods of time and some regions may be more favorable than others for the financing of ventures. However, these topics are probably better dealt with in the session on finance.

Potential founders may be influenced by the presence of role-models and by the ease with which contacts can be made with experienced entrepreneurs, professional advisors, and investors knowledgeable about technical entrepreneurship. A few recent studies have examined the presence of role-models in the entrepreneurial process. A Pittsburgh study found that 23 percent of the founders reported role-models influencing them at the time of their decisions. However, a Swedish study reported that few entrepreneurs knew of others who had taken the same step. Earlier studies of technical entrepreneurs suggested that the entrepreneurial process often was influenced by the presence of role-models with whom the would-be founder could identify.[30]

It was reported that second-generation entrepreneurship had occurred around the Innovation Center at Carnegie-Mellon, with clusters of new ventures benefiting from apprenticeship and from observation of experienced founders.[31] In Atlanta, it was observed that there was substantially greater interest in emerging technology firms on the part of accounting and law firms and the largest banks; this was expected to lead to a more favorable climate for the emergence of technology-based firms.[32] The presence of role models, of communication networks, and of easy access to experienced advisors seem likely to encourage entrepreneurship. However, research on these topics has been limited and spotty for both technical and nontechnical ventures.

A number of real-world experiments have been undertaken to stimulate and support entrepreneurship. Many are intended to provide the kinds of networks of support described above. These include innovation centers, incubators, and educational and assistance programs for aspiring entrepreneurs. The nature of facilities and support vary from region to region but have included the following: laboratory and office space; supporting services, such as secretarial help, model-building, and use of test facilities; seed capital; assistance in preparing business plans; contact with other entrepreneurs; and formal training and assistance in investigating the problems associated with the new venture.

Some of the most visible complexes of high-technology firms have grown up around universities, most notably Silicon Valley near Stanford and the Route 128 complex near M.I.T. In recent years studies have examined clusters of high-technology firms around a number of universities, including around Texas A & M, Carnegie-Mellon, the University of Utah, the University of Pennsylvania, and École Polytechnique in Montreal. One study identified 1,700 technology-based entrepreneurs in fifty-seven rural/university settings.[33] Many of these have involved students, professors (who may or may not have stayed with their universities), and those not connected with the university. However, there has been little recent systematic examination of university-based entrepreneurship across a number of universities, with consideration of why some universities or academic departments have higher rates of entrepreneurial activity than others.

It has been suggested that entrepreneurship courses and innovation centers make entrepreneurship credible to students and that attitudes of department heads and senior faculty can influence whether other faculty see this as a desirable activity. A survey of forty-two Canadian academic entrepreneurs reported that they perceived their "pure science"-oriented faculty colleagues to be relatively more hostile toward their ventures than other colleagues. The same survey disclosed that only 26 percent of the founders thought their universities had been supportive, with the remainder feeling that their universities had been indifferent or not helpful.[34]

Earlier research on high-technology entrepreneurship showed a variety of patterns in the extent to which universities had functioned as incubators, with students or staff spinning off to start new firms. M.I.T. was apparently a source of many founders but, in Silicon Valley, only six of 243 firms founded in the 1960s had one or more full-time founders who came directly from a university.[35] In that complex the role of the university as an incubator appeared to have been relatively more important in earlier years. For nontechnical firms, one recent study suggested that universities may play a relatively minor role as incubators.[36]

Other environmental influences, including the economics of location and the importance of quality-of-life have not received much attention for high-technology firms. At Pittsburgh, it was observed that the founding of high-technology companies led to the formation of specialized suppliers, which resulted in advantages for subsequent entrepreneurs. The development of a complex of related firms presumably leads to economic benefits through access to pools of trained labor, specialized suppliers, and the ability to work closely with nearby customers. Although rising real estate and labor costs may be somewhat offsetting, this is another way in which past entrepreneurship may make future entrepreneurship more likely. Quality-of-life is thought to be particularly important for this kind of venture, with its reliance on highly mobile technically trained people. However, technical entrepreneurs do not tend to move much at the time of founding, even to more attractive areas. The process may work primarily through desirable areas attracting branch plants and laboratories, which then subsequently serve as incubators. However, there has been little systematic examination of how quality-of-life may influence directly or indirectly the process of technical entrepreneurship.

NEW HIGH-TECHNOLOGY FIRMS

The high-technology firms which result from these processes tend to have distinctive characteristics. They often are positioned in markets that are rapidly growing and changing. Product life-cycles can be short, making product and process development important competitive weapons. As infant industries develop and mature, the bases of competition change, often in the direction of greater emphasis upon cost control and more standardized manufacturing operations. These turbulent conditions create opportunities but can also threaten the positions of established firms.

As in any new venture, there is great dependence on a few key people. Because the firm's competitive advantages are so embodied in the skills of the founders, there must be particular emphasis on attracting and retaining good people. The founders and key employees often are unusually competent in particular areas of technology. However, their skills in management, and even recognition of the need for those skills, may vary widely.

Although success is by no means assured, the typical young high-technology firm probably grows much more rapidly than its non-technical counterpart. Growth can present challenges, as management struggles to retain control and the same "feel" for the market that may have been critical to earlier success. An important and often unrecognized problem relates to the evolving roles of the founders as the company grows.[37] For instance, should an unusually creative design engineer devote more and more time to management or should his primary contributions continue to be in engineering? There are, of course, also problems in financing growth, particularly when there is concern about maintaining market share in the face of substantial industry growth and competitive pressures.

The resulting high-technology firms seem to do relatively well. One study of 250 Silicon Valley start-ups found that, as of 1980, when the median firm in the study was fourteen years old, only 37 percent had discontinued, whereas 32 percent had been acquired and 31 percent survived as independent firms.[38] These findings are similar to those from a study of 234 high-technology firms in the Boston area, in which in the first four to five years after founding, only 20 percent discontinued.[39] These are, of course, much lower discontinuance rates than for nontechnical firms.

OPPORTUNITIES FOR FURTHER RESEARCH

In reviewing recent research about high-technology entrepreneurship, it appears that the area of greatest activity relates to the characteristics of the entrepreneur. Further surveys of attributes, as such, may be less useful than studies that relate those characteristics to subsequent patterns of development.

Most high-technology firms are formed by teams. Many of the teams subsequently break up. More should be done in examining the team formation process, including consideration of those factors associated with more effective or more stable teams.

Formal programs to establish incubators or innovation centers clearly are receiving a lot of support. These might be viewed as experiments that are, or are not, having an impact. There should be active programs of research to monitor these programs and to draw conclusions from these entrepreneurial experiments.

Environmental factors that shape the climate for entrepreneurship have not received much attention. These include examination of the economics of location and the role of quality-of-life influences. The ways in which networks of support develop and influence the process deserve attention. It also would be interesting to examine the extent to which there exists an "entrepreneurial environment" at particular times or places. This might involve knowledge about the entrepreneurial process, knowledge about sources of assistance, awareness of role-models, and perceptions of the risks and rewards associated with entrepreneurship. It might be possible to measure the degree to which an entrepreneurial environment exists and to determine whether it can be changed.

Research on high-technology entrepreneurship has accelerated in recent years, but our knowledge base is still limited. The potential for further research is very great and the benefits—for entrepreneurs, for investors, and for our economy—can be substantial.

NOTES TO CHAPTER 6

1. Norman D. Fast, "Venture Capital Investment and Technology Development," in Karl H. Vesper, ed., *Frontiers of Entrepreneurship Research* (Wellesley, Mass.: Babson Center for Entrepreneurial Studies, 1982), pp. 288–93.

2. U.S. Small Business Administration, *The State of Small Business: A Report of the President* (Washington, D.C.: U.S. Government Printing Office, 1983).

3. Gellman Research Associates, Inc., "The Relationship Between Industrial Concentration, Firm Size, and Technological Innovation," prepared for the Office of Advocacy, U.S. Small Business Administration (SBA) under award no. SBA–2633–A–79, May 1982.

4. Arnold C. Cooper, "R&D Is More Efficient in Small Companies," *Harvard Business Review* 42: 3 (May–June 1964): 75–83.

5. Arnold C. Cooper and Albert V. Bruno, "Patterns of Development and Acquisition for Silicon Valley Startups," *Technovation* 1 (September 1982): 275–90.

6. Charles Douds and Albert Rubenstein, "Methodology for Behavioral Aspects of Innovation," in P. Kelly, M. Kranzberg, et al., *Technological Innovation: A Critical Review of Current Knowledge*, Vol. II (Washington, D.C.: U.S. Government Printing Office, 1975).

7. Michael J.C. Martin, *Managing Technological Innovation and Entrepreneurship* (Reston, Va.: Reston Publishing Co., Inc., 1984); Joseph R. Mancuso, *How to Start, Finance, and Manage Your Own Business* (Englewood Cliffs, N.J.: Prentice-Hall, 1978).

8. Arnold C. Cooper, "Strategic Management: New Ventures and Small Business," in Dan E. Schendel and Charles W. Hofer, *Strategic Management: A New View of Business Policy and Planning* (Boston: Little Brown and Company, 1979), pp. 316–27.

9. John R. Thorne and John G. Ball, "Entrepreneurs and Their Companies," in Karl H. Vesper, ed., *Frontiers of Entrepreneurship Research* (Wellesley, Mass.: Babson Center for Entrepreneurial Studies, 1981), pp. 65–83.

10. James M. Utterback, Goran Reitberger, and Andrew Martin, "Technology and Industrial Innovation in Sweden," in Vesper, *Frontiers of Entrepreneurship Research* (1982), pp. 177–88.

11. Isaiah A. Litvak and Christopher J. Maule, "Successful Canadian Entrepreneurship and Innovation," in Vesper, *Frontiers of Entrepreneurship Research* (1982), pp. 189–203; Jerome Doutriaux, "Evolution of the Characteristics of (High-Tech) Entrepreneurial Firms," in John A. Hornaday, Fred A. Tarpley, Jr., Jeffry A Timmons, and Karl H. Vesper, eds., *Frontiers of Entrepreneurialship Research* (Wellesley, Mass.: Babson Center for Entrepreneurial Studies, 1984), pp. 368–86.

12. James M. Utterback, Edward B. Roberts, Marc Meyer, Andrew Martin, and Dorothy Leonard-Barton, "Comparison of New Technology-Based Firm Formation in Sweden and Massachusetts," in John A. Hornaday, Jeffrey A. Timmons, and Karl H. Vesper, eds., *Frontiers of Entrepreneurship Research*, (Wellesley, Mass.: Babson Center for Entrepreneurial Studies, 1983), pp. 519–28.

13. Albert Shapero and Lisa Sokol, "The Social Dimensions of Entrepreneurship," in Calvin A. Kent, Donald L. Sexton, and Karl H. Vesper, eds., *Encyclopedia of Entrepreneurship* (Englewood Cliffs, N.J.: Prentice-Hall, 1982).

14. Douglas H. McQueen and J. Torkel Wallmark, "Innovation Output and Academic Performance," in Hornaday, Tarpley, Jr., Timmons, and Vesper, *Frontiers of Entrepreneurship Research* (1984), pp. 175–91.

15. Arnold C. Cooper and William C. Dunkelberg, "Influences Upon Entrepreneurship—A Large-Scale Study," Academy of Management Meetings, San Diego, Calif., 4 August 1981.

16. Patrick R. Liles, *New Business Ventures and the Entrepreneur* (Homewood, Ill.: Richard D. Irwin, Inc., 1974).

17. Albert V. Bruno and Tyzoon T. Tyebjee, "The Entrepreneur's Search for Capital," in Hornaday, Tarpley, Jr., Timmons, and Vesper, *Frontiers of Entrepreneurship Research* (1984), pp. 18–31.

18. Arnold C. Cooper, *The Founding of Technologically-Based Firms* (Milwaukee, Wis.: The Center for Venture Management, 1971); Arnold C. Cooper and William C. Dunkelberg, "A New Look at Business Entry: Experience of 1805 Entrepreneurs," in Vesper, *Frontiers of Entrepreneurship Research* (1981), pp. 1–20.

19. Albert Shapero, "The Process of Technical Company Formation in a Local Area," in Arnold C. Cooper, and John L. Komives, eds., *Technical Entrepreneurship: A Symposium* (Milwaukee, Wis.: The Center for Venture Management, 1972), pp. 63–95.

20. Thorne and Ball, "Entrepreneurs and Their Companies"; Jerome Doutriaux, and Branko F. Peterman, "Technology Transfer and Academic Entrepreneurship," in Vesper, *Frontiers of Entrepreneurship Research* (1982), pp. 430–48.

21. Ibid.

22. Norman R. Smith and John B. Miner, "Motivational Considerations in the Success of Technologically Innovative Entrepreneurs," in Hornaday, Tarpley Jr., Timmons, and Vesper, *Frontiers of Entrepreneurship Research* (1984), pp. 488–95.

23. K. B. Mayer and S. Goldstein, *The First Two Years: Problems of Small Firm Growth and Survival* (Washington, D.C.: U.S. Government Printing Office, 1961); W. M. Hoad, and P. Rosko, *Management Factors Contributing to the Success and Failure of New Small Manufacturers* (Ann Arbor: The University of Michigan, 1964).

24. Thorne and Ball, "Entrepreneurs and Their Companies."

25. Cooper and Dunkelberg, "A New Look at Business Entry."

26. Ann E. Freedman, "New Technology-Based Firms: Critical Location Factors," in Hornaday, Timmons, and Vesper, *Frontiers of Entrepreneurship Research* (1983), pp. 478–94.

27. Cooper and Dunkelberg, "A New Look at Business Entry."

28. Arnold C. Cooper, "Contrasts in the Role of Incubator Organizations in the Founding of Growth-Oriented Firms," in Hornaday, Tarpley Jr., Timmons, and Vesper, *Frontiers of Entrepreneurship Research* (1984), pp. 159–74.

29. Cooper and Dunkelberg, "A New Look at Business Entry."

30. Shapero and Sokol, "The Social Dimensions of Entrepreneurship."

31. Dwight M. Baumann, "Second Generation Innovation Center Entrepreneurs," in Vesper, *Frontiers of Entrepreneurship Research* (1981), pp. 428–42.

32. Robert G. Schwartz and Richard D. Teach, "Primary Issues Effecting the Development and Growth of a Professional Infrastructure for Emerging Technology Start-ups: The State of Georgia Experience," in Hornaday, Tarpley, Jr., Timmons, and Vesper, *Frontiers of Entrepreneurship Research* (1984), pp. 126–35.

33. Alison M. Buck, Daryl J. Hobbs, Donald D. Myers, and Nancy C. Munshaw, *Feasibility of High-Tech Company Incubation in Rural University Settings*, Missouri IncuTech, Inc., Rolla, Missouri, 1984.

34. Doutriaux and Peterman, "Technology Transfer and Academic Entrepreneurship."

35. Edward B. Roberts, "Influences upon Performance of New Technical Enterprises," in Cooper and Komives, *Technical Entrepreneurship: A Symposium*, pp. 126–49; Cooper and Dunkleberg, "A New Look at Business Entry."
36. Cooper, "Contrasts in the Role of Incubator Organizations . . ."
37. LaRue T. Hosmer, Arnold C. Cooper, and Karl H. Vesper, *The Entrepreneurial Function*, Prentice-Hall, Inc., Englewood Cliffs, N.J., 1977.
38. Cooper and Bruno, "Patterns of Development."
39. Roberts, "Influences upon Performance of New Technical Enterprises."

KEY SUCCESS FACTORS IN
HIGH-TECHNOLOGY VENTURES

Modesto A. Maidique*

The 1980s promise to become a golden age for technological entrepreneurs. An expanding economy, substantial reductions in capital gains taxes (which are likely to be sustained through the current tax changes), a shift of resources from the "sunset" industries to the "sunrise" industries, and a myriad of new product possibilities created by the deregulation of telecommunications, advances in microprocessors, factory automation, and genetic engineering have resulted in a tenfold increase in capital committed to new high-technology ventures, and in thousands of new high-tech firms. During 1983 and 1984, venture capitalists, the principal financiers of early stage high-tech firms, invested over $6 billion in high-tech ventures, and in 1984, small company high-tech entrepreneurs raised $1.2 billion through new stock issues in the over-the-counter market. These numbers represent a tenfold increase in investment activity in high-tech ventures over the past ten years.[1]

High-tech entrepreneurs such as Steve Jobs, Mitch Kapor, and An Wang have become folk heroes, replacing the traditional organization men of the smokestack industries as America's most admired industrialists. In a cover story announcing the rise of a new corporate elite, *Business Week* proclaimed, "the Organization Man is

*The author has benefitted from discussions with Professor Juan Roure, IESE, and David M. Smith, Hambrecht & Quist.

dead." In the eighties, he has been displaced by the entrepreneurs who develop and exploit the new technologies.[2]

The seas of change, however, are not altogether calm. The gush of new venture capital that has funded high technology start-ups with increasing speed has left in its wake numerous bankruptcies and near bankruptcies. The handful of well-publicized disasters—Osborne, Atari, Victor, Diasonics, and Storage Technology—as well as a host of software companies that never made it past their first year or two are only the tip of a much larger but less charted iceberg. As is usually the case, a handful of firms prospered beyond any reasonable expectation and became the focus of media attention and their founders folk heroes as sales and earnings grew exponentially, while hundreds of others failed against a climate of irrational enthusiasm. The percentages may not be that different from the previous crops of start-ups, but the absolute magnitude is now dramatically larger. There are now hundreds, not tens, of examples of optimism that in the end only yielded write-offs.

These developments give special current significance to an old but largely unresearched question, why do some high-tech ventures fail while others prosper? Successful and unsuccessful high-tech ventures have been the subject of numerous case studies that illustrate the many pitfalls to be avoided in starting a new high-tech venture.[3] Systematic research on those factors that explain high-technology new venture success (or failure), however, is as scarce today as venture capital was in the decade of the mid-seventies.

Insight on how to manage for new venture success, however, may be gained by studying two related literature streams in addition to the sparse literature on high-tech ventures: (1) new product and new venture success/failure literature; and (2) research on corporate excellence.

CORPORATE EXCELLENCE RESEARCH

The acclaimed corporate excellence studies have had a broad impact on America's business managers, including those that start new high-technology firms.[4] Ironically, this literature is nourished principally from the experiences of large successful firms (those over $1 billion in revenues) in a broad range of industries that may or may not be applicable to the unique problems of high-technology start-ups.

Second, this literature focuses only on successes and ignores the flip side, the underachieving or failing companies.

On the other hand, every study of America's "highly regarded" firms is disproportionately populated by technology-based firms such as IBM, Hewlett Packard, Wang, and DEC. Almost half of the *In Search of Excellence* sample of forty-three large companies consists of high-technology companies or companies that have a large high-technology component. By starting with a technology company focus and adding an emphasis on entrepreneurship and decisive management action, Peters and Waterman have provided what many feel is a "how-to manual" for the new breed of high-tech entrepreneurs. Perhaps this is one of the principal reasons why their book has become the best selling management book of our time.[5]

What are the implications of the *In Search of Excellence* study for high-tech entrepreneurs? Much of the "new gospel" of the new management thinkers is really a revival message.[6] The importance of leadership, closeness with customers and employees are all old lessons. Briefly put, Peters and Waterman argue that successful companies succeed not because of their strategic brilliance but because they excel in the basics: hard work, quick action, keeping things simple, sticking to what they know best, customer interaction, respect for employees, and giving meaning to their mission.

Giving meaning to the corporate mission is the principal focus of another of the best-selling management books, *The Art of Japanese Management.* These authors' principal message is that the "significant meanings or guiding concepts that an organization imbues in its members" is the most powerful success lever an organization can exercise.[7] Ouchi in his *Theory Z,* another people-oriented study, concludes that trust, subtlety, and intimacy are the fundamental determinants of organizational effectiveness.[8]

There is much behavioral wisdom and management humanism in these best-selling studies and much thinking that should be valuable to the high-tech executive. But they speak only indirectly to the specific operational issues that a high-tech entrepreneur faces in organizing a high-tech firm, or that a venture capitalist analyzes in deciding whether to fund such a venture. "Significant meanings," while of great value in uniting a large team, are secondary to a firm that has chosen the wrong target market. And, as Dave Packard once told the author, while enlightened personnel policies may be ethically satisfying, "I've met some awfully mean entrepreneurs who have been very successful."[9] Management style may be important, but it is critical to be on target.

On the other hand, at least some of these lessons from the large companies are highly consistent with the results of the literature on start-ups and new product success and failure.

NEW PRODUCT SUCCESS AND FAILURE LITERATURE

Most high-tech venture companies consist of a more or less complete management team wrapped around a more or less complete product idea. It is only the rare start-up that is based on a product line. At the outset all the efforts and all the limited resources in a new venture are sharply focused on developing a single new product and bringing it to the market. This concentration on a single product can pay off. Apple built a one billion dollar product based on the Apple II, its first product.[10] And this initial single product focus, when successful, builds disciplines and resources that are carried forward as new products are planned, developed, and introduced.

For this reason the literature on new product success and failure in the high-tech industries has considerable relevance for high-tech entrepreneurs. Initially this literature consisted of cases that probed the factors behind individual success and failure histories.

From individual cases, research in the field moved to groups of cases and to large surveys.[11] The landmark study of this latter type was Myers and Marquis's study of 567 innovations in 121 firms in five industries (railroad, railroad supplies, computer manufacturers and computer supplies, and housing suppliers), which established the primary of demand (as opposed to technological capability) as a determinant of new product success.[12] The industries in the study were selected to allow a comparison of several more and less technologically advanced products. According to Myers and Marquis, their sample was composed of innovations that were considered significantly important by the informants, usually technical people. The respondents "almost always chose an innovation which had been commercially successful in terms of return on product sales or saving in production costs."[13]

Though Myers and Marquis's large sample cut across a variety of industries and firms, the innovations they studied were predominantly commercially successful innovations. The other set, those innovations that were not commercially successful, were not studied as a control group. A second important methodological problem results from the use of "one or more technical people" as the principal informants. Cooper, for instance, has argued that the most balanced view of a product's success and failure is one free of functional bias—that is, the view of the general manager.[14]

The next major advance in the new product success and failure literature was the pioneering SAPPHO study in the United Kingdom in 1974, which used a pairwise comparison methodology that facilitates differentiation between successful and unsuccessful policies and practices by contrasting successful and unsuccessful innovations. Since then the pairwise methodology has become the methodology of choice for contemporary researchers on product development.[15]

This technique involves comparing the characteristics of two innovations, one failure and one success, to find areas of contrast and similarity. Using this methodology, the SAPPHO group studied forty-three pairs of innovations in the instruments and chemicals industries and compared them along 122 different dimensions. The study concluded that there were five general areas that discriminate between failure and success, the first two of which are generally supportive of Myers and Marquis's earlier findings: (1) understanding user needs, (2) attention to marketing and publicity, (3) efficiency of development, (4) effective use of outside technology and external scientific communication, and (5) seniority and authority of responsible managers.[16]

The first two SAPPHO findings can be further categorized into "market factors" while the last three can be viewed as "organizational variables." Their results balance earlier conclusions with their emphasis on how the company organizes and manages its new product development process.

Subsequent investigators have used the pairwise comparison methodology to reach conclusions broadly similar to the SAPPHO findings in other countries (Canada, West Germany, Japan, Finland, and Hungary) and industrial settings, though usually with smaller data bases.[17]

Rubenstein and colleagues analyzed 103 innovations in six firms in a study that included both successes and failures, and measured both technical and economic success, but used a very different methodology than the SAPPHO pairwise comparison approach. In this study, the characteristics of successful and unsuccessful innovation pairs were not statistically contrasted to identify significant differences. Rather "facilitators and barriers" to the innovation process were identified by interviewing the managers involved in these innovations and obtaining their opinions drawn from their observations and experiences. Notwithstanding these differences, their findings also coincided with SAPPHO in several major areas, such as the importance of market factors, communications, and the organization's commitment to the project.[18]

Of the pairwise studies that followed SAPPHO, Project NewProd was the most ambitious and employed the largest sample ($n = 195$; 93 failures, 102 successes). Almost 200 randomly selected Canadian industrial new products were evaluated along seventy-seven different dimensions using a mailed survey.[19] The overall results were divided into three general areas that were believed to be strongly correlated with new product success: having a unique or superior product in the eyes of the customer, having marketing knowledge and proficiency, and having technical and production synergy and proficiency.[20]

Although on the surface similar in outcome, the results of SAPPHO and Project NewProd also reflect some differences. For instance, the SAPPHO findings highlight organizational factors such as the seniority and authority of responsible managers and effective use of outside technology in addition to market factors, while largely ignoring the product itself. The conclusions drawn by Project NewProd emphasize product characteristics, in addition to the market and organizational variables. The word product, on the other hand, does not even appear in summaries of the SAPPHO work.

The Stanford Innovation Project (SINPRO), which studied 158 products in the electronics industry is the only major comparative study that used the United States as a setting.[21] This study concluded that new product success is likely to be greater when:

1. The developing organization, through an in-depth understanding of its customers and its marketplace, introduces a product with a high performance-to-cost ratio.
2. The developing organization is proficient in marketing and commits a significant amount of its resources to selling and promoting the product.

3. The product provides a high contribution margin to the firm.
4. The R&D process is well planned and executed.
5. The create, make, and market function are well interfaced and coordinated within the organization.
6. The product is introduced into the market early.
7. The markets and technologies of the new product benefit significantly from the existing strengths of the developing business unit and achieve synergy.
8. There is a high level of management support for the product from the development stage through its launch into the market place.

A comparison of these results to the SAPPHO and NewProd studies reveals broad areas of agreement and several major areas of differences. First, there is clear agreement in all these studies that no single factor, but rather a combination of factors, generally accounts for the success of a new product. Second, all three studies concluded that an in-depth understanding of the marketplace is essential for a new product success. This finding is one of the most pervasive findings of recent new product studies. The related finding, that considerable effort and skill must be employed in order to effectively communicate the characteristics of the new product offering first within the firms' organizational elements and second to the marketplace, was also a consistent theme in all the studies.

Both the NewProd and the Stanford study also emphasize the importance of the characteristics of the product—its uniqueness, particularly its value. Product "value" was measured by both the customer and the firm, respectively, through performance-to-cost ratios and contribution margins. Synergy with present capabilities—that is, the leveraging of existing market and technological strengths—was found to be highly significant in the NewProd and the Stanford studies.

NEW VENTURE SUCCESS/FAILURE STUDIES

Much of the prior evidence is only indirectly or tangentially relevant to the creation of high-technology start-ups. A handful of studies, however, *directly* address the factors that lead to success in such ventures.

A longitudinal study of Silicon Valley firms found that the more successful firms (those that survived longer) were founded by groups of founders (as opposed to a single founder) and that the more successful groups or individuals had prior experience in the markets or technologies that they addressed.[22] Furthermore the authors concluded that founders with prior experience in "large" companies (those with over 500 employees) were more likely to be successful.

In a study of thirteen software firms the authors found that start-up success was correlated with the founders' education and experience, their internal locus of control, and having a personal investment in the firm. As the authors summarized it, "Competence, confidence, imagination and commitment were the personal characteristics that distinguished between entrepreneurs of later and early stage firms."[23]

This study also concluded that success was positively correlated with having a single person in command, active involvement of top management and board members in decisionmaking, and implementing start-ups on a small scale with incremental expansion. According to these authors, the principals in the successful firms "allocate their time differently, than do their early stage counterparts. The former maintain a richer and broader network of ongoing relationships and product initiates than do the latter. They also maintain closer potential-customer relationships, have clearer goals, spend more time on internal and external communication, and deeply involve themselves and their board members in both strategic and operational decisions."[24]

In an unpublished study of venture capital investments the author concluded that the proportion of equity owned by the principals was positively correlated with success. Only two other characteristics were significantly related to the rate of return achieved: stage of development of the product at funding, and the extensiveness of the market evaluation.[25]

In a pilot study of eight experienced venture capitalists with a collective high-tech investment experience of one hundred years the authors identified several factors that seem to differentiate successful start-ups from less successful ones: (1) founders with related technology and market experience; (2) founders with advanced degrees from high quality institutions; (3) the degree to which the expertise of the founding team was complementary; (4) prior joint experience of the founding team; (5) uniqueness of the product (this could in some cases be simply the consequence of early market entry); (6) equity share of founders; (7) prior experience of board members in similar start-ups; and (8) number of buyers for product (negatively correlated).[26]

In an unpublished working paper that reviewed the strategies of ten high-technology firms the authors concluded that firms with more concentrated technological and market focus outperform other companies.[27] In a paper that reviewed the niche concept the authors likewise concluded that firms that concentrated on taking a small bite out of the market were, at least initially, more likely to be successful.[28]

Despite their methodological diversity the literature streams reviewed here have some remarkably similar implications for success in high-technology start-ups. The words may differ, reflecting the peculiarity of each subfield but the conclusions are much the same. For instance, while one researcher may say "stick to your knitting," another says "leverage existing strengths," and yet another "concentrate" or "focus," the message is the same.

The excellence studies stress communicating with customers and focus on current strengths and gradual extension of current expertise to new markets, customers, and technologies. The new product studies emphasize the quality of communication within the product team and outwards towards customers (who properly should be viewed as part of an augmented new product team) familiar to the product developers.* Not surprisingly, the new venture results conclude that experienced teams that have worked together, know the relevant customers and technologies from their previous employment, and focus their resources on carefully chosen market segments are more likely to be successful.

At the risk of oversimplification it can be argued that the underlying theme in these studies is simply that experience pays off. As Confucius once said, "In all things, success depends on prior preparation, and without such preparation there is sure to be failure."[29] Experience after all, as Oscar Wilde once quipped, is "the name men give to their mistakes."[30] And mistakes are the basis of wisdom. It is the quality of prior experience of the founding team, its relatedness

---

*One of the fundamental pieces of evidence that Peters and Waterman (note 5) cite as the basis for their conclusion that sensitivity to customers is paramount in the SAPPHO study (note 15)!

to the new business's markets and technologies, its balance and functional completeness, and the focusing of that experience on a concentrated target where the founding team has a reservoir of customer and peer networks that emerges as the principal unifying link in these varied studies.

Clearly this emerging field is so sparsely populated that there are many opportunities for research and a healthy appetite in industry and academia for the results of such studies. New work in the field, however, needs to go beyond case studies and descriptive research to rigorous testing of conceptual models by measuring the relationship between the ventures financial success and such variables as the number of founders, the number of disciplines that the founding team includes, their average number of years of related experience, and the quality of their educational experience.[31] Only through such studies will venture capital "intuition" be adequately explained.

NOTES

1. *Venture Capital Journal* (January 1985): 1.
2. "The Business Week 50," *Business Week* (21 January 1985): 63–81.
3. See for instance, M. Maidique, Course Outline, GBM 698, Managing Technological Enterprises, School of Business, University of Miami, Coral Gables (copy available on request).
4. M.A. Maidique, "The New Management Thinkers," *California Management Review* (Fall 1983): 151.
5. T. Peters and R. Waterman, *In Search of Excellence: Lessons from America's Best-Run Companies* (New York: Harper & Row, 1982).
6. M.A. Maidique, "The New Management Thinkers," *California Management Review* (Fall 1983): 151.
7. R. Pascale and A. Athos, *The Art of Japanese Management: Applications for American Executives* (New York: Warner Books, 1981), p. 307.
8. W. Ouchi, *Theory Z: How American Business Can Meet the Japanese Challenge* (Reading, Mass.: Addison-Wesley, 1981), p. 4.
9. D. Packard, personal communication, Stanford University, March 1982.
10. C. Swanger and M. Maidique, "Apple Computer: The First Ten Years," Stanford University School of Business, Case Clearing House.
11. D.A. Schon, "Champions for Radical New Inventions," *Harvard Business Review* 41: 2 (1963): 77–86; Booz-Allen & Hamilton, *Management of New Products* (New York: Booz-Allen & Hamilton, 1968); M.A. Maidique, "Entrepreneurs, Champions and Technological Innovation," *Sloan Management Review* 21: 2 (Winter 1980): 59–76.

12. D.G. Marquis, "The Anatomy of Successful Innovations," *Innovation* 1 (Nov. 1969): 28–37; S. Myers and D.G. Marquis, "Successful Industrial Innovations," National Science Foundation, Rep. NSF 69–17, 1969.

13. Ibid., p. 11.

14. R.G. Cooper, "The Dimensions of Industrial New Product Success and Failure," *J. Marketing* 43 (Summer 1979): 95.

15. R. Rothwell, C. Freeman, A. Horsley, V.T.P. Jervis, A. B. Robertson, and J. Townsend, "SAPPHO Updated—Project SAPPHO, phase II," *Research Policy* 3 (1974): 258–91; Science Policy Research Unit, "Success and Failure in Industrial Innovation," Univ. of Sussex, 1972.

16. R. Rothwell, C. Freeman, A. Horsley, V.T.P. Jervis, A. B. Robertson, and J. Townsend, "SAPPHO Updated": 259–60.

17. R. C. Cooper, "A Process Model for Industrial New Product Development," *IEEE Transactions on Engineering Management* EM–30: 1 (Feb. 1983): 2–11; for a critique of the SAPPHO study and related research see D. Mowery and N. Rosenberg, "The Influence of Market Demand Upon Innovation: A Critical Review of Some Recent Empirical Studies," *Research Policy* 8 (1979): 101–53.

18. A. H. Rubenstein, A. K. Chakrabarti, R. D. O'Keefe, W. E. Souder, and H. C. Young, "Factors Influencing Innovation Success at the Project Level," *Research Management* 19: 3 (May 1976): 15–20.

19. R. G. Cooper, "Identifying Industrial New Product Success: Project New-Prod," *Industrial Marketing Management* 8 (1979): 124–35; R. G. Cooper, "The Dimensions of Industrial New Product Success and Failure": 93–103; R. G. Cooper, "Project New Prod: Factors in New Product Success," *Eur. J. Marketing* 14: 5/6 (1980): 277–92; R. G. Cooper, "Project New-Prod: What Makes New Product a Winner?" Montreal, Canada: Quebec Industrial Innovation Centre, 1980.

20. R. C. Cooper, "A Process Model for Industrial New Product Development," *IEEE Transactions in Engineering Management* EM–30: 1 (Feb. 1983): 4.

21. M. A. Maidique and B. J. Zirger, "A Study of Success and Failure in Product Innovation: The Case of the U.S. Electronics Industry," *IEEE Transactions on Engineering Management* EM–31: (November 1984): M. A. Maidique, "The Stanford Innovation Project: A Comparative Study of Success and Failure in High-technology Product Innovation," in Proc. Conf. on Management of Technological Innovation, NSF and Worcester Polytechnic Institute, Washington, D.C., May 1983.

22. A. C. Cooper and A. V. Bruno, "Success Among High-Technology Firms," *Business Horizons* (April 1977): 16–23.

23. A. H. Van de Ven, R. Hudson, and D. M. Schroeder, "Designing New Business Start Ups: Entrepreneurial, Organizational, and Ecological Considerations," *Journal of Management* (1984).

24. Ibid.: 105.

25. Hoban, J. P., Jr., "Characteristics of Venture Capital Investments," Unpublished doctoral dissertation, University of Utah, 1976.

26. M. A. Maidique and J. B. Roure, "Key Factors in the Success and Failure of New Technological Ventures," Working Paper, Stanford University, March 1985. (To be presented at 5th Strategic Management Society Conference in Barcelona, Spain, October 1985.)

27. Marc H. Meyer and Edward B. Roberts, "New Product Strategy in Small High Technology Firms: A Pilot Study," Working Paper, Alfred P. Sloan School of Management, Massachusetts Institute of Technology, May 1984.

28. Arnold C. Cooper, Gary E. Willard, and Caroly Woo, "Strategies of High Performing New and Small Firms: A Re-Examination of the Niche Concept" (Paper for the Fourth Annual Strategic Management Society Conference, Philadelphia, Penna., 11 October 1984).

29. Confucius, *The Analects*, in *The Dictionary of Quotations* (New York: William Collins Sons & Co., 1961).

30. O. Wilde, *The Nihilists*, in *The Dictionary of Quotations* (New York: William Collins Sons & Co., 1961).

31. One such study is currently underway (note 26) and at least two proposals for related studies have come to the attention of this author within the past few months.

7 ENTREPRENEURSHIP AND TECHNOLOGY TRANSFER
Key Factors in the Innovation Process

Pier A. Abetti
Robert W. Stuart

Since the early 1970s, many key American industries have lost their international competitiveness. As a consequence their financial situation has deteriorated and employment has been cut drastically. In-depth studies have been made by the National Academy of Engineering and the National Research Council of the following industries, whose problems have had significant impact on the nation's economy: automotive, consumer electronics, ferrous metals, machine tools, and textiles.[1]

Various theories and hypotheses have been advanced to explain the fall of American industries and the rise of their foreign competitors, principally Japanese and European. Among the most popular explanations appearing in the daily press and in service club meetings, we find the oil crisis, the dumping of goods below cost by Japan, Inc., U.S. government regulations and antitrust policies, the disappearance of work ethics in American society, the deterioration of teaching in mathematics and science, and the technological obsolescence of engineers and skilled work forces. In parallel, prominent scholars and businesspersons have performed in-depth studies of the following factors:

1. Management's lack of long-term vision, imposed by short-term financial constraints, particularly in the automobile and the consumer electronics industries.[2] This climate stifles creativity and innovation, discourages risk taking, and encourages mismanagement and bureaucratic inertia.

2. The inability of many traditional, mature firms to anticipate the need for productive change and their resistance to new ideas advanced by creative people within the organization.[3]

3. The reduction in U.S. nonmilitary R&D expenditures, especially basic research, and the parallel rise of R&D expenditures in Japan, Europe, and the Soviet Union. As a result the U.S. share of world patents is declining and the number of U.S. patents granted to foreign applicants is increasing rapidly.[4]

In reaction to these bleak pictures, which at times foresee no salvation for the doomed "sunset" industries, other scholars and business people have looked for and found examples of well-managed, successful, highly competitive American firms. The business philosophies, strategies, organizational, and human resource practices of these firms are advanced as models for the American industrial renaissance. Three prominent studies of these model firms (or semi-autonomous business units within larger corporations) are:

1. Forty-three companies that Peters and Waterman classified as "excellent"[5]

2. Forty-seven "progressive" companies studied by Kanter, who then described six of these as "positive models . . . examples of how American companies can encourage innovation and prosper from it"[6]

3. A number of well-known high-technology companies of different size ($10 million to $30 billion in sales) that "appear to be fending off . . . foreign challenges successfully" and even "served as models for highly successful Japanese and European high-tech firms."[7]

In other words, to be competitive, technology must be *transferred* to useful new or improved products, processes and services, utilizing the skills of *entrepreneurship* and business management.

SCOPE: THE COALESCENCE OF INNOVATION, TECHNOLOGY TRANSFER AND ENTREPRENEURSHIP

This paper reviews the state-of-the-art knowledge on the process of technological innovation and highlights the key roles of entre-

Figure 7-1. Interrelationships of Innovation, Technology Transfer, and Entrepreneurship.

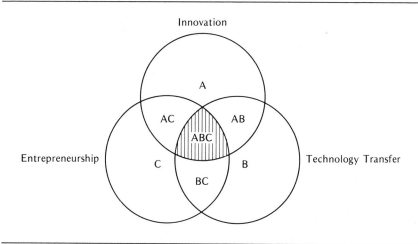

preneurship and technology transfer for ensuring the technical, commercial, financial, and social success of an innovation. Two case histories are used to illustrate our points, which are parallel case histories of successful and unsuccessful technological innovations. We will show that the probability of success of a technological innovation is enhanced by the presence of an entrepreneur who ensures effective technology transfer with the scientific/technological environment and with the marketplace. We will illustrate the necessity of horizontal technology transfer to augment traditional vertical technology transfer. We will conclude that companies must develop a *climate* conducive to entrepreneurship and technology transfer for their own success and for a reversal of the decline in America's competitive position.

The literature on entrepreneurship, innovation and technology transfer is enormous. This study concentrates on the interaction of these three disciplines, as shown by the shaded area in Figure 7-1.

Area A of Figure 7-1—Innovation

Innovation was first studied from sociological and organizational dynamics viewpoints.[8] Kanter points out correctly the importance of social and organizational innovation for today's corporations. In fact, of the thirty-four examples of innovations discussed in her book, *The Change Masters*, about three-quarters are primarily sociological and only one-quarter primarily technological.[9] Another major aspect of innovation is its relationships with creativity.[10] Even adopted innovations "involve creative use" in order to adapt them to a specific situation.[11]

Area B of Figure 7-1—Technology Transfer

Technology may be defined as a body of knowledge, derived both from theory (science) and practical experience (engineering), which expresses man's capacity to transform the physical environment. From the viewpoint of business management, technology should be considered as a *strategic resource* of the firm, in parallel with people, plant and equipment, capital, and so forth.[12] As a resource, technology may be developed (through internal or external R&D), acquired, even stolen, disposed of, sold, or simply wasted. This waste occurs when technology is left inoperative "on the shelf." Thus, in order to produce value, technology must be transferred: (1) within the firm to be embodied in actual operations, and (2) outside the firm to those users, suppliers, and members of society who will benefit. This is often a difficult and lengthy process.

While science is transferred primarily through *paper* (scientific articles, monographs, books) read by *basic* researchers, technology is primarily transferred through *people* (specifically by means of prolonged personal contacts, training, and teamwork). There are about one-half million technical reports available on government sponsored research, but *applied* researchers and development engineers do not read them. It has been estimated that 1,000 literature references lead to only one useful idea, and, of course, this pitiful yield reinforces the aversion to further search of the literature.[13]

We must distinguish between vertical and horizontal technology transfer, as first suggested by Brooks:

> Vertical transfer refers to the transfer of technology . . . from the more general to the more specific. It includes the process by which new scientific knowledge is incorporated into technology and by which a "state-of-the-art" becomes embodied into a new system. . . . Horizontal transfer occurs through the adaptation of a technology from one application to another.[14]

An example of vertical technology transfer is the development of the transistor by Bell Laboratories from basic research in solid-state physics to an electronic component, and one of horizontal transfer is the adaptation of a military aircraft engine to civilian air transport, or the diffusion of hybrid corn in the United States. In practice, vertical technology transfer takes place mostly within a company (or within a decentralized business unit). In contrast, horizontal technology transfer takes place mostly between companies (or between business units), including suppliers, manufacturers, and end-users.

The literature on vertical technology transfer, particularly from a research laboratory to operations is ample.[15] In fact, several journals frequently discuss this topic. The literature on horizontal transfer is less rich, but there is considerable interest on technology transfer across national borders and its effect on economic development.[16]

Area AB of Figure 7-1 — Technological Innovation

The interface between technology transfer and innovation—that is, technological innovation—has been studied in depth by prominent scholars with scientific, engineering, social science, and business backgrounds. The book edited by Kelly and Kranzberg, *Technological Innovation: A Critical Review of Current Knowledge* includes two ample bibliographies.[17] Tornatzky and colleagues have provided a detailed review of the literature on the process of technological innovation.[18] Other studies have been done by various U.S. government organizations and by the Organization for Economic Development (OECD).[19] Several textbooks have been written by business executives and academicians on the management of technological innovation.[20] Generally speaking, these books, with the exception of Martin, hardly mention the entrepreneur and his or her role.[21]

Studies of technology transfer do not specifically address how it contributes to technological innovation. Rather, such studies concentrate mostly on the following subjects:

1. The diffusion of innovations, after the successful introduction to the marketplace[22]
2. The transfer of technology from the customer, or prospective customer, to the manufacturer, during the early stages of the innovation process[23]

3. The improvement of horizontal transfer from government laboratories into commercial use.[24]

The interaction between vertical and horizontal transfer and the role of the entrepreneur in technology transfer appear to be of limited interest. One fact, however, comes through most consistently: Technology transfer results from individual, personal interactions, and technology is most effectively transferred by transferring people with the appropriate knowledge and skills.

Area C of Figure 7-1—Entrepreneurship

The vast body of scholarly literature on entrepreneurship includes a rapidly growing number of studies pertinent to the scope of this paper: technological entrepreneurship, and entrepreneurial innovation.[25]

Area BC of Figure 7-1—Technological Entrepreneurship

The interface between technology and entrepreneurship is defined as "technological entrepreneurship," a phenomenon first noted in the post-war years, as companies "spun-off" from MIT and Stanford technical laboratories. Many technological universities have now initiated Incubator Programs to nurture and develop high-tech entrepreneurial companies on or near the campus. The pioneer studies in this field are by Roberts and his associates, and by A.C. Cooper and his associates.[26] Many other studies have followed, and this field is well covered by several magazines.

Area AC of Figure 7-1—Entrepreneurial Innovation

Entrepreneurs are not necessarily innovators. In fact, most entrepreneurs see a business opportunity and utilize available means to serve the market. On the other hand, the more successful entrepreneurs achieve a market advantage through innovation in organization, market approach, new product development, and new technology. Kanter mentions frequently the entrepreneur as the change-master or, at least, initiator of the innovation that then diffuses through the firm. She points out that, given the resistance to change inherent in any organization or social system, an innovator cannot succeed unless he or she is also an entrepreneur. The role of entrepreneurs in innovation has also been discussed by Krasner and by Udell and others.[27]

Area ABC of Figure 7-1—Entrepreneurship and Technology Transfer in Innovation

Finally, the subset corresponding to the interaction of the three disciplines discussed above, represents the coalescence of innovation, technology, and entrepreneurship into innovative new technological ventures. Many politicians, economists, sociologists, technical and business people see these ventures as one solution, if not *the solution*, to the many economic problems of this country. However, this solution, to be effective, must be operative at all levels. That is, to reestablish our national competitive position we must have a *government policy* and *social attitude* conducive to the nurturing of innovation and progress within business; and business, in turn, must develop a *climate* for individuals to effectively complete innovative projects. As Rosenbloom has pointed out, we must consider innovation at three levels: project, company or firm, and nation.[28] Also, in consideration of innovation as ventures at the firm level, it is important to distinguish between internal or corporate entrepreneurship—that is, technological innovation in large firms[29] and external entrepreneurship, the starting up of high-tech innovative firms.[30] A recent textbook by Martin, *Management of Technological Innovation and Entrepreneurship* discusses both these aspects in two separate chapters.[31] Instead, Abetti has analyzed the similarities and differences of the process of technological innovation in large and small companies and the implications for management.[32]

Research into the characteristics of successful innovation has been most extensive at the level of individual projects. Investigations at the level of the company or firm, although less extensive, have received tremendous attention recently because of the popularity of Peters and Waterman's book on corporate excellence. Consideration at the national and international level is still quite limited but must ultimately be of interest and concern to all responsible managers and management scientists.[33] We will first consider the project-oriented research.

The role of the entrepreneur for insuring the success of technological innovations was first noted by Myers and Marquis, and later by Langrish, et al., Globe, Levy and Schwartz, Roberts and Wainer, Arnold Cooper and Komives, Rubinstein, et al., and by Litvak and Maule in Canada.[34] The other major factors noted were a user/market focus and efficient, effective technical development and technology transfer. Project Sappho and studies of European and Japanese firms have highlighted the role of "key individuals" as project champions, business innovators, executive champions, and so forth.[35] Robert Cooper's recent comprehensive studies of product success and failure emphasized the importance of product superiority, marketing factors, and technical/production synergy and proficiency but did not identify the entrepreneur as a contributing factor to new product's success or failure.[36] This may be due to Cooper's methodology, which consisted in comparing pairs of products, one successful and one unsuccessful, from the same firm. The same manager who defined the products as successful or not, replied to the questionnaire. Thus, presumably, both products were launched by the same group, possibly by the same manager. Consequently, the variable "managerial entrepreneurship" would not have appeared in the pair-wise comparison and, in fact, was not included in the questionnaire. Cooper, however, established a positive correlation between product uniqueness/innovativeness and success. Since innovation thrives when an entrepreneur is a "change-master," Cooper's results do not necessarily contradict other studies on the entrepreneur's role in the achievement of success.

Most recently Maidique and Zirger have reported on their study of innovations in the electronics industry and confirmed the importance of good market knowledge and efficient, well-coordinated engineering and marketing.[37] Again the entrepreneur/product champion was conspicuous by his absence. Maidique explains this apparent contradiction with his earlier work, which stressed the importance of entrepreneurs and product champions, by the type of innovations included in the sample.[38] Here again, the fact that innovations were being examined within the same firm may explain the lack of identification of the differential importance of an entrepreneur.

Moving to the level of the firm, Peters and Waterman's book on excellence in corporate America emphasizes an entrepreneurial climate as one key factor of success in both technological and quite "low-tech" firms.[39] This entrepreneurial climate was also identified by Maidique and Hayes in their study of "high-tech" firms.[40] They contrast this entrepreneurial culture with organizational cohesion, in a fashion similar to Peters and Waterman's "loose-tight" property.

In the last fifteen years, many successful high-tech new ventures have been created as a result of spinoffs, not from university laboratories but from large established, and in many cases progressive and innovative, firms. These spinoffs were precipitated by these firms' rejection of an innovative idea because of bureaucratic resistance to change, perceived high risk and, sometimes, lack of fit with the existing organization. The frustrated innovators, by necessity, became entrepreneurs or joined with entrepreneurs and started their own companies, which often competed successfully with their previous employers. This phenomenon is illustrated dramatically by Vesper's "Fairchild Begat Tree," which shows how no less than thirty-five high-tech new ventures originated from Fairchild in only thirteen years.[41]

Also, the performance of new ventures started by individuals, is significantly better, in terms of sales growth, return on investment and cash flow, than the performance of internal ventures started by large firms.[42] However, the traditional separation of small-firm and large-firm technological development and of their organizational vehicles for innovation is beginning to fade.[43] Large firms are trying to duplicate the stimulating climate of an independent entrepreneurial venture, while small firms are drawing more heavily from the management assistance available from universities and experienced businesspersons, such as through the MIT Forum.[44] Venture capitalists are also well aware of the fact that the "lead entrepreneur" is the key to success of new high-tech ventures that they finance, and they prefer one with previous business experience in the industry.[45] Regardless of the dichotomy and/or coalescence of technological innovations between large and small firms, Roberts' statement of 1969 still rings true: "In the large firm as well as in the foundling enterprise, the entrepreneur is the central figure in successful technological innovation."[46]

Using a case study approach, it is possible to investigate in more detail the specific roles of the entrepreneur in carrying the process of technological innovation forward to success, and controlling the nature, amount, and timing of technology transfer, both vertical and horizontal, within the firm and from and to the environment.

Figure 7-2. A Linear Model of the Process of Technological Innovation.

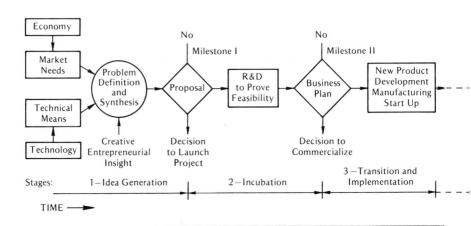

THE CASE OF THE MISSING ENTREPRENEUR: NON-IMPACT MAGNETIC PRINTER

Several large mature firms, including some at the forefront of technological progress, have a well-defined and fairly complex organization for developing new technologies in their R&D laboratories and for transferring these technologies to the operating business units. The process of technological innovation in such firms may be followed by using a linear (or "pipeline") model, as shown in Figure 7-2. This was derived by Abetti from his experiences in managing two laboratories of a large high-tech company, which at that time, presented a "segmented" rather than an "integrative" organization.[47] Thus, in order to bring an innovation to market, specific tasks, separated by clearly defined milestones, had to be accomplished in serial fashion. Technology was transferred by in-place mechanisms assigned to three separate organizational components:

1. The "liaison" function was primarily responsible for maintaining contacts with the engineering managers of the operating units,
2. The "transition analysis" function was responsible for making sure that the higher management, primarily the financial management, of the operating unit was ready to "accept" the technol-

Figure 7-2. continued

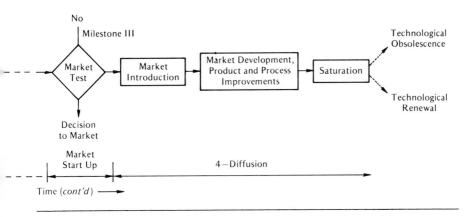

ogy to be transferred and to apply adequate resources to bring the innovation to market,

3. A "consultant" (in effect, a program manager) representing a major group of high-technology operating units was charged with making sure that the R&D laboratory was working effectively on the "right" problems.

The first case history analyzes the invention and development of the first magnetic non-impact printer. This project was technically successful in that several patents were obtained, feasibility was proven, and a successful demonstration was given at a major computer show. Yet the new product never reached the marketplace, *because it lacked an entrepreneur* who was willing to take the risk and reap the rewards.

The various phases and milestones are described below.

Stage 1—Idea Generation (1970)

The general manager of a communication division wanted to expand his market by invading the monopoly heretofore held by the Bell System. The Carterfone decision of the U.S. Supreme Court had, in fact, allowed, for the first time, the connection of "foreign equipment" to the telephone network. The general manager first looked at the transmission of information over telephone lines by facsimile as a major opportunity. The equipment then available was very slow (several minutes to transmit a page of very poor quality), produced evil smelling fumes (so that it had to be kept away from the executive offices, in "boiler rooms" accessed only by secretaries), and was subject to frequent breakdowns. Replacement by conventional impact printers, which were being produced already by the same division for data processing, did not appear to solve the problem. These printers were slow, noisy, subject to wear, and produced copies of poor quality. Also, contrary to facsimile, they could not reproduce graphs and figures. Thus, the general manager conceived the idea of a magnetic non-impact printer and, without further market analysis, asked the corporate R&D laboratory to investigate further.

Milestone I—R&D Proposal (1971)

The general manager now became an executive champion.[48] As the creator and manager of a highly successful communications business, and as a former engineer, he was well respected by the R&D laboratory management. They felt that, if technical feasibility of the proposed product could be proven, the communications division would find a "home" for it in an operating unit, which would design, manufacture, and market it successfully. Thus, the R&D management assigned to the project one of its smartest scientists, an expert in magnetic materials and magnetic phenomena, with a proven track record of inventions and patents. He was told to prepare an R&D proposal, with an estimate of required time, funds, assistance from other specialists, materials, equipment, and so forth. This R&D proposal was immediately approved and wholly funded by the R&D laboratory. (According to the charter of the laboratory, basic research was generally carried out on corporate assessed funds, product development on contract funds supplied by the interested operating unit).

Stage 2—Incubation (1972–76)

The inventor reviewed the literature on magnetic materials and domains, spoke with his colleagues in the laboratory, and investigated in series several approaches. After a couple years he conceived an original system approach basically consisting of a magnetic head, a rubber belt, and magnetic ink. An engineer was then assigned to the project, to design and develop a prototype system under the guidance of the inventor. Finally, in 1976, an engineering model was produced with much higher speed than conventional printers but poorer resolution (fineness and quality of print).

Milestone II — Business Plan (1977)

The incubation stage lasted six years, not an unusually long period for a major technological breakthrough as described above. In the meantime several major changes had taken place in the communications division:

1. The general manager, because of health reasons, had relinquished his position,
2. The market for a high-speed facsimile systems had not developed as expected, because of delays of implementation of the Carterfone decision and, more importantly, because the transmission capacity of available telephone lines was way below the printing speed of the new device,
3. The new division management was concerned with production problems in their existing product lines and assigned lower priority to new product development.

In effect, the executive champion had disappeared, and the R&D laboratory was left with an outstanding technical breakthrough without a "home." By that time, however, the management of the R&D laboratory was fully committed to the commercialization of their invention. The laboratory general manager now became the executive champion and promptly assigned to the liaison function the top-priority task of finding of a new home for the non–impact magnetic printer. This was easy, organizationwise, since one business unit of the communications division produced remote computer terminals (previously developed in-house)—that is, low-speed mechanical printers connected to a central computer through communication lines. The new printer, as pointed out above, was much faster (as much as one hundred times) and theoretically much more flexible (since it was controlled by a microcomputer, all types of fonts, foreign scripts and images could be produced with appropriate software). Thus, the new printer would address an untapped market, of unknown dimensions and characteristics, which was completely different from the OEM remote computer terminal market served by the business unit. Consequently, the business unit was reluctant to accept this innovation from the R&D laboratory, for three main reasons: lack of definition and knowledge of the market; lack of technical knowledge on magnetic printers, magnetic ink, and so forth; and the printer had been developed in the central labs as opposed to their present product line, which had been successfully developed in-house, an NIH (Not Invented Here) factor. The message of the business unit to the laboratory "technology transfer" functions was that it looks interesting, but prove to us that there is a market, and (2) you must complete a working prototype (rather than an engineering model) before we can take the project over.

Having heard these objections, the R&D laboratory management decided to commission a market study from an outside consultant and continue full speed ahead on the development of the prototype. The market study did not include interviews with prospective customers to see how the new products would meet their needs. Rather, it was a forecast of the rapidly growing computer printer market. It also concluded that, since the new printer had a performance/price ratio of "many times higher than present printers," it would sell extremely well.

Armed with this market study and with the promise that a prototype would be available within one year, the laboratory management convinced the operating unit to prepare a business plan, which received corporate approval. This plan envisioned starting production in 1981, after an expenditure of several million dollars to expand the factory and acquire new tooling.

Stage 3—Transition and Implementation (1978–79)

As soon as two working prototypes were ready, they were loaded on a company stationwagon with all the documentation. The project engineer and his assistant were told to drive to the plant of the operating unit, located several hundred miles from the laboratory, and "do not come back until the technology transfer has been completed!" The operating unit gradually built up a group of about thirty engineers and manufacturing people to plan in detail the final design and production of the new printer. However, only one marketing person was assigned to study the new market and prepare an appropriate marketing plan.

Several other prototypes were developed and pretested in the company's internal data processing operations, principally for accounting documents. Aside from frequent breakdowns, quality was judged barely acceptable, but the high speed was appreciated.

Milestone III — Market Test (1980)

In the meantime, the market and financial position of the operating unit had deteriorated significantly. Their remote computer terminals were being challenged by Japanese imports and improved domestic products, some developed by new high-tech ventures. All these products were more modern in design, had better print quality, and, most significantly, had almost a double performance/price ratio. At the same time, new models of very high-speed, high-resolution, and high-quality non-impact printers had appeared on the market launched by such major companies as Xerox, IBM, and Honeywell. These were based on electrostatic or optical rather than magnetic phenomena and thus did not infringe upon the patents protecting the magnetic printer. Although their price was about four times that of the magnetic printer, the performance/price ratios were comparable.

The operating unit management was under severe pressure to improve their earnings, short-term and long-term. Many of the managers felt that the scarce resources of the department should be applied to upgrade the competitiveness of their present product line (for which a market existed) rather than attack an uncharted market in competition with major computer companies. The advocates of the new product, spurred by the R&D laboratory management, forced the issue by announcing the product and successfully demonstrating it at a computer show. The reaction of the technical and trade press was very favorable, and the demonstration was witnessed by many potential customers and many competitors. However, no orders were received, because the software was lacking and the prospective customers were unwilling to develop it; the resolution was insufficient to compete with the other, more expensive, non-impact printers; and the initial price was too high to compete with conventional impact printers, in spite of the higher performance which would have accrued significant savings over the life of the product.

Stage 4—Collapse (1981-82)

The operating unit did not have the resources to develop the software, improve the resolution of the hardware, and, at the same time, build the new factory. The R&D laboratory had gone beyond its charter in building and testing prototypes and could not do any further "product engineering" work. The project was abandoned. The operating unit was unable to compete in its traditional market, showed poor financial performance and worse prospects. The business was disposed of by corporate headquarters.

Stage 5—Postmortem (1985)

We can now look back and examine what went wrong with this entire process. The organization, its management, and its functions cannot be faulted. The process followed the various stages according to the company's procedures, the technology transfer function did its job, the R&D executives "championed" the product, the researchers developed an original and effective approach, and additional engineering (in contrast to R&D) work could have improved the product to meet the customers' needs. Yet, the innovation failed! Here is a 20/20 hindsight of the reasons why:

1. It is clear that the major problem throughout this twelve-year process was the lack of an entrepreneur (or entrepreneurial team) who would be responsible for the product from its original idea to its successful application in the external customer's environment. Responsibility of various phases of the project passed from one person to another during the twelve years: from inventor to project engineers to the liaison function to the engineers in the operating unit, but nobody was responsible for the entire process and nobody was *fully committed* to its success.

2. Contacts with the environment, specifically the market, as represented by prospective users and competition, were minimal. The R&D laboratory liaison functions were set up to interact with the internal "customers" (the operating business units), not with the external customers. The operating business unit, in this case, was interacting mostly with OEM manufacturers and with distributors,

not with the ultimate customer, the end-user of their product. As a result there was no input from the marketplace, and, in fact, consultants had to be hired to perform this vital function.

3. The organization was set up for *vertical* technology transfer, but *horizontal* transfer was lacking completely. Vertical technology transfer was implemented according to plan: from basic scientific principles to feasibility studies, to initial system design, to engineering models, to prototypes and finally to a successful demonstration. However, there was no transfer of technology from the sophisticated external potential users, who could have assisted in writing the specifications of the product to be developed, and tested the prototype units.[49] There was also a lack of horizontal technology transfer with potential suppliers of critical components of the product, such as ink and rubber belts. The R&D laboratory was very strong in physics and electronics but lacked expertise in the mechanical and fluid-flow aspects of the printing process. Since the new product included buying critical components from outside vendors, their assistance could have been enlisted (reversing the Von Hippel process) to develop these components and transfer the technology to the magnetic printer project.

We can conclude that the "missing entrepreneur" in this case would have played three related roles: seen the new product to completion, "come hell or high water"; obtained inputs and feedback from the marketplace; and assured horizontal technology transfer, from customers and from vendors, thereby continuously matching the product with the environment, throughout all the stages of development discussed above.

THE CASE OF THE ENTREPRENEUR AS TECHNOLOGY TRANSFER AGENT: PROJECT EXTRA-HIGH VOLTAGE (EHV)

The magnetic printer case illustrates a major deficiency of the linear model of Figure 7-2: The process of technological innovation is analyzed in isolation from the market, technological, organizational, and social environments.

Other "integrative-ecological" models instead look at the innovation process within its total environment.[50] Robert Cooper has investigated in detail the relationships of success and failure of Canadian new products (not necessarily technologically innovative) in relation to market research and coupling with the marketplace. He was able to demonstrate, as had been done by the SAPPHO studies, a significant correlation between success and "market orientation." As a result, Cooper has developed a seven-stage new product process model.[51] These stages include both technical/production activities from preliminary technical assessment to full production, *and* market activities, from preliminary market assessment to market launch. In our experience, limited to technologically intensive products and systems, the marketing stages are not as well defined as the technical stages, and, in fact, some market activities may be formally skipped altogether. This is an agreement with an earlier study by Cooper, which established that in Canada marketing research expenditures for new product development were only a few percent of R&D and engineering expenditures.[52]

We believe that, in order to ensure the success of a technological innovation, continuous interaction with the science and technology environment is as important as the continuous interaction with the market environment. A modified "integrative" model is shown in Figure 7-3. Actually, the model should also include interactions with organizational, social, and political environments, but to remain within the scope of this paper, we will concentrate on the role of the entrepreneur as a *technology transfer agent.* This will be illustrated by the case history of a major project ($10 million in 1959) managed by one of the authors.

Stage 1—Idea Generation (1956)

The general manager of the large power transformer department of a major electrical manufacturer was dissatisfied with the longer range prospects of his business. The power transformer market was inelastic (new transformers were bought for planned system expansion), technologically static (power transformers were a mature product, with basic technology stabilized around 1920), and not subject to replacement (they typically lasted forty years). The market was essentially oligopsonic (dominated by the buying practices of a few major utilities) and oligopolistic (three major suppliers had about 90 percent share). As a result, fixed market shares were held by the

Figure 7-3. An Integrative Model of the Process of Technological Innovation.

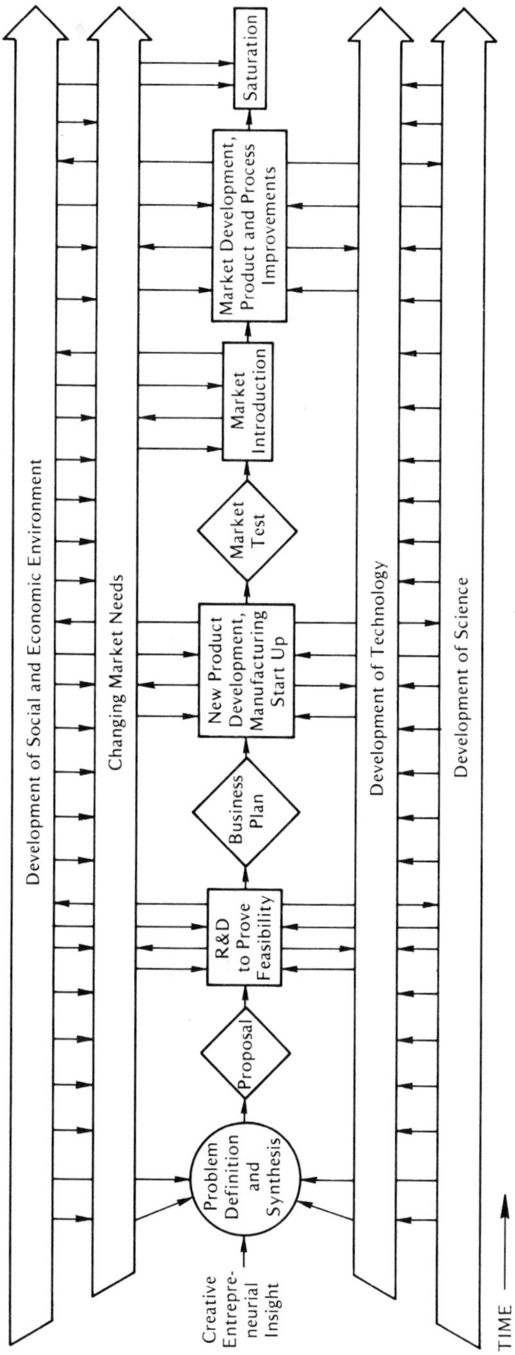

three major suppliers and price changes were not an effective way to alter these shares in the long run. Despite these handicaps, the general manager wanted to become the undisputed leader in his field. He conceived the idea of significantly increasing the maximum operating voltage of transformers. At that time the highest transmission voltage was 220KV, with a few 345KV lines being built in North America and a few 400KV lines in Europe.

The general manager felt that the superior technological image of his company coupled with a laboratory demonstration of the feasibility of higher voltages plus a renewed advertising and sales promotion (A&SP) campaign would increase his market share without provoking price cuts by competitors, unable to compete in this new technological arena for several years. In effect, there would develop a selective adjustment among the suppliers, where the general manager's department would supply the higher margin, less price-sensitive extra-high-voltage (EHV) transformers, and the two other suppliers would continue to concentrate on the more routine lower voltage transformers.

Milestone 1—R&D Proposal (1957)

The general manager charged the market development and A&SP people to prepare a preliminary proposal. It included about $1 million for R&D work in the department's high-voltage laboratory, $1 million for building a 600 to 700KV demonstration transformer within two years, and $2 million for A&SP! This proposal was approved by the corporation, and $0.5 million were authorized for initial R&D work and for the design of the prototype transformer.

Stage 2—Incubation (1957–58)

The general manager was dissatisfied with the reaction of the "segmented" organization. The R&D people were concerned with the risk of doubling the voltage without sufficient theoretical and experimental proof of feasibility, the systems engineering people (in a different company component) felt that transmission system voltages above 345KV were not needed in the United States and, in any case, if and when the electric utilities decided they were needed, there would be plenty of time for the manufacturers to respond to the customers' specifications. Therefore, the general manager decided that he needed a project manager to prove the viability of his idea and introduce it to the marketplace—that is, to the leading utilities in the United States. He chose an electrical engineer who had proven his entrepreneurial ability in introducing in the plant an integrated data processing system, based on the largest computer then commercially available. This major innovation, the first in the industry, had cut the transformer design and manufacturing planning cycle from six months to three days and paid back the $5 million investment in eighteen months.

The new project manager knew very little about EHV transmission. He found out that the research, development, and engineering people in the plant and in the company in general had some knowledge of EHV apparatus design but none of EHV systems design. An initial assessment of the market for EHV apparatus, which in turn depended on the future development of EHV systems, produced no results.

It became clear that the project could not succeed without a massive transfer of technology. There was not enough time for significant research and vertical transfer, from the corporate and the department laboratories to the project, so the transfer would have to be mostly horizontal transfer of existing technology, from outside the company. As a first step the project manager, who knew six languages (including Russian) read all available literature on the subject and even compiled a bibliography with 1,850 entries, which was later published. He also identified the leaders in the field and where they were located: none in universities, few among manufacturers and consulting engineering firms, most in utilities in Western Europe, the Soviet Union, the United States, and Canada. Fortunately, electric utilities, either private or public, are not in competition with each other and are willing to share all the available knowledge. The same was true for some European manufacturers, with whom the company had business connections.

Realizing that technology is primarily transferred by personal contact, the project manager visited practically every major utility in the United States, Canada, and Western Europe, and a few manufacturers and laboratories in Europe. The purpose of his visits were to determine the need for and the timing of EHV transmission; estimate the most probable future EHV level; find out what problems should be solved in order to persuade the utilities that this next EHV level was feasible, safe, and economic; and set up a permanent and effective network for formal and especially informal continuing technology transfer.

As a result of these trips, which lasted for about nine months, the project manager concluded:

1. Electric utilities are primarily conservative monopolies driven by financial and legal considerations (not by technology). Higher EHV voltages were needed because the total cost of transmission would be significantly reduced, and proportionately less rights of way would be needed. (Even at that time there was considerable ecological opposition).

2. Concerning the next voltage level, opinions were divided. Just as 345KV had been superimposed on 220KV, some utilities advocated 500KV as the next step. Other utilities, particularly in Europe, felt that 500KV would not bring sufficient incremental advantages, and at least double 345KV—that is, 690KV—was required.

3. The utilities were already faced with many technical problems in their present 345KV and 400KV lines such as corona loss, radio noise, lightning outages, ice formation, mechanical vibrations, stray fields, and so forth. All these technical problems, however, ultimately affected the economics, the reliability, and the ecology of the entire system.

4. A continuous informal exchange of information was vital, through continued visits and face-to-face meetings. To facilitate technology transfer two advisory boards would be required: utility planners and engineers, and consulting engineers.

Having gathered all this information the project manager realized that it would be necessary to set up a project organization that would ensure this continuing technology transfer. He built up a group of seven young engineers, several with European backgrounds. Each engineer was assigned responsibility for a specific technology (for instance: corona and radio noise, lightning performance and line configurations, mechanical design) and charged with the following responsibilities: become the leading expert in his field and technological gatekeeper for his area within the project;[53] to be responsible for developing the state-of-the-art in his field (through theoretical and experimental studies); and to be responsible in his area for all inputs pertaining to the design, construction, operation, and measurements of the experimental EHV line.

The project manager had come to the conclusion that utilities would adopt the next voltage level (and thus buy EHV transformers from the department) only after seeing proof that the *entire EHV system* worked. Therefore, building a EHV transformer prototype and conducting laboratory demonstrations was not enough. Rather, an entire experimental or prototype EHV *system* should be built, connected to the local utility system, and operated reliably for several years. The highest technically feasible voltage (as shown by laboratory experiments) was chosen—750KV nominal, 800KV maximum—on the basis of two considerations: more knowledge would be gained, which would be applicable also to the 500 to 690KV range, and the possibility of competitors demonstrating higher voltages would be preempted.

The experimental system, therefore, would not only include EHV apparatus (such as transformers, circuit breakers, lightning arresters) that the company produced, but a variety of other major components outside the company's scope: towers, substations, conductors, vibration dampers, instruments. Here again a massive horizontal transfer of technology was needed from suppliers, principally the leading manufacturers of towers and conductors. Many of these vendors responded enthusiastically and donated their engineering services and some of the equipment. Two additional advisory boards were set up: other company departments contributing equipment, and outside suppliers contributing structures, conductors, and instrumentation.

Milestone 2—Business Plan (1958)

With all inputs available a detailed project and business plan was prepared and submitted to corporate approval. There was only one problem: The total cost of the project had risen, because of the change in scope, from $4 to $10 million. Of this total, $2 million would be donated by the outside vendors; the remaining $8 million was the company's share.

By now the general manager, acting as executive champion, had rallied top executive support, and the project manager had convinced the engineering leaders of the company. With some warning from the financial people ("Don't you do this again!") the plan was approved and a consulting engineering company hired to acquire the land, design the system according to the specifications of the project team and of the suppliers, and build the entire system.

Stage 3—Transition and Implementation (1959-60)

Thanks to this massive technology transfer and especially to the "integrative" organization of the project, construction proceeded on schedule and on budget.

Milestone 3—Market Test (1960-61)

The project was officially inaugurated by high company officials in late 1960 and operated perfectly at 760KV. Utilities, the four advisory boards, and the technical press were pleased with the result and forecasted a "new era in EHV transmission." Probably the most flattering acknowledgment was the effort of the company's major competitor to copy the project, albeit on a smaller scale. One month after Project EHV reached 760KV, they went up to 770KV. The response of Project EHV was immediate: The next day 790KV was reached, and that remained the world's record for many years.

Stage 4—Diffusion (1962 to the present)

In the first three years of Project EHV operation the feasibility of a 700+KV voltage level was definitely proven. An enormous amount of data was gathered, processed and translated into design guidelines and operating practices (later all the information was published in a reference book by the utilities R&D association). Representatives from utilities, consultants, manufacturers, and government officials from all over the world visited the project, thus continuing the bi-directional technology transfer in three areas (project-utilities, project-suppliers, and project to project, including competitive projects).

The diffusion process of a technological innovation is initiated by an early adopter who, because of his or her pressing needs and willingness to take the risk, implements the innovation and becomes a leader and a role model among his or her peers.[54] A major Canadian utility was faced with the need of bringing large amounts of power across long distances, within a relatively short time. On the basis of Project EHV results, they adopted the voltage of 765KV and designed their system according to the guidelines and data furnished by the project. In 1967 this was (and still is now) the highest operating a.c. voltage in the world. Needless to say, the company's EHV transformers were installed in Canada, United States, Europe, and the rest of the world.

Project EHV, twenty-five years after its first market test, is still alive and running. It is now called Project Ultra-High-Voltage (UHV) and both a.c. and d.c. transmission up to 1500KV has been investigated. Yet, there is still considerable discussion and speculation what the next voltage step will be and when it will be introduced, probably not until the beginning of the next century.[55] Thus, the diffusion period of the Project EHV innovation will last at least forty years, an unusually long period in this epoch of accelerating technical progress.

CONCLUSION

There are important lessons to be learned by examining the innovation process. The first lesson is: The entrepreneur makes technological innovation happen, and an entrepreneur attracts and breeds other entrepreneurs.

The second lesson is: In a radical *product (or process)* innovation vertical technology transfer is a necessary condition for success, but a continuous stream of horizontal technology transfer is also required. In a *system* innovation, horizontal technology transfer is the key for success.

There is also a third general lesson, which is the combination of the first two: The entrepreneur plays a key role in the process of technological innovation through continuous effective coupling with the environment, which ensures not only transfer of market knowledge but also horizontal technology transfer.

Finally, entrepreneurship is essential to facilitate technology transfer, both vertical and horizontal, and such transfer is necessary for technological innovation. But our organizations and society must create and maintain a *climate* for innovation and entrepreneurship if we are to realize the full potential benefits available from the latent genius existing within our nation's most powerful resource: creative, intelligent and ambitious people striving for achievement and business success.

NOTES TO CHAPTER 7

1. National Academy of Engineering and National Research Council, *The Competitive Status of the U.S. Auto Industry* (Washington, D.C.: National Academy Press, 1982). Similar reports have been published in 1982–84 on the consumer electronics, ferrous metals, machine tools, and textile industries.

2. R. H. Hayes and W. J. Abernathy, "Managing Our Way to Economic Decline," *Harvard Business Review* 58 (July-August 1980): 67–77; W. J. Abernathy, "Competitive Decline in U.S. Innovation: The Management Factor," *Research Management* 13 (September 1982): 34–41; S. Rosenbloom and W. J. Abernathy, "The Climate for Innovation in Industry: The Role of Management Attitudes and Practices in Consumer Electronics," *Research Policy* 11 (1982): 209–25.

3. R. M. Kanter, *The Change Masters* (New York: Simon and Schuster, 1983).

4. "A Drastic New Loss of Competitive Strength," *Business Week* (30 June 1980); E. E. David, Jr., "U.S. Innovation and World Leadership—Facts and Fallacies," *Research Management* 8 (November 1977): 7-10.

5. T. J. Peters and R. H. Waterman, Jr., *In Search of Excellence* (New York: Harper & Row, 1982).

6. Kanter, *The Change Masters*, p. 25.

7. M. A. Maidique and R. H. Hayes, "The Art of High-Technology Management," *Sloan Management Review* 25 (Winter 1984): 17–31.

8. D. A. Schon, *Technology and Change: The New Heraclitus* (New York: Delacorte Press, 1967); T. Burns and G. M. Stalker, *The Management of Innovation* (London: Tavistock, 1961); P. R. Lawrence and J. W. Lorsch, *Organization and Environment: Managing Differentiation and Integration* (Boston, Mass.: Harvard Business School, 1967).

9. Kanter, *The Change Masters*, pp. 387–90.

10. P. L. Roe and G. Kozmetsky, *Creative & Innovative Management Bibliography*, (Unpublished.) The IC^2 Institute, University of Texas at Austin, November 1984.

11. Kanter, *The Change Masters*, p. 21.
12. H. I. Ansoff and J. M. Stewart, "Strategies for a Technology-Based Business," *Harvard Business Review* 44 (November-December 1967): 71–83; A. M. Kantrow, "The Strategy-Technology Connection," *Harvard Business Review* 58 (July-August 1980): 6–21; A. L. Frohman, "Technology As a Competitive Weapon," *Harvard Business Review* 60 (January-February 1982): 97–104.
13. R. N. Foster, "Organize for Technology Transfer, *Harvard Business Review* 48 (November-December 1971): 110–20.
14. H. Brooks, "National Science Policy and Technology Transfer," in National Science Foundation, *Technology Transfer and Innovation*. National Science Foundation, Washington, D.C., 1967 (NSF 67-5): 53–64.
15. T. J. Allen, *Managing the Flow of Technology* (Cambridge, Mass.: MIT Press, 1977); R. S. Rosenbloom and F. W. Wolek, *Technology and Information Transfer* (Boston, Mass.: Harvard Business School, 1977); W. H. Gruber and D. G. Marquis, *Factors in the Transfer of Technology* (Cambridge, Mass.: MIT Press, 1969).
16. R. G. Hawkins and A. J. Prasad, eds., *Technology Transfer and Economic Development* (Greenwich, Conn.: JAI Press, 1981).
17. P. Kelly and M. Kranzberg, *Technological Innovation: A Critical Review of Current Knowledge* (San Francisco, The San Francisco Press, 1978). (This book includes an extensive bibliography.)
18. L. G. Tornatzky, J. D. Eveland, M. G. Boylan, W. A. Hetzner, E. C. Johnson, and J. Schneider, *The Process of Technological Innovation: Reviewing the Literature* (Washington, D.C.: National Science Foundation, May, 1983). (This book includes an extensive bibliography.)
19. S. Myers and D. G. Marquis, *Successful Industrial Innovations*, National Science Foundation, Washington, D.C., 1969 (NSF 69-17); U.S. Department of Commerce, *Technological Innovation: Its Environment and Management*, Washington, D.C., 1967 (GPO: 0-242-736); Organization for Economic Cooperation and Development (OECD), *The Conditions for Success in Technological Innovation* (Paris: 1971).
20. J. A. Morton, *Organizing for Innovation: A Systems Approach to Technical Management* (New York: McGraw-Hill, 1971); L. W. Steele, *Innovation in Business* (New York: Elsevier, 1975); E. A. Gee and C. Tyler, *Managing Innovation* (New York: John Wiley & Sons, 1976); B. G. Twiss, *Managing Technological Innovation* (London and New York: Longman, 1980).
21. M. J. Martin, *Managing Technological Innovation and Entrepreneurship* (Reston, Va.: Reston, 1984).
22. P. Kelly and M. Kranzberg, *Technological Innovation*, pp. 275–98; L. G. Tornatzky, *The Process of Technological Innovation*, pp. 155–86; E. M. Rogers, *Diffusion of Innovations* (Glencoe, N.Y.: Free Press, 1983); J. E. Ettie, W. P. Bridges, and R. D. O'Keefe, "Organization Strategy and Struc-

tural Differences for Radical versus Incremental Innovations," *Management Science* 30 (June 1984): 682-95.

23. E. A. Von Hippel, "Users as Innovators," *Technology Review* 80 (January 1978): 3-11.

24. J. Gartner and C.S. Naiman, "Overcoming the Barriers to Technology Transfer," *Research Management* 7 (March 1976): 22-28.

25. C. A. Kent, D. L. Sexton, and K. H. Vesper, eds., *Encyclopedia of Entrepreneurship* (Englewood Cliffs, N.J.: Prentice-Hall, 1982). (This book includes an extensive bibliography.); K. H. Vesper, ed., *Frontiers of Entrepreneurship Research* (Wellesley, Mass.: Babson Center for Entrepreneurial Studies, 1981); K. H. Vesper, ed., *Frontiers of Entrepreneurship Research* (Wellesley, Mass.: Babson Center for Entrepreneurial Studies, 1982); J. A. Hornaday, J. A. Timmons, and K. H. Vesper, eds., *Frontiers of Entrepreneurship Research* (Wellesley, Mass.: Babson Center for Entrepreneurial Studies, 1983).

26. E. B. Roberts, "Entrepreneurship and Technology," *Research Management* 11 (July 1968): 249-66. See also Gruber and Marquis, Ref. 24, pp. 219-37; A. C. Cooper, "Spin-offs and Technical Entrepreneurship," *IEEE Transactions on Engineering Management* EM-18 (February 1971): 2-6.

27. O. J. Krasner, "The Role of Entrepreneurs in Innovation," and G. Udel, "Elaboration on Entrepreneurs in Innovation," in Kent, Sexton, and Vesper, *Encyclopedia of Entrepreneurship*, pp. 277-87.

28. R. A. Rosenbloom, "Technological Innovation in Firms and Industries: An Assessment of the State-of-the-Art," in Kelly and Kranzberg, *Technological Innovation*, pp. 215-30.

29. I. C. MacMillan, "The Politics of New Ventures," in Vesper, *Frontiers of Entrepreneurship Research* (1981), pp. 496-503; E. B. Roberts, "New Ventures for Corporate Growth," *Harvard Business Review* 58 (July-August 1980): 134-42; H. Schollhammer, "Internal Corporate Entrepreneurship," in Kent, Sexton, and Vesper, *Encyclopedia of Entrepreneurship*, pp. 209-29; R. A. Burgelman, "Managing the Internal Corporate Venturing Process," *Sloan Management Review* 25 (Winter 1984): 33-48; J. B. Quinn, "Technological Innovation, Entrepreneurship and Strategy," *Sloan Management Review* 22 (Spring 1979): 19-30; Zenas Block, "Can Corporate Venturing Succeed?," *Journal of Business Strategy* (Fall 1982): 21-33.

30. Roberts, "Entrepreneurship and Technology"; J. A. Timmons, N. D. Fast, S. E. Pratt, and W. D. Bygrave, "Venture Capital Investing in Highly Innovative Technological Ventures," *Venture Economics*, for the National Science Foundation (March 1984); K. H. Vesper, *Entrepreneurship and National Policy*, Heller Institute for Small Business, Policy Paper 3, Chicago, Ill., 1983, pp. 12-19.

31. Martin, *Managing Technological Innovation*, chapters 14 and 16.

32. P. A. Abetti, "The Process of Technological Innovation in Large and Small Companies," *Preprints*, Division of Petroleum Chemistry, American Chemical Society, 28: 4 (August 1983): 1033-44. Scheduled for publication in *Chemtech* (1985).

33. Rosenbloom and Abernathy, "The Climate for Innovation in Industry."

34. S. Myers and D. G. Marquis, *Successful Industrial Innovations*; J. Langrish, M. Gibbons, W. G. Evans, and F. R. Jevons, *Wealth from Knowledge* (London: MacMillan, 1972); S. Globe, G. W. Levy, and C. M. Schwartz, "Key Factors and Events in the Innovation Process," *Research Management* 4 (July 1973): 8-15; E. B. Roberts and H. H. Wainer, "Some Characteristics of Technical Entrepreneurs," *IEEE Transactions on Engineering Management*, EM-18 (August 1971): 100-109; A. C. Cooper and J. L. Komives, *Technical Entrepreneurship: A Symposium*, Center for Venture Management, Purdue University, Lafayette, Ind., 1970; A. H. Rubinstein, A. K. Chakrabarti, R. D. O'Keefe, W. E. Souder, and H.C. Young, "Factors Influencing Innovation Success at the Project Level," *Research Management* 6 (May 1976): 15-20; I. A. Litvak and C. J. Maule, "Some Characteristics of Successful Entrepreneurs in Canada," *IEEE Transactions on Engineering Management* EM-20 (1973): 62-68.

35. R. Rothwell, C. Freeman, A. Horlsey, V.T.P. Jervis, A. B. Robertson, and J. Townsend, "Sappho Updated—Project Sappho Phase II," *Research Policy* 3 (1974): 258-91; J. M. Utterback, T. J. Allen, J. H. Hollomon, and M. H. Sirbo, "The Process of Technological Innovation in Five Industries in Europe and Japan," *IEEE Transactions on Engineering Management* 23 (February 1976): 3-9.

36. R. G. Cooper, "The Dimensions of Industrial New Product Success and Failure," *Journal of Marketing* 43 (Summer 1979): 93-103.

37. M. A. Maidique and B. J. Zirger, "A Study of Success and Failure in Product Innovation: The Case of the U.S. Electronics Industry," *IEEE Transactions on Engineering Management* EM-31 (November 1984): 192-203.

38. M. A. Maidique, "Entrepreneurs, Champions, and Technological Innovation," *Sloan Management Review* 21 (Winter 1980): 59-73.

39. Peters and Waterman, Jr., *In Search of Excellence.*

40. Maidique and Hayes, "The Act of High-Technology Management."

41. Vesper, *Entrepreneurship and National Policy*, p. 27.

42. L. A. Weiss, "Start-up Businesses: A Comparison of Performances," *Sloan Management Review* (Fall 1981): 37-53.

43. M. Hanan, "Venturing Corporations—Think Small to Stay Strong," *Harvard Business Review* 54 (May-June 1976): 139-48; J. Friar and M. Horwitch, "The Current Transformation of Technology Strategy: The Attempt to Create Multiple Avenues for Innovation Within the Large Corporation" (Paper for the Fourth Conference of the Strategic Management Society, Philadelphia, Penna., 13 October 1984).

44. A. C. Parthe, Jr., and J. J. Schaufeld, "The MIT Enterprise Forum: A Resource for Growing Technology-Based Organizations," *IEEE Transactions on Engineering Management* EM-31 (November 1984): 204-6.

45. Timmons, "Venture Capital Investing."

46. Roberts, "Entrepreneurship and Technology."

47. P. A. Abetti, "Technology: A Challenge to Planners," *Planning Review* 12:4 (July 1984): 24-27, 45, and "Milestones for Managing Technological Innovation" 13 (March 1985).

48. M. A. Maidique, "Entrepreneurs, Champions, and Technological Innovation."

49. E. Von Hippel, "The Dominant Role of Users in Scientific Instrument Innovation Process," *Research Policy* (1976): 212-39.

50. Tornatsky, *The Process of Technological Innovation*, p. 6; F. Bradbury, P. Jervis, R. Johnston, and A. Pearson, *Transfer Processes in Technical Change* (The Netherlands: Sijthoff & Nordhoof, Alphen aan den Rijn, 1978); K. J. Schmidt-Tiedemann, "A New Model of the Innovation Process," *Research Management* (March 1982): 18-21.

51. R. G. Cooper, "A Process Model for Industrial New Product Development," *IEEE Transactions on Engineering Management* EM-30 (February 1983): 2-11.

52. R. G. Cooper, "Why New Industrial Products Fail," *Industrial Marketing Management* 4 (1975): 315-26.

53. T. J. Allen, "The World. Your Company. A Gate for Information. Who Guards the Gate?" *Innovation* 25 (1972): 1-7.

54. E. M. Rogers and F. F. Schoemaker, *Communications of Innovation: A Cross-Cultural Approach* (New York: Free Press, 1971).

55. J. J. Dougherty, "How Much Power from What Source," *IEEE Spectrum* 22 (January 1985): 41.

HOW MANY CHAMPIONS WILL AN INNOVATION CYCLE SUPPORT?

Donald D. Myers

The availability of technology is virtually unlimited. The United States Federal Laboratories perform more than $40 billion of research a year. The universities in the United States have large numbers of patents available for purchase. Many industrial corporations have established departments to license their spin-off technologies. There are large numbers of these technological ideas that have excellent potential for successful commercialization. However, many will remain on the shelf unused.

The success of transferring technology is seen in the Japanese efforts since World War II. Automobiles, steel, shipbuilding, and consumer electronics were the principal industries targeted for development. In the twenty-eight years from 1950 to 1978, Japanese organizations entered into 32,000 contracts for a wide range of technology imports to Japan at a total cost of only $9 billion.[1] This is in comparison to the United States expectant expenditures of over $100 billion a year on research and development in 1985. The significance of this Japanese story is that technology can be transferred beneficially.

Emerging technologies resulting in new products and processes provide the new jobs that hopefully will offset the jobs lost with the sunset industries. In a study using a sample of ten high-technology

211

and eight smokestack industries, it was projected that in the 1979–87 period employment gains in the high-technology sector would exceed the losses of the smokestack industries.

The smokestack sector lost about 565,000 jobs from 1979 to 1983 and is projected to regain only 227,000 by 1987. By contrast, employment in the high-technology sector grew through the recession by 217,000 jobs from 1979 to 1983. It is expected to rise another 321,000 from 1983 to 1987.[2]

New industries or major shifts in industries have typically been a result of radical innovations by a small business/inventor or a company outside of the industry. This is seen in the diesel locomotive being originated by an automotive firm, Kodachrome being originated by two musicians, xerography being originated by a patent attorney, Polaroid film being originated by an independent inventor, and nylon by a chemical firm. However, recently it is seen that companies in the chemical industry are repositioning to capitalize on new technologies.[3]

If a basic (radical) technological innovation is being introduced, there will be need for a champion to see that the new concept gets through the many knotholes. It will often require a significant market structural change. Accordingly, it makes no difference whether it is done through a large company or a small company. It will, however, impact how the champion proceeds with accomplishing the innovation.

On the other hand, incremental (step- or improvement-type) innovations may not require the forceful champion even in the large company. This is possible since it will not require the company to make major changes in the way it does business; the resistance (and justification required) will be minimized.

The issue to be discussed in this paper is whether it can be expected for a technological innovation to be successful if it requires transfer of the "baton" by several champions during the innovation cycle. This impacts the significance of technology transfer. It could not be expected that transfer of technology has importance if the innovation cycle is limited to a single champion. This would leave the burden to the inventor to insure success. However, if a series of successive champions are to be used during the cycle, it will be particularly important that the technology be transferred effectively. Only perhaps the relative level of difficulty will vary in whether the transfer is within an organization or across boundaries of organizations.

ELEMENTS OF INNOVATION

Innovation is used often to suggest the generation of a creative idea. However, in this paper it will be used in a more strict sense. Innovation will be used for technical projects and will include the complete cycle starting with the generation of a technical idea to and including commercialization of a new product, process, or service.

The technological innovation cycle has been defined as including:

1. Idea generation,
2. Synthesizing of existing knowledge and techniques to provide the theoretical basis for the technical concept,
3. Verification of the theory or design concept,
4. Laboratory demonstration (or breadboard),
5. Prototype development and field test,
6. Commercial introduction or initial operational use,
7. Widespread adoption of the innovation, and
8. Proliferation of usage.[4]

However, for successful technological innovation, more than technical creative ideas are required, creative ideas are required to develop supporting organization, financial, production, and marketing infrastructure.

It is said that "A technological innovation is like a river—its growth and development depending on its tributaries and on the conditions it encounters on the way. The tributaries to an innovation are inventors, technologies, and scientific discoveries; the conditions are the vagaries of the market place."

Technology Transfer

The completed process of the transfer of technology (or sometimes referred to as T squared, T^2) for this paper suggest that total knowledge transfer has occurred. The mere licensing of a patent would not satisfy the definition if there were more knowledge (i.e., technical know-how). It could include drawings, specifications, reports, prototypes, tooling, and so forth. The amount of knowledge available would be expected to increase as it progresses through the innovation cycle.

The process of transferring any information always results in less than perfect transmission. Accordingly, the more times technology is transferred the greater the loss or misunderstanding of the information received.

The loss in transmission becomes critical in basic innovations. At some point in the innovation cycle for a basic innovation, it is critical that the potential is recognized. It often will be the inventor who sees the need for a solution to a problem (i.e., Chester F. Carlson recognizing the need for dry copying). It then becomes necessary to also transfer the vision of application of the technology transferred. The difficulty of this process is seen in the effort by Carlson to license the basic xerography patent. A patent was granted in 1940. He went to twenty-six major companies—including IBM, A. B. Dick, RCA, Eastman Kodak—with everyone turning him down. Rights were eventually sold to Haloid in 1946. It was not until 1959 that the first Xerox machine was sold. Market research indicated the market would not exceed 5,000 units a year.[5]

Distinctions in the technological innovations have been made by differentiating between basic (or radical) innovations and incremental (or evolutionary) innovations.[6] Basic innovations often result in new products such as the diesel locomotive, xerography, jet engines. Incremental innovation tends to be product improvement or process innovations. A basic innovation generally will require many follow-on incremental innovations to be successful.

Entrepreneur

Entrepreneur, by Webster's definition, is one who undertakes to "organize, manage and assume the risk of the business." The technological entrepreneur is one whose business has a substantial technological content.

This definition provides the distinction from entrepreneur (or the intrapreneur) who champion's an innovation within the corporation but is not assuming the financial risk of the business.

Champion

An innovation champion is a highly enthusiastic and committed individual who is willing to take substantial risks to insure success of a technological innovation. The champion may be an entrepreneur or may be intrapreneur. In the case of the champion with the corporation the risks are usually related to the professional career within the corporation. The champion could also be within a governmental organization.

The importance of the champion throughout the technological innovation cycle has been recognized in small firms as well as the large organizations.[6] It has been said that "the new idea either finds a champion or dies."[7] To Schon, the champions are critical because "no ordinary involvement with a new idea provides the energy required to cope with the indifference and resistance that major technical change provokes . . . champions of new inventions . . . display persistence and courage of heroic quality."

ROLES OF THE CHAMPION

An excellent static model for considering the roles of champions in the different types of organizations was suggested by Maidique as shown in Figure D-1.[8] The organizational distinctions are based on the assumption that companies evolve through three basic stages defined as follows: (1) Entrepreneurial is where the company has a single product or single product line, with little formal structure, and controlled by the owner-manager; (2) Integrated is a single product line firm with vertically integrated manufacturing and specialized functional organizations where the owner-manager retains control of strategic decisionmaking but delegates operating decisions through policy; and (3) Diversified is a multiproduct firm with formalized managerial systems that are evaluated by objective criteria, such as rate of growth and returns on investment with delegation of product-market decisions in existing businesses. The Diversification classification was divided into the following three subcategories: (1) Dominant firms that derive 70 to 95 percent of their sales from a single business or a vertically integrated chain businesses; (2) Related business firms that diversify into related areas where there are no more than 70 percent of sales; and (3) Unrelated business firms that have diversified without necessarily relating new business to old, and where no business accounts for as much as 70 percent of sales.[9] However, this model does not account for the dynamic problem of transferring the champion role to another individual.

Figure D-1. Champions in Firms at Various Stages.

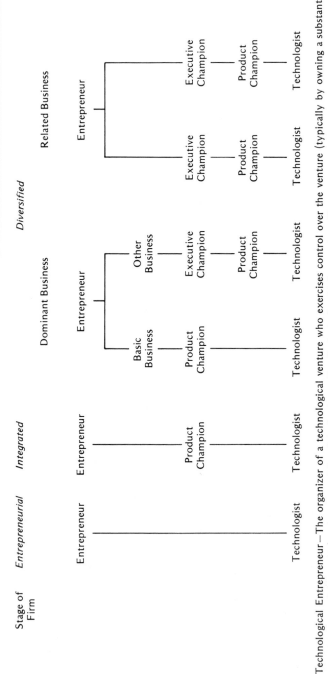

Technological Entrepreneur—The organizer of a technological venture who exercises control over the venture (typically by owning a substantial percentage of the equity) and assumes risks of the business. Usually he is the chief executive officer.

Product Champion—A member of the organization who creates, defines or adopts an idea for a new technological innovation and who is willing to risk his or her position and prestige to make possible the innovation's successful implementation.

Executive Champion—An executive in a technological firm who has direct or indirect influence over the resource allocation process and who uses the power to channel resources to a new technological innovation, thereby absorbing most, but not usually all, the risk of the project.

Source: Modesto A. Maidique, "Entrepreneurs, Champions, and Technological Innovation," *Sloan Management Review* (Winter 1980).

In the entrepreneurial firm, the entrepreneur serves as the champion for the technological innovation; this proves to be very successful as compared to the other firm stages. At this firm stage there is no need for technology transfer because the technologist is usually also the entrepreneur.

Diversified dominant basic businesses also have a reasonably successful record with new technological products. IBM's System/360, Boeing's 747, and GM's Saturn are examples of diversified-firm technological innovations. The projects are so large that they receive comparable attention to the integrated firm. Such projects have been classified as a "you bet your company."[10] However, these companies are not willing to undertake such risks again. The directors of the company have a legal obligation to protect the stockholders investment. This results in large companies gravitating away from such large short-term risks.

As the number of champions expand for a given technological innovation, the likelihood of success will decrease. Recently, large companies have tried to provide an entrepreneurial environment by setting up an autonomous operation with minimum controls. This minimizes the number of champions at any time to support the project as well as the rotation of champions.

INHERENT INNOVATION LIMITATIONS
OF TECHNOLOGY TRANSFER

Basic technological innovations would appear to require a fanatical champion. Examples of success are noted throughout history. A recent article in *The Wall Street Journal* reported the story of the Sidewinder missile and the commitment of its developer, Bill McLean.[11] This heat-seeking air-to-air missile will experience its thirtieth year in the U.S. combat arsenal. Although a government employee, McLean worked on the project part of the time in this garage and had to use discretionary funds for development. When a DOD official decreed that it be canceled because it would not work, ways had to be found to siphon money from other projects to keep it going. Similar stories are told by 3M's former CEO, Lewis W. Lehr, of firing a stubborn lab man who kept coming to work on his pet project. He was eventually rehired, the project became a division, and he became a vice-president.[12] Carlson in pursuing xerography and Land in pursuing Polaroid film exhibited similar zeal and tenacity.

The difficulty is how to develop the fanatical commitment to pursue the commercialization when the technology is transferred. The venture capitalist understands this need. Deals are structured so that the entrepreneur has made such a commitment. This positions the entrepreneur so that, when difficulties occur, the entrepreneur will see that the project is squeezed through the knothole.

All innovations must be carried out within a "window of time." If the innovation cycle is extended for significant time it is likely that the opportunity will be lost. Accordingly, if an innovation requires that technology transfer occur a number of times during the cycle, it is likely that considerable time will be lost.

The rewards must offset the risks. The motivating rewards will vary from champion to champion. The more champions in an innovation cycle the greater the diffusion of the rewards. If the risks are high, the diffusion will quickly eliminate equity for the risks. A failure at any point can result in failure of the innovation. Changing of champions results in loss of control that the champion needs to make such a commitment.

The risk of changing champions through the innovation cycle is likely to result in each champion seeing it as a short-term opportunity and attempting to use it solely as a stepping stone. If this occurs the requisite commitment will not be obtained.

SUMMARY

Technology transfer is a key factor in the success of the innovation process. It is important to remember that technology transfer is communication. With the transfer of the technical information usually there must also be communicated the opportunity for the technology.

Where there is technology push rather than a market pull the opportunity is usually not very obvious. Technological innovations, particularly basic, are generally in a technology push category. It, therefore, takes an unusual individual that recognizes and becomes committed to an opportunity that is not verifiable.

Accordingly, transfer of new technological ideas will always have severe limitations. The rewards will have to be made commensurate with the risks if successful commercialization is to occur. The Japanese have been very successful in capitalizing on technology transfer. Many excellent ideas continue to remain on shelves. The need to improve the understanding of successful technology transfer is substantial.

The case studies of technology transfer provided by Abetti and Stuart are of considerable value to understand better the relationships between the champion(s) and technology transfer with technological innovation.[13] However, theories and models for the process and content of technology transfer in technological transfer need to be developed and verified. Various frameworks for successful championing of technological innovation need to be defined. The relationship of the dynamics of market opportunities intersecting with successful and unsuccessful technological innovation need to be investigated.

The research opportunities are many. A better understanding of the principles of successful championing of technological innovation is greatly needed.

NOTES

1. William C. Norris, "Cooperative R&D: A Regional Strategy," *Issues in Science and Technology* (Winter 1985): 92–102.

2. John E. Cremeans, Gurmuikh Gill, Virgil Ketterling, Ann Lawson, and Ken Young, "Structural Change in the U.S. Economy: 1979–87 High Technology versus Smokestack Industries," 1984 U.S. Industrial Outlook, U.S. Department of Commerce, 1984.

3. Geoffrey Smith, "Culture Shock," *Forbes* (24 October 1983): 54–56.

4. James R. Bright, "Some Management Lessons from Technological Research," *Long Range Planning* 2: 1 (September 1969): 36–41.

5. John H. Dessauer, *My Year with Xerox* (New York: Doubleday Publishers, 1971).

6. William J. Abernathy and James M. Utterback, "Patterns of Industrial Innovation," *Technology Preview* (June-July 1978): 39–47.

7. Donald A. Schon, "Champions for Radical New Invention," *Harvard Business Review* (March-April 1963): 84.

8. Modesto A. Maidique, "Entrepreneurs, Champions and Technological Innovation," *Sloan Management Review* (Winter 1980): 71.

9. Ibid., p. 64.

10. T. A. Wise, "IBM's $5,000,000 Gamble," *Fortune* (September 1966): 118.

11. John J. Fialka, "Weapons of Choice: After Nearly 30 Years, Sidewinder Missile Is Still Potent, Reliable," *The Wall Street Journal*, 15 February 1985, p. 1.

12. Lewis W. Lehr, "Stimulating Technological Innovations: The Role of Top Management," *Research Management* (November 1979): p. 24.

13. Pier A. Abetti and Robert W. Stuart, "Entrepreneurship and Technology Transfer: Key Factors in the Innocation Process," *State-of-the-Art in Entrepreneurship Research Conference Proceedings*, 1985.

IV GROWTH AND ENTREPRENEURSHIP

GROWING UP BIG
Entrepreneurship and the Creation of High-Potential Ventures

8

Jeffrey A. Timmons

Entepreneurship is the ability to create and build something from practically nothing: fundamentally, a human, creative act. It is finding personal energy by initiating, doing, achieving, and building an enterprise or organization, rather than by just watching, analyzing, or describing one. Making such a personal statement about the venture requires a willingness to take calculated risks—both personal and financial—and then to do everything possible to improve the odds, thereby reducing the chances of failure. It is the ability to build a founding team to complement the entrepreneur's skills and talents. It is the knack for sensing an opportunity where others see chaos, contradiction, and confusion. It is the know-how to find, marshal, and control resources and to make sure the venture does not run out of money when it is needed most.

Entrepreneurs are driven by an intense commitment and determined perseverance. They see the cup half-full rather than half-empty. They strive for integrity. They burn with the competitive desire to excel and win. They use failure as a tool for learning and eschew perfection in favor of effectiveness. They have enough confidence in themselves to believe they can personally make an enormous difference in the final outcome of their ventures, and their lives.

WHO CAN BE AN ENTREPRENEUR?

Judging by the extraordinary variety of people, opportunities, and strategies that characterize the approximately 14 million non-farm businesses in this country, literally anyone can give it a try. Not only can they try, they can succeed and have succeeded beyond what anyone possibly could have imagined. And if they fail, no other country in the world has laws, institutions, and social norms that are more forgiving and provide a learning curve and a second—or third—chance.

Yet, while anyone can try to start a business, relatively few can grow one to beyond $1 million in sales. According to government data, only about one in thirty of those 14 million businesses had sales in 1980 of over $1 million. Trying to start a venture, and growing and harvesting it successfully, are not the same.

Creating and Building New Ventures

Today, much of the excitement about entrepreneurship is stimulated by the recent flood of high potential new ventures and the entrepreneurs who launch and build them: Compaq, Lotus 1-2-3, Quadram, and hundreds of other success stories. Understanding the forces that drive the entrepreneurial process and the practicalities necessary to get the odds in favor of success is useful for independent and corporate entrepreneurs alike. Who does it? What does it take in the way of experience, skills, know-how, and other attributes? How can one distinguish between a good idea and a real opportunity? What are the critical issues and trade-offs to be resolved? What do entrepreneurs need to know? How can it be financed? What does it take to put together a business plan that can be implemented? What analytical techniques and concepts are most useful? What are the problems and pitfalls that court failure, and how can they be avoided? Further, how can one grow successfully and conclude with a successful harvest? After all, many entrepreneurs caution from hard-won experience that achieving a capital gain and an enhanced track record is the truly hard part.

THE PROBLEM OF SURVIVAL

For the vast majority of new businesses in the country, the odds of survival are definitely not in their favor. While there is little agreement on what the precise failure and survival figures are, most agree that failure is the rule, not the exception.

Failures are not easy to define or identify. It has been said that "success has a thousand sires, but failure is an orphan." That is true of small business failures as well. Failures are very difficult to locate, and reliable statistics and databases have not been available. Success, on the other hand, is quite visible to all.

Despite these problems, there have been an unprecedented number of new company formations in the United States in the past few years. Many believe that the total number of new businesses exceeds half a million each year.[1]

High Failure Rates

What happens to these new ventures? Where the birth and death watchers do agree, the picture is rather bleak. The failure and bankruptcy rates continue at high levels. Some types of business seem to face worse odds than others. Retail trade, construction, and service businesses, for instance, account for just three of twenty-one categories reported by Dun & Bradstreet, yet they accounted for 70 percent of all failures and bankruptcies in 1980.[2]

When one attempts to summarize the overall picture, over 53 percent of all business failures and bankruptcies occur in the first five years of a new firm's life, nearly 30 percent in years six through ten, and the remaining 20 percent for firms in existence more than ten years.[3] That is not to say that all the failures need to be eliminated. A certain level of failure is part of the "creative self-destruction" described by Joseph Schumpeter. It is part of the dynamics of innovation and economic renewal. It is also part of the learning process inherent in "gaining the entrepreneurial apprenticeship." The failure of a single venture does not mean a venture career failure.

$1 Million Sales Threshhold Improves Survival Odds

In recent years some very significant new studies profiling the dynamics of new company formation have emerged. The thrust of their important messages was that a very disproportionate share—probably 70 percent or more—of the net new jobs in our country come from new and growing firms.[4] What is less well known has significant implications for would-be entrepreneurs.

By interpolating the data from these studies in terms of start-up dynamics and size, a useful "threshhold concept" emerges. There appears to be a minimum threshhold size for new firms—at least ten employees, and twenty is even better—that is closely linked to both survival odds and the promise of expansion. Roughly translated into total sales, the findings from several studies suggest that this threshhold starts at a minimum of around $500,000. (Obviously, any estimates of sales per employee vary considerable from industry to industry. A useful rule of thumb is $50,000 to $60,000 per employee annually.)

Using the number of employees as a benchmark the one year survival rates jump from 77.8 percent for firms having up to nine employees to 95.3 percent for firms with twenty to ninety-nine employees. The same trend occurs for the four year survival odds. The survival rate for firms with less than nineteen employees was 37.4 percent but increased to 53.6 percent for firms with twenty to forty-nine employees.

The message is clear: Survival odds and signs of prosperity—namely significant job creation—improve even further once the $1 million in sales level is attained. Entrepreneurs thinking about creating a new venture in which survival odds are favorable need to think big enough. An inability to achieve sales over half a million dollars within four years or so implies a business that is fragile and vulnerable to competition or one that has not focused on real opportunities. It may also mean the lead entrepreneur does not want to grow.

Exceptions to the Failure Rule

Fortunately, the record of new business failure has a notable pattern of exceptions to these national averages: Just the opposite results characterize the failure record for entrepreneurs who are able to attract start-up financing from private venture capital companies. Instead of a 70 percent to 90 percent *failure* rate, when all types of new firms are considered, these growth-minded new ventures enjoy a *survival* rate nearly that high. And their records of successes, especially in a "great bull market" such as in 1982 and 1983, are often quite spectacular.

Earlier studies of failure/success have been confirmed by more recent studies. Typically, in the portfolio of an experienced and professional venture capital firm, about 15 to 20 percent of the companies will result in total losses of the original investment. It is unusual to exceed a loss rate of 30 to 35 percent (and for it to fall below 10 percent).

A recent study analyzed 218 investments made by five prominent venture capital firms during the 1970s. They found that 14.7 percent of those portfolio companies resulted in complete losses. Another 24.8 percent experienced partial losses—roughly 50 percent. Offsetting this, much lower than the national average failure pattern, were the spectacular successes. Among the 218 investments 3.8 percent returned ten times or more the original investment in the ten-year period, and another 8.3 percent returned five to ten times, all after taxes. This translates into about 25 percent compounded return on investment after taxes.[5]

What do these talented entrepreneurs and their venture capital backers do differently? The professional venture capital investors have had a unique approach to doing their business. Successful entrepreneurs, who grow multimillion dollar firms often from scratch and sometimes with little money, understand the same things: Entrepreneurial achievement is driven by people who search for and shape superior opportunities.

THE THREE DRIVING FORCES:
A MATTER OF FIT

There are many successful entrepreneurs and there are many ways they have achieved their successes. Any undimensional model to distill their collective successes—such as a single psychological profile or characteristic, or a single idea or technology—can tell only part of the story. Instead, the author is suggesting a framework for under-

Figure 8-1. New Venture Creation: The Driving Forces.

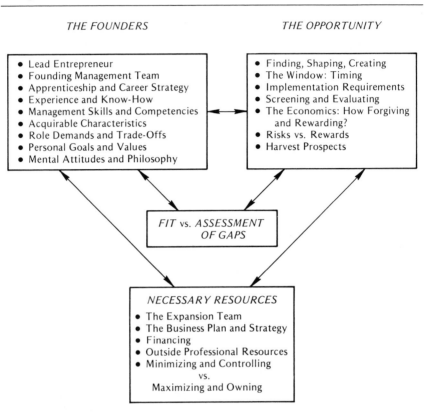

THE FOUNDERS

THE OPPORTUNITY

- Lead Entrepreneur
- Founding Management Team
- Apprenticeship and Career Strategy
- Experience and Know-How
- Management Skills and Competencies
- Acquirable Characteristics
- Role Demands and Trade-Offs
- Personal Goals and Values
- Mental Attitudes and Philosophy

- Finding, Shaping, Creating
- The Window: Timing
- Implementation Requirements
- Screening and Evaluating
- The Economics: How Forgiving and Rewarding?
- Risks vs. Rewards
- Harvest Prospects

FIT vs. ASSESSMENT OF GAPS

NECESSARY RESOURCES
- The Expansion Team
- The Business Plan and Strategy
- Financing
- Outside Professional Resources
- Minimizing and Controlling
  vs.
  Maximizing and Owning

standing successful venture creation that has emerged from earlier research and has been shaped and refined through its application in the real world and the classroom. Figure 8-1 is a summary of the three primary driving forces behind successful new venture creation—the founders, the opportunity, and the necessary resources.

Experience shows that each of these elements can be assessed and influenced in order to improve the chances of succeeding. The key is a careful and realistic assessment of these driving forces: the strengths and weaknesses of the lead entrepreneur and management team; the opportunity; and what is needed for successful implementation and eventual harvesting. The process is largely iterative, one of trial and error, learning to anticipate what it takes, where the "gaps" will be as the venture unfolds, and—of paramount importance—how to shape a good "fit."

The Team Concept

Venture capitalists feel that the two most important criteria of ventures are the lead entrepreneur and the quality of the team. Several studies have confirmed this view widely held by practitioners, including a recent study of the fifty most active U.S. venture capital firms.[6]

The same principle seems to hold true from recent research on high-technology companies formed in this country since 1967. Even in the most highly innovative technological ventures, venture capitalists still insist that they place greatest weight and emphasis on the quality and proven track record of the management team.[7]

"Apprenticeship" and Career Strategy Notion

The treatment of the lead entrepreneur and, as it is appropriate, the management team, has several dimensions. For one thing, there is the underlying notion of an apprenticeship with paths for preparation, entry strategies, and planning and managing the whole process in order to gain the relevant business experience needed. Most successful entrepreneurs do not leave this to accident or osmosis. Most have accumulated five to ten years or more of general management and industry experience prior to their first start-up. Increasingly, there is evidence from research about the career paths of entrepreneurs and the self-employed that suggests that success is linked to thoughtful preparation and planning before taking the plunge.[8]

Entrepreneurial Roots: Seeing Is Believing

There is no more powerful teacher than a good example. Seeing what has been and can be done cleanly and simply points the way and plants the seed of what is possible. No wonder then that numerous studies show a strong connection between the presence of role models and the emergence of entrepreneurs. For instance, one recent study showed that over half the new business starters had parents who owned a business. The authors summed it up this way:

> People who start companies are more likely to come from families in which their parents or close relatives were in business for themselves. These older people were examples or "models" for the children. Whether they were successful or not probably didn't matter. However, for the children growing up in such a family, the action of starting a new business seems possible—something they can do.[9]

The Experience Factor

Experience and know-how are essential for successful venture creation.[10] What are the management skills and competencies necessary for the venture? How do these fit with the strengths and weaknesses of the lead entrepreneur, based on his or her cumulative experience and track record? How do these complement possible partners? What do they say about the progress and velocity of the apprenticeship toward a successful launch? What are some effective and time-saving ways to get any needed experience? A large number of studies indicate that often 90 percent or more of founders start their companies in the same marketplace and industry they have been working in.[11]

Acquirable Characteristics and Role Demands

Another important set of factors founders can profitably consider as part of the start-up process are their own talents, attributes, and characteristics.[12] During the past several years new studies about entrepreneurs have tended to confirm what practitioners have known all along: Some characteristics and actions are in fact acquirable and learnable, and some attributes are more desirable than others, especially in the realm of high-growth ventures. Does the entrepreneur have the drive, motivation, and intensity of commitment necessary? Is he or she willing to pay the price in terms of the sacrifices and immersion demanded by the heat of the start-up role? However, beware of trying to compile a longer list of characteristics associated with success; since successful entrepreneurs seem to come in as many sizes, shapes, colors, and descriptions as is imaginable, there does not seem to be one single profile or psychological model. (And, unfortunately, the state-of-the-art in the measurement instruments has not progressed far enough to permit research that can clearly identify and distinguish these factors with reliable precision.)

Rather, what is vital is the blend and fit among the founders. Is there a talented lead entrepreneur whose capabilities are complemented by equally committed partners? Can they work together effectively? Are their collective know-how and capacities the critical ones necessary to seize and execute the opportunity? If the answers are yes to these questions, there is a good fit. Consequently, the chances for success are dramatically improved.

Mental Attitudes and Philosophy

Finally, there are some more elusive, tougher to define issues: personal attitudes and philosophy, values and ethics. While there is limited research that pinpoints the relationship of these to entrepreneurial success, practical experience does. There appear to be some important attitudes and values that more successful entrepreneurs share. They see the cup as half-full rather than half-empty. They ask, "How can I make it work?" rather than dwelling on why it won't work. No doubt about it: the vital importance of developing such attitudes is an essential part of the entrepreneurial mind-set.

AN IDEA IS NOT NECESSARILY AN OPPORTUNITY

If there is any single magnet pulling the entrepreneurial event it is the opportunity. Some recent work by Howard H. Stevenson has lent even further support to this important anchor.[13] The core problem does not seem to be the lack of ideas. Entrepreneurs and innovators bristle with new ideas. What is the problem then? Simply put, unsuccessful entrepreneurs usually equate an idea with an opportunity; successful entrepreneurs know the difference.

Judging by those earlier failure statistics, it is apparent that the vast majority of entrepreneurs run out of money before they find enough customers for their "good ideas." A novel idea is not the same as a sound business concept anchored to a marketable idea. Is there really a business opportunity or just a product or two? Further, the window on the opportunity depends upon movement in technology and competitors' thrusts. The opportunity not only has an elusive life but is a constantly moving target.

The real challenge is recognizing that an opportunity is buried in the often conflicting and contradictory data and signals and the inevitable noise and chaos of the marketplace. And often, a skillful entrepreneur can shape and create an opportunity where others see little or nothing. After all, if it were a simple matter of using available techniques, checklists, and other screening and evaluation methods we might have far more than the 470,000 or so ventures in the United States whose sales exceeded $1 million in 1979 and 1980.[14] Why? Because the literature on techniques for screening and evaluating ideas indicates that over 200 such methods have been developed and documented.

Window on Opportunity

Once an entrepreneur has spotted a viable window on opportunity the more effectively he or she can define the time frame necessary to seize it. Pulling together the essential parts of a business plan can take a few calendar months or longer, writing it down can take a hundred hours or more. So being quite sure, before beginning to prepare a formal plan, that a serious and compelling opportunity exists can save valuable time in the end. Knowing which, among a continual flow of opportunities, to focus on, and which to say no to, is key. Equally important is knowing when one does not need, or cannot afford the time necessary to prepare, a full-blown business plan; there are times when action is more appropriate. The voice of experience says that the most important move is to get to that window before it shuts.

An Opportunity for Whom?

Quite frequently one hears in the venture capital business the old adage, "One man's meat is another man's poison." Different investors will investigate the same venture and come to opposite conclusions. The same is true of opportunities facing entrepreneurs and companies considering internal ventures. For every manager, engineer, sales or technical person that sheds the "bronze" or even "golden" handcuffs to join a new venture—inside or out—there are always several that do not view the opportunity as so compelling. Why is this so?

Sizing Up the Opportunity

Defining a good opportunity is no easy matter. Experience teaches that the sine qua non is this: It must be something that the entrepreneur really wants, and which he or she and the team have the capacity to do—otherwise, why bother? A good opportunity depends on a whole host of considerations. Some of the more important issues to address include:

- What are the principal driving forces and competitive vacuums creating the opportunity? What is behind it? What are the underlying reasons, and can these be articulated? And how long will they last?

- For whom is the opportunity desirable and doable? The personal values and life style of the founders enter heavily into the definition of a good opportunity.

- Is there a real need for the product or service? Have the customers been identified, are they reachable, and are they enthusiastic? In short, is there a market?

- What are the economics of the opportunity? Are the gross margins and profits sufficient and durable enough to provide a forgiving cushion for error during the steep learning curve characteristic of the heat of start-up and necessary for sustained growth? How long will it take to reach a positive cash flow and breakeven? And how much capital will be required to do this?

- Given the alternatives, do the risk-reward trade-offs work in the entrepreneur's favor? What needs to be done to shift the balance in the right direction? The upside may be exceedingly attractive, but is the downside bearable, should that occur, both in terms of dollars and the psychological stress?

Implementation Makes the Difference

Never should a sound business plan be mistaken for a successfully operating venture. Though venture capitalists across the country remark on the high quality of business plans being submitted now, compared to ten years ago, they know that writing the plan is the easy part (although entrepreneurs may not think so when they are doing it).

It is in the implementation where the real work, and challenge, begins. What investors, bankers, customers, and prospective key employees want to know is how to make it work. Having a superbly prepared document may be a necessary, but far from sufficient, condition for launching and building a million dollar plus venture.

THE ENTREPRENEURIAL APPROACH TO RESOURCES

The third element in this model of new venture creation is the resources required to execute the opportunity, both in starting and growing the company. These include the very important concepts of a team and a business plan as key tools and talents for identifying, attracting, and managing necessary resources, both inside and outside the business. If the founder is credible and has articulated the opportunity, the chances of attracting key people and financing soar once the vision is pulled together into a cohesive strategy and implementable business plan.

The Expansion Team

Without a team it is extremely difficult to raise venture capital. It is now well established that most experienced investors consider a proven management team as the most critical success ingredient. But what is not so well known is the importance of a team to the chances of survival and expansion in new ventures, whether or not they are candidates for venture capital. As shown earlier, the exceptions to the failure pattern were most favorable for those firms who managed to grow beyond twenty employees or roughly $1 million in sales. In a large majority of businesses it is quite difficult to do this without a team of at least two key contributors.

One final point about the importance of building a team with a good "fit" should be made. There is growing evidence that having the right partner(s) can be invaluable in coping with the high degree of loneliness and stress associated with entrepreneurship.[15]

The Business Plan and Entry Strategy

The necessity for a business plan is widely accepted today, whether it is to launch an independent venture or one within a larger corporation. How important is a business plan? Very. If it is not done, one misses the chance for a "dry run" and the opportunity to get a handle on the odds for success. Further, without it the chances of raising venture capital or other formal or informal financing, or gaining corporate approval for your project, are nearly impossible.

Minimizing and Controlling Resources

Entrepreneurs seem to have a quite different mentality when it comes to resources, especially in contrast to resource driven, large, established companies. They know that they can improve the chances of attaining their business plan and personal goals without having to own the assets and resources. Their approach often is to push ahead with minimum, rather than maximum resources. This is also a good way to reduce the early risk and exposure, while working through the trial and error process of finding out if there really is an opportunity and whether it is quite certain to succeed. Both independent and corporate entrepreneurs who lead higher potential ventures appear to work this way.

Entrepreneurial middle managers and innovators in large companies, according to Rosabeth Moss Kanter, excel in a similar fashion: Entrepreneurs and entrepreneurial organizations always operate at the edge of their competence, focusing more of their resources and attention on what they do not know . . . than on controlling what they already know."[16]

Early stage entrepreneurs also position themselves so that they can control the resources, which they view as more important than owning the resources. Most large corporations are quite likely to view it just the opposite way.[17] For example, start-up entrepreneurs know they can stretch limited cash and new capital by renting or leasing new equipment, vehicles, or buildings instead of buying them. They will take cuts in pay in order to plow funds into growing the business. They work exceptionally hard in the early stages, often sixty hours or more a week, and thereby minimize the need for additional people resources. And once the business is on a solid footing it often requires two or three new hires to get nearly the same results in the jobs held initially by the founders.

Outsiders: An Often-Neglected Resource

Over a decade ago, an entrepreneur/academic argued persuasively that the careful selection of key outsiders—a banker, a CPA, a lawyer, a board of directors, informal advisors—was key to growing a successful venture.[18] Oddly, this important resource has only recently been given the emphasis it deserves.

Today, the entrepreneur seeking outside advisors, as well as advice on how to use them properly, has many places to look. Major accounting firms prepare free documents on the services they can offer to ambitious start-ups. A pioneering course on "the entrepreneurial lawyer" at George Washington University offers insight and training to attorneys wishing to become actively involved with emerging companies. Several well-circulated articles discuss how to go about choosing a board of directors, formal or informal. The challenge to the entrepreneur is to select, among the many advisors available, the ones necessary to his or her venture at a particular stage in its growth—and to learn how to benefit the most from their counsel.

Risk Capital Financing

What are the most critical ingredients needed to launch a successful new company? When asked, most people include money among the top three items, if not first. No doubt about it, you cannot go far without it. After all, it is the fuel in the gas tank of a car that makes it go. Yet, in this model it is deliberately included *last*. Why? Because an entrepreneur's capacity to raise the money is a result of having the other parts of the act together. The financing does not cause these other things to happen; in most instances it follows good people who have spotted good opportunities and who demonstrate that they clearly grasp the driving forces that will govern success. Today there is no serious shortage of risk capital. Ironically, there continues to be more venture capital available than there are new ventures with all the pieces in place.

The same appears to be true of non-venture capital and internal corporate financing as well. Increasingly sophisticated bankers, financial institutions, internal corporate reviewers, and informal investors back people who have demonstrated that they understand how the driving forces fit together and how to succeed in the proposed business.

TO: ENTREPRENEURS, CORPORATE VENTURE MANAGERS, POLICYMAKERS, AND EDUCATORS

The visible and continuing revival of entrepreneurship and its contagious effects on corporate America are fuelling the search for better answers in the question: How can the type of innovative activity embodied by new venture creation be encouraged and sustained? The process of successful venture creation can be analyzed, up to a point: the make-up of the founding team, the assessment of the opportunity, and the assembling of the resources necessary for implementation. However, the proof of the pudding lies in the synthesis—the fit—that pulls these driving forces together, and no single formula will suffice. After all, the truth is that the entrepreneurial event is a moving target composed of parts that are also in perpetual motion. The challenge to aspiring entrepreneurs, corporate venture managers, policymakers and educators, is to become familiar with the emerging body of knowledge and practice and to choose the right mix, depending on circumstances and aspirations.

Experience, thought, and action inform each other at every stage in the process of venture creation. The process of finding "the fit" resists simple description, but it is easy to label: It is entrepreneurship.

NOTES TO CHAPTER 8

1. "The State of Small Business: A Report of the President to the Congress," (Small Business Administration, March 1983).

2. Dun & Bradstreet, Business Economics Division, "The Business Failure Record, 1980" (New York, 1982).

3. The most complete summary of these is reported by Albert N. Shapero and Joseph Giglierano, "Exits and Entries: A Study in Yellow Pages Journalism," in K. Vesper, ed., *Frontiers of Entrepreneurship Research* (Wellesley, Mass.: Babson Center for Entrepreneurial Studies, 1982), pp. 113–41.

4. See David L. Birch and Susan MacCracken, "Corporation Evolution: A Micro-Based Analysis," prepared for the SBA by MIT, Washington: January 1981; Michael B. Teitz, et al., "Small Business and Employment Growth in California," Working paper No. 348, University of California, Berkeley: March 1981; and Catherine Armington and Majorie Odle, "Small Business—How Many Jobs?" *Brookings Review* (Winter 1982).

5. J. A. Timmons, et al., *New Venture Creation* (Homewood, Ill.: Richard D. Irwin, 1977), pp. 10-11.

6. J. A. Timmons and D. E. Gumpert, "Discard Many Old Rules for Raising Venture Capital," *Harvard Business Review* (Jan.-Feb. 1982).

7. J. A. Timmons, N. D. Fast, S. E. Pratt, and W. D. Bygrace, "Venture Capital Investing in Highly Innovative Technological Ventures," *Venture Economics* (March 1984).

8. See Robert Ronstadt's and Howard Stevenson's studies reported in J. A. Hornaday, J. Timmons, and K. H. Vesper, eds., *Frontiers of Entrepreneurship Research* (Wellesley, Mass.: Babson Center for Entrepreneurial Studies, 1983).

9. Arnold Cooper and William Dunkelberg, "A New Look at Business Entry," (San Mateo, Calif.: National Federation of Independent Business, 1984).

10. Karl H. Vesper, "New Venture Ideas: Don't Overlook the Experience Factor," *Harvard Business Review*, reprinted in *Growing Concerns* (New York: John Wiley & Sons, 1984), pp. 28-35.

11. Robert H. Brockhaus, "The Psychology of the Entrepreneur," chapter 3 in C. A. Kent, D. L. Sexton, and K. Vesper, eds., *Encyclopedia of Entrepreneurship* (Englewood Cliffs, N. J.: Prentice-Hall, 1982), pp. 50-55 provides a good summary of some of these studies.

12. J. A. Timmons, "Careful Self-Analysis and Team Assessment Can Aid Entrepreneurs," appeared in D. E. Gumpert, ed., *Growing Concerns* Section under "Building and Growing the Smaller Business" of the *Harvard Business Review* (New York: John Wiley & Sons, 1984), pp. 43-52.

13. See his "Paradigm" paper in the proceedings from the 75th Anniversary Symposium on Entrepreneurship, July 1983 (Boston: Harvard Business School, 1984).

14. This includes about 33,000 proprietorships and 37,000 partnerships in 1980, and just under 400,000 corporations in 1979, out of a total of nearly 17 million businesses, according to *The State of Small Business 1982*, SBA, Washington, D.C., 1983, pp. 199–200.

15. David Boyd and David E. Gumpert, "Stress, Loneliness and The Entrepreneur," in J. Hornaday, F. Tarpley, J. Timmons, and K. Vesper, eds., *Frontiers of Entrepreneurship Research* (Wellesley, Mass.: Babson Center for Entrepreneurial Studies, 1984).

16. See R. M. Kanter, *The Change Masters* (New York: Simon & Schuster, 1983), pp. 27–28.

17. This important notion is well developed by Howard H. Stevenson of Harvard in his "Paradigm" paper (note 15).

18. Patrick R. Liles (Ph.D. dissertation, Harvard Business School, 1970).

9 PROGRESS IN RESEARCH ON CORPORATE VENTURING

Ian C. MacMillan

The field of enquiry into corporate venturing has developed a long way since the first publications in the mid-1960s. Research on the phenomenon of corporate venturing has evolved from single-sample case studies to the stage where in some cases researchers were able to pursue causality—via formal hypotheses testing in rich longitudinal studies. Comparisons of research results, however, are impossible if there is lack of agreement on fundamental definitions. In the area of corporate venturing, there currently appear to be two major problems of definition: definition of scope (What is corporate venturing?) and definition of success (When do ventures succeed or fail?).

PROBLEMS OF DEFINITION OF SCOPE

There appear to be several ways in which comparison of any research results on corporate venturing are confounded by problems of definition of scope. The first has to do with delineating the stage in the innovation process that venturing actually takes place. When does new product development stop, and where does venturing start? Clearly product line extensions are not ventures, but what about the introduction of new products? Or does the study of corporate venturing focus only on the creation (and performance) of a separate department or division? Alternately, is it only corporate venturing if the activity will take the firm into entirely new businesses?

To illustrate the problems of scope definition let us look at Vesper's categorization of ventures. In his pilot study, Vesper uses three dimensions to classify corporate entrepreneurship activities:

1. The extent to which the activity is a strategic departure from the firm's current activity,
2. The extent to which the activity is the result of bottom-up versus top-down initiatives,
3. The extent to which the activity is assigned to an autonomous unit.[1]

In his analysis of seventy-seven ventures, Vesper found every combination of each of these dimensions. Clearly there are many dimensions to the phenomenon. In their study, MacMillan and George attempted to delineate a scale of venturing, in which each increment indicated an additional major increment in difficulty.[2] This is depicted in Table 9-1 and further serves to show how wide the ranges of activities are that could be classed as venturing.

The definition problem is compounded by another facet of scope—the degree to which the venturing is done by the firm as opposed to other entities. Is a joint venture venturing, or is the definition con-

Table 9-1. Levels of Corporate Ventures.

Level 1: New enhancements to current products/services (not really venturing—lowest point on scale).

Level 2: New products/services that could be sold to current customers/markets within two years.

Level 3: Existing products/services that could be sold to new customer/markets within two years.

Level 4: New product or service concepts that can be sold to current markets but will take more than two years to reach commercialization stage.

Level 5: New product/services that are really unfamiliar to the firm but are already being produced and sold to unfamiliar markets by other firms.

Level 6: Product/services concepts that do not exist today but which could be developed to replace current products/services in current markets or create entirely new markets.

fined only to corporate start-ups? What percentage of the start-up activity can be done by other firms to disqualify the activity as a start-up? Is an acquisition a venture? What about acquiring a patent and starting from there—how early in the life cycle of the acquisition is the dividing line between an acquisition that qualifies as a corporate venture and one that does not?

These appear to be major definitional problems that will plague researchers if they seek comparability of results across studies. They even can create problems of comparability of results *within* studies.

PROBLEMS OF DEFINITION OF SUCCESS AND FAILURE

Another definitional problem that is sure to contribute to controversy is the issue of how and when to define success and failure. Is a venture a failure if it is killed or only if it is not killed "in time"? If having to kill a venture indeed signals failure, during what stage of the process must it be killed to be a failure? Even if it is not a failure, when is it a success? When it is making profits? or positive cash flow? or meeting targets? or merely making revenues? Maidique and Zirger point out in their study time and again that a prior venture failure sows the seeds of a later spectacular success.[3] So do we define success only in monetary terms? Until we can find ways of tying down the definitions of success and failure, researchers will continue to argue past one another on issues of what makes ventures succeed.

The most integrative underlying theme for discussing research is the theme of what helps or hinders the success of corporate venturing. The major factors relating to the success and failure of ventures appear to be: culture, climate, and support; venture mission, strategy, and environment; structure/design of venture activity; staffing and reward systems for venture management; and planning, monitoring, and evaluation of results.

CULTURE, CLIMATE, AND CORPORATE SUPPORT

Schon was one of the first researchers to argue explicitly that new venturing activity is up against a significant and a very natural resistance in existing organizations.[4] The fact of the matter is that the organization *must* build a high commitment to existing products and technologies or it would be "perpetually and fruitlessly shifting gears." He points out that radical change creates radical disruption. This is the anathema of the bureaucracy, which acts to protect and reestablish the status quo, stifling venturing effort.

In her rich study, Kanter points out another reason why modern organizations tend to stifle venture activity—the large modern organization has erected huge barriers to the exercise of entrepreneurial initiative by overspecialization and compartmentalization of jobs, administered by an onerous hierarchy that confines lower level members to very narrow, specified activities.[5]

MacMillan, Block, and Subba Narasimha find that among the most intractable obstacles to success reported by their sample of corporate ventures were lack of support, lack of commitment by senior management, lack of mission, internal competition for resources, lack of fit with corporate strategy, and sheer lack of entrepreneurial talent in the firm.[6] Not only were these major obstacles, but they were ones that firms do not seem to be able to improve on, even with repeated experience.

In the light of these findings, researchers have made it clear that corporate venturing success is highly dependent on the creation of a supportive entrepreneurial culture in the corporation. In the literature, there appear to be three major components to this: top management commitment, top management support, and top management style.

Top Management Commitment

Fast and Pratt ascribe lack of top management commitment as a major contribution to the failure of dozens of attempts at corporate venturing in the 1970s.[7] Regardless of the size or stage of evolution of the firm, venturing will probably fail if top management is not committed to change. Indeed, the only thing that changes with size is the nature of the entrepreneurial network linking top management to the venture managers. Quinn and Mueller suggest that it goes beyond mere statement of commitment—that it takes tough minded and constant attention to fostering change in the organization to prevent it from becoming comfortable with the status quo.[8] What is also required is long-run persistence; creating an entrepreneurial environment is not a short-term project. Unless top management is prepared to demonstrate this commitment by paying significantly more than pro rata attention to venturing activity, such activity should not even be started since it only raises aspirations and precipitates later frustration and disruption.

Top Management Support

To reinforce management commitment there is a need for top management support. In his comprehensive study, Fast identified that support for venturing activity can be given in a variety of important ways: in budget allocations (funds and staff); in indirect budget allocations (making other departments commit resources); in supporting venture management's proposals; and in siding with venture management when arbitrating conflicts.[9] Formal CEO recognition of the entrepreneur could also be added to this list.

Fast goes on to suggest that such support is a delicate issue. Too much support alienates the venture managers from the rest of the organization and exposes them politically.

On the other hand, Fast and Pratt insist on a long-term commitment of *funds* (ten to twelve years). They also suggest that the firm commit up front to providing additional funding on a timed basis, so that as ventures pass each critical milestone they need not have to fight, or wait, for the next budget approval. They argue that this staggered commitment of funding emulates the procedure used by venture capitalists, who are expert in supporting venturing activities and have learned that this is the best way to handle the funding issue.

Others argue that another, critical way of providing support is to assure that potential ventures have access to a variety of funding channels rather than a single formal route to necessary funds.

Top Management Style

According to researchers the most critical issue in fostering an entrepreneurial culture lies in the management style. Kanter's research results indicate that internal entrepreneurship cannot thrive in the absence of a flexible and collaborative style. Maidique and Hayes's multicase study suggests that this open, collaborative climate be accompanied by a management style that encourages rapid attacking of problems, is more tolerant of failure, has high levels of communication across *and* between levels, provides individual workers time to pursue their own ideas, and encourages hands-on management.[10]

To this Roberts would add:

- Create an environment where the burden of proof lies on the people who want to stop a new idea.

- Do not discourage competition for new product development between divisions; some duplication of effort is better than complacency.[11]

MISSION, STRATEGY, AND ENVIRONMENT

By far the greatest body of research literature focuses on strategy and environment issues, and their implications for venture selection and success. For convenience one can divide this literature into five classes: mission, environmental factors, product/market strategy, entry strategy, and alternatives to full-scale corporate venturing.

Mission of Venturing Activity

One of the major obstacles to venturing success appears to be lack of clear mission on the part of the corporation encouraging the venture. In deciding this mission, the key question is what the purpose is of the venturing activity. Vesper suggests that for a corporation this may go beyond a simple need for increased profits—that the firm may decide to venture in order to participate in, or exploit, new technologies or to diversify away from traditional markets.[12] In 1973, Vesper and Holmdahl surveyed companies in order to determine the purpose of their venturing activity and found a variety of reasons, the most common of which were diversification, exploitation of new developments, creation of an entrepreneurial climate in the rest of the firm, retention of talented people, and utilization of surplus capacity.[13]

The problem of mission—what should be the scope and reach of new venturing activity—is a knotty one. Hill and Hlavacek found in their 1972 study that a broad mission was an important correlation of venturing success for new venture teams.[14] Yet by 1977, Dunn found that the failed venture divisions in his study had all been given very broad missions.[15]

Fast's research suggested that *relatedness* to the firm's current activities was important in defining mission. The further away from base, the more likely it was that the firm would run into problems. He suggested that the main reasons for this are that the more related activities benefit from three major advantages: maximal skills transfer is possible, the new activity can be implemented with small incremental cost, and high levels of commitment from management are secured with minimal effort.

However, the closer the venture is to base, the more likely it is to be seen as infringing on the activities and prerogatives of the existing business. It seems that the challenge lies in finding the correct balance between purpose of corporate venturing in the first place and the cost/benefit trade-off of venturing too near or too far from "home."

Environmental Factors

The major work that has been done in the area of assessing the effect of environment on subsequent venture performance has been done for new product development. Through a number of studies, it has been possible to place environmental characteristics into the two following classes.[16]

Inhibiting environmental conditions were:

- Very competitive, dynamic markets,
- Markets with rapid rates of new product introduction,
- Markets in which there are a high proportion of satisfied customers,
- Highly fragmented markets,
- Industries with a recent major technological innovation.

Facilitating environmental conditions were:

- High market growth rates,

- Customers who knew, and interacted intensively with, the parent firm,
- Markets that are rich in technological opportunities,
- Markets in which there are dominant competitors,
- Markets where customers initiated the new product idea.

One of the most important market characteristics, which appear to permeate all the studies, is the degree to which the venture satisfies a market's user need. Von Hippel found two successes out of three satisfied a market need, while six failures out of six attempted to "sell" a technical capability.[17] Maidique and Zirger point out that a particularly beneficial combination for venturing is a market where the customer base is well known, interaction between the firm and customer is intense, and there is a real market need—so that the emerging venture can create a product or service where benefit to cost is clearly identifiable to both venturers and their customers. Von Hippel found that the best of all worlds occurs when the user need has high proximity to the firm's technological strengths.

Obviously, selection of the most appropriate market environment in which to venture is a major strategic choice. However, there are other strategic issues that have been identified with successful ventures that have to do with selection of product strategies, discussed next.

Product/Market Strategy

Successful ventures, when compared to failing attempts, had the following differences:

- Product uniqueness and superiority,
- Superior marketing research,
- Superior marketing proficiency (i.e., experience and skill at marketing to customer),
- Superior technical proficiency (i.e., skill and experience in technology and production),
- Greater experience with the customer base,
- Superior marketing skills, particularly sales force and advertising strength,

- Strong marketing communication skills,
- More effort at user education.

In addition, it appears that high R&D expenses are positively correlated with new product sales, but with highly diminishing marginal returns.

Entry Strategy

Having decided on the strategy, the next issue is *how* to enter. The first thorough longitudinal study of corporate venturing entry strategies was conducted by Biggadike.[18] His results indicated that aggressive scale of entry was highly correlated with superior returns on investment. This was supplemented by the results of Hobson and Morrison, who showed that aggressive marketing moves were correlated with success in market share gain.[19]

It appears that scale of entry may end up as a self-fulfilling prophecy, at least for the type of large manufacturing firm represented in the PIMS start-up data base from which these studies were drawn. As a result of aggressive share objectives, companies select marketing and investment strategies that allow them to capture the share they seek and, having captured large share, also capture economies of scope and scale that makes them more profitable than more timid market entrants.[20]

There is another entry issue reported in the literature, and that is whether success is correlated with early entry into markets. Here the results are ambiguous.

Alternatives to Full-Scale Corporate Start-ups

There is another major strategic option for corporate venturing: the *mode* of venturing.

Roberts identifies a range of possible alternatives to full-scale corporate start-up: starting with internal ventures, through joint ventures, through participation in venture capital markets. He suggests that the firm is ill advised to attempt venturing in areas where there is a mismatch between the prerequisites for competing and the firm's skills and experience. Fast goes further and suggests that inexperienced firms should start off by participating in venture capital funds to learn and observe venturing before starting to venture themselves.[21]

MacMillan et al. found that every obstacle to successful corporate start-up was rated *less* of an obstacle for joint venturing. This is not to say that joint ventures do not have other obstacles, but it does suggest that organizations with little experience in venturing could consider building up their venturing capabilities by starting with modest scale joint venturing efforts and using the experience benefits to develop proficiency at corporate start-ups. That experience benefits are in fact achievable is suggested by their results, which found a significant improvement in coping with most venturing obstacles, but generally only after the *third* attempt at venturing. This reinforces the advisability of using joint venturing to build venturing experience.[22]

Another major alternative to corporate start-ups is via acquisition. There seems to be a definite difference in performance between independent, venture capital backed start-ups and data for corporate start-ups. On average, the independents reach profitability twice as fast and end up twice as profitable.

So if effectiveness at venturing is more desirable than protection of pride, full-scale corporate start-ups may not be the most effective route, particularly if the purpose of venturing is to diversify or gain access to new technologies/markets. Furthermore, it is important to note that pursuing corporate start-ups does not preclude acquisitions and vice versa. In fact, the more venturesome firms seem inclined to do more of both than the less venturesome ones.

As far as strategy is concerned, it appears that the path to success is indicated by several major guidelines:

- Selection of a growing market in which the customer base is well known,
- Creation of a superior or unique product or service,
- Satisfying a real user need,
- Drawing from the firm's strengths in technology,
- Supporting the product with superior marketing,
- Entry on a realistic but aggressive scale.

STRUCTURE AND DESIGN
OF VENTURING EFFORT

The issue of how to structure for successful corporate venturing has received widespread attention in the literature. Perhaps the best way to put this issue in perspective is to review the highlights of the corporate venturing process as espoused in a masterful longitudinal study by Burgelman.[23] In his study, he identified several major venturing process functions that are conducted by critical players at different levels of the organization. The failure of these processes could lead to total failure of the venturing process.

Burgelman identifies three levels in the venturing hierarchy: the venture manager, the venture division management, and the top management.

The critical functions of the venture manager are:

- *Linking:* identifying a user need in the market and linking it with the necessary internal skills and capabilities to produce a viable product.

- *Product championing:* developing sufficient momentum and enthusiasm in the firm to give the new idea sufficient impetus so that technical and marketing development is started; also, creating a *market* interest in the idea.

- *Strategic forcing:* concentrating intense effort on penetrating the market as rapidly as possible to build the momentum necessary to break through the attention barrier of the organization and cause senior levels in the organization to take an interest. This gives the venture access to needed resources and also allows it to acquire significant assets (which then commits the organization to the venture).

- *Strategic neglect:* Unfortunately a common byproduct of strategic forcing is that the venture manager neglects the administrative duties and is sometimes replaced for internal mismanagement.

The critical functions of the *venture division management* are:

- *Strategic building:* the articulation of a master strategy for the broader field of new business development that has been opened up by the venture manager through the agglomeration of additional new businesses with the venture. This makes the venture increasingly important to the organization as a whole.

- *Organization championing:* maintaining contact with top management, keeping them informed and enthusiastic about the emerging area of opportunity, and communicating where the current development is leading and why it is important for the overall corporation.

- *Delineating:* delineating in clear and organizationally attractive terms the context and potential of new *fields* of opportunity that slowly emerge from the *agglomerated* successes of individual ventures. In other words, it is an important role for venture management to show the organization how to see beyond the individual ventures (the trees) to a whole new field of organizationally feasible opportunities (the woods).

The *corporate management* roles consisted of:

- *Rationalizing:* deciding whether or not the successful new initiatives constitute an organizationably acceptable activity and, if so, building it into the organizational strategy or rejecting it. By their conferring legitimacy to the activity, the venture gains political clout and can start to command more rapid access to resources.

- *Building structural context:* defining the autonomy and status of the new venture division, the definition of position and responsibility and authority of its members, and the establishment of criteria for measuring and evaluating the venture managers, and the venture management division as a whole.

In this study of one hundred new product developments, Souder found that four out of six major characteristics associated with success had to do with "lubricating" the processes Burgelman identified: (1) the individual responsible for carrying out the venture had a clear mandate; (2) these individuals received the support and sponsorship from members higher in the organization; (3) the venture managers were accorded enough discretion to act fast and flexibly; and (4) the venture was located at the correct location in the firm—high enough for the venture managers to be able to command the attention from functional areas when they need it, yet low enough to protect it from being "helped to death" by senior management.[24] These results reflect all the needs in Burgelman's model.

It becomes clear from Burgelman's study that in reality senior management can only play a limited positive role in the actual discovery and creation of new business opportunities, but can do much to help—*and a great deal more to hinder*—such activity by the structural context it creates.

Block goes further.[25] He suggests that there are two distinct and equally important management challenges that *must* be resolved if venturing is to succeed. The first is the management of the ventures per se, which is obvious. The second is management of entrepreneurship—a critical top management function of creating the right context, structure, and systems to foster entrepreneurship. His position strongly supports Burgelman's process model.

What also seems clear from Burgelman's study is that the processes of organizational championing and product championing are critical. This has been reinforced in many other studies for different types of organizations, for different sizes of organizations, and for different stages of evolution of organizations.

As far as venturing success is concerned, two critical organizational issues are degree of separation from the rest of the firm and degree of autonomy.

Separate Venture Business Unit or Not?

Researchers are unanimous that a high degree of autonomy be accorded to those charged with venturing. Shapero is a particularly strong proponent of autonomy and cites situations where increased autonomy dramatically increased performance of ventures.[26] Ten out of eleven mediocre corporate ventures grew dramatically after they were spun off from the main body of the firm to become autonomous business units, and fifteen out of seventeen ventures that were started as independent business unit exceeded management expectations.

Others have been strongly in favor of multidisciplinary venture teams, recruited from the divisions of the business, to take charge of the venture as an autonomous mini-business. However, on the macro level, Hill and Hlavacek lean towards the creation of a new venture division at the same level as other divisions. Roberts argues that there should be a new product development department associated with each of a large number of relatively small divisions: (1) because corporate entrepreneurship and venturesome activity is inhibited by large size; and (2) because such a structure promotes more venturing in the whole organization.

There may be another more fundamental reason than organizational flexibility that makes it important for firms seeking a venturesome environment to have small autonomous divisions. The more divisions there are, the more "boundaries" there are and therefore the more people in the firm there are to fulfill the crucial boundary spanning and gate keeping roles that Tushman found as significant correlates of innovativeness in firms.[27]

As for the design of the venture team, Hill and Hlavacek cited several characteristics from their study of one hundred venture teams that may be relevant. They found that venture teams were separated from the operating organization, multidisciplinary, were truly teams in the sense that there was diffuse authority, were given a broad mission, had direct access to senior management, and were not subjected to tightly defined time deadlines.

Interestingly, Dunn's study five years later found that the characteristics of ten failed venture teams were that their mission was too broad, too few constraints were placed on their activities, they received too much functional autonomy, expectations of venture managers were raised too high, venture groups were too expensive (they developed expensive methods of operating and accumulated large multidisciplinary staffs), and groups were not put under enough pressure to produce, so productivity was low.

It is clear that many of these problems could have been precipitated by firms doing too much of a good thing as far as autonomy is concerned. (It may also be a warning to researchers to seek for comparisons between good and poor performers, rather than study only the attributes of good performers.)

Dunn's results show some of the problems that can be created by creating too much autonomy and suggest that senior management cannot abdicate responsibility but has to monitor the venturing activity more closely. Whether this can be done without interfering in the process is an issue discussed below.

Other serious byproducts of creating a highly visible, elite, and autonomous venture group is the organization disruption it creates, particularly to those who remain behind in the traditional business, and the problem of "digesting" the new venture once it has reached a size where it makes sense to incorporate it into the ongoing business.

Finally there are the disturbing results of Hisrich and Peters, who found no significant difference in sales from new products of firms with new business venture units and firms without.[28]

PLANNING, MONITORING, AND EVALUATION OF VENTURES

Block identifies five major concepts that shape the venturing process in an organization: dramatically higher uncertainty than in the ongoing business; dramatically higher failure rates than in the ongoing business; increased need for commitment from both senior and venture managers to foster and support the embryonic ventures; and entrepreneurial talent to take on these greater risks. As a result, the required planning, control, and evaluation process are dramatically different from the ones used in the conventional business. In this section the literature that addresses these differences is reviewed.

It is the lack of corporate knowledge upon which to anchor the plan that is the critical difference between conventional planning and planning for new ventures—and hence lies at the heart of the monitoring and control of new ventures. The conventional business has a fairly good idea of market conditions, operating procedures, and competitive actions on which to base its plan, and yet firms *still* have difficulty in meeting plan.

So in the face of the almost complete ignorance of market and production conditions that the venturing firm faces, it is absurd to expect the venture manager to match accomplishments with a set of prearranged deadlines. In the corporate world, the extent to which this is accepted varies. Vesper and Holmdahl found in their survey that the following control systems were in effect for corporate venturers:

- Regular meetings to discuss management of the venture: 43 percent,
- Regular meetings to review budget: 21 percent,
- No restraints except around budget review: 18 percent,
- Complete freedom to control resources: 18 percent.

Clearly, it is necessary to strike a balance between imposing some fiscal and management discipline, and the ludicrousness of forcing venture managers to produce blindly according to a set of projections made in ignorance. The solution to this problem lies in how the *independent* entrepreneur is handled by the banks and venture capitalists. For instance, Shapero has suggested that monitoring and control of the venture be handled in much the same way as the banker handles the small business entrepreneur. The bank does not attempt to get involved in the day-to-day operation of the business but controls by imposing key performance goals and then setting a limited number of financial controls with rather broad boundaries on the actions the business can take. The idea is that as long as the entrepreneurs operate within these constraints, they are free to act as they please, but once these limits are exceeded a meeting with the banker is required.

Quinn suggests something similar.[29] His position is that the resource rationing approach, which is the basis of conventional planning, be replaced by an opportunity-seeking approach for venture planning. He eschews detailed control too soon and argues that evaluation be conducted in much the same way as the venture capital community would approach the problem: "first evaluate the problem in conceptual terms only, using very broad figures, then through careful appraisal of the team making the proposal; and finally by the company's capacity to support the concept if it is successful. Only if the concept passes muster as a high potential idea would more detailed analysis be used." He suggests that the control system be adjusted to measure performance along "mission lines." The overall mission of each venture is defined in terms of how it will contribute to the firm's strategy—and thus the venture's time horizon, its payout, its risk category, the market and product area it will be required to support, and other criteria will be set in directions appropriate to the specific strategy. The point Quinn makes is that the control system should be built around the intended role of the venture in the firm's portfolio of activities, not just its short-term profitability.

Fast takes a somewhat different but complementary approach. He points out that "one of the major difficulties of venturing within a large corporation is the setting of realistic budgets and benchmarks against which performance can be measured. An entrepreneur who starts a venture and receives venture capital funding is aware that he must perform credibly to make his company attractive for the next round of financing. Consequently, performing exactly as planned is not critical in his case. In the corporate environment, however, the venture's performance is typically evaluated by how closely it adheres to a plan. As a result, there is a much greater emphasis on doing what was promised rather than opportunistically adapting and responding to the unforeseen.

Block proposed this as a critical issue in his analysis of the planning problems of corporate ventures. He strongly recommended that planning be structured around the achievement of *event milestones* rather than dates. He also acknowledged that there are critical linkages between activities—that some activities cannot be started (delivery of orders) before others are completed (plant completed)—so that there is a time dimension to venture planning, but that this is time dimension imposed by linkages between events rather than performance to specific dates. In his final analysis, he recommends that the only dates that be imposed be ones that are imposed by event linkages or by *externally imposed* deadlines (like competitive actions or agreements with customers, distributors, or suppliers). Venture management should then be evaluated on their ability to perform or adapt, as the case may be, as each milestone *event* is achieved rather than enforcing adherence to a projection in a plan based on high uncertainty.

There is one other element to the plan execution process that is very significant for ventures: the learning opportunity. In a profound and highly insightful longitudinal follow-up of their original study, Maidique and Zirger have identified a critical benefit of the venturing process that has only been recognized implicitly in other research so far.[30] This is the learning benefit. They suggest that the venturing process is characterized by three highly beneficial learning processes that take place as the venture progresses:

- *Customers and distributors "learn by using"*—i.e., only by using the product do they begin to understand its benefits and limitations, and thus does the venturing firm learn what the real needs are.

- *The firm "learns by doing"*—i.e., only by making the product and delivering it to the market does the firm learn the technical and marketing challenges it faces.

- *The firm "learns by failing"*—i.e., even with failure so much can be learned that in this failure the seeds of future successes can be sown.

The implications of this are obvious. Block and MacMillan argue that a key component of the planning process, and the subsequent evaluations of performance, be to set learning objectives for each milestone so that, as each milestone is reached, new information is deliberately secured and analyzed.[31] The decision to proceed to each step is taken on the basis of ever harder information—the plan starts off on the basis of assumptions and is completed or aborted or redirected on the basis of facts learned, as deliberate learning objectives, set for each milestone in the plan. Management is then evaluated not on how they conformed to plan but on how they replanned in the light of unfolding information.

Of particular importance in planning is the need for rapidly developing an understanding of the ill-defined market and vaguely determined market needs. In study after study, this has been cited as a critical challenge. Therefore, one would expect that a significant proportion of the early milestones should revolve around flushing out market information.

In addition to insuring that venture managers are not bound to ill-advised attempts to meet unrealistic projections, milestone planning has one other advantage. At each milestone a decision point is reached; in the next step of the venture may be approved, accelerated, slowed down, aborted, or redirected based on a realistic assessment of the new information that has been obtained since the last milestone.

STAFFING AND REWARDING VENTURE ACTIVITY

Many authors and researchers have described the desirable characteristics of the venture manager, or product champion, who will be responsible for the change. By way of introducing the topic it is interesting to specify what researchers say that are *not.*

Block suggests that successful corporate venturers are:

- Not gamblers (they take calculated risks);

- Not necessarily successful managers of existing divisions; and
- Not necessarily the idea generators (in fact, the generators of the idea are often poorly qualified to implement it).

Von Hippel in his study found that the successful venturers were not necessarily highly dedicated to the venture, nor did they see their future as lying with the growth of the venture. Rather they saw the venture as a project that was part of a career in the company. He also found that successful venturers were not from high positions. In fact, he found a significant negative correlation between success and size of the venture management's budget and staff before taking on the venture. He suggests that senior, high position managers feel disquieted and never become comfortable with running a riskier job, with less resources and staff than they are used to. Interestingly he cites similar results for R&D managers.

When it comes to identifying characteristics of successful internal venturers, several important and recurring themes emerge. First, there is unanimity among all researchers that team building and persuasive skills are vital. As Kanter points out, entrepreneurs cannot afford to be "lone rangers" in the corporate environment because there is just not the resource support. They must be able to go beyond the limits of their authority to secure support. Souder suggests that they have a reputation for "spreading credit around."

Second, there is unanimity regarding the need for political sensitivity and political skills. Souder's results suggest a need to be well-known in the firm and a skill at forging alliances with other members of the firm, yet at the same time avoiding the reputation as an empire builder. Kanter and Burgelman both stress the need for entrepreneurs to be able to build coalitions at both their levels and levels above them, without angering superiors. Fast suggests that the individual should have worked in several divisions so that there is an established contact and influence network. Others have found a high correlation between venture failures and the fact that the manager was an outsider who was brought in to run the venture but did not have the connections.

This raises a dilemma for the firm that is new to venturing. If outsiders are likely to fail, how do we find suitable insiders? Block suggests seeking out young managers who have demonstrated some skill at accomplishing a purpose under uncertain conditions. For example, sales people who have developed new territories, engineers who have created and built new plants from pilots and so on could be developed by assigning them to more challenging, uncertain tasks.

There is another major dilemma with these corporate entrepreneurs. Due to their attention to critical championing activities, the entrepreneurs may end up having to be replaced because of internal mismanagement; they become a sacrifice to their own success. Block suggests that this can constructively be handled by recycling—that is by creating for these managers a career as venture starters.

Reward Systems for Venture Managers

Given the incentives and career dangers for the venture manager in taking on the task, the question now becomes: How shall venture managers be rewarded? Though little research has been done on the subject, common sentiment suggests that venture managers should be richly rewarded for all the uncertainty and career danger they expose themselves to in starting a venture. However, the results of the survey by Vesper and Holmdahl indicate that management does not share this sentiment. In their survey, Vesper and Holmdahl found that 43 percent of the companies give no special compensation to venture managers, 34 percent gave some cash bonus, and only 27 percent gave stock options. Current work by Ornati and Block would seem to indicate that not much has changed in twelve years since the above figures were about the same in 1984.[32]

Researchers, however, still suggest that special reward structures be created to increase the venturers personal stake in the venture or, by offering a variable compensation for performance, to increase the level of commitment to the ventures success. There is little hard evidence to indicate one way or another whether special reward systems make a difference. Perhaps many venture managers see the venture as yet another challenging project in their corporate career, or the greatest reward of all is to be allowed to try again, on another venture. Whatever the reason, it is clear that research in the area of effectiveness of reward systems for corporate venturing is a major hole in our knowledge of corporate venturing.

Research in the area of corporate venturing has progressed considerably, particularly since about 1975. There is a growing, increasingly rich body of descriptive research but considerably less research that has systematically explained causal linkages between corporate venturing variables and performance. Though expensive and time consuming, the greatest potential lies in multicase, longitudinal studies, particularly if we wish to tease out causal linkages between venture variables and venture performance.

NOTES TO CHAPTER 9

1. K. H. Vesper, "Three Faces of Corporate Entrepreneurship: A Pilot Study," in J. Hornaday, F. Tarpley, J. Timmons, and K. Vesper, eds., *Frontiers of Entrepreneurship Research* (Wellesley, Mass.: Babson Center for Entrepreneurial Studies, 1984), pp. 294–320.

2. I. C. MacMillan and R. George, "Corporate Venturing: Challenges for Senior Managers." *Journal of Business Strategy* 5:3 (Winter 1985): 34–44.

3. M. A. Maidique and B. J. Zirger, "The Stanford Innovation Project, Phase I: A Study of Success and Failure in High Technology Innovation." *IEEE Transactions on Engineering Management* EM–31: 4 (November 1984): 192–203.

4. D. A. Schon, "The Fear of Innovation." *International Science and Technology* 14 (November 1966): 70–78.

5. R. M. Kanter, *The Change Masters* (New York: Simon & Schuster, 1983).

6. I. C. MacMillan, Z. Block, and P. N. Subba Narasimha, "Obstacles and Experience in Corporate Venturing," in J. Hornaday, F. Tarpley, J. Timmons, and K. Vesper, eds., *Frontiers of Entrepreneurship Research* (Babson College, 1984), pp. 341–63.

7. N. D. Fast and S. E. Pratt, "Individual Entrepreneurship and the Large Corporation," in K. Vesper, ed., *Frontiers of Entrepreneurship Research* (Wellesley, Mass.: Babson Center for Entrepreneurial Studies, 1981), pp. 443–450.

8. J. B. Quinn and J. A. Mueller, "Transferring Research Results to Operations," *Harvard Business Review* (January-February 1963): 49–66.

9. N. D. Fast, "The Future of Industrial New Venture Departments," *Industrial Marketing Management* 8 (1979): 264–73.

10. M. A. Maidique and R. H. Hayes, "The Art of High-Technology Management," *Sloan Management Review* (Winter 1984): 17–31.

11. E. B. Roberts, "New Ventures for Corporate Growth," *Harvard Business Review* (July-August 1980): 134–42.

12. K. H. Vesper, "Ten Questions for Corporate Venture Climate Analysis." *Working Paper: University of Washington*, February 1984.

13. K. H. Vesper and T. G. Holmdahl, "How Venture Management Fares in Innovative Companies," *Research Management* (May 1973): 30–32.

14.   R. M. Hill and J. D. Hlavacek, "The Venture Team: A New Concept in Marketing Organization," *Journal of Marketing* 36 (July 1972): 44–50.

15.   D. T. Dunn, "The Rise and Fall of Ten New Venture Groups," *Business Horizons* (October 1977): 32–41.

16.   R. G. Cooper, "The Dimensions of Industrial New Product Success and Failure," *Journal of Marketing* 43 (Summer 1979): 93–103; R. Rothwell, "Factors for Success in Industrial Innovations," in *Project SAPPHO—A Comparative Study of Successes and Failures in Industrial Innovation* (Brighton, Sussex: SPRU, 1972); and R. Rothwell, C. Freeman, A. Horsley, V.T.P. Jervis, A. B. Robertson, and J. Townsend, "SAPPHO Updated—Project SAPPHO Phase II." *Research Policy* 3 (1974): 258–91.

17.   E. Von Hippel, "Successful Industrial Products from Customer Ideas," *Journal of Marketing* (January 1978): 39–49.

18.   R. Biggadike, "The Risky Business of Diversification," *Harvard Business Review* (May-June 1979): 103–11.

19.   E. L. Hobson and R. M. Morrison, "How do Corporate Start-up Ventures Fare?" in J. Hornaday, J. Timmons, and K. Vesper, eds., *Frontiers of Entrepreneurship Research* (Wellesley, Mass.: Babson Center for Entrepreneurial Studies, 1983), pp. 390–410.

20.   I. C. MacMillan and D. L. Day, "Having Your Cake and Eating It: Some Indications of the Dynamics of Corporate Venturing in the Manufacturing Sector," *Working Paper: New York University Center for Entrepreneurial Studies*, January 1985.

21.   N. D. Fast, "Pitfalls of Corporate Venturing," *Research Management* (March 1981): 21–24; Roberts, "New Ventures for Corporate Growth."

22.   Macmillan, Block, and Narasimha, "Obstacles and Experience in Corporate Venturing."

23.   R. A. Burgelman, "A Process Model of Internal Corporate Venturing in the Major Diversified Firm," *Administrative Science Quarterly* 28 (1983): 223–44; and "Corporate Entrepreneurship and Strategic Management: Insights from a Process Study," *Management Science* 29: 12 (December 1983): 1349–64; "Managing the New Venture Division: Research Findings and Implications for Strategic Management," *Strategic Management Journal* 6: 1 (January-March 1985): 39–54.

24.   W. E. Souder, "Encouraging Entrepreneurship in the Large Corporations," *Research Management* (May 1981): 18–22.

25.   Z. Block, "Concepts for Corporate Entrepreneurs." *Proceedings of the Texas A & M Business Forum*, January 1985.

26.   A. Shapero, "Intracorporate Entrepreneurship: A Clash of Cultures." *Working Paper: Ohio State University*, 1984.

27.   M. L. Tushman, "Special Boundary Roles in the Innovation Process," *Administrative Science Quarterly* 22 (December 1977): 587–605.

28. R. D. Hisrich and M. P. Peters, "Internal Venturing in Large Corporations: The New Business Unit," in J. Hornaday, F. Tarpley, J. Timmons, and K. Vesper, *Frontiers of Entrepreneurship Research* (Wellesley, Mass.: Babson Center for Entrepreneurial Studies, 1984), pp. 321–342.

29. J. B. Quinn, "Technological Innovation, Entrepreneurship and Strategy," *Sloan Management Review* (Spring 1979): 19–30.

30. M. A. Maidique and B. J. Zirger, "The Success-Failure Learning Cycle in New Product Development." *Working Paper: Department of Industrial Engineering, Stanford University Terman Engineering Center*, July 1984 (in review at *Research Policy*).

31. Z. Block and I. C. MacMillan, "The Paradox of Planning for New Ventures." *Working Paper: New York University Center for Entrepreneurial Studies*, January 1985.

32. O. Ornati and Z. Block, "Compensation of Corporate Venture Managers." *Working Paper: New York University Center for Entrepreneurial Studies*, January 1985.

THE CORPORATE ENTREPRENEUR REVISITED

John A. Hornaday

As Ian MacMillan has clearly stated in his paper in this volume, a strong approach to a study of the area of the corporate entrepreneur is division of the task into two parts: reviews of methodologies and definitions related to corporate venturing, and consideration of the major factors associated with success in corporate venturing as indicated by review of the literature. It is evident that we have a focus on the trends in early studies of this subject that have concentrated on specific, descriptive, or very limited findings of the kind that a great number of research persons carry out. MacMillan's plea is for an integration of these separate, factual studies into a cohesive whole with a theoretical structure from which, in turn, additional assumptions can be derived and tested. It is time, he says, to move toward a more fully encompassing statement of corporate entrepreneurship theory. Figure D-2 below may express the relationship of the separate, factual studies to the development of theoretical structure.

The base line, with many circles, represents the relatively large number of descriptive, cross-sectional, sometimes single-case, sometimes multiple-case studies. Some studies contribute to the theoretical superstructure; some do not (as represented by those straggling out at the end). They lend themselves to relatively simple statistical analyses, and they do not derive from a priori hypotheses. They do allow for a posteriori deductions especially when two or more of these studies are sufficiently similar in structure and in definition to

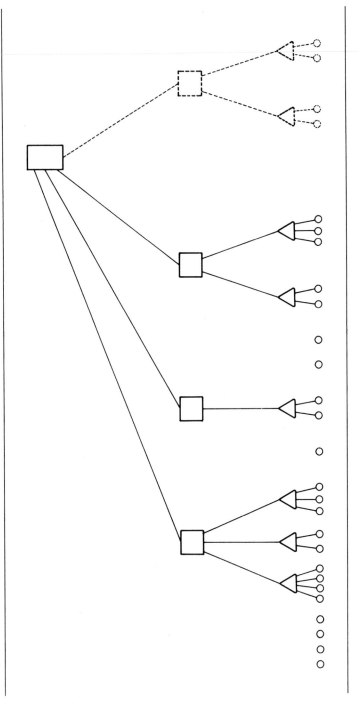

Figure D–2. Levels of Development in Theoretical Structure.

allow for generalizations. The second line upward, here represented with triangles, represents such generalizations. They draw from one or, better, several such studies and thus move toward some general statements, but, in spite of that, the structure is still not highly integrated. When there are a sufficient number of these well-supported generalizations—supported by empirical studies that are carefully and intelligently derived without *excessive* generalization—*then* we can develop an even higher order of thinking about the theoretical structure of corporate entrepreneurship. That would be at the level represented by the squares in the diagram, and we can say we have "theories." From these several theoretical statements, again well supported and carefully drawn (so that a misdirection does not undermine the whole structure), we can derive a still higher order theoretical statement here represented by a rectangle.

We see lines that recede in one direction and extend forward in the other direction. Whereas the two-dimensional structure without these lines represents a snapshot of the relationship at any one point in the time continuum, the receding and advancing lines represent the time line, and they emphasize the effectiveness of longitudinal studies. As the structure advances through time, it will also grow, extending its roots and branches as if it were growing, which indeed it is.

At this point it behooves us to begin working back down, represented here with dotted lines rather than solid lines. This depicts the derivation of additional subtheories and, at the lower level, heretofore unstated generalizations that would hold as a logical development if the rest of the structure is correct. From the downward development, we eventually then derive observable facts or empirically testable relationships that must hold, based on the previous structure—and those we then test in turn. If they prove to be correct, that further strengthens our confidence in these higher order theoretical statements; in fact, if sufficient evidence and support are gathered, causing these dotted lines to become solid, we might even say that the statement represented by the rectangle is a "law of corporate entrepreneurship."

Ian MacMillan's complaint in the early part of his paper is the lack of advanced theoretical constructs in this field and the lack of testable deductions. We certainly have no *laws* of corporate entrepreneurship at this time. We have, he says, a plethora of the basic circles, many simply standing alone, others with some theoretical superstructure that has not yet been assimilated into the whole.

In an effort to correct this weakness in the way in which research in this field has been dealt with, MacMillan applied the procedures he recommends to the area of success versus failure in corporate entrepreneurial ventures. Immediately it is evident that one must put various specific studies into a common language; if the definitions are not compatible, this hypothetico-deductive structure becomes a tower of Babel. He does deal with definitions, at least in two cases; "scope" and "success and failure."

In the second part of his paper, MacMillan reviewed a fairly wide selection of studies and derives some generalizations, some more advanced theories, and some order from them. The result is his development of the six *issues* relating to the success and failure of corporate ventures: culture, climate, and support; mission; venture strategy environment; structure/design of venture activity; staffing and reward systems; and planning, monitoring, and control. With his summaries of each of these sections (except mission, which was included only as subparts of three of the other topics), he develops the second level and perhaps begins to move up into the third level of development of the structure we have cited. The summaries clearly and succinctly express correctly the state of each of these areas, and the support for his statements in the summaries can be found in the material cited; of course, one can go back to the original studies where desired.

On the other hand, one might wish for more in MacMillan's paper to which the present is a reaction. He does cleverly integrate material to develop a higher order of thinking about corporate entrepreneurship, especially in the areas that relate success or failure to other factors, but this eclectic study did not go into the derivation of new, testable statements and then, in fact, test them. The portion of Figure D-2 represented as dotted lines was not attacked in his paper.

MacMillan's final statement—that the greatest potential lies in multicase, longitudinal studies that tease out causal linkages—is well supported. One might wish beyond MacMillan's present paper that he had pointed to *specific* hypotheses that might be fruitful and which would lead to insights that in turn would allow for the higher order development of generalizations, theoretical constructs, and even "laws" of causal linkages in corporate entrepreneurship ventures.

MacMillan has an optimistic view of the future of corporate entrepreneurship. This optimism is implicit rather than explicit in his paper, but I believe it is there. Somewhat less optimistic is a report by John E. Bailey.[1] Bailey asks the question: Are programs that move toward creating intrapreneurs and intrapreneurial cultures likely to become sources of high-growth start-ups? He does not answer negatively but reflects considerable reservation about the possibility in his paper. The fact that he is in Australia may have been sufficient reason to omit the study, but Bailey speaks of "worldwide" trends—it would have been preferable to have MacMillan cite that study and perhaps refute it rather than ignore it.

Another study that raises caveats in Mack Hanan's.[2] It would have been interesting to be able to read MacMillan's evaluation of and reaction to Hanan's conclusions, which are not entirely in line with MacMillan's own.

In spite of my relatively minor complaints that I would have wished for more in discussing MacMillan's paper, his paper is bold, demanding, and stimulating. This discussant is confident that the "more" will be forthcoming both from the author and from those who are inspired by his work.

NOTES

1. John E. Bailey, "Intrapreneurship—Source of High Growth Start-ups or Passing Fad?" in J. Hornaday, P. Tarpley, J. Timmons, and K. Vesper, eds. *Frontiers of Entrepreneurship Research* (Wellesley, Mass.: Babson Center for Entrepreneurial Studies, 1984), pp. 358–67.

2. M. Hanan, "Venturing Corporations—Think Small to Stay Strong," *Harvard Business Review* (May-June 1976): 139.

V RESEARCH AND EDUCATION

10 A UNIFIED FRAMEWORK, RESEARCH TYPOLOGIES, AND RESEARCH PROSPECTUSES FOR THE INTERFACE BETWEEN ENTREPRENEURSHIP AND SMALL BUSINESS

Max S. Wortman, Jr.

One of the most exciting new research areas in business in the past five years has been that of entrepreneurship. However, business historians have been researching individual corporations and outstanding entrepreneurs for at least fifty years. As a research field, small business has garnered the attention of business researchers for approximately thirty years. During that period of time, little or no significant progress has been made until the identical five-year period that has spurred the interest in entrepreneurship research. Indeed, many of the researchers who have found a niche in entrepreneurship research also had or continue to have a strong interest in small business research.

During this period researchers have also attempted to define the interface between small business and entrepreneurship.[1] Although they have proposed typologies and taxonomies in both entrepreneurship and small business, the focus in most of these has been to delineate differences in the areas or to defer interfaces.[2] As a result of narrowly focused typologies, taxonomies, models, and frameworks, the research efforts in both fields have not progressed as far as they would have if there had been a unified focus in either or both of the fields. Such a unified focus would have provided a framework within which to integrate the diffuse research studies and furnished guidance for neophyte researchers in both fields.

273

The purposes of this overview of the interface between entrepreneurship and small business are: (1) to provide a framework for the study of entrepreneurship and of small business; (2) to establish a research typology for both entrepreneurship and small business; (3) to critique the research work in both fields in the light of the two typologies established; (4) to analyze the research interface between the two fields; and (5) to establish a research agenda for both fields based upon the typologies.

A UNIFIED FRAMEWORK AND
RESEARCH TYPOLOGIES

To facilitate the efforts in providing more comprehensive views of both fields, a unified framework as well as a more inclusive typology is needed. Although all entrepreneurship and small business researchers would not agree with the following research framework and typologies, it is one effort to systematize the research efforts. Indeed, it is an initial step toward a more complete structuring of current research and toward the research needed in both areas.

Framework for the Interface between
the Two Fields

Based upon the empirical research, a suggested framework for the analysis of entrepreneurship and small business was formulated (see Figure 10-1). Figure 10-1 shows a clear interface between individual entrepreneurship and small business and a fairly clear absence of interface between corporate entrepreneurship and small business. In addition, in governmental units and nonprofit organizations, there is also an area that is basically oriented to the same topical research as the interface between individual entrepreneurship and small business *and* the interface between corporate and individual entrepreneurship. These topics are environment (micro and macro) and entrepreneurial behavior (both individual and organizational).

Based upon the following suggested typologies, some research areas are not involved in these interfaces including the structure and the operations under individual entrepreneurship and business functions under small business. However, the behavioral patterns of entrepreneurs and owner-managers and the environment are involved in the interface.

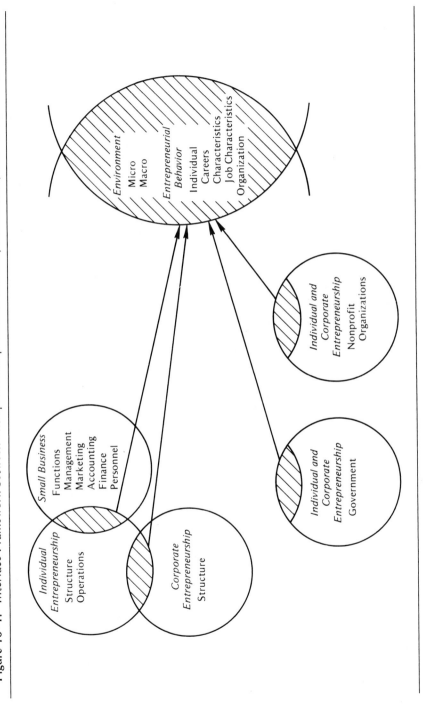

Figure 10-1. Interface Framework between Entrepreneurship in Small Business, Government, and Nonprofit Organizations.

Research Typologies of Entrepreneurship and Small Business

In the development of the two typologies, there has been an effort to consider inclusiveness as a major criterion. It is quite clear that certain areas of both fields have been overinvestigated while many subareas have not been studied.

In comparing the typology for entrepreneurship and the typology for small business (see Table 10-1), there are clearly a number of conceptual and research areas that are quite similar in nature. For example, the theoretical development of both fields requires work on theories, frameworks, definitions, and models (both process and content). Historical and environmental aspects of entrepreneurship and small business need to be considered in any comprehensive frameworks.

Differences in these two typologies occur when the larger field (entrepreneurship) is considered in its many organizational contexts. Today there are researchers in government and nonprofit organizations that are utilizing entrepreneurship concepts.[3] Moreover, the functional classification of each typology is different. The functional classification in corporate entrepreneurship deals primarily with corporate structure and behavior and in individual entrepreneurship deals primarily with individual structure and behavior. In the small business functional classification, there is an effort to deal with the business functions of management (operations and strategic), marketing, accounting, finance, and personnel. Others, namely historians and economists, have also found the area to be fruitful for research.

Classification of Research Studies

In addition to using the typologies, several other criteria were employed. First, studies utilizing students were not considered. Students may be significantly different than persons serving in real organizations and may contribute bias in the studies.

Second, no case studies were utilized because the small business field has been overwhelmed by exploratory studies and the field has passed the time for mass use of the case study.

Third, no studies of small business institutes, small business development centers, service corps of retired executives, active corps of executives, and similar management assistance agencies were included.

Fourth, research on the two fields included only the United States and Canada. Other countries were excluded at this time.

Lastly, only data-oriented research studies on entrepreneurship and small business were included in this analysis. The research studies were classified by type of organization studied, sample size, research methods and/or instruments employed, statistical methods used (if any), issues studied, and content of the study. Variables were not identified as either independent or dependent because many of the studies did not attempt to explain relationships between variables.

Clearly, other criteria could have been utilized, other typologies established, and other classifications employed. As the years pass, other schemata will undoubtedly be suggested and used.

CRITIQUE OF RESEARCH ON INDIVIDUAL ENTREPRENEURSHIP

Since this study was oriented to the interface between entrepreneurship and small business, only individual entrepreneurship was examined (see Table 10-2). Almost all of the studies on individual entrepreneurship have been carried out in small businesses. In most of the studies, the small businesses have cut across a number of different industries and geographical settings. Sample sizes and populations vary widely. However, as researchers began to discover that larger sample sizes automatically provided some type of significance in their studies, more and more researchers have utilized larger sample sizes.

Throughout these studies, the use of mail questionnaires *and* interviews with structured or nonstructured schedules is the overwhelming type of research methods used by most researchers. When specific instruments are used, they are either developed by the researchers or are behavioral instruments which have found their way into the field of entrepreneurship. For example, Rotter's locus of control, the Myers-Briggs Type Indicator, Job Description Index, Levinson locus of control, Miner Sentence Completion Scale, and Allport-Vernon-Lindzey *Study of Values* are all time-honored instruments from psychology that are now being utilized in the study of entrepreneurship behavior. Practically no instruments specifically dedicated to the study of entrepreneurs have been developed.

Table 10-1. Comparison of a Typology for Research on Entrepreneurship and a Typology for Research on Small Business.

Typology for Research on Entrepreneurship	*Typology for Research on Small Business*

I. Theoretical
  A. Theories of entrepreneurship
    1. Corporate
    2. Individual
  B. Frameworks
    1. Comprehensive
    2. Psychological
    3. Sociological
    4. Economic
    5. Political
    6. Social
  C. Definitions of entrepreneurship
  D. Models of entrepreneurship
    1. Process
    2. Content
II. Historical
  A. Corporate entrepreneurship
  B. Individual entrepreneurship
III. Environmental
  A. Macroenvironment
    1. International and national
  B. Microenvironment
	I. Theoretical
	  A. Theories of small business
	  B. Frameworks of small business
	  C. Definitions of small business
	  D. Models of small business
	    1. Process
	    2. Content
	II. Historical
	III. Environmental
	  A. Macroenvironment
	    1. International
	    2. National
	  B. Microenvironment
	IV. Occupational
	  A. Careers of owner-managers
	  B. Characteristics of owner-managers
	V. Functional
	  A. Management
	    1. Operations
	      a. Macro
	      b. Micro
	    2. Strategic

IV. Organizational entrepreneurship
   A. Business
   B. Government
   C. Nonprofit
V. Functional
   A. Corporate entrepreneurship
      1. Structure
         a. Venture formation
         b. Innovation
         c. Technology
         d. Public policy
      2. Behavior (Total organization)
   B. Individual entrepreneurship
      1. Structure
         a. Operations
         b. Associations and external groups
      2. Behavior
         a. Careers
         b. Characteristics
         c. Job characteristics
VI. Future of entrepreneurship

   B. Marketing
      1. Operations
         a. Macro
         b. Micro
      2. Strategic
   C. Finance
      1. Operations
         a. Macro
         b. Micro
      2. Strategic
   D. Accounting
      1. Operations
         a. Macro
         b. Micro
      2. Strategic
   E. Personnel
      1. Operations
         a. Macro
         b. Micro
      2. Strategic
VI. Future of small business

Table 10-2. Classification of Empirical Studies on Individual Entrepreneurship Based upon a Typology for Research on Entrepreneurship.

Entrepreneurship Segment Studied	Author(s)	Types of Organization Studied	Sample Size
I. Theoretical			
A. Frameworks			
1. Comprehensive	Pennings (1982) AMJ Vol. 25, No. 1	High-tech industry	70 SMSA 3 high-tech industries
II. Environmental			
III. Organizational			
IV. Functional			
A. Corporate Entrepreneurship			
1. Structure			
a. Venture formation	Brockhaus (1980) JSBM Vol. 18, No. 1	Small business	93 owners
	Stoner & Fry (1982) JSBM Vol. 20, No. 2	Small business	76 entrepreneurs
	Hoy, Vaught, & Buchanan (1982) Proc. SMA	Retail trade association	23 store owners
	Hoy & Carland (1983) FER	Small business	16 entrepreneurs; 57 non-entrepreneurs

Table 10-2. continued

Research Method/ Instrument	Statistical Method	Issues Studied	Content of the Study
	Factor analysis; correlation; multiple regression	Population; industry size; quality of life (economic, political, environmental, health, educational, social)	Examination of quality of life on entrepreneurial activity. Both economic and noneconomic aspects must be used to improve entrepreneurial activity.
Questionnaire; Job Description Index	Chi-square	Relationship of job satisfaction to decision to start a business	Dissatisfaction with the actual work appears to be the major "push" toward the decision to start a business.
Questionnaire	t-test	Job satisfaction and its relationship to starting own business	Work experiences fit the dissatisfaction model of entrepreneurial motivation.
Questionnaire		Corporate growth and development	Stages of transition may be fertile ground for future research on small business development.
Myers-Briggs Type Indicator questionnaire	t-test	New venture formation	An attempt to differentiate owners based upon personality characteristics measured by Myers-Briggs did not support earlier study.

(Table 10-2. continued overleaf)

Table 10-2. continued

Entrepreneurship Segment Studied	Author(s)	Types of Organization Studied	Sample Size
a. Venture formation *(continued)*	Russell (1983) Proc. ICSB	Petroleum industry	30 firms
	Enbiyaoglu (1984) DAI Vol. 45, No. 3	Educational software	14 small firms
	Katz (1984) FER	Restaurants	22 start-ups 21 buyouts 22 resurrections
	Van de Ven, Hudson, & Schroeder (1984) JOM Vol. 10, No. 1	Educational software	12 firms
d. Public Policy	Everett (1984) DAI Vol. 45, No. 6	Small business owners; city council members; lobbyists	3 groups in Arizona
2. Behavior	Miller, D. (1983) Mgmt. Science Vol. 29, No. 7	Small and medium size	52 firms

Table 10-2. continued

Research Method/ Instrument	Statistical Method	Issues Studied	Content of the Study
Interview		Joint ventures	Examines use of joint ventures to enter offshore petroleum drilling.
Interview; questionnaire		Entrepreneurs' experiences; business planning activities; business idea characteristics	Analyzes how a company's pre-start-up stage relates to its future performance.
Interview; free response questionnaire		Entry strategies; individual level characteristics; organizational outcomes	Develop a scale of entrepreneurial initiative.
Interview; questionnaire; customer evaluation form	F-ratio; correlation	Design of new business start-ups	Performance and stages of development of new firms viewed from three perspectives: entrepreneurial, organizational, and ecological.
Questionnaires	Ranking; correlation	Small business influence on decisions; quality of city council performance	Examines attitudes of 3 groups as to extent of small business influencing city council decisions.
Questionnaire; interview; Rotter locus of control	Cronbach alpha F-ratio; t-test; product moment correlation; multiple regression	Environment; organization structure; decisionmaking style; strategy; entrepreneurship	Entrepreneurial activity of firm (simple, planning, and organic); different firms require very different types of forces to stimulate entrepreneurship.

(Table 10-2. continued overleaf)

Table 10-2. continued

Entrepreneurship Segment Studied	Author(s)	Types of Organization Studied	Sample Size
B. Individual Entrepreneurship 1. Structure a. Operations	Pelligrino (1980) DAI Vol. 23, No. 2	Retail and service	20 female entrepreneurs
	Gasse & d'Amboise (1981) FER	Small manufacturing	107 entrepreneurs
	Bracker (1982) DAI Vol. 43, No. 6	Small business	265 firms
	Hisrich & O'Brien (1982) FER	Small business	284 women entrepreneurs
	Pellegrino & Reece (1982) JSBM Vol. 20, No. 2	Small business	20 female entrepreneurs

Table 10-2. continued

Research Method/ Instrument	Statistical Method	Issues Studied	Content of the Study
Case study; transcripts; interview	Content analysis	Formative and operative problems of female entrepreneurs	Perceived formative and operations problems encountered by female entrepreneurs.
Interview	Ranking	Managerial problems	Acquire knowledge of everyday managerial problems of owner managers or entrepreneurs. Problems appeared to be: scarcity and delivery of raw materials and recruitment of skilled production personnel.
3 industry-specific performance measures	MANOVA; multiple comparison technique	Strategic planning practice; performance	Analyzes relationship of strategic planning, type of entrepreneur, and financial performance. Three most important competencies were: knowledge of customer needs, oral and written communications; and knowledge of industry entered.
Questionnaire		Women entrepreneurs	Women entrepreneurs experience particular problems in financing and these problems do reflect to some extent the type of business they are in.
Interview; questionnaire		Formative problems; operational problems	Identifies formative and operational problems of women entrepreneurs.

(Table 10-2. continued overleaf)

Table 10-2. continued

Entrepreneurship Segment Studied	Author(s)	Types of Organization Studied	Sample Size
b. Associations	Hutt (1984) FER	Small business	18 companies
2. Behavior			
a. Careers	Scanlan (1980) DAI Vol. 40, No. 8		64 entrepreneurs
	Dunkelberg & Cooper (1982) Proc. AOM	Small business	1,805 firms
	Kent, Sexton, Van Auken, Young (1982) FER	Small business	111 managers 1,259 entrepreneurs
b. Characteristics	Brockhaus (1980) Proc. AOM	Small business	

Table 10-2. continued

Research Method/ Instrument	Statistical Method	Issues Studied	Content of the Study
Interview; interview guide	Mean; rank order	Entrepreneurs' organizations	Ascertain activities for new organization.
Interview; Vocational Preference Inventory; Levinson's Attitude Statement Survey		Self-employment; career options; entrepreneurship	Route of opportunistic entrepreneur is more conscious and direct than craft entrepreneur who has greater number of work experiences after becoming self-employed.
Questionnaire	Correlation; multivariate analysis	Patterns of small business growth	Assesses impact of owner background and objectives and of firm characteristics on compound annual growth rate in employment.
Questionnaire	Discriminant analysis; MANOVA	Lifetime experience including demographic characteristics, formal education, post-secondary education extracurricular activities, and preadult work experiences	Lifetime experiences taken as a whole are significant predictors of whether an individual becomes an entrepreneur or a manager. Little significance attached to any single lifetime experience in differentiating venture initiators over managers.
Rotter locus of control; Job Description Index; Risk Taking	Discriminant analysis	Successful and unsuccessful entrepreneurs	Successful entrepreneurs had more internal locus of control, less satisfied with previous jobs, more fearful of dismissal from previous jobs, and more likely to be married than unsuccessful entrepreneurs.

(Table 10-2. continued overleaf)

Table 10-2. continued

Entrepreneurship Segment Studied	Author(s)	Types of Organization Studied	Sample Size
b. Characteristics *(continued)*	Brockhaus (1980) AMJ Vol. 23, No. 3		31 entrepreneurs; 31 transferred managers; 31 promoted managers
	McCaleb & VanFleet (1980) Proc. SMA	Food service stores	12 managers
	Mescon (1980) DAI Vol. 40, No. 11	Real estate	31 independents; 20 franchisees
	Gasse (1981) Proc. AOM	Small manu- facturing	51 owner-managers
	Hisrich & O'Brien (1981) FER	Small business	21 self-employed women

Table 10–2. continued

Research Method/ Instrument	Statistical Method	Issues Studied	Content of the Study
Wallach & Kogan Choice Dilemmas Questionnaire	Analysis of variance; Kolmogorov confidence band	Entrepreneurial risk preference	Level of risk taking does not distinguish new entrepreneurs either from managers or general population.
Myers-Briggs Type Indicator; Levinson locus of control; Torrance test, managerial ratings	Correlation	Problem-solving styles; creativity	Relationships were found between experience and locus of control with profitability.
Jackson's Personality Research Form; Rotter locus of control; interview; questionnaire		Entrepreneurship	Independent brokers scored higher on endurance and locus of control; both groups felt they were masters of their own destinies.
Interview; questionnaire	t-test	Entrepreneurial characteristics	Cultural analysis of French and English Entrepreneurial characteristics and practices.
Interview; interview schedule		Women entrepreneurs	Indicates women entrepreneurs have particular problems in obtaining lines of credit, weak collateral position, and overcoming society's negative attitudes about women.

(Table 10–2. continued overleaf)

Table 10-2. continued

Entrepreneurship Segment Studied	Author(s)	Types of Organization Studied	Sample Size
b. Characteristics (continued)	Mescon & Montanari (1981) Proc. AOM	Real estate	51 real estate brokers
	Sexton & Kent (1981) FER	Small business	45 executives; 48 entrepreneurs
	Thorne & Ball (1981) FER	Small business	51 entrepreneurs
	Carland, J.W. (1982) DAI Vol. 23, No. 6	Small business	77 owner-managers
	Ray (1982) DAI Vol. 43, No. 4	Retail trades	136 entrepreneurs, franchise owners; managers
	Schere (1982) Proc. AOM	Small business	52 entrepreneurs; 65 managers

Table 10-2. continued

Research Method/ Instrument	Statistical Method	Issues Studied	Content of the Study
Interview; questionnaire	ANOVA	Personalities of entrepreneurs	Comparisons made between independent and franchise entrepreneurs on personality and socioeconomic variables.
Interview; questionnaire		Female executives and entrepreneurs	Female executives and entrepreneurs tend to be more similar than different.
Questionnaire	Correlation; regression analysis	Entrepreneurs; new company formation	Provides profile of entrepreneurs, their companies, and institutional environment.
Panel of experts		Personality characteristics of entrepreneurs and small business owners	Entrepreneurs do not vary when contrasted with owners on personality characteristics Entrepreneurs higher on innovative behavior and have different management styles.
Questionnaire	Multiple discriminant analysis; multiple regression	Entrepreneurial characteristics and venture performance	Developed profiles of entrepreneurs, franchise owners, and managers. No correlation with profiles and venture performance.
Budner's scale of ambiguity intolerance; questionnaire	F-test; ANOVA	Tolerance of ambiguity	Entrepreneurs had a higher tolerance for ambiguity than top executives or middle managers.

(Table 10-2. continued overleaf)

Table 10-2. continued

Entrepreneurship Segment Studied	Author(s)	Types of Organization Studied	Sample Size
b. Characteristics (continued)	Smith, McCain, & Warren (1982) FER	Small business	76 female entrepreneurs
	Welsch & Young (1982) Proc. ICSB	Small business	143 women business owners; 55 men business owners
	Gartner (1983) DAI Vol. 43, No. 10	Small business	106 entrepreneurs
	Gasse (1983) Proc. ICSB	Small manu- facturing	51 owner-managers
	Hisrich & Brush (1983) FER	Small business	468 women entrepreneurs

Table 10-2. continued

Research Method/ Instrument	Statistical Method	Issues Studied	Content of the Study
Entrepreneurial type questionnaire		Crafts-oriented entrepreneur; opportunistic entrepreneur	Comparison of constructed types of male and female entrepreneurs. Female entrepreneurs differ from males in behavior and attitudes with a clear tendency to be more opportunistic.
Questionnaire	t-test	Personality characteristics; business problems; information sources	Profile of women entrepreneurs to male entrepreneurs is relatively similar. Women were younger, more educated, more interested in information sources.
Questionnaire	Ward's hierarchical clustering algorithm	Entrepreneurial behavior	Entrepreneurial behaviors varied widely among entrepreneurs — more than between entrepreneurs and non-entrepreneurs.
Interview; item analysis	Correlation	Ideology dimensions	Measures nine dimensions of business and managerial orientation of managers and entrepreneurs.
Questionnaire		Profile of women entrepreneurs	Analyzes women entrepreneur profiles and indicates weaknesses in finance, marketing, and business operations.

(Table 10-2. continued overleaf)

Table 10-2. continued

Small Business Segment Studied	Author(s)	Types of Organization Studied	Sample Size
b. Characteristics *(continued)*	Knight (1984) FER	Small business	105 franchise operators; 102 owner/operators
	Rezaian-Yazdi (1984) DAI Vol. 45, No. 4		Male and female entrepreneurs in U.S. (Iranian)
	Smith & Miner (1984) FER	Small business	51 entrepreneurs; 20 non-entrepreneurs
	Stone & Schweser (1984) Proc. ICSB	Small business	154 female entrepreneurs
	Unni & Nappi (1984) Proc. ICSB	Small business	61 minority entrepreneurs; 69 non-minority entrepreneurs
c. Job characteristics	Diffley (1982) DAI Vol. 43, No. 6	Service and retail industries	106 self-employed women

Table 10–2. continued

Research Method/ Instrument	Statistical Method	Issues Studied	Content of the Study
Questionnaire		Personal character-istics of small business owner/operator sources of information; franchise operations	Independent entrepreneurs appear to be more self-reliant than franchise entre-preneurs, and also have more experience.
Allport-Vernon-Lindzey *Study of Values*	*t*-tests; ANOVA	Theoretical, eco-nomic, aesthetic, social, political, religious values	Showed significantly dif-ferent values profiles.
Miner Sentence Completion Scale; innovative technology survey questionnaire	*t*-tests	Self-achievement; avoiding risk; feedback of results personal innovation future orientation	More successful entre-preneurs exhibited much greater task or achieve-ment motivation on MSCS than entrepreneurs with slow growth and non-entrepreneurs.
Questionnaire	Correlation; rank order	Success factors; success descriptors	Identified factors to aid in understanding of success by female entrepreneurs.
Management Style Diagnosis Test		Management styles	Both minority and non-minority entrepreneurs seemed to be using "less effective" styles.
Survey	*Chi*-square; ranking	Entrepreneurial competencies	Three most important competencies were: knowledge of customer needs; oral and written communications; and knowledge of industry entered.

(Table 10–2. continued overleaf)

Table 10-2. continued

Small Business Segment Studied	Author(s)	Types of Organization Studied	Sample Size
c. Job characteristics *(continued)*	Knight (1984) JSBM Vol. 22, No. 2	Small business	105 franchisee entrepreneurs; 102 independent entrepreneurs
	Ray & Hand (1983) Proc. SMA	Retail stores	52 retail entrepreneurs; 74 retail managers
	Gomolka (1984) Proc. SMA	Female owned business	231 female entrepreneurs
	Gomolka (1984) Proc. ICSB	Small business	223 minority owned businesses
	Hisrich & Brush (1984) JSBM Vol. 22, No. 1	Small business	468 women entrepreneurs
	Jeromin (1984) DAI Vol. 45, No. 2	Precision metal-working company	100 Los Angeles based and 100 national

Table 10-2. continued

Research Method/ Instrument	Statistical Method	Issues Studied	Content of the Study
Questionnaire		Personal characteristics; management skills; financing required; outside support services	Franchisees better recognized for their lack of management skills more than the independents.
Questionnaire	Kolmogorov-Smirnov two-sample test	Characteristics of retail entrepreneurs and retail managers	Determines extent to which there are differences in characteristics of retail entrepreneurs and retail managers and how they differ from technical entrepreneurs.
Questionnaire		Female entrepreneurial characteristics	Comparison with previous male entrepreneurial studies showed females to be younger, less foreign-born, same in educational level, similar in economic and social background.
Questionnaire	Chi-square	Entrepreneurial succession; minority entrepreneur characteristics	Analysis shows low level of succession planning. Identifies relationships between succession patterns, individual characteristics, and company characteristics.
Questionnaire		Type of business venture; past experience; self-appraisal of management skills	Provides composite picture of women entrepreneurs and types of business engaged in.
Survey; questionnaire		Skills training	Identifies underlying reasons for skills shortage as related to management's entrepreneurial characteristics, attitudes, and perceived responsibility toward training.

(Table 10-2. continued overleaf)

Table 10-2. continued

Small Business Segment Studied	Author(s)	Types of Organization Studied	Sample Size
c. Job characteristics *(continued)*	Boyd & Gumpert (1983) FER	Small business	281 entrepreneurs
	Boyd & Gumpert (1984) FER	Small business	249 chief executive officers

Journal abbreviations are given at the end of Table 10-3, p. 322.

During the past five years, there has been little change in the use of statistics in studying individual entrepreneurship. Strangely enough, entrepreneurship researchers are still using raw data in many of their studies with an emphasis upon percentages. Considering the level of statistical sophistication in the past twenty-five years, it is surprising that more efforts at explanation of the data in terms of relationships and cause-and-effect have not been attempted. When statistics are used, they generally are at a relatively unsophisticated level such as means, standard deviations, ranking, t-tests, and linear correlation.

There is little balance in the issues studied by entrepreneurial researchers. Over one-half of the studies are examining the characteristics of entrepreneurs. With the stress on potential minority involvement and female involvement in entrepreneurship and small business by the government, researchers have moved toward studying characteristics in these areas. Venture formation and creation seems to be the second major issue studied. However, the investigation of

Table 10-2. continued

Research Method/ Instrument	Statistical Method	Issues Studied	Content of the Study
Bio-data questionnaire; Jenkins activity survey	Mean; standard deviation	Stress behaviors; job satisfaction; performance	Although founders exhibited high degree of stress, symptoms did not adversely affect job satisfaction. When founders were grouped by age of firm, there was no significant variation in stress symptoms.
Questionnaire	Correlation	Loneliness; stress	Analyzed relationship between loneliness and stress among start-up entrepreneurs. Correlation between the two was significant.

entrepreneurial-behavior is so overwhelming that it almost precludes any other type of research on individual entrepreneurship. Regardless of the type of study in individual entrepreneurship, practically every one of the studies suffers from the same problem—the lack of a clearly defined relationship to a comprehensive framework of entrepreneurship.

As a distinct type of research, doctoral dissertations on individual entrepreneurship and small business are not found primarily in business schools. These dissertations are being written in cultural anthropology, history, political science, education, sociology, mass communications, and economics. A major failing of abstracts published in *Dissertation Abstracts International* is the absence of critical information (i.e., sample size, statistics used, variables, etc.).

Based upon the suggested typology, there are truly many gaps in the research on individual entrepreneurship. This presents many opportunities for new research streams.

Table 10-3. Classification of Empirical Studies on Small Business Based upon a Typology for Research on Small Business.

Small Business Segment Studied	Author(s)	Types of Organization Studied	Sample Size
I. Theoretical A. Theories	Paulson (1980) AMJ Vol. 23, No. 2	Retail stores	77 general managers
	Dollinger (1983) DAI Vol. 44, No. 3	Small business	84 owner/operators
	Geeraerts (1984) ASQ Vol. 29, No. 2	Manufacturing; service; construction	37 owner/founders; 61 owner/successors; 28 managers
II. Environmental A. Macro	Wilson (1980) JSBM Vol. 43, No. 3	Small business	180 owners or managers
	Wilde (1982) DAI Vol. 43, No. 3	Business firm	
	Chrisman & Archer (1984) Proc. ICSB	Small business	62 managers; 32 nonbusiness persons

Table 10–3. continued

Research Method/ Instrument	Statistical Method	Issues Studied	Content of the Study
Interview	Correlation; multiple regression	Size, task scope, horizontal differentiation, and complexity	Levels of size related to horizontal differentiation and change in task scope related to horizontal differentiation, but not as important as size. Size more important than technology in explaining complexity.
Survey; LISREL	*Chi*-square test of goodness of fit	Boundary spanning activities; organizational performance	Stable environment is needed for boundary spanning activity to be effective in small business.
Interview	Correlation; multiple regression	Size; horizontal differentiation; formalization; specialization; decentralization	Relationship between size of firm and its structure is modified by management; control and socialization may be related.
Interview; phenomenological method		Responsibilities to customer, employees, ethics, community, profits	Survey of social responsibility of small business.
Questionnaire		Attitudes of small business owners toward social responsibility accounting	Analysis of attitudes toward social responsibility accounting; should be concerned citizens but not collect social data.
Questionnaire	Wilcoxon rank order test; ranking; Kruskal-Wallis test	Competitive performance; social responsibility	Small business and non-business individual perceptions of small business social responsibility are similar.

(Table 10–3. continued overleaf)

Table 10-3. continued

Small Business Segment Studied	Author(s)	Types of Organization Studied	Sample Size
A. Macro (continued)	Sigarodi (1984) DAI Vol. 45, No. 5	Small business	25 executives
	Peterson, Kozmetsky, & Ridgway (1984) JSBM Vol. 22, No. 1	Small business	1002 small business; 522 general public
III. Occupational A. Careers	Cooper & Dunkelberg (1981) FER	Small firms	1805 owner/ managers
B. Characteristics	Unni (1980) Proc. SMA	Small business	132 owner/managers
	Hoy, Judd, & Vaught (1981) Proc. SMA	Retail grocery stores	379 stores
	Lindecamp (1981) DAI	Retail	109 owner/operators; 127 retail firms

Table 10-3. continued

Research Method/ Instrument	Statistical Method	Issues Studied	Content of the Study
Survey		Environmental factors; innovation	Identification of environmental variables perceived by small business executives to contribute most to decline of innovation.
Telephone survey; questionnaire		Government regulation of small business	Small businesses should have less regulations than large businesses.
Questionnaire		Family background, career paths, incubator organization characteristics, attitudes, motivations	Substantial differences in their backgrounds, depending upon how they became owners and depending upon their industry.
Questionnaire	Mean	Managerial assumptions of small business managers	Small business managers were found to be conservative and leaning toward Theory X.
Questionnaire	Correlation	Owner characteristics; small business success	Provides limited support for existence of differences between owners of more and less successful firms, using selected financial measures.
Personal Values Questionnaire; Myers-Briggs Type Indicator; interview	Ranking	Personal values; business success	Examines personal values and business success.

(Table 10-3. continued overleaf)

Table 10-3. continued

Small Business Segment Studied	Author(s)	Types of Organization Studied	Sample Size
B. Characteristics *(continued)*	Welsch & Young (1982) JSBM Vol. 20, No. 4	Small business	53 owners
	Castaldi (1983) DAI Vol. 44, No. 4	Small furniture manufacturing	10 chief executive officers
	Hope (1983) DAI Vol. 43, No. 12	Small business	19 owner/managers
	Carland & Carland (1984) Proc. SMA	Small firms	56 owners; 21 entrepreneurs
	Carsrud, Olm, & Thomas (1984) Proc. ICSB	Retail building supply	96 owners
	Min (1984) DAI Vol. 45, No. 1		159 Korean families

Table 10-3. continued

Research Method/ Instrument	Statistical Method	Issues Studied	Content of the Study
Questionnaire	Correlation	Personality characteristics; information sources	Significant differences were found across personality traits and information sources. There are different information seeking preferences among entrepreneurs.
Brunswick lens model	ANOVA	Work roles of chief executive officers in small firms	Relative importance of operational and strategic related work roles as related to technology, competition, and CEO tenure.
Diary; questionnaire; telephone survey		Management tasks and skills	Examines nature of owner-manager; allocation of time between work and leisure, and role of formal education in developing owner/ manager.
Myers-Briggs Type Indicator	MANOVA: discriminant analysis	Profiles of entrepreneurs and small business owners	Entrepreneurs are extroverted, intuitive, thinking, perceptive, and innovative; owners are extroverted, sensing, feeling, and judging.
Questionnaire; Work and Family Orientation Inventory	Correlation; multiple regression	Productivity; owner personality; organizational success	Work, mastery, and interpersonal competitiveness, percentage of ownership, and level of cooperativeness interact in predicting small business success.
Case study; questionnaire	*Chi*-square test; multiple regression	Status of Koreans in small business; urban segregation	Explains social phenomenon of Koreans concentration in small business.

(Table 10-3. continued overleaf)

Table 10-3. continued

Small Business Segment Studied	Author(s)	Types of Organization Studied	Sample Size
B. Characteristics (continued)	Triana, Welsch, & Young (1984) JSBM Vol. 22, No. 4	Small business	81 owners
IV. Functional A. Management 1. Operations a. Macro	Goad (1980) DAI Vol. 41, No. 2	Small business	41 executives
	Hoy & Vaught (1980) JSBM Vol. 18, No. 1	Small business	105 owner/managers
	Schary (1980) JSBM Vol. 18, No. 3	Small manufacturing	201 firms
	Vozikis & Glueck (1980) Proc. AOM	Sr ll retail and service businesses	117 firms
	Vozikis (1980) DAI Vol. 40, No. 11	Retail and service	

Table 10-3. continued

Research Method/ Instrument	Statistical Method	Issues Studied	Content of the Study
Questionnaire	Correlation	Personality characteristics; information sources; and problem categories	Significant correlations were found between psychological variables and information sources between problem categories and information sources.
Questionnaire	Chi-square	Organization development	Examines problem-solving technology of organizational development as related to small business problems.
Interview; questionnaire		Major problems of rural entrepreneurs	Survey of the major problems of the rural entrepreneur.
Questionnaire	Mean; ranking	Transportation decision areas and transportation problems	Identified importance of transportation costs, model choice, problems encountered, and attitude toward transportation service.
SBDC files; panel of judges	Chi-square; Cramer's statistic	Small business problems and stages of development	Determines that stage of development should be determined by small business owner to find out strategic advantage or disadvantage profile.
	Chi-square; Cramer's statistic	Stratetic disadvantage profile	Empirical analysis of internal small business problems at different stages of development.

(Table 10-3. continued overleaf)

Table 10-3. continued

Small Business Segment Studied	Author(s)	Types of Organization Studied	Sample Size
a. Macro (continued)	Franklin, Fulmer, & Goodwin (1981)	Small business	249 firms
	Franklin, Fulmer, & Goodwin (1981)	Small business	249 firms
	Senchack (1981) JSBM Vol. 19, No. 1	Small manu-facturing	260 firms
	Unni (1981) Proc. SMA	Small business	43 managers
	Unni (1981) Long Range Planning Vol. 14, No. 2	Small business	62 minority and 58 non-minority businesses
	Jones (1982) JSBM Vol. 20, No. 3	Small business	79 firms
	Jones (1982) Proc. SMA	Small business	69 firms

Table 10-3. continued

Research Method/ Instrument	Statistical Method	Issues Studied	Content of the Study
Questionnaire		Succession strategies	Focuses on preparation and planning process for managerial succession.
Questionnaire		Management succession	Succession is considered a major concern, but little formal planning is implemented.
Questionnaire		Incidence of R&D intensity of R&D activity; source of funds	Survey of small manufacturing R&D activities.
Questionnaire	Correlation	Corporate planning; entrepreneurial success	Age, experience, and education were related to planning. Lack of knowledge of planning is major barrier to planning use.
Questionnaire	*Chi*-square; Pearson Product moment correlation	Strategic planning; company characteristics; success criteria (profit satisfaction and sales growth satisfaction)	Lack of planning was most serious obstacle.
Questionnaire	*t*-test	Planners; informal planners	Examines differences between user of formal versus informal planning methods.
Questionnaire	Correlation; *t*-test	Planners	Survey of planning in small businesses. Characteristics of planners versus non-planners.

(Table 10-3. continued overleaf)

Table 10-3. continued

Small Business Segment Studied	Author(s)	Types of Organization Studied	Sample Size
a. Macro *(continued)*	Lindecamp & Rice (1982) Proc. ICSB	Retail stores	102 owner/managers
	Mehra (1982) Proc. SMA	Small business	70 firms
	Robinson, R. (1982) AMJ Vol. 25, No. 1	Retail, service and manu-facturing	101 small firms (SBDC); 101 Robert Morris Associates; 61 bookkeeper services
	Schell (1982) Proc. ICSB	Small manu-facturing	35 firms
	Ambrose (1983) JSBM Vol. 21, No. 1	Small business	53 owner/managers
	Bracker (1983) Proc. SMA	Small business	265 firms
	Franklin & Goodwin (1983) JSBM Vol. 21, No. 2	Small business	670 firms
	Raymond (1983) Proc. ICSB	Small manu-facturing	139 owner/managers

Table 10-3. continued

Research Method/ Instrument	Statistical Method	Issues Studied	Content of the Study
Interview questionnaire	Correlation	Size; formal planning; control	Larger businesses use more formal planning and control techniques than smaller businesses.
Questionnaire		Operational problems	Develops a data base for analyzing operational problems, timing of these problems, and needed training programs.
	Chi-square; MANOVA Duncan's multiple range test	Dimensions of effectiveness; growth; profitability; productivity; employment	Effectiveness of small firms engaging in outsider-based strategic planning was significantly higher than firms not engaging in such planning.
Questionnaire	Correlation	Management training; growth	Professional management does have significant impact upon job growth.
Questionnaire		Transfer of family-owned business; importance of accounting systems	Family-owned businesses must select between transfer and termination. Options must be understood.
Questionnaire	MANOVA	Operations/production management in small firms	Addresses total operating system performance in light of operations management techniques.
Questionnaire	Ranking	Small business problems; sources of information	Survey of problems of small businesses and information sources.
Questionnaire	Correlation; multiple regression	Management information system success	Explores influence of various organizational, individual, and technical factors on MIS success.

(Table 10-3. continued overleaf)

Table 10-3. continued

Small Business Segment Studied	Author(s)	Types of Organization Studied	Sample Size
a. Macro *(continued)*	Robinson, R. (1983) Proc. ICSB	Small manufacturing	32 senior executives
	Robinson, R. & Pearce (1983) SMJ No. 4	Banks	85 banks
	Stoner (1983) JSBM Vol. 21, No. 1	Small manufacturing	62 firms
	DeLone (1983) DAI Vol. 44, No. 6	Manufacturing	93 small Los Angeles firms
	Ackelsberg & Arlow (1984) Proc. SMA	Small business	172 firms
	Bartley & Cell (1984) Proc. ICSB	Small and large businesses	
	Churchill & Lewis (1984) JSBM Vol. 22, No. 2	Small business	1057 firms

Table 10-3. continued

Research Method/ Instrument	Statistical Method	Issues Studied	Content of the Study
Questionnaire		Strategic planning; decisionmaking; outside sources of information	Determines importance of outside assistance in key decision areas.
Questionnaire	*t*-test	Formal strategic planning; financial performance	Small banks performed equally well regardless of whether or not there was a formal planning system.
Questionnaire; interview	Mean	Planning; short-term objectives; long-range plans; information sources	Survey of planning in small business.
Two questionnaires		Computer success in small business	Chief executive knowledge of computers and his/her involvement are directly associated with computer success.
Questionnaire	*t*-test; correlation	Planning; economic performance; external environmental uncertainty	Reveals that planners had better economic performance than nonplanners. External turbulence causes small business to intensify planning efforts.
Questionnaire		Quantitative techniques	Study showed only slight correlation between techniques being taught and those being used.
Questionnaire	Ranking	Effects of economic conditions upon small business during recession	In recessions, owner/managers do act to reduce impact of external forces upon operations.

(Table 10-3. continued overleaf)

Table 10-3. continued

Small Business Segment Studied	Author(s)	Types of Organization Studied	Sample Size
a. Macro (continued)	Grablowsky (1984)	Small business	94 firms
	Robinson, R. et al. (1984) JSBM Vol. 22, No. 2	Small business	51 firms
	Saladin & Nelson (1984) JSBM Vol. 22, No. 2	Small business	60 firms
	Salem, et al. (1984) Proc. SMA	Retail food stores	81 independent stores
b. Micro	Chamard, Catano, & Beresford (1983) Proc. ICSB	Small manufacturing	98 firms
	Duffus (1984) Proc. ICSB	Garment and furniture industries	80 chief executive officers

Table 10-3. continued

Research Method/ Instrument	Statistical Method	Issues Studied	Content of the Study
Questionnaire		Inventory control	Found that small business owners are a long way from achieving reliable control of inventory.
Panel of judges	Inter-rater reliability; MANOVA; correlation	Stage of development; effectiveness; strategic planning intensity	Improvement in effectiveness is not contingent upon stage of development. Basic planning has a positive impact upon firm performance.
Questionnaire		Operations Management	Small business is confused about what productivity is and do not understand impact upon operations.
Questionnaire	Correlation	Long-range planning; short-range planning	High levels of operational planning were associated with significantly higher performance for three of four performance measures used.
Questionnaire; interview		Fitness; lifestyle awareness	Are aware of fitness and lifestyle improvement and feel companies would benefit from such programs.
Questionnaire	ANOVA; Tukey multiple comparison test	Foreign exchange shortages	Nonexporters believe foreign exchange shortages have more inhibiting effect on export performance than do exporters.

(Table 10-3. continued overleaf)

Table 10-3. continued

Small Business Segment Studied	Author(s)	Types of Organization Studied	Sample Size
b. Micro (continued)	Reid (1984) Journal of Bus. Rsch. Vol. 12, No. 2	Metal fabrication; furniture machine manufacturers	89 firms
	Dart (1980) JSBM Vol. 18, No. 2	Advertising agencies	128 agencies
	Farah (1983) Proc. ICSB	Retail stores	59 sales managers
	O'Dea, Pynn, Eaton (1983) Proc. ICSB	Retail stores	40 firms
2. Strategic	Kaynak & Kothari (1984) Mgmt. Intl. Review Vol. 24	Manufacturing	308 firms in Texas (196 nonexport: 112 export) 176 firms in Canada (72 nonexport; 104 export)
C. Finance 1. Operations a. Macro	Patillo (1981) JSBM Vol. 19, No. 2	Small manufacturing	Chief financial officer

Table 10-3. continued

Research Method/ Instrument	Statistical Method	Issues Studied	Content of the Study
Instrument developed	Guttman scalogram analysis; Pearson product moment correlation; regression analysis	International predisposition and intention of exporting	Small firms do not operate on a limited information basis, but use alternative cheaper sources.
Questionnaire	Mean, standard deviation	Advertising agency problems with small clients	Identification of the difficulties using an advertising agency.
Questionnaire	t-test; Chi-square	Attitude; product knowledge; selling skills	Analyzes successful and less successful sales personnel based on sales volume and total earnings in attitudes, product knowledge, and selling skills.
Questionnaire; interview	Standard deviation	Advertising management practices	Incur real and substantial costs by not effectively managing advertising.
Survey	Ranking; means		Cross-national study of export behaviors; points out difference between exporters and nonexporters; examines strategic approaches to marketing.
Interview		Capital investment policies; capital investment techniques	Examines capital investment practices of American versus multinational manufacturers.

(Table 10-3. continued overleaf)

Table 10-3. continued

Small Business Segment Studied	Author(s)	Types of Organization Studied	Sample Size
a. Macro (continued)	Sexton, Van Auken, & Hardy (1982) Proc. ICSB	Small firms	344 firms
	Chaganti & Chaganti (1983) JSBM Vol. 21, No. 3	Small manufacturing	192 firms
	Scott (1983) DAI Vol. 45, No. 6	Small business	2,171 minority businesses 2,044 non-minority businesses
	Gasse (1984) FER	Small business	36 owner/managers; 30 entrepreneurs
b. Micro	Herrmann (1984) Proc. ICSB	Small business	396 loans

Table 10–3. continued

Research Method/ Instrument	Statistical Method	Issues Studied	Content of the Study
Interview; questionnaire		Sell-out techniques	Most had strong preference for concrete sell-out approaches based on asset valuation.
Questionnaire	Wilks lambda; Chi-square	Strengths and weaknesses of profitable versus unprofitable firms; business operations and profitability	Innovativeness, know-how, and creativity are important for success in small business. Managerial competence also is important.
	ANOVA	Financial indicators	Minority firms which do not receive assistance were found to have the same performance characteristics as non-minority firms on profitability, indebtedness, and liquidity.
Interview schedule		External financing	Comparison of the two groups shows differences relative to most important perceived factors influencing potential investors, and the extent to which owner-managers would take advantage of such an investment program.
Loan files; loan applications	Multiple regression	Loan maturity; loan repayment	Financial variables are most useful in explaining loan performance than experience or other variables.

(Table 10–3. continued overleaf)

Table 10-3. continued

Small Business Segment Studied	Author(s)	Types of Organization Studied	Sample Size
b. Micro (continued)	Holman & Young (1984) Proc. ICSB	Small business	
D. Accounting			
1. Operations			
a. Macro			
b. Micro	Anderson, E. (1980) DAI Vol. 40, No. 12	Small business	
	Finnerty & Krzystofik (1984) Proc. ICSB	Small and large businesses	74 small business; 74 large business
	Knutson & Wichmann (1984) JSBM Vol. 22, No. 1		236 accountants
E. Personnel			
1. Operations			
a. Macro			
b. Micro	Osborn (1980) DAI Vol. 41, No. 1	Retail	25 retail managers
	Cox, Moore, & Van Auken (1984) JSBM Vol. 22, No. 4	Small business	220 husband-wife teams

Table 10-3. continued

Research Method/ Instrument	Statistical Method	Issues Studied	Content of the Study
Economic Report of the President	Econometric analysis; multiple regression; coefficient of determination	Small business failures; small business financing	Factors affecting failure of small business and public financing of such firms.
Questionnaire	Correlation	Accounting information	New managers do not make financial plans; cannot use accounting data effectively.
Questionnaire COMPUSTAT	Multiple regression	Accelerated cost recovery system; investment tax credit	Small and large businesses fared equally well under provisions of ERTA in terms of using ITC & ACRS.
Questionnaire	t-test	Disclosure requirements	Disclosure requirements less important for private than public firms; less important for small private than large private firms; considered same for all public firms.
Interview; questionnaire		Training needs for retail managers	Determinants of training needs; financial skills and marketing skills more deficient.
Questionnaire	Mean; t-test	Equality and harmony of working relationships of couples in small business	Survey of working relationships in small business of couples. There is a positive relationship or beneficial impact upon marriage.

(Table 10-3. continued overleaf)

Table 10-3. continued

Small Business Segment Studied	Author(s)	Types of Organization Studied	Sample Size
b. Micro (continued)	McEvoy (1984) JSBM Vol. 22, No. 4	Small business	84 managers

Abbreviations for Journals:

AMJ — Academy of Management Journal
JSBM — Journal of Small Business Management
DAI — Dissertation Abstracts International
FER — Frontiers of Entrepreneurship Research
ASQ — Administrative Science Quarterly
Proc. SMA — Proceedings, Southern Management Assn.
Proc. ICSB — Proceedings, International Council for Small Business
Proc. AOM — Proceedings, Academy of Management

CRITIQUE OF RESEARCH ON SMALL BUSINESS

In analyzing the research on small business, the most commonly used types of industry are retail stores and manufacturers (Table 10-3). Most of the other studies cut across all types of industries and geographical settings. These types of studies are similar to those on individual entrepreneurship. Although sample sizes vary widely, most of the sample sizes are large enough for critical statistical significance.

In almost every study, some type of mail questionnaire or combination of interview and questionnaire was employed. Only a few studies used instruments or tests of any type. Behaviorists have not used as many psychometrically designed instruments and tests in small business studies as they have in entrepreneurship studies. When instruments are used, they are the same types used in studies of individual entrepreneurship. In fact, many of the same authors are involved in the same types of studies on both entrepreneurs and small business owner-managers. As in the case of entrepreneurs, seldom

Table 10–3. continued

Research Method/ Instrument	Statistical Method	Issues Studied	Content of the Study
Questionnaire interview		Personnel practices in small firms	Survey of personnel practices in small business.

has an instrument been specifically designed for small business owner-managers or small businesses.

In the past five years, there has been a significant shift in the number of studies on small business using statistical techniques. In 1980, eight studies noted in this analysis were statistical compared to twenty-six studies in 1984. But the researchers are still producing a significant number of studies using raw data or percentages. In fact, the relative percentage of studies employing statistical techniques versus those using raw data or percentages has been relatively constant over the past five-year period. Although means, ranking, t-tests, and correlation are still used, there has been a significant upgrading in the level of sophistication in type of statistic employed during the past five years. Far more researchers are using sophisticated parametric and nonparametric statistical techniques, including multivariate analysis of variance, different types of multiple regression, and nonparametric statistics.

With respect to the issues studied in small business research, there is a difference between small business and individual entrepreneurship research. Only a few studies are related to the characteristics of owner-managers. Most of the studies in small business are related to usage of given business functions in operating small business (e.g., management, production, marketing, finance, accounting, and personnel). Furthermore, most of these studies are oriented toward truly operational (micro) issues as contrasted to macro issues. Few of the studies are oriented toward the strategic components of the major functional areas. Throughout the entire set of studies analyzed, there is an overwhelming feeling of confusion—as if these studies belonged to a field but had not yet found a framework within which to fit. A well-defined framework for small business research has not yet been proposed and widely adopted.

Although the field of entrepreneurship (individual and corporate) is larger than that of small business, the content (set of topics) of small business research covers a much broader area than the content of individual entrepreneurship research. Some of the topical areas in small business have not been covered in depth, but there definitely is a broader set of issues than that found in individual entrepreneurship.

Based upon the suggested typology for small business research, there are still many different topical areas that need to be studied. New challenges for significant research exist.

RESEARCH INTERFACE BETWEEN INDIVIDUAL ENTREPRENEURSHIP AND SMALL BUSINESS

In terms of the interface areas noted in Figure 10-1, there has been very little research in the environmental area. Neither the macro-environment (international and national) nor the microenvironment have received significant amounts of research attention. In both areas, some authors could argue that they have indeed studied the microenvironment (internal to the organization) through their studies on the characteristics of entrepreneurs and small business owner-managers. But most of these studies are still primarily oriented to the characteristics of entrepreneurs or owner-managers and not to the environments in which they operate. Part of this lack of attention may be due to the complexity of external environmental issues and part may be due to the absence of comprehensive sub-frameworks on the environment.

With respect to the characteristics of entrepreneurs and owner-managers, we may already have a sufficient number of the types of questionnaire survey design to provide directions toward far more sophisticated inquiry into the makeup of these individuals. Moreover, these studies again are not related to any systematic framework of either entrepreneurship or small business. Through meta-analysis, significant variables could be singled out for further research.

Many potential research topics in individual entrepreneurship and small business have not been attacked. These include studies that develop theories, frameworks, definitions, and models of the entire fields and the subcomponents of these fields. Historical and longitudinal studies are rare.

The overriding factor for the development of both fields appears to be the need for comprehensive frameworks that provide the impetus for systematic research on all parts of both fields.

RESEARCH PROSPECTUS ON INDIVIDUAL ENTREPRENEURSHIP

From a comprehensive overview, many different topics exist for research in the area of individual entrepreneurship. But there are other overriding issues that should be examined before proceeding to individual topics or topical areas within the field. For example, the issue of why only certain types of organization have been investigated still exists. Perhaps the simplistic answer is that certain types of small business are much easier to analyze because the data are available. There may be more complex answers to the question of why certain types of small businesses were examined to the exclusion of others. Some of the questions that need to be answered are:

- Why are so many of the studies oriented to retail stores and to manufacturing? and

- Why have specific types of business not been investigated rather than always seeming to take in all the small businesses in the surrounding area?

With respect to research design, perhaps the field has reached the point at which fewer exploratory studies should be conducted on individual characteristics, and at which more well-designed studies which relate to an overall framework should be conducted. The design of these studies should not only relate to an overall framework of individual entrepreneurship but should also be targeted to a specific population or sample (instead of all venture firms, all small businesses, etc.) and utilize appropriate statistical techniques that would lead to the external validity of the studies. Moreover, statistical techniques to check the reliability of the data and of the instruments used should be employed.

Studies that have been providing raw data or percentages should employ increasingly sophisticated techniques of analysis and be tied to a unified framework. Certainly, some elemental descriptive statistics such as t-tests, correlation, and *Chi*-square could be used to provide more practical use (as well as theoretical use) of these studies. In addition, these studies could be truly useful in adding to the scientific knowledge base of individual entrepreneurship.

Studies that have been utilizing sophisticated statistics should be tied to a unified framework of entrepreneurship so that others may build upon their works. If this step is not taken, the field will continue to be a quagmire of unrelated or seemingly unrelated topics and subtopics.

In the following sections, some suggested research questions based upon the individual entrepreneurship typology have been raised. These are just a few samples of topics that have not been examined or only slightly analyzed.

Theoretical Studies

There have been few systematic attempts to frame out what we know about individual entrepreneurship from the literature into a comprehensive theory of entrepreneurship. If this framework were based upon present research and proposed research, a theoretical framework could be formulated that would demonstrate the gaps in the field and provide the challenge to fill in those gaps.

What is needed is not just what is happening in each of these sub-components but a systematic analysis of the research (e.g., psychological) in each sub-framework followed by a theoretical framework which would demonstrate the interconnectedness of the parts of the sub-framework and of the sub-framework to the comprehensive framework.

Agreement upon a short, common definition of entrepreneurship (corporate and individual) is probably more needed than additional definitions of entrepreneurship. Moreover, models of entrepreneurship on both process and content bases need to be developed and related to a comprehensive, understandable framework.

Environmental Studies

Few environmental studies have been completed, and those that have been are usually related to psychological characteristics of the individual. Therefore, studies examining environmental factors are needed on both macro and micro bases. This would permit the relationships between environment and individual characteristics of entrepreneurs to be analyzed. Questions that should be asked about the environment include:

- What internal and external environmental factors have an impact upon the effectiveness of an entrepreneur?

- What relationships exist between environmental factors and individual characteristics of an entrepreneur?

- What differences exist in internal environments for entrepreneurs in owner-managed companies versus large-scale companies?

- What environmental differences are there in business, governmental and nonprofit organizations for entrepreneurs?

Organizational Studies

Although studies of individual entrepreneurship in business firms, government agencies, and nonprofit organizations do exist, there are few comparative studies. As a fruitful area of comparative analysis in entrepreneurship, several illustrative questions emerge:

- Are entrepreneurs different in different types of organizations including business, government, and nonprofit organizations?

- Are individual entrepreneurs affected by the management processes involved in different types of organizations?

- Do entrepreneurs serve similar or dissimilar roles in different types of organization?

- What impact do entrepreneurs have in the different types of organization?

Functional Studies

The present types of study of characteristics of individual entrepreneurs should be halted until a systematic analysis of previous studies has been set in an overall framework of entrepreneurship. At that point, additional sophisticated statistical studies should be undertaken. Presently there is a question of how useful the research on characteristics has been and whether additional studies may actually be harmful rather than helpful. However, studies on the careers in a theoretical context and studies on job characteristics (as contrasted to individual characteristics) of entrepreneurial jobs could be quite useful. Examples of the types of research questions that would be useful in functional studies are:

- What relationship does an entrepreneur have to the actual structure of the organization within which he or she functions?

- Are entrepreneurs better at one or more of the usual functions of an organization? How are these related to the success of the organization?

- What roles do other business functions (other than long-range planning) play in the development of entrepreneurial organizations?

- What generalizable factors are possible for individual entrepreneurs (based upon all the previous research studies)? How are these factors related to organization, role, and environment?

RESEARCH PROSPECTUS ON SMALL BUSINESS

Many of the same conclusions could be drawn about future research on small business that have been drawn about research on individual entrepreneurship. There are differences in the emphases laid upon particular topics in the two fields. Both fields have overemphasized the research in certain areas, although not the same area, and have completely neglected other parts of the fields.

First, there has been a tremendous amount of small business research in one area—that of the operations of small business. Second, there has been extensive research on the individual characteristics of owner-managers. Although a moratorium is not suggested on the research in these two areas, there should be a call for significantly improved research designs throughout the field with an even stronger emphasis upon sophisticated research designs.

Different types of business should be investigated on an individual basis rather than on a mass basis. Although statistical analysis has improved substantially in the past five years in small business research, there is a clear need to move away from the reporting of raw data with little or no statistical analysis.

Theoretical Studies

Redundancy could be the theme of this section. The call for conceptual studies of all types that was issued for individual entrepreneurship research could also be issued for small business research. These conceptual studies are necessary to provide us with the theories, frameworks, models, and definitions that would give us the impetus to improve the structuring of the field of small business. Each theory, framework or sub-framework, model, and definition needs to be related to an overall framework of the field. Although researchers in this field are constantly formulating their own definitions of small business, there is little consensus on the definition of small business from an operational point of view.

Environmental Studies

Since few environmental studies have been initiated, many such studies could be undertaken if they were tied to a comprehensive framework for the small business field. Questions of environment (both macro and micro) were asked in the individual entrepreneur research section, and similar questions could be asked in the small business context. Other questions related to environment that could be investigated include:

- What environmental factors, if any, differentiate between entrepreneurs and owner-managers?
- Do entrepreneurs and owner-managers operate in similar internal or external environmental contexts?
- Are there any environmental contexts (external or internal) in which small business owner-managers are more successful? Less successful?

Occupational Studies

Although significant numbers of studies of owner-manager careers and of the characteristics of owner-managers have been conducted, additional studies could be undertaken if they were related to a comprehensive framework. Moreover, these studies should not be the reporting of raw data and percentages but should be far more sophisticated in their statistical analysis. This analysis is indeed possible today if we would examine all of the exploratory studies that have already been completed. Some research questions that could be asked include:

- What generalizable factors have led to the concept of the owner-manager? How diffuse are these factors?
- Are there any significant occupational backgrounds which have led individuals to become owner-managers?

Functional Studies

Many studies of operations in small business have already been completed. However, there are many facets of management, marketing, accounting, finance, and personnel that have not been examined in-depth in a small business context. For example, planning as a topic in small business should be relegated to a long moratorium because so many studies have already been completed. If studies in this area are continued, they should be far more complex in design if they are to derive any usefulness for small business owner-operators. Many structural and behavioral facets of the functional areas of business remain as virgin territories for researchers in small business.

Strategic components of management, marketing, finance, accounting, and personnel remain untouched as significant research areas for small business researchers. A few sample questions follow:

- Are entrepreneurial chief executive officers different than owner-manager chief executive officers?
- How do owner-managers become strategic managers? Are there differences between strategic managers and entrepreneurs?
- Are there differences between strategic managers and entrepreneurs in change-seeking behavior, risk propensity, divergence in problem solving, and innovativeness?

CONCLUSION

An interface exists between entrepreneurship and small business. However, there is little interface between small business and corporate entrepreneurship. What is needed most is the development of a comprehensive set of frameworks for both areas. If such a framework were developed, it could lead to significant advancement in the fields of individual entrepreneurship and small business.

NOTES TO CHAPTER 10

1. Arnold C. Cooper, "The Entrepreneurship-Small Business Interface," in Calvin A. Kent, Donald L. Sexton, and Karl H. Vespter, eds., *Encyclopedia of Entrepreneurship* (Englewood Cliffs, N.J.: Prentice-Hall, 1982), pp. 193-205; Justin G. Longenecker, "Commentary on the Entrepreneurship-Small Business Interface," in Kent, Sexton, and Vesper, eds., *Encyclopedia of Entrepreneurship*, pp. 206-7.
2. Kenneth E. Loucks, "A Survey of Research on Small Business Management and Entrepreneurship in Canada," in Vesper, *Frontiers of Entrepreneurship Research* (Wellesley, Mass.: Babson Center for Entrepreneurial Studies, 1981), pp. 111-129; Karl H. Vesper, "Scanning the Frontier of Entrepreneurship Research," in Vesper, *Frontiers of Entrepreneurship Research*, pp. vii-xiv; William C. Dunkelberg and Arnold C. Cooper, "Entrepreneurial Typologies: An Empirical Study," in Vesper, *Frontiers of Entrepreneurship Research, 1982*, pp. 1-15; Jo Ann C. Carland and James W. Carland, "A Taxonomical Approach to Small Business," *Proceedings*, Southern Management Association, 1983, pp. 338-40.
3. Barbara H. Moore, ed., *The Entrepreneur in Local Government* (Washington, D.C.: International City Management Association, 1983); E. I. Rudd, "Responding to the Challenge of Fiscal Stress: The Public Entrepreneurial Approach the Answer? A Study of the Use of Entrepreneurial Management Strategies, in Municipal Park and Recreation Departments in Southern California," *Dissertation Abstracts International* 44: 11 (May 1984): 3490A.

11 ENTREPRENEURSHIP RESEARCH
Directions and Methods

Neil C. Churchhill
Virginia L. Lewis

The state-of-the-art of entrepreneurial research methodology was surveyed in a paper presented at the 1981 Baylor Conference by Paulin, Coffey, and Spauldin.[1] Their philosophy: " . . . it is of prime importance that the research should focus on significant questions." Their paper takes the position that research should be as carefully and systematically designed as possible, given the topic and practical circumstances. In the paper the emphasis is on describing:

- The way the area of inquiry of the research interacts with the methodology.

- The extent to which the research attempts to contribute to the improvement of practice, the improvement of theory (understanding), or the improvement of methodology—and thus, derivatively, to both practice and theory.

- The centrality of the research to the core issues and problems of the field.

Motivation for such an approach comes from two sources: a belief that research in the entrepreneurial and small business areas has developed to a point where more systematic attention to key problems will be fruitful for both theory and practice, and the need to recognize and deal with two characteristics of the field:

1. Individuals actively involved in entrepreneurship have related more to the practitioner than to the university. Thus they are somewhat outside the mainstream of academic activity and are perceived as taking more from the academic community than they return to it.

2. Entrepreneurship is viewed as a very applied field and unsuitable (fraught with danger) for the teaching and research activities of young scholars.

BACKGROUND

Words used to describe the field of entrepreneurship research are "young,"[2] "at a formative stage,"[3] and "still in its infancy."[4] Even the definition of entrepreneurship is neither agreed upon nor static. It is restricted by some to new ventures, viewed by others to necessitate personal risk, and more recently has come to include initiatives in any organization that involve innovation, a new strategic direction involving risk, and a significant new combination of strategic "factors of production."[5] The field is young, complex, involved in a process of discovery and transition, and the recipient of increased attention and the basis for economic hope. It is a field involving, appropriately, considerable discovery-oriented research; hence, it is no wonder that its research directions are fragmented, creative, and diverse.

These observations are not unique unto entrepreneurship but have been applied to other fields of management study. Thus it seemed appropriate to examine entrepreneurial research with lenses polished by the research activities of the similar but slightly more mature fields of business policy (strategy) and marketing. Business policy was chosen because it is relatively new, still struggling with the problems of complexity, and a field from which a number of entrepreneurial researchers have moved. Marketing was chosen because it has recently examined the state of its research and methodology and, like the field of entrepreneurship, has shown signs of a growing tension between those who would serve practice and those who would serve theory.

The Field of Business Policy

There is general consensus that the field of business policy (or strategic management) (a) is at an early stage of development, (b) possesses complex phenomena, (c) that are subtle, and (d) has a plethora of facts but a lack of theory. It is a field in which the underlying constructs are not well formulated, where many of the compelling research problems have not been adequately defined, and where theory development is of primary concern.

In addressing the research methodologies appropriate in the policy/ strategy field, most writers agree that considerable exploratory, theory-building research is needed. This is put the most strongly by Duncan, who states: "Policy research has been more concerned with asking questions about complex, relevant problems organizations face in terms of strategic decision-making and policy formulation than with research rigor." He criticizes inappropriate rigor by saying: "Policy questions in their relevant scope have tended to be ignored by organizational theorists who have been more concerned about rigor," and that "organizational theorists seem to learn more and more about less and less."[6]

This theme is picked up by Hatten, who states: "Quantitative research methods have had little impact on Business Policy so far," and "the most important quantitative research issue in policy is to establish just what the different findings mean and to develop a rigorous theory describing how they are linked."[7]

In a survey of strategic planning research, Hofer found the four principal research thrusts to be: hypothesis formulation; surveys, sometimes accompanied by limited interviews, to understand phenomena; field studies in depth in a limited number of companies; and experiential treatments (vignettes) of "how it is done" in different companies under different circumstances. Hofer criticized strategic planning research in general for lacking validity, failing to build on what had gone before, and introducing "spurious causality" through the researchers' implicit hypotheses.[8] This latter point is a concern of Duncan, who refers to it as the "enactment problem" in field research—a situation where a researcher with questionnaires or interviews can create a structure in the mind of the interviewer that never existed before the question was asked. This means that, in the absence of considerable understanding, researchers must be careful in evaluation of responses to refrain from deducing what someone really does (*theory in use*) from what the individual says he does (*espoused theory*). In ill-structured field situations, the researcher may have more influence on the research results than is realized.

Hofer summed up research needs in strategy by stating:

> Because of the subtlety and complexity of the strategic planning process, there always will be a need for some in-depth field studies. The fact that more of the theory and research findings in the strategic planning area is situational or contingent in nature indicates that larger samples will be needed to assure the external validity of any set of findings. At the same time, questions of causation and the time dimensions associated with most strategic planning issues and processes will continue to require that most studies be longitudinal. Taken together, these factors imply that new approaches to research design and methodology will be needed to support new research in this area.[9]

The implications of the business policy research literature for entrepreneurial research are:

- Entrepreneurial research is also at an early stage with little theory to guide it. Thus considerable emphasis on exploratory research is warranted to provide insights and build theories for subsequent testing.

- Rigorous methodology for rigor's sake is inappropriate.

- Care must be taken in field research not to produce "enactment problems." This is particularly relevant to research contacts with action-oriented entrepreneurs who are not always inclined to introspection.

- Case studies or "experiential vignettes" have considerable use but should be carried one step further by (a) utilizing what has gone before, and (b) generalizing from the particular to the general so that others have something upon which to build.

The Field of Marketing

The field of marketing was chosen, in part, because of a recent examination of its theoretical status in the Fall 1983 *Journal of Marketing*. Review of the marketing field could thus be limited to this issue.

From these papers it can be seen that although the university community is properly concerned with research, science, and theory, its members are influenced by the evaluations of their peers and concerned that they too be viewed as engaged in "scientific study." Unfortunately, too many academicians view science strictly from the limited view of science as an inquiry system that produces objectively proven knowledge, rather than any socially organized information-producing activity. Too narrow a view of what is "science" can, on the margin, hold back investigations into the core of complex, applied problems that are not easily "proven objectively" and can restrict the choice of problems to those that are amenable to the "scientific method." On the positive side, it encourages considering the relationships between the field under investigation and the broader problems of society.

In addition to the conflict between the differing views of science three other constructs important to entrepreneurship emerge from marketing's introspection:

1. There are two classes of theoretical developments that are relevant to almost any field of study. One is improvements in the understanding of the field itself (*substantive theory*); the other is improvements in the methodologies relevant to the field (*methodological theory*).

2. In an applied field (such as marketing or entrepreneurship) there are two classes of substantive theory: *theory for understanding* and *theory for use*. The first aims at increasing the simplicity of explanation and the breadth of fundamental understanding of the broad concepts of a field; the second, at discovering ways to improve practice and to synthesize complex phenomena for the use of practitioners in the field.

3. Marketing, along with business policy, is concerned with improving the present state of substantive theory in the field and with focusing a majority of these improvements on "theory for understanding."

A final comment from marketing deals with the conflict between attempting to understand the basic concepts of the field and trying to understand and deal with the vast complexity of the problems faced by the practitioner in the field. Anderson observes:

Traditionally, marketers have viewed their discipline as an applied area concerned largely with the improvement of managerial practice. However, the broadening concept makes it clear that marketing is a generic human activity which may be studied simply because it is an intrinsically interesting social phenomenon. On this view, the *exchange process* [emphasis added] itself becomes the focus of attention in much the same way that communication is the focus of communication theorists and administration is the focus of administrative scientists. The interest must lie in understanding and explaining the phenomenon itself, rather than understanding it from the perspective of only one of the participants.[10]

STRUCTURE OF THE ANALYSIS

Looking at the state-of-the-art of business policy and marketing research suggested that a similar analysis of research in entrepreneurship should take into account three concepts that relate to methodology but which transcend "methodological" classification in any narrow sense:

1. The *objective* of the study: whether its purpose is to improve the understanding of entrepreneurship (*theory*), to enhance the *practice* of entrepreneurship, or to advance *methodology* appropriate to research in the field;
2. The *topic* of the study, and
3. The extent to which the research is *central*—directed toward the core problems and questions (issues) of the field.

Objective of the Research

Any theory that attempts to further understanding of the practice of entrepreneurship is without argument desirable in a new and essentially pragmatic and exploratory field. Practice-oriented studies can serve several important purposes. They can provide feedback to the researcher on the accuracy of his or her perceptions; they can, if done properly, add to the understanding of entrepreneurs and entrepreneurship; and they can, of course, contribute to the development of successful entrepreneurial activities in both new and established firms.

There are, however, some disadvantages to a disproportionate leaning toward a theory of practice. Although adding to the knowledge of entrepreneurship, such a focus rarely contributes to the understanding of broader aspects of economic, organizational, or managerial behavior. This means that practice-oriented research *takes from other disciplines while returning little to them.* This is detrimental both to the discipline and to the academic community itself, for issues that require interdisciplinary understanding—and whose investigation could generate real insights for both entrepreneurship and for allied fields—may never be addressed due to lack of cross-fertilization of scholarly pursuits.

An advantage of theory-directed research is, however, that insights gained in looking at entrepreneurial organizations may be (and should be) compared with the theory base developed from studies of large, traditional organizations. Such comparisons can enhance understanding of both entrepreneurial and general management theory.

Finally, there are subtle costs to the individuals aligning themselves with a discipline that focuses primarily on practice. Since a focus on practice contributes little toward generic understanding, it fails to provide a base upon which theoretical understanding can build. Further, since the methodology appropriate to practice-based research tends to be informed observation and exploratory studies in field situations, the research tools required are primarily an understanding of entrepreneurial practice and the vocabulary of the entrepreneur.

The third research objective, methodological theory or improvement of methodology, also presents some peculiar challenges for the field of entrepreneurship. In entrepreneurial research—perhaps more than in any other field—the most severe methodological shortcoming is at present lack of data in organized or accessible form. Thus, any systematic research must be preceded, in most cases, by an extensive data collection effort.

The position of the authors with regard to research is that extensive topical analysis of research in entrepreneurship is less important than the concept of centrality to the core issues of the field.

Centrality to the Core Issues of the Field

Given the increasing attention being paid entrepreneurship by business schools, the approach taken was to look at current research from the standpoint of its proximity to what might be considered

Figure 11-1.   Convergence toward the Core Issues and Problems.

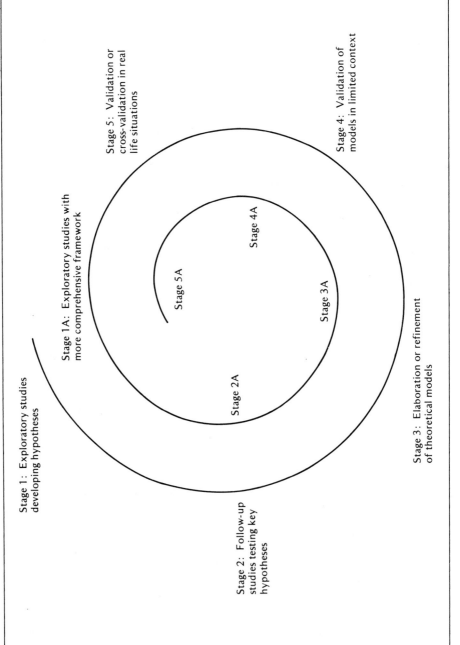

Stage 1: Exploratory studies developing hypotheses

Stage 1A: Exploratory studies with more comprehensive framework

Stage 5: Validation or cross-validation in real life situations

Stage 4: Validation of models in limited context

Stage 5A

Stage 4A

Stage 3A

Stage 2A

Stage 2: Follow-up studies testing key hypotheses

Stage 3: Elaboration or refinement of theoretical models

the *central questions* or *core issues* of the field. This required both considering what core issues are and finding a method for determining centrality.

Core Issues. Taking a broad, inclusive view of the research topics, we included almost all the research that addressed itself to: characteristics of the entrepreneur, characteristics of the entrepreneurial organization (whether small or large), the environmental factors conducive or nonconducive to entrepreneurship, and the impact on society as a whole of entrepreneurial activity. This view excluded only the most peripheral studies, since the concern was whether or not the study was done in a way that enabled it to contribute to understanding the critical (core) issues and problems of the field.

Centrality. Centrality is defined as the extent to which the research study *converged* on the core issues of the field rather than addressing peripheral aspects of either theory or practice and thus draining resources and detracts from more important (i.e., core) issues. This centrality or convergence is independent of the methodology used. If McGrath's programmatic concept is adapted somewhat, the picture of convergence shown in Figure 11–1 emerges.[11] Thus, exploratory studies lead to development of hypotheses, to hypothesis testing, and to validation and cross-validation—and these in turn lead to the development of (perhaps) simpler, more lucid, and more comprehensive hypotheses, to a second (and third, and so on) level of "exploration" in an ever-tightening concentric motion toward the core of the issue, problem, or phenomenon. This can be a test of either theory, practice, *or* methodology, for the test of a "convergent" methodologically oriented study would be the "power" of the methodology for supporting core research in either an explanatory (theoretical) or operationally useful (practical) way.

ANALYSIS OF DATA

To understand how entrepreneurship research was being conducted on the *methodology, objective, topic,* and *centrality* dimensions, two sets of data were developed from primary entrepreneurship or small business publications (e.g., the *Journal of Small Business Management*) as well as from other journals that are secondary sources for entrepreneurship research (e.g., the *California Management Review*). The first set of data was constructed through computer search of the ABI/INFORM data base (Dialog Information Services). More out of curiosity than anything else, we requested a count of all entries in the data base (which begins with 1971) that contained any variation of four keywords—entrepreneur, small business, corporate-venturing, and intrapreneur. There were 6,322 such entries. The search was then limited to the period of interest, 1981 through 1984, to determine the extent of entrepreneurship research published since the 1981 Baylor Conference. A search on all publications for this period produced 3,694 entries. Since 1981, almost three-fifths of the total publications related to this field have been published.

To develop a data base more amenable to analysis, the final search was limited to ten journals (Appendix 11-A) that contain, if not most, a good representation of the research studies in the entrepreneurial field. This produced 298 abstracts containing one or more variations of the four keywords. These abstracts form the "Journal Data Base."

The second data set was composed of articles published in the proceedings of the four Babson Conferences (1981 through 1984) and the 1983 Harvard Symposium on Entrepreneurship (see also Appendix 11-A). The conferences were chosen both to round out the study and to capture the newer developments in the field, which in many cases had not yet been published in the traditional journals. The 150 research papers presented at the conferences and symposium form the "Conference Data Base."

The first step in the analysis of the data was to classify each item in the data bases. This was done by methodology, topic, research objective, and centrality to the core issues in entrepreneurship. The second step was to evaluate these analyses both by means of cross-classifications and comparisons between the data bases. The third step was to evaluate the results. The way in which the basic classifications were made varied to some extent by data base due to their very different natures. Thus the classification procedures are described separately for the two sets of data.

Journal Abstracts

Each of the 298 abstracts of journal articles on entrepreneurship and small business in the "Journal Data Base" were classified as according to general *topic* and *research methodology used.* The six methodological classifications utilized (Appendix 11–B) were an abbreviated version of those used in the prior survey on entrepreneurial research methodologies.[12] A total of fifteen groupings were used (Appendix 11–B). This was a compromise between capturing the diversity of the research studies examined and doing so with a tractable number of classifications.

The next classification performed on each study was *research objective*—improvement of *understanding (theory)*, improvement of *practice*, and improvement of the *methodologies* relevant to entrepreneurial research. These classifications were made with somewhat less precision than topic or methodology due to the limitation the use of abstracts placed on our judgmental ability. This was even more pronounced when we began the fourth classification—*centrality*, or convergence of the study toward the core issues in the field. For this reason an intermediate category of *almost convergence* to the core was added to *convergence* and *non-convergence*—and some 21.5 percent of the journal studies fell into this borderline classification.

Conference Proceedings

A similar classification process was carried out on the 150 conference papers forming the "Conference Data Base." The topical headings were those developed in the analysis of journal abstracts, and the same steps were followed. There is somewhat less subjectivity in these categorizations since complete research reports were used.

Analysis of the Classifications

Topic. There was, as expected, considerable diversity in the concentration of research in the fifteen topical categories (see Table 11–1). The category encompassing the most studies (69) was *Domestic Operations*—a "how to" manage entrepreneurial enterprises better and more effectively in domestic markets. The three categories with the lowest total number of studies were *International Operations, Entrepreneurial Climate* and *Buying, Selling and Valuing* with twelve, thirteen, and fourteen studies respectively. (The average of 448 studies on any of fifteen topics would be, of course, thirty.)

Table 11-1. Analysis of Research Topics.

Topic	Journals		Conferences		Row Total	Row Percent
	No.	%	No.	%		
Entrepreneurial Climate, Relation to Society	7	2.3	6	4.0	13	2.9
Personal Characteristics of Entrepreneurs	16	5.4	37	24.7	53	11.8
Management Characteristics of Small or Entrepreneurial Firms	21	7.0	8	5.3	29	6.5
Start-ups, incl. data on	17	5.7	22	14.7	39	8.7
Financing and Venture Capital	11	3.7	20	13.3	31	6.9
Buying, Selling, and Valuing	12	4.0	2	1.3	14	3.1
High Technology	6	2.0	14	9.3	20	4.5
Strategy and Growth	23	7.7	1	0.7	24	5.4
Corporate Venturing	7	2.3	13	8.7	20	4.5
Crosscultural	11	3.7	6	4.0	17	3.8
Interface with Government: Regulation and Legislation	38	12.8	11	7.3	49	10.9
International Operations	12	4.0	0	0.0	12	2.7
Domestic Operations, incl. Computerization and Management Assistance	69	23.2	0	0.0	69	15.4
Accounting, Tax	39	13.1	0	0.0	39	8.7
Entrepreneurial Education	9	3.0	10	6.7	19	4.2
Column Total	298	100.0	150	100.0	448	100.0

Table 11-2. Analysis of the Research Methodology.

| Methodology | Source of Data | | | | | |
| | Journals | | Conferences | | Row Total | Row Percent |
	No.	%	No.	%		
Observ./Contemp. Theory	162	54.4	34	22.7	196	43.8
Survey	70	23.5	79	52.7	149	33.3
Survey Using Public Data	11	3.7	14	9.3	25	5.6
Field Study	10	3.4	5	3.3	15	3.3
Computer Sim./Modeling	0	0.0	2	1.3	2	0.4
Vignette or "Reportage"	45	15.1	16	10.7	61	13.6
Column Total	298	100.0	150	100.0	448	100.0

Of considerable interest is the difference in research focus between the studies published in the journals and those given at research conferences. Four topics accounted for 48 percent of the journal papers but less than 1 percent of the conference studies. On the other hand, four different topics accounted for 61 percent of the conference studies and only 17 percent of the journal papers. The predominant topics of the journal articles were the "how to" subjects of *Domestic Operations*; *Accounting, Tax*; and *Interface with Government.* The least studied were *High Tech, Corporate Venturing*, and *Entrepreneurial Climate.*

In the conference reports the four most emphasized topics were *Personal Characteristics of Entrepreneurs, Start-Ups*, and *Financing and Venture Capital.* This strongly emphasizes the need to consider both journals and conference proceedings in order to understand what is occurring in a rapidly moving research field such as entrepreneurship.

Methodology. An examination of the methodologies utilized in the research studies, Table 11-2, shows a preponderance (77 percent) of *Observational and Contemplative Theory-Building* and *Surveys —* and few (less than 4 percent) *Field Studies* or examples of *Computer*

Modeling. Compared with topics studied, methodologies used were far less divergent as between data sources—but there was over twice as much use of *Observational and Contemplative Theory-Building* in the journal studies as in conference studies, while the conferences produced over twice the incidence of *Survey* methodologies.

The relative lack of field-based research—3.3 percent—is surprising for such a practice-based field, although this lack is mitigated to some extent since the vignettes are field-based and quite a few of the surveys involved field interviews as well as questionnaires. This may be attributed to some extent to an academic bias that views such studies as not being "research" or to the writers' failure to relate the case studies and field situations to the general problems or underlying theories of the field. These and the "how it was at the XYZ Corporation" were classified as Vignettes or "Reportage" in this survey. More troublesome, but not surprising, is the very small number of studies that utilized *public data.* The lack of surprise is due to widespread awareness of the paucity of good data on entrepreneurship and small business growth, development, and demise. One positive note in this area is the presence of six *methodological* research studies in the research data base—with three in the latest conference proceedings.

Topic-Methodology. While the topic classifications were sufficiently broad so that no topic had more than 15 percent nor less than 3 percent of the total studies, the methodologies used were more concentrated—44 percent of the studies used *Observational and Contemplative Theory-Building* and 33.3 percent used *Survey* (Table 11-2). Here again, methodological use was different between the journal and conference data sources.

Table 11-3 shows a varied pattern of topic and methodological pairings. Due to the dominance of two methodologies, we calculated a "threshold metric" of one-and-one-half times the average use of a methodology and used this in analyzing the crosstabulated data. Looking at topics, eight of them were predominately studied by a single methodology—only one that crossed the "threshold." Studies in, for example, *International Operations* and *Accounting, Tax* both used *Observational and Contemplative Theory-Building* some 75 percent of the time (1.71 times the average), but no other methodology was used even at an average level. In contrast, studies of two topics, *Corporate Venturing* and *Domestic Operations* never exceeded the "threshold" at all—indicating a broad approach to these problem areas. Looking at the cross-tabulation by methodology, there are few overall differences. No methodological use "crossed the threshold" in fewer than two nor more than four topics.

Objective. As expected in a practice-oriented field, by far the majority (63 percent) of the 448 research studies, Table 11-4, dealt with improving the *practice* of entrepreneurship. A contrast existed between studies published in journals (75 percent) and those in proceedings, where only 36 percent of the papers dealt with practice. Not surprisingly, there were only six studies, all presented at conferences, that dealt primarily with methodological improvements—for the most part with building data bases.

Examination of research objective by topic studied, Table 11-5, reveals that research into some topics is exclusively, or almost exclusively, practice-oriented. Five such topics are the subject of over half—144—of the 282 practice-oriented studies, but only of five theory-oriented ones—the last four listed in Table 11-5, plus *Buying, Selling, and Valuing.* If *Interface with Government, etc.* is added, the numbers are 184 practice and 18 theory. On the other side, *Personal Characteristics of Entrepreneurs, Entrepreneurial Climate,* and, to a lesser extent, *Corporate Venturing* are predominantly theory-oriented—with a ratio of fifty-two theoretical to twenty practice-oriented studies.

Centrality. Before examining the data on the centrality of the research, it is important to recall the subjectivity with which these judgments are made—particularly in our ability to apply the criteria to the journal abstracts. Thus the following analysis should be approached with "a modicum of humor."

Looking first at the data in total and by data source, Table 11-6, almost half (46 percent) of all the studies were central (convergent) to the core issues of entrepreneurship; 37 percent were not central; and 17 percent were almost central or ambiguous as to centrality. For studies reported upon at conferences 57 percent were central and 35 percent were noncentral. The numbers for journal articles showed essentially the same percentage of nonconvergence—41 percent and 38 percent, respectively. There was a considerably higher percentage of almost-convergent articles in the journals than in the conference reports. This may be due to some underlying factors but

Table 11-3. Analysis of Topic and Methodology of the Research.

Topic	Obs./Cont. Theory		Survey		Survey-Pub. Data		Field Studies		Computer Sim.		Vignette		Row Total	Row Percent
	No.	%	No.	%	No.	%	No.	%	No.	%	No.	%		
Entrepreneurial Climate, Relation to Society	8	61.5	2	15.4	3	23.1	0	0.0	0	0.0	0	0.0	13	100.0
Personal Characteristics of Entrepreneurs	11	20.8	36	67.9	1	1.9	0	0.0	1	1.9	4	7.5	53	100.0
Management Characteristics of Small or Entrepreneurial Firms	13	44.8	15	51.7	1	3.4	0	0.0	0	0.0	0	0.0	29	100.0
Start-ups, incl. data on	15	38.5	11	28.2	6	15.4	2	5.1	1	2.6	4	10.3	39	100.0
Financing and Venture Capital	6	19.4	20	64.5	4	12.9	1	3.2	0	0.0	0	0.0	31	100.0
Buying, Selling, and Valuing	8	57.1	2	14.3	0	0.0	0	0.0	0	0.0	4	28.6	14	100.0
High Technology	5	25.0	9	45.0	2	10.0	1	5.0	0	0.0	3	15.0	20	100.0
Strategy and Growth	15	62.5	4	16.7	2	8.3	3	12.5	0	0.0	0	0.0	24	100.0
Corporate Venturing	11	55.0	8	40.0	0	0.0	1	5.0	0	0.0	0	0.0	20	100.0
Crosscultural	4	23.5	2	11.8	1	5.9	3	17.6	0	0.0	7	41.2	17	100.0
Interface with Government: Regulation and Legislation	11	22.4	11	22.4	3	6.1	1	2.0	0	0.0	23	46.9	49	100.0

Methodology

	No.	%	No.	%	No.	%	No.	%	No.	%	No.	%	Total	%
International Operations	9	75.0	3	25.0	0	0.0	0	0.0	0	0.0	0	0.0	12	100.0
Domestic Operations, incl. Computerization and Management Assistance	44	63.8	13	18.8	1	1.4	3	4.3	0	0.0	8	11.6	69	100.0
Accounting, Tax	29	74.4	5	12.8	1	2.6	0	0.0	0	0.0	4	10.3	39	100.0
Entrepreneurial Education	7	36.8	8	42.1	0	0.0	0	0.0	0	0.0	4	21.1	19	100.0
Column Total/Percent	196	43.8	149	33.3	25	5.6	15	3.3	2	0.4	61	13.6	448	100.0

Table 11-4. Analysis of the Objective of the Research.

| | Source of Data | | | | | | | |
| | Journals | | Conferences | | | Row Total | Row Percent |
Topic	No.	%	No.	%			
Theory	73	24.5	87	58.0		160	35.7
Practice	225	75.5	57	38.0		282	62.9
Methodology	0	0.0	6	4.0		6	1.3
Column Totals	298	100.0	150	100.0		448	100.0

Table 11-5. Analysis of Topic and Objective of the Research.

| | Source of Data | | | | | | | | | | | | |
| | Journals | | | | Conferences | | | | Subtotals | | | Row Total |
Topic	T	P	M	Total	T	P	M	Total	T	P	M	
Entrepreneurial Climate, Relation to Society	4	3	0	7	5	0	1	6	9	3	1	13
Personal Characteristics of Entrepreneurs	8	8	0	16	31	6	0	37	39	14	0	53
Management Characteristics of Small or Entrepreneurial Firms	11	10	0	21	6	2	0	8	17	12	0	29
Start-ups, incl. data on	7	10	0	17	8	11	3	22	15	21	3	39
Financing and Venture Capital	5	6	0	11	13	6	1	20	18	12	1	31
Buying, Selling, and Valuing	1	11	0	12	1	1	0	2	2	12	0	14
High Technology	4	2	0	6	6	8	0	14	10	10	0	20
Strategy and Growth	12	11	0	23	1	0	0	1	13	11	0	24
Corporate Venturing	4	3	0	7	9	3	1	13	13	6	1	20
Cross-cultural	5	6	0	11	3	3	0	6	8	9	0	17
Interface with Government: Regulation and Legislation	9	29	0	38	4	7	0	11	13	36	0	49

International Operations	2	10	0	12	0	0	0	0	2	10	0	12
Domestic Operations, incl. Computerization and Management Assistance	0	69	0	69	0	0	0	0	0	69	0	69
Accounting, Tax	1	38	0	39	0	0	0	0	1	38	0	39
Entrepreneurial Education	0	9	0	9	0	10	0	10	0	19	0	19
Column Total	73	225	0	298	87	57	6	150	160	282	6	448

Table 11-6. Analysis of the Centrality of the Research.

	Source of Data					
	Journals		Conferences		Row Total	Row Percent
Centrality	No.	%	No.	%		
Convergent	122	40.9	85	56.7	207	46.2
Almost Convergent	64	21.5	13	8.7	77	17.2
Non-Convergent	112	37.6	52	34.7	164	36.6
Column Totals	298	100.0	150	100.0	448	100.0

Table 11-7. Analysis of Topic and Centrality of the Research.

Topic	Centrality						Row Total	Row Percent
	Convergent		Almost Convergent		Non-Convergent			
	No.	%	No.	%	No.	%		
Entrepreneurial Climate, Relation to Society	8	61.5	5	38.5	0	0.0	13	100.0
Personal Characteristics of Entrepreneurs	6	11.3	15	28.3	32	60.4	53	100.0
Management Characteristics of Small or Entrepreneurial Firms	18	62.1	5	17.2	6	20.7	29	100.0
Start-ups, incl. data on	19	48.7	9	23.1	11	28.2	39	100.0
Financing and Venture Capital	26	83.9	0	0.0	5	16.1	31	100.0
Buying, Selling, and Valuing	6	42.9	4	28.6	4	28.6	14	100.0
High Technology	12	60.0	1	5.0	7	35.0	20	100.0
Strategy and Growth	14	58.3	8	33.3	2	8.3	24	100.0
Corporate Venturing	16	80.0	4	20.0	0	0.0	20	100.0
Cross-cultural	11	64.7	2	11.8	4	23.5	17	100.0

Interface with Government: Regulation and Legislation	22	44.9	8	16.3	19	38.8	49	100.0
International Operations	0	0.0	7	58.3	5	41.7	12	100.0
Domestic Operations, incl. Computerization and Management Assistance	21	30.4	6	8.7	42	60.9	69	100.0
Accounting, Tax	21	53.8	1	2.6	17	43.6	39	100.0
Entrepreneurial Education	7	36.8	2	10.5	10	52.6	19	100.0
Column Total	207	46.2	77	17.2	164	36.6	448	100.0

Table 11-8. Analysis of Research Objective and Centrality.

Abstracts of Articles from Journals

Centrality	Improve the Theory		Improve the Practice		Improve the Methodology		Row Total	Row Percent
	No.	%	No.	%	No.	%		
Convergent	53	72.6	69	30.7	0	0.0	122	40.9
Almost Convergent	17	23.3	47	20.9	0	0.0	64	21.5
Non-Convergent	3	4.1	109	48.4	0	0.0	112	37.6
Column Totals	73	100.0	225	100.0	0	NA	298	100.0

Papers Presented at Conferences

Centrality	Improve the Theory		Improve the Practice		Improve the Methodology		Row Total	Row Percent
	No.	%	No.	%	No.	%		
Convergent	58	66.7	22	38.6	5	83.3	85	56.7
Almost Convergent	8	9.2	4	7.0	1	16.7	13	8.7
Non-Convergent	21	24.1	31	54.4	0	0.0	52	34.7
Column Totals	87	100.0	57	100.0	6	100.0	150	100.0

All Studies

Centrality	Improve the Theory		Improve the Practice		Improve the Methodology		Row Total	Row Percent
	No.	%	No.	%	No.	%		
Convergent	111	69.4	91	32.3	5	83.3	207	46.2
Almost Convergent	25	15.6	51	18.1	1	16.7	77	17.2
Non-Convergent	24	15.0	140	49.6	0	0.0	164	36.6
Column Totals	160	100.0	282	100.0	6	100.0	448	100.0

also may be caused by the difficulty in determining centrality from abstracts. If the near-convergent studies are ignored, the percentage of convergence of journal studies is 52 percent as compared to 63 percent for conference reports—and is 56 percent overall. Either figure, 46 percent or the 56 percent convergence on the core issues, is respectable but leaves ample room for improvement.

In examining centrality by topic studied, Table 11-7, the range is from over 80 percent centrality in two topics to zero percent in one and 11 percent in another. (It should be noted that the zero-centrality topic had a high percentage of studies in the *Almost-Convergent* category.) Six other topics had over 50 percent of their studies in the *Convergent* category, and three additional ones were over 40 percent. On the other hand, three topics had over 50 percent of their research studies in the *Non-Convergent* category, and two more had 40 percent or over in this same classification. For two topics, *Corporate Venturing* and *Entrepreneurial Climate*, all the studies were either central to the core issues or almost there.

There is some suggestion in this analysis that the more applied topics fared less well on the centrality measure. This is examined in Table 11-8, which cross-tabulates centrality by research objective. This exhibit shows that studies that attempt to extent our understanding of theory have a higher degree of convergence toward the core issues and problems than studies dealing with practice. And this is true across both data bases. Whether this result is due to a bias in our classification or is a commentary on the difficulty of conducting "good" practice-oriented studies is a matter that must be left to further investigation. What is apparent is that there can be studies central to the main problems of entrepreneurship in either theory- or practice-oriented research, with perhaps a bit more effort required for the latter to be central.

One last observation on the data: The six studies aimed at methodology were all presented in conferences and were all central (or almost central) to the core issues. This is primarily definitional, for only studies aimed at expanding our general data capability were assigned to a "methodological objective" category. Given the paucity of data in the field of entrepreneurship, this made them almost de facto central to the core of our concerns in entrepreneurial research.

OVERVIEW AND RECOMMENDATIONS

Analysis of the data revealed some interesting patterns and suggested some directions for future research into entrepreneurship.

Sources of Research Studies

Both journal publications and conference proceedings were included in the study in order to obtain a complete picture of the research activities taking place in entrepreneurship. Conferences were included since conferences with proceedings usually restrict papers presented there from being published elsewhere and usually report on more recent works, thus capturing the more current trends in research. This latter point was reinforced in the study, for when the 1984 Babson conference was entered into the data base, it added thirty-seven (9 percent) to the 411 articles tabulated up to that time—yet contributed 35 percent to the articles on *Start-Ups*, 33 percent to those on *Corporate Venturing*, and 27 percent to those on *Entrepreneurial Education*. When this is combined with the great differences found in *topic, methodology used*, and *research objective* between the data sources (which may be due to the focus of the conferences in contrast to the more eclectic nature of the journals), it emphasizes the need to consider both sources of material in any examination of the entrepreneurship field.

Topic-Methodology

The examination of both topics and methodologies indicates: (1) that survey techniques and a combination of informal and reflectional observation are used more often than all other methodologies, (2) that most topics are investigated by concentrated use of one or two methodologies, (3) that field research is less predominate and often does not lead to generalization, and (4) that the state of organized data on entrepreneurship leaves much to be desired. It appears that available data, along with lack of good theory and a "comfortableness" with proven methodologies, are influencing what is studied and even the nature and the objective of the investigation.

Objective and Centrality

Until recently, the field of entrepreneurship has focused on independent, start-up business entities. With the current focus expanded to include "corporate venturing"—entrepreneurial endeavors within large corporations—one may contrast the management of these entities to management within small independent businesses and to non-entrepreneurial management of large organizations. This can expand the knowledge of entrepreneurship, enable researchers directly to utilize and relate to the theories of business and business organizations and directly challenge these established theories and management practices that have primarily developed from the study of large companies. This cross-cultural "study of a foreign language" provides entrepreneurial research with a bridge to the larger business research community for improved two-way communication of ideas, insights, and problems.

Centrality

In determining centrality 63 percent of the studies were classified as central or almost there. This was higher for studies aimed at theory than those oriented toward practice. This could be attributed either to the classification process or to the added difficulty of doing studies that both address immediate, practical problems and also contribute to the solution of key ones. Thus some consideration as to what these key problems or issues might be would be helpful. What might also be helpful is the use of new methodological approaches to aid in our understanding of entrepreneurship. As a start, we have the following suggestions.

Suggestions for Improving Entrepreneurial Research

An eclectic view of topics was taken in determining the centrality of the research studies under the belief that it was more appropriate to evaluate how well the research converged toward fundamental problems or issues than to evaluate the nature of the topic chosen. In the process, after forming an opinion on what is key and what is not, and in consultation with others, five broad categories of problems and issues in entrepreneurship were developed that appear to lie at the core of the field. Some aid understanding of entrepreneurship, some improve the practice, and most do both. These key issues and problems are:

• What enables the entrepreneur to move quickly and economically into new opportunities?

• Are the above factors unique to the entrepreneurial organization? If so, why? If not, to what extent can they be duplicated in larger organizations? And if installed in larger organizations, how do these "entrepreneurial" organizations differ from independent entrepreneurial entities?

• What are the aspects of entrepreneurial organizations that are good for society?

• What are the critical factors, environmental or other, for the development/nondevelopment of entrepreneurial firms or prosperity/failure of entrepreneurial firms?

• What are the critical factors for the development/nondevelopment or the prosperity/failure of "entrepreneurial entities" in large organizations?

While all may not agree on these particular issues or problems, it is suggested that a focus on topics whose solution increases understanding of the key issues and problems of the field will help advance entrepreneurship, contribute to understanding of both managerial and economic processes and organizations, and, in general, aid in economic well-being.

Research Methodologies

The scarcity of research using already available data pointed to a major difficulty with entrepreneurial research, a difficulty increasingly addressed in more recent studies. In part because of the lack of available data, a large number of studies—33 percent—used one or a combination of questionnaire and interview techniques. Not all of these studies fell into the "convergent" category due, to some extent, to the limitations of these techniques. A new source of data for entrepreneurial studies comes from the micro data studies of David Birch. This is a development that warrants serious attention from the entrepreneurship research community.

Micro Data

Our new development for broadening the understanding of small firms and the emergence of new ones has been the development of the Dun & Bradstreet credit files by David Birch and others into a viable new- and small-business data base that has already had a significant impact on entrepreneurship research.[13] According to Birch, this impact can be attributed to:

Sheer Size. Depending on the years for which data are requested, the data base contains four to upwards of six *million* records on individual U.S. establishments, an estimated 80 to 85 percent of all those in existence (smaller law and dental partnerships, nonprofit organizations in the social service sector, and many smaller schools are among those firms "missed"). Even after meticulous editing of raw data relatively few records have to be eliminated—usually between 3 and 5 percent.

The Longitudinal Nature of the Data. The Birth data trace individual firms over time rather than using aggregate or cross-sectional data (snapshots) of groups of firms or industries at particular points in time.

Policy Impact. Microanalysis already is having and will continue to have significant impact on national policy. The studies relating share of jobs to share of job creation by sector and size and kind of firm have already exerted a large influence on public policymaking by pointing clearly to areas where resources should be directed to serve the greatest overall economic good.

Understanding Problem Solving and Creativity

Research into artificial intelligence has produced a considerable body of empirical evidence about the processes that people use to think, to solve problems, and to do so "creatively."

This problem-solving literature provides entrepreneurial research with a new methodology for dealing with some key problems:

- Delegation: Do entrepreneurs get more satisfaction by solving problems themselves or by influencing others to solve them? How can we test for this proclivity?

- What is the information that successful entrepreneurs have accumulated? Do they differ between entrepreneurs and managers? If so, how?

- What heuristics aid the individual in "recognizing the differences" when they occur and how can these best be learned?

This is a challenging new methodological development for research into entrepreneurs and entrepreneurship.

NOTES TO CHAPTER 11

1. William L. Paulin, Robert E. Coffey, and Mark E. Spaulding, "Entrepreneurship Research: Methods and Directions," in Calgin A. Kent, Donald L. Sexton and Karl H. Vesper, eds., *The Encyclopedia of Entrepreneurship* (Englewood Cliffs, N.J.: Prentice-Hall, 1982).

2. Rein Peterson, and Deszo Horvath, "Commentary on Research in the Field of Entrepreneurship," in Kent, Sexton, and Vesper, *The Encyclopedia of Entrepreneurship.*

3. Ray Perryman, "Commentary on Research Methodology in Entrepreneurship," in Kent, Sexton, and Vesper, *The Encyclopedia of Entrepreneurship.*

4. Donald L. Sexton, "Research Needs and Issues in Entrepreneurship," in Kent, Sexton, and Vesper, *The Encyclopedia of Entrepreneurship.*

5. Karl H. Vesper, "Three Faces of Corporate Entrepreneurship," *Working Paper*, University of Washington, 1984.

6. R. B. Duncan, "Qualitative Research Methods in Strategic Management," in D. E. Schendel and C. W. Hofer, eds., *Strategic Management: A New View of Business Policy and Planning* (Boston: Little, Brown, 1979).

7. Kenneth J. Hatten, "Quantitative Research Methods in Strategic Management," in Schendel and Hofer, *Strategic Management.*

8. Charles W. Hofer, "Research on Strategic Planning: A Survey of Past Studies and Suggestions for Future Efforts," *Journal of Economics and Business* 38: 3 (Spring–Summer 1976): 261–87.

9. Ibid.

10. Paul F. Anderson, "Marketing, Scientific Progress, and Scientific Method," *Journal of Marketing* 47 (Fall 1983): 18–31.

11. J. E. McGrath, "Toward a Theory of Method for Research in Organizations," in W. W. Cooper, H. J. Leavitt, and M. W. Shelly, eds., *New Perspectives in Organizational Research* (New York: John Wiley, 1964).
12. Paulin, "Entrepreneurship Research."
13. David Birch, *Using the Dun & Bradstreet Data for Micro Analysis of Regional and Local Economies*, MIT Program on Neighborhood and Regional Change, 1979.

APPENDIX 11-A
CONTENTS OF DATA BASES USED IN ANALYSIS

Journal Data Base — Abstracts of articles appearing between 1981 and 1984 in the following journals (n = 298):

- *Academy of Management Journal* (6)
- *Academy of Management Review* (5)
- *Administrative Science Quarterly* (3)
- *American Journal of Small Business* (95)
- *Business Horizons* (12)
- *California Management Review* (4)
- *Harvard Business Review* (42)
- *Journal of Business Strategy* (8)
- *Journal of Economics and Business* (3)
- *Journal of Small Business Management* (120)

Conference Data Base — Papers presented at the following conferences (n = 150):

- Babson College Entrepreneurship Research Conference, 1981 (38)
- Babson College Entrepreneurship Research Conference, 1982 (34)
- Babson College Entrepreneurship Research Conference, 1983 (32)
- Babson College Entrepreneurship Research Conference, 1984 (37)
- Harvard Symposium on Entrepreneurship, 1983 (9)

APPENDIX 11–B
DESCRIPTION OF RESEARCH METHODOLOGIES
AND TOPICS USED FOR CLASSIFICATION

Methodologies

Observational and Contemplative Theory-Building: Either anecdotal or formal theory that is based on one or more of the following: contemplation, experiential learning, hypothesized relationships between or among variables, or literature review (general).

Survey: Surveys using for the most part random sampling of larger populations based on questionnaires, tests, interviews, or a combination thereof.

Survey—Public Data: Surveys based upon review of data from public sources; e.g., Dun & Bradstreet credit files, industry data bases ("archival survey" of Paulin et al.).

Field Study: Direct observation of phenomena in natural settings, usually longitudinal in nature (see Paulin, note 1, p. 361).

Computer Simulation or Modeling: Mathematical theory-building allowing manipulation of variables in a nonexperimental way (see Paulin, note 1, p. 361).

Vignette or "Reportage": Refers generally to organizational or personal histories; case studies without conclusions, generalizations, or hypothesis-building; journalistic reporting of events or circumstances, or about people and/or organizations; and to a more or less straightforward setting forth of the facts, particularly with regard to new or proposed legislation, government programs, etc. (in the latter case without bringing forth discussion of policy issues in a broader sense).

Laboratory Experiment: A controlled test which allows for internal validity of conclusions and emphasizes replicability and reliability of observation (Paulin et al., 1982). No laboratory experiments were encountered in our analysis.

Topics

Entrepreneurial Climate, Relation to Society: Broad philosophically based articles relating to the climate for entrepreneurship as well as related topics such as small business ethics and social responsibility. Articles which relate to the climate for entrepreneurship in a more specific way, e.g., the financial climate (availability of capital), are categorized under the more specific topic (that is, financing and venture capital).

Personal Characteristics of Entrepreneurs: Articles on the psychological characteristics of entrepreneurs and other traits which relate to the entrepreneur as an individual or as a particular type of individual (e.g., the entrepreneur and stress or loneliness). Also articles which relate to particular groups of entrepreneurs such as women and minorities.

Management Characteristics of Entrepreneurial Firms: Entrepreneurial characteristics as they relate to management of the firm. These may include discussions of critical managerial factors (e.g., the ability to delegate), management techniques (e.g., budgeting) as they relate to small firms, or ways of dealing with environmental factors (e.g., managing during recession).

Start-ups, Including Data On: Articles on the environment conducive to starting new ventures, on assessing potential success, discussion of entry decisions and barriers to entry, success/failure data (e.g., bankruptcies), and data base building on exits and entries.

Financing and Venture Capital: All-inclusive of the financial environment both for new firms and for ongoing small businesses.

Buying, Selling, and Valuing: Both "how to" and theoretical articles on buying or selling a business (including broad studies of acquisition and deacquisition patterns—usually regional in scope), valuing a business both for buying/selling purposes and with regard to stock price. Also includes a few articles on "giving employees a piece of the business" (ESOPs).

High Technology: While articles on high-tech firms also appear elsewhere in the data base (e.g., under start-ups) this topic is made up for the most part of articles which deal with the role high-tech plays in the broader economic picture (e.g., is high tech the "savior" of the U.S. economy?).

Strategy and Growth: Articles relating the tools of the academic discipline of strategic planning/business policy to the small firm (narrow definition); articles pertaining to the desirability of growth, growth strategies, sustainable growth rates, etc. (broader definition).

Corporate Venturing: Entrepreneurial activities in large firms ("intra-preneurship").

Cross-cultural: Again, articles which are cross-cultural in nature may appear under other topics in the data base (i.e., a study of delega-tion in U.S. vs. Swedish firms would appear under the primary topic of Management Characteristics.) Articles appearing under Cross-cultural are primarily those which deal with the environ-ment for entrepreneurship in other countries (e.g., France or Poland).

Interface with Government: Regulation and Legislation: Articles dealing with government programs, including case studies; descrip-tions and discussion of new or proposed legislation; discussions of both specific regulations and the "small business regulatory bur-den" (i.e., the regulatory environment with which small and entre-preneurial firms must cope); and miscellaneous government state-ments and pronouncements (e.g., "Excerpts from the President's Report to the Congress on the State of Small Business").

International Operations, Domestic Operations, including Computeri-zation and Management Assistance, and Accounting, Tax: All three topics include the "how to" literature on starting and man-aging a small business or beginning (managing) aspects of inter-national operations. Almost half the "Domestic Operations" topic is represented by articles on how to "computerize" the small business. The "Accounting, Tax" category is largely "Fifo vs. Lifo," "Lease vs. Purchase," "ACRS vs. Straight Line Deprecia-tion," "Expense or Capitalize," etc. (These are by definition "non-research;" hence they fall out in the Conference data base.)

Entrepreneurial Education: Includes articles on both research and pedagogical needs in entrepreneurial education, on the "teacha-bility" of entrepreneurship, and on related topics such as surveys of alumni (e.g., to judge effectiveness of programs).

ENTREPRENEURSHIP
Research in Quest of a Paradigm

Alan L. Carsrud, Kenneth W. Olm,
and George G. Eddy

The concern with the definition of an entrepreneur has long been an issue in the research literature. For example, Schumpeter stated that the entrepreneur was the individual whose function it was to carry out, or manage, the new combination of the means of production and credit that we call enterprise.[1] J. B. Say was credited by Schumpeter as among the first to state that the entrepreneur's function was to combine various production factors into a viable entity. This is similar to the later definition adopted by Schumpeter in his own work.

While numerous works continue to restate theoretical definitions of entrepreneurship and who is an entrepreneur, Brockhaus and Horwitz in this volume have succinctly noted that no generic definition of an entrepreneur has yet to emerge from the literature. This lack of a generally agreed upon definition is a shortcoming that misdirects research efforts and leads to a lack of a coherent body of research literature.

The failure by researchers in recent years to arrive at an agreed upon theoretical definition of the entrepreneur and entrepreneurial behaviors is exemplified by a number of recent articles that purport to distinguish between managers and entrepreneurs.[2] The rise of the concept "intrapreneurship" or corporate entrepreneurship to imply that employees who are innovative are to be classified as entrepreneurial seems only to further confuse the issue. Entrepreneurs may be innovative and creative managers, but these unique managers are not entrepreneurs because they lack ultimate personal responsibility and risk for their actions.[3] This view is somewhat contrary to that held by Wortman (see Chapter 10).

A theoretical definition of an entrepreneur that reflects the current research knowledge and that can be easily operationalized is clearly needed. In fact, an effective operational definition would be useful in developing a theoretical definition that has widespread acceptance by researchers. One such definition would be that an entrepreneur is "an individual who is willing and able to engage in personal risk taking and responsibility, while at the same time combining the means of production and credit, in the expectation of realizing profit and/or other specific objectives such as power and prestige." Expected correlates, but neither necessary nor sufficient conditions, include creating new forms of business organization, production or service innovations, or some process of change. This definition would remove the corporate manager, academic researcher, consultant, and passive investor from the definition of an entrepreneur.

The lack of convergence in the conceptualization of entrepreneurial behaviors has also contributed to the general lack of a widely accepted operational definition of an entrepreneur. As Cartwright has pointed out, operational definitions serve to coordinate constructs to specific empirical data, while avoiding any "surplus" meaning.[4] Conceptual, or theory-based, definitions place various concepts in a system of ideas that can be examined by logic. Operational definitions and conceptual definitions cannot be developed independently of each other; both must occur to represent successfully any given incident or case. Effective research demands that both exist and that operational definitions be used to improve communications between researchers. Lacking operational definitions, most research cannot be replicated with precision, nor can subsequent research build upon previous work.

For example, McClelland's seminal work has been widely cited and yet he is criticized for the inclusion of non-entrepreneurs in his sample because individual researchers disagree with his operational definition.[5] The distinction between the entrepreneur and the small business owner/manager is an example of a theoretical position that is difficult to turn into an objective, operationally based, definition with which to do empirical research. For example, doesn't an active entrepreneur manage? Thus, why should there be any significant difference between a successful entrepreneur and a successful manager in many psychological factors (such as achievement motivation) if much of their job tasks are the same? As Wortman notes, the current typologies used in the study of entrepreneurship and small business management are too simple to be of effective use to the researcher.

Brockhaus and Horwitz have noted the definition of the characteristics of a successful, or unsuccessful, entrepreneur must also include an understanding of the type of business the individual owns and actively manages and the amount of the equity of the business owned. For example, Carsrud, Olm, and Thomas found that the strongest effects of multidimensional achievement motivation on business success occurred in those male owner and managers who owned less than 50 percent of the business.[6] Also, in a sample of entrepreneurs drawn from the same industrial sector (retail building supply dealers), those having multiple partners were more successful (as defined by gross sales revenues and employee productivity) than those who owned 100 percent of their firms and who tended to be preoccupied with other businesses or activities. This pattern was somewhat different in female entrepreneurs, in that percentage of ownership had less of an effect on their success.

Many of the studies reported in the literature assume that the entrepreneur in a traditional heavy manufacturing setting has the same personality, motivations, and skills that one would have in a personal service or technical service activity or in a high technology industry. This grouping of entrepreneurs into broad, overgeneralized classifications, such as Female Entrepreneurs, without regard to the specific businesses and economic sector they have chosen (and why) only increases the imprecision of the research results and interpretations generated. Hisrich (see Chapter 3) claims that the reason that female entrepreneurs are not as successful as male entrepreneurs is due to the fact that they generally have less experience and specialized education than male entrepreneurs.

This conclusion may be limiting in the conceptualization of the causes for differences between men and women. For example, little research has been done on the effect of sex-role orientation on the selection of a business venture. Likewise, the role of gender-dominate personality characteristics (such as instrumentality and expressivity) has received only limited research attention. Therefore, the gross differentiation between male and female biological gender may "hide" many interesting aspects of entrepreneurial behavior.

Again, Hisrich notes the fact that women are more highly represented in the personal service sectors than they are in manufacturing businesses and the high-technology sectors. The reasons women are less "successful" could be because they (1) are women; (2) are in lower paying, more highly competitive industrial sectors; (3) have different personal motivations and personality structures; (4) have less relevant experience; (5) have less experience in business; and/or (6) have been in business less time than their male counterparts. Using only demographic data, the interpretations and the proposed remediations for shortcomings are potentially confounded.

Dunkelburg and Cooper propose that no one single pattern for entrepreneurial success may emerge.[7] That is, there may be a multitude of different patterns for entrepreneurial success that are dependent on owner background, education, process for becoming an owner, personality, regional economic differences, and the nature of the industrial sector in which the owner/manager choose to operate. This position, while more complex, more adequately reflects the nature of the phenomena of entrepreneurship.

OPERATIONAL DEFINITIONS OF PREDICTORS AND CRITERIA

Related to the above discussion concerning the need for operational definitions of what is an entrepreneur, there is a similar set of needs to define operationally those factors that significantly influence success and exactly how the researcher defines success. Entrepreneurial theory should determine the breadth and richness of these concepts, but these concepts must be made into specific, measurable events or stimuli if reliable and valid interpretation of their effects is to take place.

For example, the researcher needs to define success operationally in terms of specific, measurable events such as gross sales, net profit, years in business, market share, return on assets, or return on equity such as Cuba, Decenzo, and Anish have attempted to do.[8] Each measure of success may mean very different things, especially if they relate to a specific goal of an entrepreneur, as noted by Hornaday and Treken in their interviews of famous entrepreneurs.[9] Therefore, when researchers discuss the successful entrepreneur, one needs to be very specific as to how that success was measured, especially if, as in some research studies, it merely means survival. Each operational definition of success is potentially very different. What predicts one criteria may or may not predict another.

The patterns of success and their related causes may also shift over time, a view held by Churchill.[10] For example, in a recent study by Helmreich, Sawin, and Carsrud, personality factors played no role in predicting job performance of a group of non-entrepreneurs during the initial months of employment but did have a consistent effect after a "honeymoon" period had been completed.[11] A similar shift in the patterns of prediction was found in a simulation study of entrepreneurs. Carsrud, Olm, Thomas, and Dodd found that students' personalities and achievement motivation predicted sales revenues in the first three-quarters of a computer-based business simulation game, but as the game progressed, these effects dissipated.[12] Similar relationships of predictors to success criteria may exist for "real" entrepreneurs. An interesting side note to this study is that students in the simulation study showed a different pattern of responses than that found in studies involving actual entrepreneurs.

RESEARCH METHODOLOGIES AND STATISTICAL ANALYSES

A number of writers in this volume have lamented the lack of long-term studies of entrepreneurs. McClelland is often cited as the model for this type of research.[13] Yet most of the research on the effects of predictor variables are studies that try to discriminate between groups of entrepreneurs and non-entrepreneurs or provide excessive descriptive statistics concerning a specific entrepreneurial group or elaborate case study approaches.

Although these research approaches are valuable sources of information concerning specific aspects of the concepts involved in entrepreneurship, they are still largely descriptive studies and do not provide adequate causal inferences. That is, these descriptive research approaches are unable to provide information concerning the relative direct, indirect, and interactive causal effects of various microlevel and macrolevel variables on business success adequately. The studies now being conducted every five years on the alumni of the Harvard Business School promise to yield rich data for analyses.

Although true experimentation may not be possible or ethically desirable, certain methodological and statistical approaches to inferences in field research are possible. One approach would be more extensive use of multivariate regression analyses when both the predictors and the criterion measures of "success" can be defined on a continuum. Thus the researcher would be provided with information concerning the relative effects of various predictors on various measures of business success such as profitability or length of time the business has been operated. As Wortman notes, the level of methodological and statistical sophistication in most data-based studies of entrepreneurship and small business ownership is quite low. Likewise, computer simulation business games provide an interesting methodology to test entrepreneurial variables within certain controlled settings.

In the "real world of business" it is possible for different mixes of predictors to produce the same result of success. If this is the case, linear-based models may not provide sophisticated enough statistical tools to reflect this complex interactive process. What may be needed are statistical tools such as Data Envelopment Analysis, which allows for both micro- and macrolevel data (including nominal, ordinal, and interval data) to be combined in any number of ways to produce optimal utility functions. This approach has potential utility to the study of entrepreneurship by having success predicted by a wide variety of variables in differing combinations.

CONCEPTUALIZATION OF PSYCHOLOGICAL VARIABLES

Brockhaus and Horwitz have provided an extensive review of the research literature on the relationship of entrepreneurship to various psychological concepts. However, much of this research, as cited, has not kept pace with the reconceptualizations and advances in the research areas of personality and social psychology. For example, most of the research cited by Brockhaus and Horwitz with regard to the need for achievement (or achievement motivation) reflects the view that the variable is a unidimensional construct. This assumption could lead one to assume that individuals possessing an identical single score would act in this same manner.

However, research by Spence and Helmreich has shown that achievement motivation is not unidimensional but multidimensional.[14] Those dimensions are mastery, work orientation, and interpersonal competitiveness. Interestingly, when individuals are high in all three components, they do less well in job performance than if they were high in work and mastery but low in interpersonal competitiveness. Competitiveness seems to be a positive factor only when one is low in the other two, or the job tasks are such that the individual works in isolation.[15]

Recent work by Carsrud, Olm, Thomas, and Dodd on a uniform group of male entrepreneurs found that despite being high on competitiveness as a group, the trait was a negative predictor of "business success" (in a regression analysis).[16] Success in these studies was defined as per-employee gross revenues. This result is similar to that found by Helmreich in predicting the performance of male, commercial airline pilots.[17] Any use of a unidimensional scale would have hidden that relationship, and any causal inferences made from descriptive statistics would have led to the false notion that competitiveness was a positive predictor of success. This only points out the need for care in making generalizations about causal relationships or remedial measures to be taken, when using only descriptive statistics of gross classifications. In a related vein, much of the literature cited by Brockhaus and Horowitz concerning the use of the locus-of-control measure or risk taking fail to note the major reconceptualizations, or methodological changes, that personality and social psychological research has undergone during the last ten years.

It would seem advisable for researchers in entrepreneurship to expand their research teams to include personality and social psychologists who are familiar with the contemporary research in those fields. That is, entrepreneurial research needs to become an interdisciplinary research area.

CONCEPTUALIZATION OF ORGANIZATIONAL VARIABLES

Most of the research in entrepreneurship cited by Wortman has typically focused on three basic areas: (1) the personal, or psychological characteristics, of the entrepreneur; (2) the nature and role of venture capital; and (3) the role of public policy. There is a need for more research related to the organizational structure of the entre-

preneurial venture, such as cross-utilization of employees, job sharing, job-task redesign, and levels or complexity of management that
may interact with personal variables to influence the success of the
business venture. Studies such as those by Aldrich and Zimmer (see
Chapter 1) are examples of approaches to organizational variables
that could prove very useful. Some research is being done that
attempts to bridge the gap between micro and macro variables by
looking at the characteristics of the organization (entrepreneurial and
bureaucratic) and how they relate to the motivation to manage those
organizations. Interestingly, Smith and Miner found only minor differences between managers and entrepreneurs and only suggestive
findings related to the concept of the organizational life cycle.[18]

There is a clear need for more systematic research into the interaction of micro- and macro-variables as they affect success, including degree of equity ownership.

CONCEPTUALIZATION OF ENVIRONMENTAL VARIABLES

The role of environmental variables such as venture capital, economic
factors, governmental policies, and demographic changes in the
American society have been discussed by many authors including
MacMillan and Abetti (see Chapters 7 and 9). Although these discussions are valuable, there has been a serious lack of research into how
individual entrepreneurs have dealt with these strong environmental
factors. What research has been done in these areas has tended to be
individual cases, and not empirically based, large sample studies with
appropriate inferences concerning the relative influence of various
variables. Although this line of investigation, with its integration with
micro-oriented variables, is most difficult both conceptually and
statistically, such an integration could provide useful information as
to how an individual overcomes potentially lethal constraints to business success.

PROPOSED RESEARCH PARADIGM

The need for a model, or paradigm, to direct entrepreneurial research
has been discussed in terms of the need for common operational defi-

Figure D-3. A Proposed Paradigm for Entrepreneurial Research.

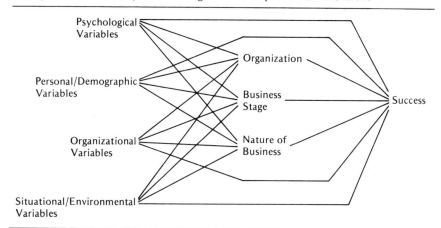

nitions of entrepreneurial success. All researchers certainly aspire to the ideal of systematic research, although most attempts tend to be post hoc in nature. The model presented below is an attempt to integrate the current research knowledge in order to encourage a more systematic investigation. The proposed model is not to be viewed as a totally inclusive one of all the variables that have an effect but as an outline to direct systematic investigation in this area. The model is proposed as a path-analytic model, although the relationships need not necessarily be linear nor consistent in their effects over time.

The model proposed is used by the Research Group on Entrepreneurship at the University of Texas at Austin. Although the model is not exhaustive of the factors involved, systematic attempts have been made, or are currently underway, to examine the interaction of four general categories of primary causal factors: psychological variables, personal/demographic variables, organizational/sociological variables, and situational/environmental variables.

These factors have direct and interactive effects on secondary predictor variables such as current business stage and type of business operation and industrial sector. These primary and secondary factors have both direct and indirect influence on various outcome measures of success.

The current psychological variables under investigation at the University of Texas are multidimensional achievement motivation, type A/B stress proneness, and gender-predominate personality characteristics (instrumentality and expressivity). Proposed research will look at intelligence, risk taking, self-esteem, and personal responsibility.

Personal/demographic variables currently under study are the role of mentors, age, gender, education, family support system, personal constraints (children, family), birth order, and previous experience. Future studies will continue to focus on these variable plus the nature of previous business experience of family and the role of formal education in business.

The current organizational variables being researched are the number of employees, the industrial sector, and the percentage of ownership. Future studies will also address the role of organizational structure and job design in effecting entrepreneurial success.

The situational/environmental variables currently under investigation are financial resources available to the entrepreneur, local governmental policies, and economic conditions (both local and national). Future studies will examine governmental policies that serve as encouragement and constraints (such as licensure).

The secondary factors currently under investigation are the age of the business when acquired, how the business was acquired, the type of partnership, the mode of delivery of the service or product, and the nature of the industrial sector chosen. Future research will focus on the role of venture capital in this process.

The outcome measures being employed in the current studies include the length the business has been in existence after acquisition or start-up, capital worth, the degree of gross/net profits, and market share. Future work will look at degree of political power and influence, return on investment, and return on equity as measures of success.

Adoption of this model, or some similar paradigm, would go a long way to insure that more of the research being conducted could be replicated. In addition, the adoption of a paradigm would encourage new research to build more effectively on that which has been done previously. What entrepreneurship needs is researchers willing to be more entrepreneurial in their approaches to the topic.

NOTES

1. J. A. Schumpeter, *The Theory of Economic Development* (Cambridge, Mass.: Harvard University Press, 1934, reprinted 1959), p. 74.

2. J. W. Carland, F. Hoy, W. R. Boulton, and J. C. Carland, "Differentiating Entrepreneurs from Small Business Owners: A Conceptualization," *Academy of Management Review* 9: 2: 354–59.

3. H. Schollhammer, "Internal Corporate Entrepreneurship," in C. A. Kent, D. L. Sexton, and K. H. Vesper, eds., *Encyclopedia of Entrepreneurship* (Englewood Cliffs, N. J.: Prentice-Hall, 1982).

4. D. Cartwright, "Lewinian Theory as a Contemporary Systematic Framework," in S. Koch, ed., *Psychology: A Study of a Science, Study 1. Conceptual and Systematic, Volume 2. General Systematic Formulations, Learning, and Special Processes.* (New York: McGraw-Hill, 1959), pp. 7–91.

5. D. C. McClelland, *The Achieving Society* (Canada: Free Press/Collier-McMillian, 1961).

6. A. L. Carsrud, K. W. Olm, and J. B. Thomas, "Small Business Productivity: Relationship of Owner's Personality to Organizational Success," *Proceedings of the International Council for Small Business*, 1984, pp. 18–24. See also, A. L. Carsrud, K. W. Olm, and J. B. Thomas, "Predicting Entrepreneurial Success: Effects of Multi-Dimensional Achievement Motivation, Levels of Ownership, and Cooperative Relationships," *Academy of Management* (August, 1984).

7. W. C. Dunkelberg and A. C. Cooper, "Entrepreneurial Typologies," in K. H. Vesper, ed., *Frontiers of Entrepreneurship Research* (Wellesley, Mass.: Babson Center for Entrepreneurial Studies, 1982), pp. 1–15.

8. R. Cuba, D. DeCenzo, and A. Anish, "Management Practices of Successful Female Business Owners," *American Journal of Small Business* 7: 2 (1983): 40–46.

9. J. A. Hornaday and N. B. Treken, "Capturing Twenty-one Heffalumps," in J. Hornaday, J. Timmons, and K. W. Vesper, eds., *Frontiers of Entrepreneurship Research* (Wellesley, Mass.: Babson Venter for Entrepreneurial Studies, 1983), pp. 25–29.

10. N. C. Churchill, "Entrepreneurs and Their Enterprises, A Stage Model," in Hornaday, Timmons, and Vesper, *Frontiers of Entrepreneurship Research* (1983), pp. 1–14.

11. R. L. Helmreich, L. L. Sawin, and A. L. Carsrud, "The Honeymoon Effect in Job Performance: Temporal Increases in the Predictive Power of Achievement Motivation." Under review in *Journal of Applied Psychology.*

12. A. L. Carsrud, K. W. Olm, J. B. Thomas, and B. G. Dodd, "Business Profitability: A Simulation Study of Personalities and Organizational Success," *American Psychological Association*, August, Toronto, Canada.

13. D. C. McClelland, "Need Achievement and Entrepreneurship: A Longitudinal Study," *Journal of Personality and Social Psychology* 1: 389–92.

14. J. T. Spence and R. L. Helmreich, *Masculinity and Feminity: Their Psychological Dimensions, Correlates, and Antecedents* (Austin, Texas: University of Texas Press, 1978).

15. R. L. Helmreich, L. L. Sawin, and A. L. Carsrud, "The Honeymoon Effect in Job Performance."

16. A. L. Carsrud, K. W. Olm, J. B. Thomas and B. G. Dodd, "Business Profitability."

17. R. L. Helmreich, "Personality and Social Factors in Flight Crew Performance," in R. M. Guion and J. Barron (chs.) proceedings, "Scientific and Professional Contributions to Air Safety," *American Psychological Association* August 1982.

18. N. R. Smith and J. B. Miner, "Motivation Considerations in Success of Technological Innovation Entrepreneurs," in J. Hornaday, F. Tarpley, J. Timmons, and K. Vesper, eds., *Frontiers of Entrepreneurship Research* (Wellesley, Mass.: Babson Center for Entrepreneurial Studies, 1984), pp. 488–95.

12 NEW DEVELOPMENTS IN ENTREPRENEURSHIP EDUCATION

Karl H. Vesper

Five years ago the principal trends in entrepreneurship education appeared to be the following:

- Increasing number of schools with entrepreneurship courses.
- Engineering as well as business schools starting courses.
- Varied teaching approaches being used.
- Series, concentrations, and majors being initiated.
- Almost no formal educational research being published.
- Endowed chairs being added.
- Centers being started.
- Few research projects being conducted.

Today most of these trends seem to be continuing. While the pace of academic research has accelerated considerably, little of the research seems to be reporting upon the educational activities.

In 1975 entrepreneurship courses were offered in 104 colleges or universities across the United States. By 1980, the number had increased to 163, and in the last five years, an additional ninety schools have begun offering entrepreneurship courses bringing the total to 253. This information is based upon periodical studies reported in

Entrepreneurship Education and published by the Center for Entrepreneurship at Babson College.

The most recent (1985) update is based upon questionnaires sent to 570 schools of business and 267 schools of engineering. Replies were received from 48.8 percent of the former and 46.1 percent of the latter. The results added eighty-five to the list of business schools with entrepreneurship courses and subtracted ten from the list, for a net addition of seventy-five schools making the total 212 business schools. For the engineering school list there were twenty additions and two subtractions to leave a total of forty-one. Undoubtedly there were some schools missed in both the additions and subtractions. Past indications have been that the former are probably more numerous than the latter, so that the number of schools with entrepreneurship courses is probably somewhat understated.

If the number of inquiries currently being received by those persons responsible for courses or programs from those considering starting courses is indicative of future offerings in additional schools, the number of course offerings should increase at an expanding rate over the next few years.

The 253 schools (212 of business plus 41 engineering) with entrepreneurship courses are located at 245 institutions of higher education, eight having such courses in both their business and their engineering schools. As this trend has moved forward some other effects have also emerged. One has been a rise in the amount of academic research on entrepreneurship. Another has been the emergence of entrepreneurship majors and areas of concentration in entrepreneurship at some schools, while other schools have continued to explore variations in individual courses and related activities. These include the following:

1. More well-supported programs. A total of about fifteen endowed chairs are now in place at a number of schools, and more are being added each year. Harvard and Wharton have especially well-financed and massive programs of activity, and Baylor now has three endowed positions in entrepreneurship. Centers for entrepreneurship have been established or are expected soon to be at other schools including Arizona, Arizona State, Babson College, Baylor University, Carnegie-Mellon, Case-Western, De Paul, James Madison, New York University (NYU), University of North Carolina, Rensselaer Polytechnic, University of Southern California, and Wichita State.

An evolution that will be interesting to watch is the successful variety of strategies now emerging. For instance, Babson has become a major focal point for information and publications concerning the academic activities of entrepreneurship, Carnegie-Mellon has begun its center with emphasis on rendering assistance to startups, NYU has selected a focus on corporate internal entrepreneurship, and Wichita State has established a clearinghouse for information about student entrepreneurship clubs.

2. More doctoral activities associated with entrepreneurship are underway, particularly at the Harvard Business School. In the past there have been occasional doctoral theses on the subject from schools such as Harvard, Georgia, Michigan State, Washington, Wharton, and others, but they were relatively rare and scattered. Harvard seems to be stepping up the pace and developing as the leading institution.

3. Spread to nonmetropolitan schools. It is easier to offer entrepreneurship courses in metropolitan areas, partly because there are more entrepreneurs to choose from as guest lecturers (an element most instructors consider highly important to their courses) and partly because there are more start-up opportunities to study, attempt to exploit, help others exploit, or simply discuss, nearby. However, students in nonurban areas also want to study the subject, and nonurban communities also want start-ups. So notwithstanding some handicaps, there are reasons for nonurban schools to develop effective ways of offering the subject. Baylor University established the first program in a nonmetropolitan area in 1980. Others seriously taking up this challenge are Texas A&M, the University of Illinois at Champaign-Urbana, James Madison University, and Eastern Montana College.

4. Spread abroad. There had been considerable academic attention and effort applied to entrepreneurship in England for many years. Now the activity seems to be cropping up more in other countries such as Ireland, Australia, and those of continental Europe. INSEAD, for instance, appears in this volume for the first time.

COURSES

Most schools start with a "standard" entrepreneurship course consisting of venture design projects, case studies, readings, and lectures by guest speakers and the instructor. Some move on to a logical second course such as a "project only" course in which those students who started a project in the first course are provided an opportunity to carry the project further. Such a second course can work very well and actually produce start-ups.

Introducing other entrepreneurship courses beyond that, however, tends to raise some problems. One concerns specialty versus survey courses and whether the same students should take both. Another is how redundancies between entrepreneurship courses and other courses in the curriculum can be reduced. Is there a full courseworth of difference between entrepreneurial marketing and other marketing courses, or between venture capital and other finance courses, for instance, and if so, what is it?

Schools which are exploring this important frontier include Babson, Baylor, Calgary, Southern California, and Wharton. Some of the course possibilities include the following:

- Venture Finance (Babson, Baylor, Calgary, Harvard, Northwestern)
- Venture Marketing (Baylor, Calgary)
- Entrepreneurial Management (Harvard)
- Innovation Management (Drexel, Ecole Polytechnic, MIT, RPI)
- Product Design and Development (Dartmouth, MIT)
- Feasibility Analysis (Arizona State, Rhode Island, Wichita State)
- Economics of Entrepreneurship (Economic Development) (Hawaii)
- Psychology of Entrepreneurs (Case-Western)
- Entrepreneurial History (Wisconsin)
- Internal Corporate Entrepreneurship (Interpreneurship, Intrapreneurship, Corporateurship, or . . .) (UCLA, NYU, Wichita State)
- Venture Accounting and Taxation (Baylor)
- Academic Fields of Entrepreneurship (Babson)
- Venture Law (Calgary)
- Real Estate Ventures (Harvard)
- TV for Credit Entrepreneurship (Wichita State)

Two other especially interesting directions of exploration are: (1) introduction of entrepreneurship in other courses of the curriculum at the University of Oklahoma; and (2) the use of entrepreneurship courses as a "capstone," a mission usually performed by business policy courses, at Pace University. Both these ideas had been suggested before. The first had often been dismissed with the observation that injection into other courses had mainly failed when it was tried with international business topics, and the latter had been challenged on the basis that it might represent a broader subject with only one of its subareas and therefore be inappropriately underscoped for its mission. Hopefully, these trials will make a better case one way or the other. If they do, it should be a valuable contribution.

Course Composition

Within courses yet another collection of interesting approaches is being tried, including the following:

- Use of personal computers in venturing planning (Babson, Baylor, Northwestern)
- Development of product prototypes, not just paper designs, as part of the course (University of Nevada, Reno)
- Using feasibility studies as class projects (Arizona State, Baylor)
- Using videotapes of entrepreneurs (De Paul, Wichita State)
- Using live, as opposed to written entrepreneurship cases (Tulsa)
- Using a live entrepreneurial case for the final examination (Berkeley)
- Having students cross-evaluate each other's venture plans
- Having venture capitalists evaluate students venture plans (Baylor)
- Having students keep diaries of their venture study activities (Virginia)
- Trying a series of different entrepreneurship texts to see which work best (East Carolina)
- Adopting a grading policy under which any student who manages to raise $10,000 or more on the basis of a venture plan developed in the course receives an automatic "A" (Marquette)

- Scholarships specifically for students of entrepreneurship (Baylor, Wichita State)

Class Composition

Who the students should be in an entrepreneurship course seems to be a question with many possible answers. Among the possibilities currently in process are the following:

- Combining undergrad and grad students in the same classes (Wright State)

- Combining nonstudents and students in the same classes (Delaware, New Mexico, Rochester, SMU)

- Opening or offering entrepreneurship classes to student with majors other than business or engineering (Clarkson, Rhode Island, Wright State)

- Offering entrepreneurship in a liberal arts college (Macalester, St. Thomas)

Entrepreneurship courses seem typically to be relatively high in student popularity. This sometimes makes it hard for instructors who hate to say "no" to students who want to get in on an overload basis, but it also permits instructors to be selective in admissions and thereby recruit highly motivated students. At the University of Southern California, selection is based on personal interviews. At the University of Washington students self-select because they must use cherished course priority privileges to gain entry. At Long Island, the course is required.

EXTRACURRICULAR ACTIVITIES

Student entrepreneurship clubs have been created at a host of schools. Some reported in the survey for this review were at Arizona State, Case-Western, Clarkson, Oregon, Stanford, Texas A&M, Virginia, Washington, Wichita State, and Willamette. More information about these clubs is available from Wichita State, which has formed an association of such clubs. It organized a national convention of club representatives at MIT in 1984 and is planning another to be held in Dallas in March, 1985.

Outreach activities that involve students working to help entrepreneurs develop business plans, conduct market research, and the like are among the things these clubs do, as have been the organizations of local entrepreneurship symposia or one-day conferences for would-be entrepreneurs from around town.

The idea of creating venture capital funds for the financing of student-designed ventures is also being explored at several schools, including Clarkson, Northwestern, and the University of Southern California.

Operating speaker series as a complement to entrepreneurship courses is being used at the University of Virginia (where it is a daytime lecture series), at San Diego State (where it is run as a dinner series), and at Wichita State (where it is part of an annual "Entrepreneur in Residence" affair).

At least two schools, Southern California and Wichita State, are now publishing periodic newsletters specifically focused on their activities in entrepreneurship.

Research

The stream of university research papers presenting new data on entrepreneurship has continued steadily and grown since the State-of-the-Art Research Conference at Baylor in 1980. This has been followed by additional conferences at Babson in 1981, 1982, and 1983, at Georgia Tech in 1984, and at Wharton in 1985, where over sixty papers were submitted. Proceedings of all these conferences are available from the Center for Entrepreneurial Studies at Babson. However, few research publications seem to be treating the subject of performance in entrepreneurship education.

This survey attempted to lay groundwork for assessing the productivity of schools in spawning start-ups by employees, students, and alumni. At 28.1 percent of the business schools and 53.6 percent of the engineering schools, respondents indicated they could name enterprises started by employees and/or students. The ratio of those who felt the climate of their schools would tend to encourage versus oppose faculty start-ups was 3.6 to 1 in business and 5.6 to 1 in engineering. The ratio of schools collecting information on which alumni were self-employed versus those not doing so was 1.4 to 1 in business versus 2.1 to 1 in engineering. In short, a majority of schools appear to have basic data that could be analyzed to determine the extent to which their alumni end up self-employed, and at what occupation. But almost no follow-up of those questions is being performed.

That is not to criticize faculty of the courses. They have plenty to do with running the courses plus performing other research on entrepreneurs and how they work. Faculty of other courses do not follow up their courses with educational research either, except in rare instances. Faculty put their efforts where the incentives are. And if there is to be more such research there will have to be incentives to perform it that can compete with the fun of doing research on other aspects of entrepreneurship, the research funding available for studying other aspects of it, and the consulting and business income incentives of working on other problems.

Another topic deserving of some research attention, in fact, may be the question of how faculty time is spent in entrepreneurship versus other types of courses and what the utilities of that time application are from the viewpoints of both faculty and students. Presumably the answers would in part vary with schools. Publish-or-perish schools would likely have a different set of utilities for the instructor than heavy teaching load schools that would influence course design and what students get out of it. And the answers might be different for part-time lecturers than for full-time professors who teach it as a sideline versus mainline of academic interest. (It is true that entrepreneurs are more effective teachers of the subject than straight academics? Those two groups have predictably disagreed in prior surveys on that question, but their opinions have never been systematically tested.)

Some other questions that might benefit from more methodical research include the following:

- What should be the most meaningful measures of course performance? (Is course popularity really "it"?)

- What should be the measures of instructor performance? (Student popularity, or student ratings, or . . . ?)

- What balance or mix should students be getting from the course of such things as (1) factual content, (2) practice in creative and hard-headed business thinking, (3) self-discovery, (4) practice in teamwork, and/or (5) inspiration, motivation, or feeling good about the subject of entrepreneurship?

- What meaning(s) should students ascribe or not ascribe to the grades they receive in an entrepreneurship course?

- How much importance should students ascribe to the mechanical elegance and literary quality of the business plan? (And versus what else about a proposed venture, judged how by whom?)

Answers to these questions will always be uncertain, if for no other reason than the fact that they will vary among both schools and classes and they will vary over time. It will probably be helpful, however, to keep worrying about them and to explore them in some systematic ways.

But the responsibility for doing so should not be dropped on faculty without recognizing the importance of incentives. If the pay-offs for faculty are higher elsewhere they should not be blamed for neglecting such questions any more than faculty in other fields are. Arranging incentives should be the concern of administrators, funding agencies, alumni who influence schools' directions by their financial contributions, as well as peers who rate and thereby set standards for each other's performance.

HARVARD'S EXPERIENCE WITH A NEW ENTREPRENEURSHIP PROGRAM

Howard H. Stevenson

The Harvard Business School (HBS) has had a long but ambivalent history of interest in the subject of entrepreneurship. This interest has taken the form of both research scholarship and course development. Many great teachers have been devoted to the field at one time or another in their careers: Mace, Hosmer, Liles, and Tucker. The Center for the Study of Entrepreneurship was the focal point of business history in the forties and is considered by many to be the nursery at which many of the best current business history scholars were trained under Schumpeter and Cole. In spite of this tradition, however, the seedling never took root in the same fashion as other more discipline-oriented subjects. Schumpeter's center was disbanded. The courses in entrepreneurship endured with an ambivalent focus on small business and on the new high potential venture. Staffing has exemplified this ambivalence. Entrepreneurial management is the only area that historically has had a significant portion of the teaching load carried by nontenure track faculty. These individuals have often served as remarkably inspiring teachers but have not had the time nor incentives to build a balanced base of teaching, course development and research.

THE SAROFIM-ROCK INITIATIVE

In October 1981, two graduates of HBS, Fayez Sarofim and Arthur Rock, established the Sarofim-Rock Chair to encourage the school to exploit more fully the interests of its students and alumni in the study and pursuit of entrepreneurship. As befits the field, the establishment of the chair was the recognition of a major opportunity but was provided without constraints of fitting to an existing resource base. The message was clear: Identify the territory and make progress toward staking an intellectual claim. The challenge was substantial: Many basic questions remained to be answered. What is entrepreneurship on an individual and organizational level? How does it differ from "small business"? Traditional definitions are no longer adequate to handle today's complexity. New behaviorally oriented definitions need to be developed that rest on a psychological foundation that is more than one-dimensional.

This task is important as more entrepreneurs start companies and as more individuals within existing organizations attempt to renew existing firms. The substantial number of self-employed HBS alumni as well as the growing interest in entrepreneurship on the part of MBA students lend the efforts a particular urgency. These needs are being addressed by a growing interest of colleagues with specialization in the traditional discipline-based fields.

Freedom was given to pursue the field as an "interest group" without the normal constraints of area and discipline. Neither administration nor the chair donors imposed a particular view of the desired outcomes. There was simply a recognition of the importance of the concept of entrepreneurship to students and alumni, to the school, and to society. It was left to those interested to define the means by which such an important topic should be pursued.

The Colloquium

In order to define better the agenda in the field of entrepreneurship at HBS, the core faculty was invited to prepare "an agenda-setting colloquium." Since it was the first colloquium with such a goal, even the colloquium itself proved to be an entrepreneurial venture. The meeting was designed around small, action-oriented discussion

groups to promote the maximum amount of interaction and to minimize the stifling effect of a traditional presentational meeting. The
purpose of the colloquium was to provide an opportunity for discussion and interaction regarding the future directions in the teaching of
entrepreneurship. The papers presented in the proceedings, *Entrepreneurship: What It Is and How to Teach It*, were largely designed
to stimulate thought rather than to serve the more traditional role of
conveying knowledge. To this end, they presented a variety of perspectives and experiences on the conceptual and pedagogical components of entrepreneurship.

In organizing the colloquium and the curriculum, all the traditional dilemmas had to be faced, These included the balance between
academics and practitioners, between the role of theory and the experience of practice, and between conceptual rigor and a focus on
action. These dilemmas were faced in both the design of the colloquium and in the definition of the expected outcomes. The resolution was to invite a highly qualified group of participants who were
balanced between academics and practitioners. The goal dilemmas
were resolved by focusing on five questions:

1. What is the future of entrepreneurship in the decade ahead?
2. What concepts, skills and attitudes should be developed in MBA
    candidates who intend to pursue entrepreneurial careers?
3. What concepts, skills, and attitudes should be included in pro-
    grams for continuing education of entrepreneurs?
4. What can be done to increase the mutual benefit of projects
    carried out jointly between academic institutions and business
    organizations?
5. What are the most important research subjects for increasing our
    knowledge of entrepreneurship?

The history of entrepreneurial education at HBS. would not be
complete without noting the continuing role of the alumni. In addition to the Sarofim-Rock initiative, there have been many others
who have provided a continuous reminder of the interest and tangi-
ble support available to the school in this area. Money, time, case
sites, and forums for expression have all been freely made available.

Goals for the Development of Entrepreneurship at HBS

It is fitting to examine the goals in this field as they relate both to the internal activities at HBS and as they have impact on the world beyond the school. Although the former is relatively more controllable, ultimately it is the latter that is critical to the long-term success of the individuals participating in unfolding this agenda, to the growth of the knowledge base in entrepreneurship, and to establishing leadership in this field.

Internal goals fall into traditional categories: course development, teaching, faculty development, and research. The goals for external impact are more difficult to assign to such distinct categories. They do, however, relate to other schools, to the business community, and to processes in government and society at large. The colloquium participants outlined goals in each of these areas. Among the goals they articulated were the following:

Internal

1. Development of new courses in the social psychology of entrepreneurship and in entrepreneurial finance;
2. Including entrepreneurial situations into the general MBA curriculum of finance, organizational behavior, marketing, control, and business policy;
3. Development of material for practicing managers regarding building and sustaining an entrepreneurial climate in established organizations;
4. Continuing to meet the MBA demand for courses with competent instruction and new relevant material;
5. Providing for the development of faculty sensitivity to issues of growth, change, and pursuit of opportunity through consulting, directorships, and field case writing;
6. Providing for student involvement in field-based research in entrepreneurial firms;
7. Developing a body of research-based knowledge that can provide a valid basis for:

   - recommendations for public policy that result in social benefit,

- the formation of educational policy and course content,
- initiating effective and innovative methods of instruction.

External

1. Providing a central core of pedagogic materials for other schools interested in the teaching of entrepreneurship, including cases, technical notes, and teaching aids;
2. Promoting the legitimacy of entrepreneurship as a critical element of business management;
3. Emphasizing the ethical element in entrepreneurial management;
4. Engaging in the public debate regarding social, tax, and regulatory policy through research, public speaking, and publication;
5. Developing Harvard's national reputation for innovative development of the concepts of entrepreneurship that will underlie the legitimacy of entrepreneurship as an academic discipline.

These goals are far-reaching and can never be deemed to have been fully attained. They, in a sense, represent a mission for the existence of an institution rather than the task for a few individuals.

Substantial progress has been made on all of the goals outlined above. The strategy of those interested in the field has been to proceed on all fronts rather than putting 100 percent effort behind any single goal. The reasoning behind such a strategy was straightforward: such an entrepreneurial venture can only succeed if it rests upon solid ground in student support, research credibility, and demonstrable service to a broad audience.

It is perhaps easiest to review internal progress by examining the teaching, research, and faculty development issues separately. These three elements are both mutually supportive and inextricably linked. Nonetheless, the dimensions of progress can be assessed separately.

Teaching

Teaching is perhaps the easiest dimension on which to see the impact of the last two years' efforts. The interest group has followed the colloquium's recommendations closely. There are now six offerings in the entrepreneurial interest group. These are as follows:

Entrepreneurial Management.   This course is the largest offering of the group. For 1984–85, there were 650 students who attempted to enroll with places provided for 510. The course has, since 1982, been completely revised with thirty-five new cases and twelve technical notes completed. The course focuses on five critical areas:

- Defining opportunity
- Developing a resource plan
- Acquiring control over resources
- Operating problems
- Managing the harvest

The course has been compiled into a book published in March 1985 by Irwin. The book, *New Business Ventures and the Entrepreneur*, includes cases, text, and a 310-page instructor's manual.

Entrepreneurship, Creativity and Organization.   This course is being offered for the first time in 1985 as a full course. It features thirty new cases, twelve videos, new team exercises, and fifteen industry and technical notes. The course, which has attracted 182 students, is organized to study the following issues:

- The entrepreneur
- Partnerships and teams
- Managing creative resources
- Project-team management
- Human resource management in the entrepreneurial firm
- Corporate entrepreneurship
- The entrepreneurial process

This course is responsive to the stated goal of developing a course in the social psychology of entrepreneurship. It builds from a study of the individual entrepreneur to the study of the large firm attempting to maintain an atmosphere of entrepreneurship.

Entrepreneurial Finance.   This course is being offered for the first time as a one-half credit seminar. Thus far, sixteen new cases, and two industry notes have been developed for the course, which has attracted 420 initial registrants. It builds strongly on the concept of value creation through financial strategy. The course is developed around the following issues:

- Start-up financing
- Financial management in a rapidly growing firm
- Venture creation in a large firm
- Management during financial distress
- Public offerings, leveraged buyouts, and realizing value

This course provides a basis for the student to examine in some detail "operational finance" as distinguished from the currently more highly emphasized study of capital asset pricing.

Field Studies in Entrepreneurial Management. This course is designed for those who have identified a new business venture that they desire to pursue. It has attracted sixteen student project teams with sixty-five members. These students have submitted a detailed proposal regarding the nature of the venture, their research plan, and the proposed business outline. In addition to close supervision of the field study activity, an eight-case series has been developed to raise detailed questions regarding the "normal" progress of a start-up venture. In 1983, four companies were started based on work initiated in the field studies course.

Real Property Asset Management. This course has been established since 1972. It is currently one of the most popular at HBS. It has 420 students vying for 210 slots. The course focuses on the analysis of real property investment and development.

Field Studies in Real Property. This course has been established to give the students the opportunity to work on projects provided by major development firms and individuals with substantial real property holdings. The teams of four to six are organized to deal with a specific problem of investment with both the faculty sponsor and with the sponsoring individual or organization.

In addition to the MBA courses, two other activities have emerged. These include a one-week President's Seminar, which is offered to the presidents of growing firms. The seminars have focused on the management of growth as seen from differing functional and general management perspectives. In the last two years, there have been approximately 320 attendees. The doctoral activities have focused upon the development of a cadre of interested doctoral candidates. At present, three candidates are doing work of substantial relevance to the entrepreneurial management area.

Research

Research activities are well underway. Publication has thus far been limited to proceedings of the Babson Conference on Entrepreneurship in 1983 and 1984. The major thrusts are centered in the following areas:

The Individual Entrepreneur. Through analysis of the alumni data base, many startling conclusions arose as to the actual employment history of HBS graduates, the reward structure, and their job satisfaction. This work continues, and, in addition to publications already in print, the work will be reported in several scholarly journals.

There is extensive work on the individual entrepreneur, including a large control group study comparing successful professional managers with successful entrepreneurs on the basis of in-depth interviews and psychological tests. The studies are being extended to examine age as a factor in the results.

The work in this field is aimed at development of a theory of entrepreneurship based on distinctions between opportunity-based or resource-driven personal strategies. It extends early psychological work.

Entrepreneurship and Organizations. The thrust here is to extend the conceptual framework of opportunity-driven versus resource-driven to the analysis of organizational imperatives for entrepreneurship. The first published results appeared in the *Harvard Business Review* in the March–April 1985 issue.

A current D.B.A. candidate has done some exciting work that has statistically validated the discriminating power of the conceptual framework. This work was done through structured questionnaires administered in a variety of organizational and cultural settings. The tests indicate a robust structure underlying the work being done. This validation holds out considerable promise for having impact well beyond the confines of the entrepreneurial-management group.

Entrepreneurship and the Capital Markets. The thrust in entrepreneurial finance is focusing on the problems inherent in the assumption of efficient markets. The problems of "Capital Market Myopia" are being studied through a systematic analysis of the disk drive industry. Other work is being conducted regarding the perspectives on future value of research and development expenditures as seen through accounting, financial, and entrepreneurial perspectives. Another research topic is risk management with the emphasis upon anticipation of good and bad news and with the structuring of preconceived options for expansion and abandonment.

Faculty Development

Considerable effort and expense is going into faculty development. Although senior-level faculty interest is still problematic, much is occurring at the junior faculty, the adjunct faculty, and the doctoral level. Junior faculty are being systematically exposed to problem situations through the mechanism of the President's Seminar, through participation in joint research activities, and through the encouragement of new course development. This exposure, in turn, is leading to the encouragement of the doctoral level research. At the present time, there are one full professor, one associate professor, two assistant professors, and three doctoral candidates with substantial commitment to this field. In addition, there are a number of assistant professors who are making commitments to the study of individual situations that fall within this purview.

Adjunct faculty are still an important element of the manning table. Currently five half-time faculty are involved in teaching and course development. By all measures, these are extremely successful and involved members of the group. They represent a wide variety of disciplines and backgrounds. Each, however, is committed to both teaching and intellectual capital building. They have, in total, supervised or written eleven cases in 1984–85. Their involvement in the development of the courses is critical for the maintenance of the forward momentum in the field. The collective teaching experience of this group is large.

Economics of the Effort

Although the fundamental purpose of the activity is noneconomic, in practice, the development of the entrepreneurship area has been an economic contributor. The clear items include the following:

Estimated Revenues	
M.B.A. Tuition	$ 900,000
President's Seminar (net)	180,000
Endowment Income	90,000
TOTAL INCOME	$1,170,000
Estimated Costs	
Salaries	$ 400,000
Doctoral and Research	75,000
Overhead and Expenses	475,000
TOTAL EXPENSES	$ 950,000
Estimated Contribution	$ 220,000

These estimated are obviously extremely rough since the true overhead factor is not generally calculated. The benefits are also understated since some of the time of the faculty is spent on course development, other teaching in executive and doctoral programs, and on administrative matters. In addition, there is no credit claimed for incremental alumni contributions. There has been money raised directly to support the doctoral work, and we believe that, as noted later, the thrust is clearly being supported by large and concentrated alumni gifts.

Impact beyond HBS

The impact of the activity is as yet difficult to measure with any precision. There are strong signs that the work is both being noticed and having an effect. Among the areas of impact are the following:

Adoption of Course Materials. The material from the Entrepreneurial Management course will be published in March by Irwin as *New Business Ventures and the Entrepreneur.* This book of text and cases is apparently going to be widely adopted by those teaching case-method entrepreneurship courses. Course materials from the Entrepreneurial Finance and Entrepreneurship, Creativity and Organization courses have also been widely requested, indicating good potential as well.

Perhaps one of the most important indications of successful infusion of the materials into the basic curriculum is the inclusion of an "Entrepreneurial Management" section in the ninth edition of *Policy Formulation and Administration*. With all cases, extensive conceptual notes and teaching notes are being provided in addition to the case material. The entrepreneurial management faculty has also been active in helping the materials developed for the course to be used in executive education programs here at the School.

Alumni Relations. The core faculty group in entrepreneurial management has made considerable effort in building alumni relationships through entrepreneurship conferences and speeches before alumni groups. In addition, there has been considerable coordination with the Executive Council of the Alumni. They have proven to be useful in development and maintenance of the case and research contacts.

Participation in Policy Discussions. The core entrepreneurial management faculty has been involved in activities as diverse as the President's Commission on Industrial Productivity, the S.E.C. Business-Government Forum on Small Business, the MIT Enterprise Forum, the Eleventh World Congress on Small Business, and Brussels' C.I.M. Research Program in Entrepreneurship. These involvements include both reporting of research findings and active discussion of both industry and governmental policy options. There is considerable interest in the field and a paucity of both hard data and imaginative policy alternatives.

Other Outside Activities. The faculty group involved has focused their outside activities on the real world problems of change and on growing companies. Board work and problem solving consulting have been the major activities rather than outside teaching. This problem focus provides both for the development of the intellectual capital of the area and for a positive role mode for other faculty. This is sometimes a risk, since the demands are high, but thus far, the payoff in increased sophistication regarding the appropriate questions has also been high. The list of companies and organizations which have cooperated and which are providing cases, research data bases and experiential learning is developing rapidly.

Looking forward, there are clear goals ahead. They are in the basic categories of course development, teaching, research, and faculty recruitment and development.

Course Development Goals.   Work remains to be done in developing Entrepreneurial Finance into a full course. The major challenge will be intellectually to differentiate this course from the current course offerings in finance. This differentiation will occur through a focus on the operational financial issues which are not totally expressed in capital market terms. The course—Entrepreneurship, Creativity and Organization—has now been expanded to a full course. Work remains, however, in both polishing the individual class units, adding new cases that explore important conceptual issues, and in refining the conceptual unity of the course so that it can be measured as providing "creative course development" according to the standards for promotion.

Further work in the Entrepreneurial Management course is being undertaken both to expand the range of situations studied and to place more emphasis upon the operational aspects of the entrepreneurial firm. Expansion of the concept of entrepreneurial management to the larger firm is also important to the agenda.

The field studies activities in both Real Property Asset Management and in Entrepreneurial Management are well launched. If staffing were available, it would be advisable to give more opportunity for project involvement of individuals without an interest in immediately forming their own business. That opportunity is largely a function of the staffing availability.

Teaching.   The primary goal of teaching must be to insure continued quality instruction in all course offerings. To do this, the entrepreneurship interest group must focus on the entry slots. Those starting cannot be left to fend for themselves but must be provided with teaching aids and personal help. The Price-Babson Fellows Program will provide one such form of help, but each teacher must recognize the personal involvement that will be necessary to create meaningful entry-level slots. To a certain extent, entrepreneurship education has always been the slot for the seasoned practitioner or the senior faculty. If it is to develop a broad base, the school must also provide a mechanism for new, discipline-trained junior faculty to enter and to succeed in the entrepreneurship course offerings.

Research. The future direction in research has been largely set by the activities of the past year. The expected product will be both academic papers and practioner-oriented books. The faculty involved have an interest balanced between teaching and research. The goals for the research activity are clear: It must be built on faculty strengths; it must be tied to discipline-based thinking and methodologies. The goals are impact publications that will be integrated into the teaching and course development of the entrepreneurship interest group and of the other faculty members.

Faculty Development. Obviously, the task is formidable. The agenda of entrepreneurship is limited primarily by the scope of hours available to do quality work. Much effort has been expended in order to attract younger faculty, excellent adjunct faculty, and doctoral candidates. These efforts will continue.

Success requires a constant search for the best people who desire to contribute substantially to the most exciting area of intellectual involvement at the School. Only as people at all levels of experience are identified and recruited can those involved be certain of the continuity of effort required for success.

The concrete progress exhibited to date is just the beginning. With continued hard work, a little luck in recruitment, and continued positive involvement of friends, colleagues, and other interested people, the work can be one of the shining stars of Harvard Business School.

The future is built on a real need. It is fed by an enthusiasm that is both practical and academic. It must be strengthened by building a credible research base. In sum, it is a life's work for many individuals, but the time frame within which it must be accomplished is considerably shorter.

INDEX

ABOUT THE SPONSORS

IC² INSTITUTE

The IC² Institute at the University of Texas at Austin is a major research center for the study of Innovation, Creativity, and Capital (hence IC²). The institute studies and analyzes information about the enterprise system through an integrated program of research, conferences, and publications.

IC² studies provide frameworks for dealing with current and critical unstructured problems from a private sector point of view. The key areas of research and study concentration of IC² include: the management of technology; creative and innovative management; measuring the state of society; dynamic business development and entrepreneurship; econometrics, economic analysis, and management sciences; the evaluation of attitudes, opinions, and concerns on key issues.

The Institute generates a strong interaction between scholarly developments and real world issues by conducting national and international conferences, developing initiatives for private and public sector consideration, assisting in the establishment of professional organizations and other research institutes and centers, and maintaining collaborative efforts with universities, communities, states and government agencies.

IC^2 research is published through monographs, policy papers, technical working papers, research articles, and three major series of books.

CENTER FOR ENTREPRENEURSHIP
BAYLOR UNIVERSITY

The Center for Entrepreneurship in the Hankamer School of Business at Baylor University has three major thrusts: entrepreneurship education, business outreach activities, and entrepreneurship research.

Within the area of entrepreneurship education, Baylor University is one of only three schools in the nation that offer degree programs in entrepreneurship at both the graduate and undergraduate levels. The entrepreneurship major began at the B.B.A. level in 1980 and followed with an M.B.A. concentration in 1981.

Business outreach activities include a venture assistance program and an innovation evaluation program. The venture assistance program is a modification of the Small Business Institute in that assistance is in the development of business plans prior to the initiation of the venture. The innovation evaluation program evaluates initiation of the venture. The innovation evaluation program evaluates the commercial or market feasibility of inventions.

Approximately fifty to sixty would-be entrepreneurs are assisted with business plans each year. The program has evaluated over 600 inventions since the innovation evaluation program was established three years ago.

Research efforts have been directed primarily in the areas of psychological characteristics of entrepreneurs and in the prevalence of strategic planning in small business.

RGK FOUNDATION

The RGK Foundation was established in 1966 to provide support for medical and educational research. Major emphasis has been placed on the research of connective tissue diseases, particularly scleroderma. The foundation also supports workshops and conferences at educational institutions through which the role of business in American society is examined. Such conferences have been co-sponsored with the IC^2 Institute at the University of Texas at Austin and the Keystone Center in Colorado.

The RGK Foundation Building, which opened in October 1981, has a research library and provides research space for scholars in residence. In the past year, the building's extensive conference facilities have been used to conduct national and international conferences. Conferences at the RGK Foundation are designed not only to enhance information exchange on particular topics but also to maintain an interlinkage among business, academia, community, and government.

LIST OF CONTRIBUTORS

Pier A. Abetti is a professor in the School of Management of Rensselaer Polytechnic Institute in Troy, New York.

Howard Aldrich is a professor of Sociology and chairman of the Industrial Relations Curriculum at the University of North Carolina at Chapel Hill.

Robert H. Brockhaus, Sr. is a professor of Management at St. Louis University and president of Progressive Management Enterprises, Ltd., a management consulting firm that he founded.

David J. Brophy is associate professor of Finance at the Graduate School of Business Administration of the University of Michigan and director of the University of Michigan Banking and Financial Services Executive Program.

Albert V. Bruno is the Glenn Kimek Professor of Business at Santa Clara University.

Alan L. Carsrud, co-founder of University Research Associates of Austin, Texas, is on the faculty of the Graduate School of Business at the University of Texas at Austin.

Neil C. Churchill is the Distinguished Professor of Accounting and director of the Caruth Institute of Owner-Managed Business at Southern Methodist University.

Arnold C. Cooper is the Louis A. Weil, Jr. Professor of Management at the Krannert Graduate School of Management, Purdue University.

George C. Eddy is a senior lecturer in Management at the University of Texas at Austin.

Yvon Gasse is associate dean and professor of Organization Theory and Behavior at Laval University in Quebec, Canada.

Robert D. Hisrich is the Bovaird Chair Professor of Entrepreneurial Studies and Private Enterprise and professor of Marketing at the University of Tulsa.

John A. Hornaday is professor of Management and Organizational Behavior and director of the Center for Entrepreneurial Studies at Babson College.

Herbert E. Kierulff is the Donald L. Snellman Professor of Entrepreneurship in the School of Business at Seattle-Pacific University.

Virginia L. Lewis is senior research associate and adjunct faculty of the Caruth Institute of Owner-Managed Business at Southern Methodist University.

Ian C. MacMillan is the director of the Center for Entrepreneurial Studies and professor of Management at the Graduate School of Business of New York University.

Modesto A. ("Mitch") Maidique is professor of Management and director of the Innovation and Entrepreneurship Institute at the University of Miami.

Donald D. Myers is associate professor in the Engineering, Management Department and director for the Center for Technological Development at the University of Missouri–Rolla.

Kenneth W. Olm is professor of Management in the Graduate School of Business at the University of Texas at Austin.

Howard H. Stevenson is the Sarofim-Rock Professor of Business Administration at the Harvard Business School.

Robert W. Stuart is a doctoral candidate and current instructor in the School of Management at Rensselaer Polytechnic Institute.

Jeffry A. Timmons is professor in Entrepreneurial Studies at Babson College.

Karl H. Vesper is a professor of Business Administration and of Mechanical Engineering and Chairman of the Management and Organization Department at the University of Washington.

William E. Wetzel, Jr., is professor of Business Administration at the Whittemore School of Business and Economics, University of New Hampshire.

Max S. Wortman, Jr. is the William B. Stokely Professor of Strategic Management and director, Institute for Strategic Management, at the University of Tennessee, Knoxville.

Catherine Zimmer is a doctoral candidate in Sociology at the University of North Carolina at Chapel Hill.

ABOUT THE EDITORS

Dr. Donald L. Sexton is director of the Center for Entrepreneurship and holder of the Caruth Chair of Entrepreneurship at Baylor University.

A native of Ohio, Dr. Sexton was formerly an associate professor of Business Administration in the Graduate Business Administration Program at Sangamon State University. Dr. Sexton worked in business for fifteen years prior to joining the academic community. His last eight years in industry were at executive level positions. He was known as a "turnaround" specialist, having successfully managed four firms from losses to profitable operations. He continues to maintain contact with businesses through his activities at the center, consulting, and membership on four boards of directors.

He received his bachelor's degree in Mathematics from Wilmington College and his M.B.A. and Ph.D. from Ohio State University.

Dr. Sexton has been active in the Academy of Management, the International Council for Small Business and the International Symposium for Small Business. He has served on the editorial review board of the *Journal of Small Business Management*, the *Journal of Venturing*, and the *Academy of Management Review*.

He has written and presented numerous papers on the various aspects of small business and entrepreneurship, is a frequent speaker on the topic, and has published three text books: *Encyclopedia of*

Entrepreneurship, with Calvin Kent and Karl Vesper; *Experiences in Entrepreneurship and Small Business Management*, with Phil Van Auken; and *Starting and Operating a Business in Texas*, coauthored with Michael Jenkins.

Dr. Raymond Smilor is the associate director of the IC^2 Institute, the University of Texas at Austin, and a member of the faculty in the Department of Marketing in the College of Business Administration. He also holds the Judson Neff Centennial Fellowship in the IC^2 Institute.

He has served as a research fellow for the National Science Foundation for an international exchange program on computers and management between the United States and the Soviet Union. He has been a leading participant in the planning and organization of many regional, national and international conferences, symposia, and workshops.

He serves as a consultant to business, government and the non-profit sector. He is president of the Management Strategies Group and a director of the Texas LYCEUM Association. He appears in *Who's Who in the South and Southwest*.

Dr. Smilor's academic works have covered a wide variety of interdisciplinary subjects. He has taught courses on the graduate and undergraduate level in management and currently teaches a course on Marketing, Technology, and Entrepreneurship. His research interests include science and technology transfer, regional economic analysis, marketing strategies for high-technology products, and creative and innovative management techniques. He has edited or coedited a number of books, the most recent of which is *Corporate Creativity: Robust Companies and the Entrepreneurial Spirit* (Praeger, 1984). He is coauthor of *Financing and Managing Fast-Growth Companies: The Venture Capital Process* (Lexington, 1985). He is coauthor of the forthcoming book, *New Business Incubators* (Lexington, 1986) and coeditor of *Improving U.S. Energy Security* (Ballinger, 1985) and the forthcoming *Take-Off Companies* (Praeger, 1986). Dr. Smilor earned his Ph.D. in U.S. History at the University of Texas at Austin.